A professional economist, Gavin ... Finance at Heriot-Watt Universi... include *The Military in the Th... *Captain Cook* (1978), *Burden* ... *in NATO* (1979) and *Defense Economics* (1983). His biography of Bligh, which won the *Yorkshire Post* literary award, was published in 1978.

# CAPTAIN BLIGH

## the man and his mutinies

Gavin Kennedy

**CARDÍNAL**

FOR PATRICIA

A CARDINAL BOOK

First published in Great Britain by Gerald Duckworth & Co. Ltd 1989
Published by Sphere Books Ltd in Cardinal 1990

Reproduced, printed and bound in Great Britain by
The Guernsey Press Co. Ltd, Guernsey, Channel Islands.

ISBN 0 7474 0679 0

Sphere Books Ltd
A Division of
Macdonald & Co. (Publishers) Ltd
27 Wrights Lane, London W8 5TZ

A member of Maxwell Pergamon Publishing Corporation plc

# Contents

# Plates

William Bligh, attributed to John Webber
Elizabeth Bligh by John Webber
Sir Joseph Banks
John Fryer by Gaetano Calleyo
Robert Tinkler
Peter Heywood by J. Simpson
The crew of the *Bounty* loading breadfruit at Tahiti
'Collecting the breadfruit' by Thomas Gosse
William Bligh, engraving by H. Adlard from J.A. Russell's
    portrait
John Adams by R. Beechey
William Bligh, engraving from a portrait by J. Smart
William Bligh, miniature silhouette
Harriet Bligh
John Macarthur
George Johnston by Henry Robinson Smith
William Bligh, Vice-Admiral of the Blue

# Foreword

by Stephen Walters

> Just before Sun rise Mr. Christian, Mate, Chas Churchill, Ship's Corporal, John Mills, Gunner's Mate, and Thomas Burkett, Seaman, came into my Cabbin while I was a Sleep and seizing me tyed my hands with a Cord behind my back and threatened me with instant death if I spoke or made the least noise …

So wrote Lieutenant William Bligh some hours after the now notorious event on that sultry Pacific morning, 28 April 1789. In so doing he stirred an avalanche of comment and controversy that has run to this day. With five films, a score of radio and television plays and innumerable articles, books and pamphlets, the public's interest in the mutiny has never lapsed.

And yet there have only ever been three satisfactory biographies of William Bligh. The first was George Mackaness's scholarly two-volume *Life of Vice-Admiral William Bligh RN, FRS*, first published in Sydney in 1931 and condensed into one volume for an American edition shortly thereafter. A revised edition appeared in 1951, but has long been out of print. Then in 1936 Owen Rutter, the principal collector of Bountiana in the thirties, published his *Turbulent Journey: a life of William Bligh, Vice-Admiral of the Blue*. This too has long been unobtainable. Finally, Gavin Kennedy, a professional economist with a strong interest in eighteenth-century seamanship, produced what has come to be regarded as the definitive biography, *Bligh* (1978). Along with a new assessment of all the earlier material, it brought together the results of research since the war.

Dr Kennedy's book was itself an inspiration for new research. New views and new information have come to light in the last decade. The publication of *Bligh: the man and his mutinies* coincides with the bicentenary of the mutiny. It brings to a wide readership a true summation of the current state of Bligh scholarship.

North Aston                                                                                    S.W.
1 January 1989

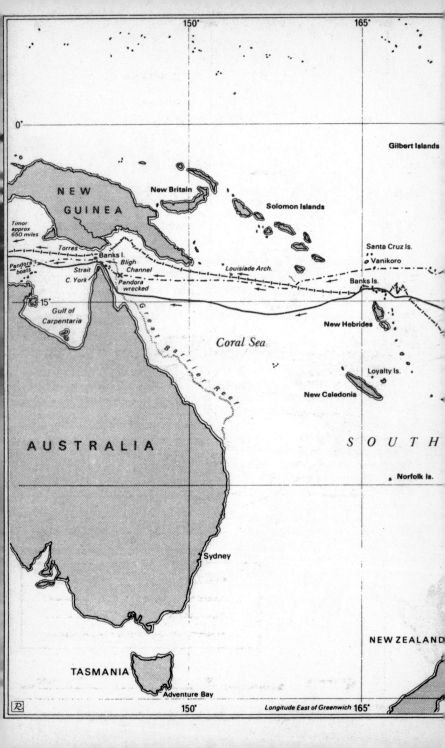

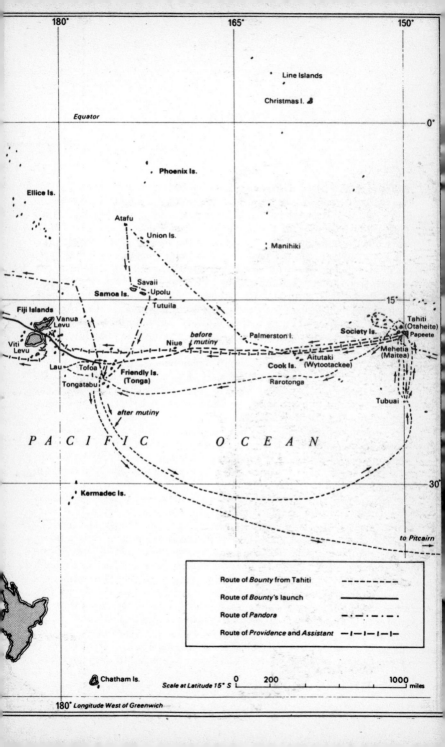

# Preface

William Bligh's name will be assured of notoriety forever by the mutiny two hundred years ago of his friend and protégé, Fletcher Christian, on board His Majesty's Armed Vessel *Bounty*, just after 4.30 am on 28 April 1789, about 30 miles off the Pacific island of Tofoa. There were other, more bloody, more dramatic, mutinies in the history of the Royal Navy, but none have stirred the passions of so many people as the relatively insignificant mutiny on *Bounty*. For brutality as a cause of mutiny we need look no further than the mutiny in 1797 of HMS *Hermione*, Captain Hugh Pigot. This man, almost unknown today, drove his men so hard with senseless floggings (a thousand lashes in a year) that they rose and murdered him and nine other officers, including a 13-year-old midshipman. By contrast, *Bounty*'s mutiny was a placid affair. Emotions certainly ran high that fateful morning, but it was more like a family arguing, albeit heatedly, than a group of men bent on murderous revenge.

The *Bounty* mutiny has achieved notoriety, in spite of its humble place in the larger history of the Royal Navy, because it encompasses the drama of an almost inexplicable conflict between two men: one ambitious, determined and talented, and the other less experienced, less ambitious, less determined, though every bit as talented: Bligh, out to make his name, and begrudging the delay in achieving the recognition he believed he deserved; Christian, out to find a new life and begrudging the sudden change in his family's fortunes that prevented him following a career of his own choice.

The causes of the mutiny were as simple and as complicated as the fact that these two men clashed, and one broke. For two hundred years authors have pored over every nuance of their relationship, and some, in missing the mundane, have found, instead, numerous 'explanations', ranging from the naive to the bizarre. Among the former we can include all assertions that Bligh was a harsh disciplinarian in the Pigot mould. Among the latter there is an assertion that Bligh and Christian were homosexual lovers who fell out when Christian indulged himself in heterosexual liaisons at Tahiti. This is unconvincing for, apart from the total lack of evidence in support of the assertion, we know that Christian was an active ('foolish', as one witness put it) heterosexual on the two voyages he made with Bligh before *Bounty*. Indeed he was treated for VD before *Bounty* reached Tahiti. If they were engaged in such an affair, there was no way it could be kept secret on *Bounty*, and, in all the streams of invective that emerged from the men on board, none of them accused Bligh of homosexuality (which surely would have finished him).

Both naive and bizarre explanations for the mutiny are occasioned by the fantasies of Hollywood scriptwriters, who turned the *Bounty* story into a stereotyped clash between a brutal and unfeeling captain (played by Mayne Lynton, Charles Laughton and Trevor Howard), complete with keel-hauling, senseless floggings, mastheadings and drought-stricken punishments, and a noble-minded gentleman (played by Errol Flynn, Clark Gable and Marlon Brando). Given that their entertaining concoctions had no basis in fact, these imaginative writers created a popular image of Bligh and Christian devoid of historical content. It is almost as if, in two hundred years' time, the popular imagination will come to believe that Mother Teresa was a food racketeer. The latest film version, played with Anthony Hopkins in Bligh's role and Mel Gibson in Christian's, moved the focus of the clash between them closer to the truth.

The rows between the two men in real life were less deep, though no less wounding, for Christian. Bligh was merciless with people who he found did not match up to his standards. His great asset, according to one of his protégés, was his foresight, manifesting itself in the way in which he took every precaution before committing his ship to anything.

People who are obsessive about precautions are worriers; they cannot abide any slackness that might, no matter how remotely, endanger their plans. In its worst manifestations, when they detect a subordinate performing below the norm they expect they target him for special vigilance, often of a kind not much different from nagging; they chase, and chase again, all and any signs of lack of attention to detail or dereliction of duty. 'It may not matter to you, Sir,' bawls Bligh, 'but it does matter a great deal to me!' The sense of outrage at a subordinate's irresponsibility is intensely personal. He feels it passionately, almost in a state of paranoia, as if the offender had deliberately neglected his duty. And it makes no difference whether the offence is large or trivial – any small neglect is a sign of a proclivity to a larger slackness, and slackness, Bligh preached endlessly, is what sinks ships. Bligh believed that slackness was caused either by neglect or malice ('Did I not tell you a thousand times to check the details?'). Bligh did not appreciate that bullying the alleged slackers, justly or not, eventually provokes resentment, and that, in a weaker person, perhaps too haughty, perhaps lacking in the tolerance that comes from experience, perhaps because of the confines of a long voyage in a small ship, it also risks mutiny. We know that he was genuinely astonished at Fletcher Christian's behaviour, just as he was totally unaware of Frank Bond's true feelings later on *Providence*.

I believe the explanation for what happened to Fletcher Christian lies in this area of human tension. He was a young man lacking in sea experience (only four voyages in three ships under only two captains), and he was also troubled by the unexpected turn in his fortunes – from gentleman scholar to the harsh realities of serving in His Majesty's Royal Navy (no bed of roses at the best of times, and certainly not with a man like William Bligh).

Christian had no more idea of what he had to do to please Bligh than Bligh had that he was pushing the young man too far. For Bligh, his strictures were intended to lick Christian into good shape for promotion to Lieutenant; for Christian, the process devalued his ambition to become one. In brooding in *Bounty* after a glorious five months at Tahiti over whether it was worth becoming a Lieutenant, he must also have reviewed his future prospects in the distant islands off the north-west coast of Europe known as Britain. He decided that he preferred to throw up everything and remain in the islands of the Pacific.

His original intention was to slip away by himself to a nearby island and seek his destiny there. He was tolerably proficient in Tahitian and probably believed he knew how to enter into the life and culture of a Polynesian community, even though he would arrive among them with nothing of any value to them. That he revised his plan, under the influence of a striking sentence spoken to him by George Stewart, Midshipman, to involve everybody on board, except Bligh and three others, is a fact of history. That he was to be disappointed in his expectations – most of the crew preferred to take their chances with Bligh – within hours of his fateful decision, and later had to revise them again when 16 of the 25 men who stayed on board preferred to risk the doubtful mercies of British justice by waiting on Tahiti, are also facts of history. No wonder that in his despair at the world he had come from, and from which he was forever barred, he was to remark that he never wanted to see a European again, except the final eight who went with him to Pitcairn.

Bligh's behaviour over his entire life seems to have been of a kind that did not vary much (allowing for the poor health from *Bounty*'s open boat voyage that dogged him to his death). Yet though he provoked Christian into mutiny, Fryer to mutiny's brink, Bond to vowing never to serve with him again, Frazier to court-martialling him for abuse and oppression and Macarthur into orchestrating a military coup, he could still receive warm support from people for the many dutiful kindnesses he committed. Those who testified to his good character and impartiality at George Johnston's court martial in 1811 had to sail round the world to do so and at some considerable inconvenience and expense to themselves.

Two hundred years later it is still almost impossible to write a book on the life of Admiral Bligh without being forced into judgments about human errors and vanities, not just in his person but in all those whose lives he touched. In fact feelings still run high whenever Bligh and the *Bounty* are discussed. When my biography of Bligh was published (*Bligh*, Duckworth, 1978) it attracted an enormous correspondence, some of it extremely kind, while others verged on the abusive. Obviously I have stirred some very Bligh/Christian-like people in the past ten years.

Among these correspondents, I must mention Rolf Du Rietz of Uppsala, Sweden. He has made many original contributions to the serious study of the causes of the *Bounty* mutiny. Some of his monographs were published in the 1960s (see *Studia Bountyana*, 1965; 1966) and he continues to fire his broadsides at those who dispute his version of the cause of the unhappy events (see *Banksia 1*, 1979; *Banksia 2*, 1981; and *Banksia 3*, 1986). Like William Bligh, Du Rietz combines a withering fire at the works of others, including my own, with an 'emollient plaster' to soften the hurt that his often hasty and verbally violent strictures are likely to cause in his targets. His habit of excusing the failings of others who broadly accept his views is slightly more irritating, as well as revealing. Nevertheless Du Rietz's approach and some of his ideas have influenced my own, though I expect that he will continue to regard me as wayward in many respects because I disagree with his interpretations of certain human tensions fought out in the midst of known historical events.

Other correspondents claimed to be descendants of some of the people on *Bounty*, such as of Peter Linkletter, Quartermaster; John Adams, Seaman; Robert Tinkler, Midshipman; George Stewart, Midshipman, through his Tahitian wife, 'Peggy'; James Morrison, Boatswain's Mate; and Thomas Denman Ledward, Assistant Surgeon. They clearly were proud of their ancestors, irrespective of whose side they took on *Bounty*, and provided me with additional information. Glynn Christian, a direct descendant of Fletcher Christian from his last days on Pitcairn, also crossed my path, though via third parties; his beautiful book, *Fragile Paradise, the discovery of Fletcher Christian, Bounty Mutineer* (1982), is highly recommended, even though he occasionally disagrees with my assessments! I have met only one descendant of William Bligh's, the Countess of Devon, his great-great-great-granddaughter, during an exhibition of Bligh memorabilia at her home in England, of whom I risk venturing the view that I could see something of the Admiral in her bearing (though not of course in her language and manners!).

Of those connected with Bligh, though not with *Bounty*, I had the pleasure of dining with Sir George and Lady Home, in Scotland, whose forebear's ship, *Defiance*, mutinied in 1795, and which mutiny Bligh helped to put down (it was particularly poignant to be eating off the same dinner service as used by Captain Sir George Home on *Defiance*). My research on Bligh's time in New South Wales as Governor brought me into contact with John Macarthur, a direct descendant of the famous Captain Macarthur who caused Bligh and, it must be accepted many others, so much grief. The generous access provided by his descendant to the family papers, and permission to quote from them (until then, 1982, severely restricted), is warmly acknowledged.

I first started reading about Bligh and the *Bounty* in 1973, and in the ten years since *Bligh* (1978) was published I have continued to read and reread material in my own collection and in those of various institutions. All Bligh scholars are indebted to the vast Bligh, Banks and Macarthur collections of original materials held at the Mitchell Library, Sydney, Australia (call-numbers are listed in the text as ML). Other libraries and their staffs have also been most helpful, including the Public Record Office at Kew, London (listed as PRO); the National Maritime Museum, Greenwich, London; the Admiralty Library, Fulham, London, the British Library, London, the National Library of Scotland, Edinburgh; and the Alexander Turnbull Library, Wellington, New Zealand.

I have also drawn from time to time on the detailed knowledge and private collections of Stephen Walters, Oakley, Bucks; I know of no other person who has been so willing to give up his time, and to take so much trouble while doing so, to answer any query or speculative thought I might have had over the years since we made contact. His knowledge of Bligh materials, and of the *Bounty* voyage, is unrivalled.

Others who have contributed to my work on William Bligh include Lieutenant-Commander Andrew David, of the Hydrographic Department, Taunton; Terry Martin, Blairgowrie; and the many authors whose books I have consulted, especially George Mackaness and Owen Rutter.

As with all occasions when we use, or misuse, the works of others, we must enter a disclaimer that they are in no way responsible for any of the failings and errors of our own work; but, in justice, they may claim credit for any of its achievements.

Lastly, the contribution of my family. Authorship is always a great consumer of time and patience (of which apparently I have not sufficient), and I can best describe my debts to Patricia and the children by asserting that if, like Bligh, my temperament occasionally gave them much cause to recoil, they coped with my temper more maturely, and ultimately more sensibly for everybody concerned, than Fletcher Christian on *Bounty*, John Fryer in the *Bounty*'s launch, Frank Bond on *Providence*, Matthew Hollister on *Director*, John Frazier on *Warrior*, and George Johnston of the New South Wales Corps.

Edinburgh, April 1988                                                                 G.K.

# 1

# A Young Gentleman

William Bligh's place of birth is variously stated as St Tudy, near Bodmin, and Plymouth. For certain he was baptized in St Andrew's Church, Plymouth, his birthday being recorded as 9 September 1754. His father, the fifth son of John Bligh who held the Manor of Tinten in St Tudy, came of a distinguished Cornish line which in the years 1505-88 provided Bodmin with five mayors. More recently it had produced General Edward Bligh (1635-1775), who distinguished himself in Britain's foreign wars, though he retired amidst controversy, and Admiral Sir Richard Rodney Bligh (1737-1821). Of the same line came the Earls of Darnley, who from favour received an Irish peerage, 'promoted' not long after to an English peerage. In later years William Bligh used the coat of arms of the Darnleys as his personal seal and was on social terms with the family. The Darnleys were active in the Customs Service (then a sinecure) in Plymouth from 1648 to 1663; Bligh's father was a customs officer in Plymouth and named his son after the William Bligh who had held the same post and fathered the Darnley line.

William Bligh's mother, Jane, was a widow when she married Francis Bligh. Her son-in-law, John Bond, was a surgeon in the navy when he married her daughter (William's step-sister) from her previous marriage, Catherine Pearce. The Bligh and Bond families were close; they exchanged family 'news' throughout their lives. On his second 'Breadfruit' voyage in HMS *Providence*, he made a point of taking his nephew, Francis Godolphin Bond, as his First Lieutenant. Bligh's mother died before he was 16; his father made two later marriages and died on 27 December 1780.

Bligh's formative years were spent in the naval centre of Plymouth, where his father's post as Customs Officer assured his family a modest standard of living and family connections were available to open doors to the Royal Navy. It is not known where Bligh learned his mathematics, but that he was gifted in this subject we know from his rapid progress when he came to apply himself to the science of navigation. Traces of his early career in the Royal Navy include the appearance of his name as 'Captain's Servant' on the muster roll of HMS *Monmouth* in 1762 (on

which John Bond was serving as Surgeon). Bligh was only 7 at the time.
This kind of arrangement was not unusual for the sons of well-connected
parents. The practice did not mean that the navy countenanced child
labour on its ships. The parents would persuade captains to place their
sons' name on the muster; the captain could draw both extra rations and
servants' pay to supplement his own if they did not actually go to sea, or,
if they did, they would be taught by a midshipman designated
schoolmaster and would generally familiarise themselves with life on
board. Captain Cook on his voyages to the Pacific placed his sons' names
on the roll once the ship had left port and removed them abruptly when
he was near home on his return. It was a harmless fiddle. Naturally this
arrangement was not open to the families of seamen, and it tells us
something of the social standing of Bligh's father that he was able to
arrange this for his 7-year-old son. It is not known whether Bligh actually
went to sea at this early age. That his name went on the roll he owed to
John Bond (his brother-in-law). His name remained on the roll for six
months. In 1774 Bond also got his 9-year-old son, Frank, as a 'surgeon's
assistant', on the muster of HMS *Torbay*, in which he was also serving as
Surgeon.

On 27 July 1770, at the age of 15, after his mother died, Bligh was
entered on the roll of HMS *Hunter*, a 10-gun sloop. He was rated as Able
Bodied (AB). Prospective officers, midshipmen, – 'young gentlemen' –
were officially supposed to have two years' experience at sea and be at
least 13 (11 if they were the sons of naval officers). Recruitment of
midshipmen was left to the captains, but their number per ship was
prescribed by regulations. If a captain took more than the offical quota on
board he rated them as ABs though he messed them with the
midshipmen. As a vacancy arose he promoted accordingly from among
the young gentlemen rated as ABs. This is what happened in Bligh's case,
and also in that of Cook, Troubridge, Nelson and thousands of others,
including Fletcher Christian.

Within six months of joining *Hunter*, on 4 February 1771, Bligh was
discharged from the ship on the orders of Admiral Sir Richard Spry and
re-entered the next day as a midshipman. On 22 September 1771 he was
transferred to the larger HMS *Crescent*, a 36-gun frigate, on which for the
next three years he learned his navigation and seamanship. On 23
August 1774, he was paid off the *Crescent*, and he entered HMS *Ranger*
on 2 September 1774, first as an AB volunteer and then, on 30 September
1774, as a midshipman. *Ranger* was employed in searching for
contraband among ships in the Irish Sea, based at Douglas in the Isle of
Man. He completed his six years as a midshipman on *Ranger* and must
have shown outstanding promise, for Captain Cook, then fitting out for
his Third Voyage, passed over more senior and experienced men and
chose Bligh to be the Master of HMS *Resolution* on 20 March 1776.

This appointment was remarkable. Bligh was unknown, yet he was offered the responsible post of Master, in charge of the ship's seamanship and navigation. Cook, who never suffered fools gladly, must have had a high opinion of the potential of the untried Bligh or, alternatively, a high opinion of whoever recommended him. Perhaps Cook was impressed by Bligh's midshipman's journals, including his charts, which he would have sent to the Admiralty for inspection. Bligh, as Master, was bound to work closely with Cook: too closely, perhaps, for the liking of some. To have gone with *Resolution* at the invitation of Cook, without promotion, would have been incentive enough; to go as Master was a creditable beginning for an ambitious young officer. A good performance under Cook would assure Bligh of early promotion to Lieutenant and, perhaps, to Post-captain, the crucial rung on the seniority ladder to Flag Officer's rank. Once Bligh made Post-captain he would move up the lists as men above him died or disgraced themselves. It was a ghastly lottery; news of tragedies at sea and the loss of captains signified a general move towards Flag Rank for the survivors on the list.

At 22 Bligh was still a long way from Post-captain. To complete the formalities of his Midshipman's service he sat the Lieutenant's examination before joining Cook on *Resolution*. His certificate of passing is dated 1 May 1776. Bligh was ready for the first major test in his turbulent career.

# 2

# The Death of Captain Cook

James Cook had entered the Royal Navy as an AB after a career in the merchant service. Once in the Royal Navy, he at first made rapid progress, moving from AB to Master's Mate in a month (July 1755), and to Master on 30 June 1757, but he then stood still for ten years and was not commissioned Lieutenant until 1768 when he was 40. In that rank he made his first voyage, and in his second he went out, as Commander, to the Pacific. On his first voyage he took with him a young amateur botanist, Joseph Banks, who was to play a crucial role in the life of William Bligh.

It was for his third and final voyage that Cook chose Bligh. On this expedition were several other men whose names later became linked with Bligh's. Among them was Lieutenant James Burney (later Admiral Burney) who became a close friend of Bligh's and edited his account of the voyage of the *Bounty* in 1792. But for the moment we are concerned with two main aspects of the voyage: Cook's conduct of the expedition, and the circumstances of his death.

The facts of the voyage are straightforward. Cook had a remarkable record in preserving the life of his crew on long voyages. It was not uncommon to lose a dozen or more men on an Atlantic crossing lasting weeks, yet Cook managed to sail for years with very few deaths. His 'secret' was regular and reasonable food combined with insistence on personal cleanliness and exercise. He overcame resistance from the ever-conservative seamen by example and firm discipline, and on one occasion had two seamen flogged for refusing to eat meat. Cook also introduced a three-watch system on his ships, giving the seamen eight hours' rest between duties instead of the traditional four. He was elected to the Royal Society in 1776 for his improvements to health at sea, and was awarded the Copley Gold Medal for a paper on the subject. Yet Cook's recommendations were not widely accepted. Bligh was one of the first to introduce Cook's methods on all his ships, and he met with similar resistance to new diets and habits. He learnt much from Cook about management; he may also have been influenced to imitate Cook's personal mannerisms, for Cook's violent fits of temper on the third voyage were notorious. (The crews referred to them as 'heivas', after a

4

particularly energetic Tahitian dance.) Bligh later exhibited similar behaviour.

The major discovery of Cook's third voyage was the Hawaiian island group in the north Pacific. Cook named them after the Earl of Sandwich and they were known as the Sandwich Islands into the nineteenth century. It was here that Cook was killed by Hawaiians on the morning of Sunday 14 February 1779. The story of the death of Cook is one of misunderstandings between sailors and Hawaiians, hasty decisions and violent disagreements afterwards about who was to blame; but Bligh comes out of it well. I will give only the main details of the episode here, highlighting Bligh's part and its effect on his career. The full story, with a detailed discussion of the primary manuscript accounts of the people present, is given in my book, *The Death of Captain Cook* (1978), where I show that Cook's overconfidence, his temper and his belief that one shot would clear the beach of Hawaiians were largely to blame for his tragic death.

Cook's ships, *Resolution* and *Discovery*, had come upon the Sandwich Islands on their way north to the Bering Strait in 1778, and after a fruitless search for the fabled North-West Passage to Europe he brought them back to the islands for a rest, and to survey his new discovery. On this visit the ships stayed at the eastern end of the island group, on the large island known as Hawaii, at a place called (today) Kealakekua Bay. After a stay of some weeks they left the bay and went exploring, but heavy storms forced them to return to Kealakekua for major repairs to *Resolution's* foremast.

Initially Cook had been welcomed by the Hawaiians. He was identified by them with a legendary god Lono who had disappeared to sea in ancient times and who, they believed, would return to them bearing gifts in canoes decorated with white streamers (a passable image of the European ships). But relations between the Polynesians and the Europeans deteriorated, The sailors ate large quantities of the local produce, and were pleased to discover that the local women would have sex for an iron nail. Iron and other objects that could not be bargained for were often 'stolen' by the Hawaiians. (In Polynesian society ownership of property had a different meaning from that common in Europe.)

On 13 February some Hawaiians rolled large lava stones down the hillside to the well where some seamen were drawing water for the ships. A little later a Hawaiian stole some tongs from *Discovery*; he was caught and flogged. Then another stole them again, and this time got away. He was chased ashore, and the result was a mêlée on the beach between a few unarmed Europeans and several hundred Hawaiians armed with clubs and stones. By the time things were sorted out, a ship's boat had been ransacked and its oars broken.

During the night, some Hawaiians removed one of *Discovery's* boats from its anchorage in the bay. This was a serious loss for an expedition that used ships' boats for work near uncharted shores. Lieutenant Clerke, captain of *Discovery*, informed Cook of the theft at approximately 6.30 am. Cook had been extremely vexed by the previous incidents and this was the last straw; he decided to show the Hawaiians how dangerous it was to trifle with him. He issued orders to blockade the bay and seize the Hawaiians' canoes. On previous occasions in the Pacific he had taken both islanders and property hostage to recover stolen items, usually with success. Accordingly he ordered Clerke to send two boats 'well manned and armed' (specifying that ball shot be issued, not the less lethal small shot) to the southern point to stop any canoes escaping, and he ordered two of his own boats from *Resolution* to the northern point with the same orders (PRO Adm. 55/22-3;51/4561/217). While his orders were being implemented, a large ocean canoe was sighted making its way out of the bay. The only boat ready-manned and armed was *Resolution's* cutter, commanded by William Bligh. Cook ordered Bligh after the canoe, and Bligh set off immediately. He soon caught up with it and tried to persuade its crew to go ashore, but no notice was taken, so he ordered his men to fire their muskets. No one was was hit, but the noise of the muskets caused the canoe to veer towards the southern shore. There the Hawaiians beached their canoe and ran off inland. *Discovery's* guns were also fired at a canoe.

Soon after, Cook decided to go to the village on the north shore to visit the Hawaiian king, Terreeoboo, with the intention of getting him on board and using him as a hostage for the return of the boat. This did not fit well with his first plan, as the gunfire in the bay would have alarmed the Hawaiians, and the men needed to take Terreeoboo by force were now scattered about the bay keeping in the canoes. But at about 7 am Cook left for the north shore with a Marine Lieutenant, two NCOs and seven armed marines. Just before he left his attention was drawn to Bligh's boat, which by then had chased the escaping canoe ashore. It was suggested by an officer that if Bligh had the same trouble as the boat party the day before he would be in difficulties. Cook dismissed the idea, saying that Bligh was armed and one shot would clear the beach (BM Add. MS 8955). Once on shore, Cook found Terreeoboo just getting up, and invited him to accompany him to the boats with a view to going on board *Resolution*. At first Terreeoboo agreed willingly, but on his way to the shore he was persuaded by his wife and some of the crowd that rapidly gathered to change his mind.

Cook insisted and the crowd resisted. The situation worsened; news came to the Hawaiians that one of their chiefs had been killed in the bay while trying to penetrate the blockade. Cook, however, refused to abandon his plan. The Hawaiians became more and more insolent and threatening, and Phillips, the Lieutenant of Marines, asked permission to line up his men along the shore in case fire was needed. Cook agreed and this was done, but they formed up some paces behind Cook. The sequence of events from this point becomes less clear, but it is fairly certain that a Hawaiian threw something – a stone or a breadfruit – at Cook, which struck him in the face (PRO Adm. 55/122). Either then or shortly after, Cook fired his double-barrelled piece, first small shot and then ball shot, and killed at least one Hawaiian, either in rage at the insult and with the intention of making an example of one of the islanders, or in self-defence. A general assault now began; the marines fired once and then turned and fled for their lives into the water, abandoning their muskets. Phillips and the sergeant soon followed (PRO Adm. 55/22-3). The pinnace that had brought the shore party was waiting just off shore, but could not give a good supporting fire as it was severly rocked by marines clambering on board. Cook and some of the party were left on the rocks, and were quickly overrun by Hawaiians.

Cook was struck down by an Hawaiian club and stabbed repeatedly with knives. Four marines who could not swim were dragged out of the water, stabbed and beaten to death with clubs. The Hawaiians were dispersed for a short time by fire from *Resolution*'s guns, but some quickly crept back and dragged off the corpses, which were later dismembered and stripped of their flesh, as was the custom.

One person who could have helped and did not was Lieutenant Williamson, of *Resolution*, who had gone to the north point with an armed party of seamen in the launch, as part of the blockade, and had then been ordered by Cook to join him for the shore expedition. Instead of coming in closer and giving supporting fire at the crucial moment when the marines deserted their posts, he moved his boat further out, and would not allow his men to fire, even though they wanted to. Nor did he make any attempt to recover the bodies during the time that the shore was empty of Hawaiians (BM Egerton MS 2591).

With Captain Cook dead, Captain Clerke of *Discovery* took command. His immediate problem was to safeguard the shore camp at the southern part of the bay where Lieutenant King was making observations and guarding *Resolution*'s foremast; he sent Bligh in *Discovery*'s cutter to inform Lieutenant King of what had happened, with orders to break camp and bring on board the ship's timekeeper, essential for navigation.

King departed for *Discovery* in the cutter, leaving Bligh in charge of *Resolution*'s mast, and while he was away Bligh's party was attacked by stone-throwing Hawaiians. Bligh ordered his men to fire and repelled them successfully. Reinforcements soon arrived, with all the available armed men from both ships, and orders from Clerke to bring everything on board as quickly as possible. This was managed; once Bligh had demonstrated that they were prepared to stand and fight, the Hawaiians left them alone. By 11.30 am everything was safely on board. It took several days to recover parts of Captain Cook's body, and these were committed to the deep before the ships left Hawaii.

Surprisingly, Williamson was promoted on the voyage and eventually became a Post-captain. Bligh did not criticise him in his own account of Cook's death, which suggests he was being protective of Williamson. One explanation is that there may have been a masonic connection (then fairly common among officers in the Royal Navy) between Bligh and Williamson (who is known to have been a mason; and a portrait of Bligh as a young man shows him wearing a masonic-like symbol). Certainly Williamson's behaviour at Kealakekua was covered up by some of his fellow lieutenants and the Admiralty was given a highly distorted account of what happened.

Lieutenant King was awarded the prestigious task of completing Cook's account of the voyage, which was published in 1784. His influential account admitted Captain Cook's over-confidence in dealing with the Hawaiians as a contributory cause of his death, but suggested that the 'fatal turn in the affair' was afforded by the news of the death of the chief, killed by Lieutenant Rickman's boats at the southern point. King ignored the criticisms of Williamson made at the time and recorded in the Logs and Journals of the officers. Rickman was made a scapegoat for Cook's death and never progressed beyond Lieutenant in the Navy. Samwell, also present at Kealakekua, perhaps more convincingly, called Willtamson's conduct 'the fatal turn in the affair'.

William Bligh marked in the margins of a copy of King's version of Cook's third voyage many bitter comments on the accuracy of what King had written, not just about the death of Cook but about the whole voyage. This copy was found in the Admiralty in the 1920s and may have been written in by Bligh during his service in the hydrographic office in 1804.

King edited out of the official account Bligh's contribution to the voyage. As Master of *Resolution* Bligh had done much of the navigation and had also drawn a large number of charts under Cook's supervision. King infuriated Bligh by using some of his charts in the book and ascribing them to Henry Roberts. Bligh wrote on the title page: 'None of the Maps and Charts in this publication are from the original drawings of Lieut. Henry Roberts; he did no more than copy the original ones from Captain Cook, who besides myself was the only person that surveyed and laid the coast down, in the Resolution. Every plan & Chart from C. Cook's death are exact Copies of my Works.' Evidence in support of Bligh's claims is provided by the division of the profits from the sale of King's official account; he received one-eighth of the proceeds but no acknowledgment, a typical case of a junior being paid off by his seniors.

Bligh's most caustic comments were reserved for the account of Cook's death. He wrote: 'The Marines fire[d] & ran which occasioned al[l] that followed for had the[y] fixed their bayonets & not have run, so frighte[ned] as they were, they migh[t] have done all before t[hem]' (letters in square brackets indicate where a binder cropped the unbound sheets across Bligh's remarks; they have been interpolated following R. T. Gould, 'Bligh's Notes on Cook's Last Voyage', *The Mariner's Mirror*, vol.

14, no. 4, October 1928, pp. 371-85). He went on to describe the conduct of Lieutenant Molesworth Phillips, represented in the official account as heroic, as a most 'ludicrous performance', and called King's version of what Phillips did during the attack 'a most famous lie'.

If, as seems likely in the small society of ships on a long voyage, King and Phillips became aware of Bligh's views during the remainder of the voyage, it explains why he was excluded from the general promotion on the ships' return to Britain in 1780. If King could cover up for Williamson (whom even Phillips did not excuse; the recriminations between both men flared up into a duel at the Cape of Good Hope), if he could shift the blame implicitly onto young Rickman and miscredit charts and drawings of Bligh to Roberts, he was surely capable of blocking Bligh's promotion. With King's account established as the offical story of the voyage, Bligh could only fume in private.

Bligh found one consolation for his failure to gain promotion when he revisited the Isle of Man on his return. He had probably met the Betham family when he was stationed at Douglas before the voyage. The Bethams had an unmarried daughter, Elizabeth, aged 27, and William and Elizabeth became engaged. The Bethams were rich and influential: Elizabeth's father, Richard, was a close friend of the Scottish philosopher David Hume and the Scottish economist Adam Smith. Her grandfather, Dr Neil Campbell, had been principal of Glasgow University and chaplain to the King. Her uncle, Duncan Campbell, was a wealthy and successful merchant, who owned several merchant ships plying between the West Indies and Britain, and was a contractor to the Royal Navy and managed the prison hulks on the Thames, which were to feature as an important consideration in the future colonisation of New South Wales.

Bligh married Elizabeth in the Isle of Man on 4 February 1781. He gained the loyal and lasting support of a strong-willed, intelligent and well-educated woman, and was also brought into touch with people influential in and around the Royal Navy.

# 3

# A Great Goodness

When *Resolution* and *Discovery* returned in 1780, Britain was fighting another war with her continental rivals. There was the added complication of the revolt of the American colonies. It was a world war, which was fought in Europe, America and in the Atlantic. Though Britain was forced out of the American Colonies (but not Canada), she remained the premier power in Europe. Rodney's great victory in the Caribbean against the French, in 1782, following the British surrender at Yorktown, was regarded as more significant than the loss of a continent, because it gave command of the Atlantic once again to the Royal Navy. But in a day when serious debate took place over whether to take Guadeloupe Island in exchange for Canada in a peace settlement, it is perhaps less surprising that an empty ocean was preferred to an empty continent.

Bligh participated in two naval events at the tail end of the war; he missed a third by being delayed in port. On 14 February 1781 he was appointed Master of HMS *Belle Poule*, Captain Philip Patton, a captured French frigate put into the King's service. The main duty of Admiral Parker's fleet was to keep an eye on the Dutch and also to escort British merchant ships to and from the Baltic. *Belle Poule* spent some time crossing and recrossing the North Sea. In April she captured a small French prize, *La Cologne*, which was taken to Leith in Scotland.

On 5 August 1781 a British convoy, escorted by seven line-of-battle ships and five frigates, including *Belle Poule*, met a Dutch convoy, escorted by eight Dutch warships, near the Dogger Bank. Parker ordered the merchant ships to cut and run for home. The wind, a north-easterly, favoured the British squadron, with the Dutch lying to the south-west. In the rush to catch the Dutch the Admiral misjudged the pace of the ships, and they approached the enemy in some disorder. Frigates by convention did not engage line-of-battle ships, so *Belle Poule* did not take part in the main assault, but would be used to give assistance, pass on signals and act as support if needed. Bligh's job was to control the sailing of the ship, and the fact that he was promoted to a larger ship after the battle suggests that he distinguished himself in his work when other ships were sailing around in confusion. The battle raged for just over three and a half hours, causing about equal damage and casualties.

The British lost 104 killed and 339 wounded and the Dutch 142 killed and 403 wounded. A Dutch ship later sank in shallow water; but apart from this the damage was slight to both sides.

On 5 September 1781 Bligh was transferred from *Belle Poule* to HMS *Berwick*. He was promoted Lieutenant 'from Mr Keith Stewart's partiality to me from my services' on 5 October 1781. *Berwick*, Captain John Fergusson, had been a ship-of-the-line at the battle of the Dogger Bank, and Bligh served in her for only a few months before being transferred again, as Fifth Lieutenant, to HMS *Princess Amelia*, another ship-of-the-line at Dogger Bank. He served in her from 1 January to 19 March 1782 and was then transferred to HMS *Cambridge*. In *Cambridge* Bligh was Sixth Lieutenant, and he served in her until 13 January 1783.

*Cambridge* was assigned to Vice-Admiral Barrington's fleet, but during April 1782 she underwent repairs. Owing to what Bligh considered 'a want of effort' on the part of the shipwrights and other artificers, *Cambridge* was held in port while the fleet under Barrington captured a convoy of supply ships. Those who participated in the action gained prize-money in proportion to their rank, while those who missed out, such as the men in *Cambridge*, did not. In Bligh's case he thought his prize-money would have been worth £200, or about three years' wages as Lieutenant.

*Cambridge* did, however, take part in the relief of Gibraltar, which was under siege from a combined force of French and Spanish ships and troops. The Governor, General Elliot, had successfully held them off but was in desperate straits from want of supplies. Lord Howe's fleet left Spithead on 11 September 1782 and reached Gibraltar on 13 October. The French and Spanish fleets came out to meet him, but may have been daunted by the size of Howe's fleet (149 ships and 34 ships of the line). They remained too far off to present any obstacle to Howe's entrance into Gibraltar. He brought enough provisions to last for a year; Gibraltar was secured for another two centuries.

The fleet returned to Spithead on 14 November, and on 13 January 1783 Lieutenant Bligh was paid off and placed on half-pay, along with thousands of other officers, as the great war fleets were stood down for the ensuing peace.

In the months after his return Bligh was with his wife and his new baby daughter, Harriet Maria, at Douglas, Isle of Man. His half-pay was 2 shillings a day, hardly enough to feed and clothe his family. Elizabeth's uncle, Duncan Campbell, had a number of merchant ships for which he needed experienced and reliable officers, and he advised Bligh to get a written clearance from the Admiralty to go into the merchant service and leave the country. Bligh's earlier three years of Royal Navy experience in the West Indies (1771-4) probably helped him gain employment with Campbell. Bligh completed the formalities by July 1783 and shortly afterwards embarked on his temporary mercantile career. He sailed

Campbell's ships for four years, and acted as his commercial agent in Jamaica.

Bligh commanded *Lynx*, then *Cambrian* and then, in 1787, *Britannia*. It was in *Britannia* that he took on as a volunteer a young midshipman, Fletcher Christian, following recommendations made to him by Captain Taubman, and some persuasion from Christian himself. Although Bligh had his full establishment on board and had declined to take Christian as Master's Mate, Fletcher, according to his brother Edward, wrote to Bligh with the following offer: 'Wages were no object, he only wished to learn his profession, and if Captain Bligh would permit him to mess with the gentlemen, he would readily enter the ship as a foremast man, until there was a vacancy among the officers. "We midshipmen are gentlemen, we never pull on a rope; I should be glad to go one voyage in that situation, for there may be occasions when officers may be called upon to do the duties of a common man" ' (Edward Christian, 1794). Fletcher Christian made at least two voyages with Bligh to the West Indies and they became friends.

On returning home from what was to be his last voyage in *Britannia*, Bligh found some good news awaiting him. Due to the patronage of Sir Joseph Banks, he had been appointed to command an expedition to the Pacific.

The government had been persuaded to send an expedition to Tahiti to procure breadfruit plants for transport to the West Indies. The breadfruit was a Pacific island plant which explorers had reported on for years. The islanders ate it regularly and it was the closest thing to bread that Europeans had discovered in the Pacific. Seamen became accustomed to it and, as it grew in abundance without cultivation and was easy to cook, it attracted the attention of plantation owners in the West Indies as a possible food for slaves. In 1786 Hinto East, a West Indian planter, was in Britain lobbying Sir Joseph Banks, who soon became convinced of the case. He had been under pressure for years to persuade the government to undertake the scheme. The idea had the backing of the scientific community and of commerce, a powerful combination; it was also the right time for it politically, as attention shifted from the losses in America to the possibilities of the Pacific. Sir Joseph put the scheme to George III at one of their meetings, and the King made the necessary orders for a ship to be assigned to the task. Sir Joseph, having been a prominent member of Cook's first voyage to Tahiti, and being an eminent botanist and President of the Royal Society, was charged with the arrangements for the expedition, which included some influence in the appointment of the commander. It would be a plum job for a young unemployed lieutenant. A voyage lasting two years or more, with the opportunities for discovery, would mean almost certain promotion to Post-captain.

Why was Bligh selected? Since the demands for the expedition came from the West Indies, and since Bligh had been sailing to and from there for the previous four years, meeting planters, government officials and Admiralty personnel, his name was no doubt mentioned in discussions. That Duncan Campbell lobbied Sir Joseph is suggested by a letter he wrote to his cousin on 2 May 1787, in which he wished Bligh 'home soon, as thereby he may stand a chance of employment in his own line'. Bligh also knew Tahiti, having been there with Cook, and he had sailed the greater part of the route. Bligh's navigational skills were known and he was junior enough in rank to regard the job as a prize. Perhaps for these reasons the Admiralty agreed to Sir Joseph's recommendation. The decision to go ahead was made in May but Bligh only received the news in August, a few days before the official confirmation of his appointment. He wrote immediately to Sir Joseph Banks to thank him (Mackaness, 1951, p. 37):

I arrived recently from Jamaica and should have instantly paid my respects to you had not Mr. Campbell told me you were not to return from the country until Thursday. I have heard the flattering news of your great goodness to me, intending to honour me with the command of the vessel which you propose to go to the South Seas, for which, after offering you my most grateful thanks, I can only assure you I shall endeavour, and I hope succeed, in deserving such a trust.

# 4

# The King's Bounty

On 5 May 1787 Lord Sydney, a Principal Secretary of State, wrote on behalf of George III to the Lords Commissioners of the Admiralty and officially informed them of the King's intentions about a South Sea voyage for breadfruit. These intentions were set out explicitly:

The Merchants and Planters interested in His Majesty's West India possessions have represented that the Introduction of the Bread Fruit Tree into the Islands in those Seas to constitute an Article of Food would be very essential Benefit to the Inhabitants, and have humbly solicited that Measures may be taken for procuring some Trees of that Description from the place of their present Growth, to be transplanted in the said islands.

His Majesty desirous at all Times to promote the Interests of so respectable a Body of his Subjects, especially in an instance which promises general Advantage, has thought fit that Measures should immediately be taken for the procuring some Bread Fruit Trees and for conveying them to the said West India Islands, and I am in Consequence to signify to your Lordships His Majesty's Command that you do cause a Vessel of proper Class to be stored and victualled for this Service, and to be fitted with proper Conveniences for the Preservation of as many of the said Trees as from her Size can be taken on Board, giving the command of her to some able and discreet Officer, and when she shall be ready for sea, your Lordships are to direct the said Officer to proceed in her to the Society Islands, situated in the Southern Ocean in the Latitude about 18 Degrees South and Longitude about 210 Degrees East of Greenwich, where according to the accounts which are given by the late Captain Cook, and Persons who accompanied him on his Voyages, the Bread Fruit Tree is to be found in its most luxuriant state.

It is proposed that the Vessel which your Lordships are to despatch upon this Service should proceed round Cape Horn and after she shall have arrived at the Society Islands and as many Trees and plants have been taken on Board as may be thought necessary, to proceed from thence through Endeavour Streights (which separate New Holland from New Guinea) to Princess Island in the Streight of Sunda, or if it should happen to be more convenient, to pass on the East Side of Java, to some port on the North side of that island, where any Bread Fruit Trees which may be injured or have died may be replaced by Mangosteens, Duriens, Jacks, Nancas, Lansas, and in short all the fine fruits of that Quarter, as well as the Rice Plant which grows upon dry land. From Princess Island she should

14

proceed round the Cape of Good Hope to the West Indies, calling on her way thither at any Places which may be thought necessary, and deposit one half of her Cargo at His Majesty's Botanical Garden at St. Vincent for the Benefit of the Windward Islands, and from thence to carry the other half down to Jamaica.

As from Analogy it appears that the Monsoons prevail in the Seas between New Holland and New Guinea, the easterly Winds will commence in March or April. It is therefore judged proper that the Vessel should sail from thence in the month of September next.

Mr David Nelson and Mr William Brown, Gardeners by Profession, have from their Knowledge of Trees and Plants been hired for the Purpose of selecting such as appear to be of a proper Species and Size and it is His Majesty's Pleasure that your Lordships do order those Persons to be received on board the said Vessel and to be borne for Wages and Victuals during the Voyage.

The *Bounty* voyage was a botanical 'collect and carry' mission (see Knight, 1936, pp.183ff). In the great pageant of British history it was hardly more than a footnote in the maelstrom of contemporary events.

Within a week of receiving Lord Sydney's letter the Lords Commissioners, having no suitable vessel available, issued instructions to purchase a vessel of not more than 250 tons. The Navy Board opened tenders for the purchase of a ship and requested that the various offerings be inspected by a person who was to sail on the ship, as well as by their own officials. This was a sensible suggestion. In the event, however, it was Sir Joseph Banks and David Nelson, one of the gardeners, who inspected the short-list of two vessels, *Bethia* and *Harriet*, the other vessels (including the 300-ton *Lynx* from Duncan Campbell, which Bligh had commanded in 1783) having been rejected by the Admiralty inspectors. This ensured that the chosen ship was at least seaworthy and that it could be adapted to carry the plants; but, in the absence of the views of its commander, the only person qualified to judge a ship's suitability for the proposed voyage, which included perilous passages round Cape Horn and through Endeavour Straits, it left open the question of whether the chosen vessel was appropriate to meet the King's intentions. As it was, Bligh had not yet been appointed, and considerable expense was undertaken, making the purchase and fitting-out decisions irrevocable.

On 23 May 1787 the Deptford Yard officers estimated the value of *Bethia* to be £1820 12s 8d. against the asking price of £2600 tendered by its owners, Welbank Sha[i]rp and Brown. A negotiated price of £1950 was agreed, and *Bethia* passed into the Royal Navy and into Deptford Dock for extensive alterations and repairs. The wooden sheathing was replaced with copper (to combat the notorious pest *Teredo navalis*), the masts and rigging altered to shorten the sail area and the main cabin altered, under Sir Joseph Banks' advice, to accommodate the plants. The Admiralty asked for a report on the number of men that the ship could take, and on 6 June the yard reported that the ship could accommodate 20 men in addition to the officers. On 8 June the Admiralty informed the Navy Board that the *Bethia* was to be listed 'as an Armed Vessel by the name of *Bounty*', and was to have an establishment of 45 men – 25 ABs plus the officers.

The *Bounty* was ready for service on 14 August 1787. Bligh's appointment as commander was confirmed two days later. When Sir Joseph Banks visited *Bounty* at Deptford and met Bligh, he thought him a 'very deserving man'; but he was somewhat put out to find 'he knew he was to go to the S. Seas & some other places but he knew little or nothing of the object of his voyage had no Idea of going to the East Indies or to the West Indies in short he was about to sail the latter end of this month with little or no information or knowledge of the Object of his Voyage'. In the same letter to Sir George Young he offered the advice: 'I will not suppose but that Mr Nelson the Gardiner may have had Full instructions but you will excuse me for saying that unless you do interest the Captain himself or instruct him & inspire him with the spirit of the undertaking it is to very little purpose the vessel would sail' (ML A78-4, vol. 5).

That Bligh knew a great deal more about the voyage than he was prepared to reveal to Banks is almost certain, if only from his connection with Duncan Campbell, who was fully informed. But he chose to imply ignorance, which in the services is often the wisest stance, and would naturally defer and be extremely polite and circumspect to his new patron, waiting for Banks to offer information rather than volunteering the port gossip himself. There is also a hint that the Admiralty did not regard the voyage with any degree of urgency; they were carrying out the King's instructions but were hardly imbued with the enthusiasm evident among the botanists, or the plantation owners, who had engaged the ear of the sovereign.

Bligh's manner appears to have paid off, for Banks gives an account in his letter of how he remedied Bligh's apparent lack of knowledge:

> I had above an hours discourse with him, he enterd into the plan with Spirit was delighted with the Idea of rendering such service to his Country & mankind but declared if it had not been for my visit he never should have known any thing of it … I have promised him extracts from all my official papers on the subject he enters into it with pleasure has even begd to be assisted in studying the subject.

The relationship that Bligh built by his consummate handling of his first meeting with Banks lasted his entire life, and Banks never failed him as a friend and sponsor.

Due to the parsimony of the Navy Board and the ignorance of the botanists, an extremely small ship had been foisted on Bligh. *Bounty* weighed only about 215 tons; in comparison, Cook's *Endeavour* weighed 368 tons, *Adventure* 336 tons and *Resolution* 462 tons. In fact *Bethia* was the smallest of the ships offered to the Navy. It was some 87 feet long, 11 feet 4 inches deep in the hold, and 24 feet 4 inches wide. The bow carried a figure of a woman in a green riding habit. But the major feature was its smallness, whose consequences were twofold. First, the ship's company, larger than the inspectors allowed for, lived on top of one another even more than usual, and secondly the ship's complement was reduced below the minimum needed for such a long voyage; in particular the officer structure was diluted and no marines were carried. The ship was simultaneously overcrowded and undermanned.

With £4456 worth of alterations costing more than the price paid for the ship, the unreasonableness of what was proposed caused some hot debate. In September Bligh wrote to Lord Selkirk on the subject of manning and Lord Selkirk, after consulting other opinions, took up his points with Sir Joseph Banks in a letter sent on 14 September 1787:

> An officer of the navy ... happens to be here just now on a visit; who tells me that this Establishment of Blighs vessel is that of a Cutter & says it is highly improper for so long a voyage; only 24 Able Seamen & 21 of all others, without a Lieutenant, or any Marines, with only a Surgeon without a surgeons Mate, which arises from it being considered as a Cutter, whereas in a Sloop of War they have besides Lieut a Surgeon & his Mate, tho they be put on the Channel Service, where if a Surgeon dies, they can have help at every Port but if Blighs Surgeon meets with any accident they must wait for all Medical assistance God knows how long... And for this Establishment of a Cutter poor Bligh must be deprived of his preferment, for its seems a Lieut. cannot command a Sloop, & a Master & Commander is above taking command of a Cutter (ML A78-4, vol. 5).

Bligh continued his efforts to get promoted before sailing. He forsaw the problems that might arise on a long voyage. He was the only commissioned officer on board, the rest being warrant officers and midshipmen. He had no marines to maintain discipline. If he was promoted to Post-captain, a lieutenant would be appointed below him, thus extending the officer structure, and partly make up for the deficiencies and risks of the voyage. Selkirk, earlier in the letter quoted above, reveals some of the arguments being used by Bligh to secure his promotion:

> Mr Bligh himself is but very indifferently used, or rather really ill used: he seems to have lost hope of getting any preferment at going out, & God knows who may be at the head of the Admiralty at his return. It would have been simply Justice to him, to have made him Master & Commander before sailing; nay considering that he was, I believe, the only person that was not in some way or other preferd at their return, of all who went out with Capt. Cook, it would be no unreasonable thing to make him Post Captain now: more especially as Ld Howe made Captain Hunter Post when he went out lately to Botany Bay with Commodore Phillips. Hunter & Bligh were in very similar situations, they had both been Masters & both were refused by Sandwich to be made Lieutenant and it happened that both of

them were made Acting Lieutenant by Keith Stewart & afterwards confirmed not with Sandwichs goodwill.

A month later, on 3 October 1787, with no progress on the promotion issue, Bligh wrote to Sir Joseph Banks:

> Pray Sir, could I not hope that my Lord Howe as promotion would take place, might be prevailed on to give me rank as Master & Commander, considering that I was going out of the immediate chance of promotion, and the great advantage of being in the beginning of a War...I have been constantly in service for 18 years and I hope that may have some weight with his Lordship...As you have already been so great a Friend to me I thought I might just mention this circumstance.

Throughout November and December 1787 Bligh's letters to his patron (5 November; 6, 10, 12 December) invariably return to his lack of promotion. Banks was unable to get Bligh what he wanted and he had to reconcile himself to the situation.

Although small, *Bounty* was rated as an 'Armed Vessel' and therefore carried some weaponry. Four 4-pounders and ten swivel guns were placed on her sufficient for 'Foreign Service' under charge of a Master Gunner. To assist in the maintenance of these weapons the establishment was altered to include an armourer, making one seaman less. The rest of the ship's equipment consisted of three boats, which the Navy Board had ordered to be made at Deptford, namely a launch of 20 feet, a cutter of 18 feet and a jolly-boat of 16 feet. Deptford was too busy at this time to make the boats, so an order went to John Burr, a boat contractor, to build the launch, and the other two boats were ordered from the Navy office at Deal. These were delivered before Bligh was appointed, and Bligh asked the Navy Board to exchange the 20-foot launch for a larger one, 23 feet long, which would hold four more men. After the mutiny he was to travel 3,900 miles in this larger boat with 17 companions.

On 20 August the first appointments of warrant officers were made; first the Master, John Fryer, from Wells in Norfolk, who was two years older than Bligh. He had been a Master in the Navy since 1781 (in HMS *Camel*) and had worked his way to the grade of 3rd Rate. The other warrant officer was Thomas Huggan, the Surgeon, who turned out to be an incurable alcoholic. Presumably his condition was known to the Admiralty and somebody regarded the *Bounty* voyage as a convenient opportunity to get rid of him. Bligh tried desperately to discharge him in return, but failed; he then pleaded for an assistant surgeon, which he was eventually granted just before the ship sailed, though entered as an AB, again making one seaman less.

Two ABs were appointed on the same day. One of them, William Brown, who had been sent on the recommendation of Sir Joseph Banks, was then sent to *Ariel* on Lord Howe's order (Bligh described Brown as 'the best non-commission'd officer I had'); the other was Thomas Hayward, aged 20, from Hackney in London. Hayward was moved to Midshipman on 1 December 1787.

A week later, 27 August, the next batch of appointments was made. William Cole, Boatswain (Bo's'n), came from *Alecto*, a fireship, and William Peckover, Gunner, came from *Warspite*, a receiving ship. Peckover had sailed on all three of Cook's voyages and he knew Bligh. He also knew Tahiti and was fairly fluent in the language. He was an excellent choice. William Purcell, Carpenter, on the other hand, was a disastrous acquisition. He was to become the bane of Bligh's life. Lawrence Lebogue, Sailmaker, however, had been with Bligh on *Britannia*; he was 40 and very loyal to Bligh (and subsequently sailed with him in *Providence*).

Two ABs were appointed, Henry Hillbrant, 24, from Hanover and Michael Portman from Birmingham. Portman was on *Bounty* for two months and was discharged on 18 November at Deptford. John Samuel, from Edinburgh, aged 26, was appointed Clerk; Bligh had a high regard for Samuel and later publicly acknowledged his debt to him. Another midshipman was appointed with this batch, George Stewart from Orkney, aged 21. Bligh had met his family when *Resolution* made landfall at the Orkneys on the way back from Cook's third voyage. Bligh was later to write that because of the reception he had received from Stewart's family in 1780 he would 'gladly have taken him with me; but, independent of his recommendation, he was a seaman, and had always borne a good character' (Bligh, 1792). Stewart was re-rated AB, while keeping his status as a Young Gentleman, as was the custom, but by re-rating him Bligh was able to recruit other midshipmen, although, in consequence, because Young Gentlemen did not 'pull on a rope', it reduced the effective number of ABs yet again.

The last of the enlistments made on 27 August was of Peter Heywood, aged 15, from Douglas, Isle of Man. The Heywood family were close friends of the Bethams, and it was through this connection that Bligh was strenuously lobbied by his father-in-law to take Heywood with him. Richard Betham, Elizabeth's father, wrote to Bligh in the following terms:

> I'm much obliged to you for your attention to young Heywood, and getting him a berth on board the vessel. He is an ingenious young Lad and has always been a favourite of mine and indeed everybody here. And indeed the reason of my insisting so strenuously upon his going the voyage with you is that after I mentioned the matter to Mrs Bligh, his family have fallen into a great deal of distress on account of their father's losing the Duke of Atholl's business. And I thought it would not appear well in me to drop this matter, if it could possibly be done without any prejudice to you; as this would seem deserting them in their adversity; and I found they would regard it as a great disappointment. I hope he will be of some service to you, as far as he is able, in writing or looking after any necessary matters under your charge.

By these entreaties Bligh took on board a young boy with no experience of the sea or ships, and it was magnanimous of him to do so with *Bounty* already undermanned with experienced seamen. But, in the eighteenth century, for favours received favours had to be returned. Heywood stayed with Bligh's family while *Bounty* was fitting out and he accompanied him to the ship and about ship's business. Heywood came to *Bounty* as an AB and moved up to Midshipman on October 23.

Two important posts were filled on 29 August. William Elphinstone from Edinburgh became Master's Mate. He was 36. Peter Linkletter, from Stromness, Orkney, became Quartermaster. He was 30. Elphinstone was older than Bligh and Fryer. The Mate assisted the Master in the more routine tasks such as heaving the log, attending to the galley to stop 'wrangling' and checking on the crew to maintain cleanliness. Linkletter, as Quartermaster, was young for the job, which was normally given to an older man because the duties, while responsible, were not onerous. His role was to oversee the specialised work of others such as the helmsman, the work of stowage, the ringing of the ship's bell (to call the watches) and the distribution of the carefully weighed out provisions by the Purser (a position on *Bounty* filled by Bligh).

In the batch signed on 29 August came several ABs. The first ones were Thomas Hall, aged 38, from Durham, John Charlton, aged 23, from Sunderland, and John Cooper, aged 28, from Suffolk. Hall became the *Bounty*'s cook and the other two men deserted, Cooper within a week at Deptford and Charlton in November at Portsmouth. This happened several times before *Bounty* finally got away, presumably because the nature of the voyage became obvious from 'scuttlebut' – though the men were not told officially where they were going until *Bounty* was well into the voyage – and some men preferred to risk a flogging for desertion rather than face a long absence from home. Given the general mobilisation of the fleet in September, in anticipation of war, other captains were willing to recruit good seamen, without asking too many questions, for service nearer home.

Four more ABs signed on a couple of days later. Among them was Isaac Martin, from Philadelphia in America and aged 30. The three others jumped ship, two a month later at Deptford, and one two months later at Portsmouth. Joseph Coleman joined *Bounty* as Armourer. He was from Guildford, aged 36.

The recruitment of ABs continued into September, by now competing with the general mobilisation. On 7 September Charles Churchill, 28, from Manchester joined the ship, and was made Ship's Corporal, which task included keeping order among the crew – a singularly inappropriate appointment in this case, as Churchill was one of the worst troublemakers on the voyage, so it was probably a case of assigning the meanest-looking man to the toughest job. With him Richard Skinner, 22, from Tunbridge Wells and Alexander Smith from London were recruited. Smith, or Adams as he was really called, was 20. Samuel Sutton, 28, from Hull came on board as AB, but he deserted four weeks later.

Lord Selkirk's son, the Hon. Dunbar Douglas, was also signed on as an AB and efforts were made by Lord Selkirk to get his son's tutor, Mr Lockhead, taken on board as well! Bligh, while solicitous of the favours Selkirk could do for him – though he had failed to get him promoted – was in no mood further to dilute his inexperienced crew with tutors, and he politely but firmly refused to consider Lockhead, citing Lord Howe's establishment for *Bounty* as the excuse. Lord Howe supported Bligh on this issue and noted his 'very laudable civility' (Howe to Banks, 22 September 1787) and, within a month, the Hon. Dunbar Douglas was discharged into HMS *Royal Sovereign*.

Along with Douglas came Fletcher Christian, 22, from Cockermouth in Cumberland (though he signed on as being from Whitehaven). He was rated Master's Mate. He had, of course, sailed as a midshipman before he joined Bligh in *Britannia*, and this voyage would assure him of promotion to Lieutenant. He had left *Britannia* in August, and his sailing with Bligh on two voyages to the West Indies assured him consideration for *Bounty*'s voyage.

The batch of recruits appointed on 7 September was the largest to join *Bounty* in one day. The most important from the point of view of the *Bounty* story was James Morrison, aged 27, from London, rated Bo's'n's Mate. His was an exacting job in many ways. His main charge was the ship's rigging. He had to check on the sailmaker and on the condition of the sails in *Bounty*'s locker. He also carried out any floggings imposed as punishments on the crew. Morrison must have been an above-average seaman to get appointed as Bo's'n's Mate; his Journals show that he had considerable talent, though he often wasted it in invective and petty moaning. With Morrison came Thomas McIntosh, Carpenter's Mate, from North Shields, and John Mills, Gunner's Mate, from Aberdeen.

Robert Tinkler, 17, rated AB, came on the recommendation of the Master, John Fryer; he was his brother-in-law. Bligh would hardly refuse the Master's request in this respect. Though rated AB, Tinkler messed with the Young Gentlemen and after the mutiny he went on to become a Commander in the Royal Navy. Other ABs were Thomas Burkitt, 25, from Bath; John Milward, 21, from Plymouth; John Sumner, 22, from Liverpool; and John Williams, 26, from Stepney. Five others joined as ABs but deserted before *Bounty* sailed.

John Hallet came on board as the Second Midshipman, recommended by Bligh's wife as the brother of her friend Anne Hallet. He was only 15, from London, and combined loyalty to Bligh with a capacity to sleep on his watch. Bligh asked John Norton, 34, from Liverpool, to join as Quartermaster, having known him in the merchant service, possibly in *Britannia*. He joined on 13 October 1787.

Four more men arrived on 23 October: William Musprat, 27, from Maidenhead; Matthew Thompson, 37, from the Isle of Wight; Luke Dods,

20, from London (he deserted at Deptford); and Edward Young, 21, from St. Kitts in the West Indies. Young was a nephew of Sir George Young and was rated AB but messed with the Young Gentlemen. Very little is known about Young – he was not mentioned in the Log – yet he played a significant part in the mutiny and in the bloody events on Pitcairn.

During October 1787 other men joined the ship, some to replace those who had deserted and others to complete the complement. James Valentine, 28, from Montrose, was among these. Another Scotsman, Alexander Tyre, 23, from Arbroath, joined but deserted at Deal within four weeks. George Simpson, 27, from Kendal came as an AB but was promoted to Quartermaster's Mate a few days later.

Robert Lamb, 21, from London, joined as an AB on 8 October and Thomas Ellison, aged 19, from Deptford, another former crew member of *Britannia*, joined with him. The last few men came aboard during October: John Smith, AB, 36, from Stirling and Charles Norman of Portsmouth were among the late entrants; so was Michael Byrne of Kilkenny, rated as AB but in fact so nearly blind as to be of little use as a seaman. His main skill was as a fiddle player. Bligh recruited Byrne to keep the men exercised in the regular dancing sessions he imposed. *Bounty* was still short of ABs, so four men were sent from *Triumph*, two as volunteers and two as pressed men. The two pressed men, John McTargett and Alexander Johnston, both Scots, deserted on 5 December in Portsmouth. The last man to join the ship was Thomas Denman Ledward, rated AB, but actually the Assistant Surgeon.

In total, instead of the 25 ABs allowed in the Admiralty's establishment, *Bounty* sailed with only 13 men who were assigned to the working of the ship, and one of these was a near-blind Irish fiddler.

Nineteen men sent to *Bounty* did not sail with her, three were honourably, if inconveniently, transferred to other duties, and sixteen deserted (or 'allowed' themselves to be pressed into other ships). Their replacements included six of the hard-core mutineers, three of whom – Young, Quintal and McKoy – went with Christian to Pitcairn. Desertion before a long voyage was quite common; for instance, during the preparations for Cook's third voyage, sixty men deserted.

This then was His Majesty's Armed Vessel *Bounty*, small, overcrowded and undermanned, with a crew that was in many ways the second or third choice enlistment, or there because of special favours owed by Bligh to others. Despite Bligh's best efforts to improve the odds against the voyage's success, with one or two exceptions his recommendations failed. He was simply left to get on with it.

# 5

# The First Setbacks

*Bounty* left Deptford on 9 October 1787 and after a stop at Long Reach made Spithead on 4 November. Bligh had an opportunity to observe his men under the difficult conditions of the passage down the Channel – he was almost driven onto the French coast – and he sent his views in letters to Sir Joseph Banks and Duncan Campbell. Of the Master, John Fryer, he wrote that he 'was a very good man and gives me every satisfaction'. He was less complimentary about Huggan, the Surgeon, who while 'a very capable man' was 'unfit for the Voyage' owing to his 'indolence and corpulency'. On the whole, however, he thought it would not be long before he got his crew 'in very good order' (Bligh to Banks, 5 November 1787).

If Bligh was expecting a speedy departure from Spithead he was to be disappointed. The Admiralty had not sent Bligh's final orders to Lord Hood at Spithead, and without them he could not sail (ships of the Royal Navy do not sail at the whim and fancy of their captains), although the weather for the next three weeks was near perfect for getting down the Channel and into the Atlantic. Good weather is inevitably followed by bad, and every day lost in port added unnecessary difficulties to the voyage. The final sailing orders arrived on 24 November, two months later than planned, and after paying the men two months' wages in advance Bligh attempted a quick dash down the Channel; but he was driven back to Spithead on 3 December. He tried again on 6 December but was again beaten back by the weather. By this time he was fuming at the bureaucrats who had kept him idle while the ideal weather prevailed. On 10 December, after his two attempts to get away, he wrote to Duncan Campbell:

> If there is any punishment that ought to be inflicted on a set of Men for neglect, I am sure it ought on the Admiralty for my three weeks detention at this place during the fair wind which carried all outward bound ships clear of the Channel but me, who wanted it most. This has made my task a very arduous one indeed for to get round Cape Horn at the time I shall be there I know not how to promise myself any success & yet I must do it if the ship will stand it or I suppose my character will be at stake. Had Lord Howe sweetened

this difficult task by giving me promotion I should have been satisfied ...
The hardship I make known I lay under is that they took me from a state of
affluence from your employ with an income of five hundred a year to that of
a Lieuts pay of 4/- Pr Day to perform a voyage which few are acquainted
with sufficiently to insure it any degree of success (Mackaness, 1951, p. 48).

On 17 December he wrote to Sir Joseph Banks for advice on whether to
apply for discretionary orders in case it proved impossible to get round
Cape Horn. His original orders made it mandatory to approach Tahiti
from the Horn and return via the Cape of Good Hope. With the season so
far advanced, Bligh was concerned that the voyage should not end
prematurely in winter seas off Cape Horn. Banks contacted Lord Howe on
Bligh's behalf and it was agreed that Bligh should be allowed discretion
between the Horn and the Cape. Banks advised Bligh, however, that he
was not to give up the attempt to get round the Horn without trying.
Bligh replied by return: 'I assure you Sir I will do all that it is possible for
a Man to do to get round Cape Horn' (Bligh to Banks, 19 December 1787).

The discretionary orders were only partly helpful. Bligh calculated that
the uninterrupted voyage to Tahiti would take seven months via the
Horn and nine or ten via the Cape. The difference was between arriving
at Tahiti in July or in October. By insisting that Bligh try the Horn route
in winter, the orders implied that he might fail and therefore have to
double back across the South Atlantic, with an even greater delay, which
was in fact what happened.

In one of his last letters before he left Bligh told Duncan Campbell how
he had managed a last visit to his wife and family (one of his children had
smallpox) and how Lord Hood had 'winked at my absence'. He wrote: 'I
shall endeavour to get round [Cape Horn], but with heavy Gales, should it
be accompanied with sleet & Snow my people will not be able to stand it,
and I shall not hesitate to go to the Cape of Good Hope. Indeed, I feel my
Voyage a very arduous one, and have only to hope in return that
whatever the event may be my poor Family may be provided for.' He
added that *Bounty* was 'in the best of order and my Men & Officers all
good & feel happy under my directions' (Bligh to Campbell, 22 December
1787).

I shall use *Bounty*'s Log as the main source for my account of the
voyage. Captains were obliged to keep a Log which recorded all events,
momentous and trivial, during the voyage: punishments, the weather,
any sailing orders, such as changes in the sails, and any work the crew
carried out. The Log had to be handed to the Admiralty when the ship
returned. It was a permanent legal record of the voyage. *Bounty*'s official
Log is held at the Public Record Office, Kew (PRO Adm. 55/151). It has
also been published (in limited editions: Rutter, 1937; Bligh, 1975;
Bowker, 1978).

Naturally, a captain's Log seldom included anything disparaging about
his own conduct, and as such should be treated with caution. The

*Bounty*'s Log was written up daily from Bligh's own two-volume Log and Journal, which is in the Mitchell Library, Sydney (ML Safe 1/46 and 1/47). It is therefore a contemporary and unedited account of events before the mutiny. But comparing both versions, it can be seen how Bligh did suppress certain events that would have shown his colleagues in a worse light (he pencilled through certain passages, indicating to his clerk, John Samuel, what was to be left out of the official version), and we shall see some events which he omitted that bear on his conduct. Until the mutiny, Bligh had no knowledge that his remarks would later become important evidence for or against him; there can be no question about the authenticity of the Log's technical contents. I therefore allow Bligh, in the 'neutrality' of the undoctored Log, to present his version of the proceedings before the mutiny. I shall leave till later a detailed discussion of the errors and omissions in Bligh's own accounts and in those of his critics written after 1792. Which Log I am quoting from should be clear from the text.

On 23 December 1787 Bligh finally got *Bounty* away and into the Channel. The ship was lashed by gales and heavy seas; this was the second test of the ship and its crew, and Bligh was pleased by the performance of both. Two days later, on Christmas day, rum was issued with beef and plum pudding. The storms built up, and soon everybody and everything was wet. Bligh tried to minimise the discomforts of the weather, but the best that could be done for the crew at the moment was the issue of more grog 'to make up for their Wet uncomfortable Situation' (Bligh's private Log, 27 December 1787).

In the storms *Bounty* suffered a great deal of damage. The ship's boats were stove in and almost lost overboard; only the determined action of the crew saved them. Seven barrels of beer were washed away and a large part of the 'bread' (biscuit) store was destroyed by seawater. All hands were set to salvage what remained of the biscuit by picking out the uncontaminated pieces. This task was so important that everybody was kept busy at it for several days. Bligh decided to ration the remainder of the biscuit store by cutting the daily ration by a third. Given the uncertainty over the time needed to get to Tahiti, even by the Horn, and the possibility of further losses from storms or vermin, this was a sensible decision, if not fully appreciated by the seamen. It proved a prudent decision because not only did *Bounty* eventually have to take the longer route, but hundreds more pounds were damaged by seawater in the south Atlantic. Having logged his decision, Bligh ensured that the crew became entitled to short allowance money from the Admiralty on their return (which those who returned with him received).

When the storm abated, as soon as the ship's stove could be lit, Bligh organised the drying of clothes. Two men were assigned from each watch to do nothing else. The fires provided hot water for washing clothes, and when the weather permitted the hatches were opened to let air into the

*Captain Bligh*

ship. Until Tenerife was reached on 5 January 1788, the daily routine consisted of washing between the decks and cleaning clothes. Vinegar was used to wash the beams; the bedding was aired on deck, and everybody was inspected by Bligh on Sunday musters for personal cleanliness. These methods, learned from Captain Cook, combatted the combined effects of dirt, foul air and cramped living conditions which proved fatal on so many eighteenth-century ships. Bligh had with him a copy of Lynd's *On the Health of Seamen, On the Scurvy*.

At Tenerife *Bounty* interrupted its journey to take on fresh supplies, but it was a bad time of year for what was most wanted, such as fresh fruit and wine. Without substantial supplies at Tenerife *Bounty* had to fall back on its own resources, which were meagre.

Another innovation of Cook's which Bligh copied was the three-watch system (or four hours duty in twelve). Most ships operated a two-watch system (or four hours duty in eight). With two watches efficiency could rapidly deteriorate. Interrupted sleep (all hands on deck in a storm or other emergency), constant effort, exhausting work aloft and the normal debilitating effects of rain and wind all led to a weary crew, and a weary crew led to accidents and perhaps disasters. Three watches did not turn a dangerous and difficult job into a safe an easy one. But it helped the men to cope with their work and minimised additional dangers. Bligh recorded in his Log (11 January 1787):

> I have ever considered this [three watches] among Seamen as Conducive to health, and not being Jaded by keeping on Deck every other four hours, it adds much to their Content and Chearfulness.

For most of his crew this was an innovation, and no doubt some of them considered it an imposition and a new-fangled idea. The others who had sailed with Bligh before would have retorted that it was normal practice in his ships.

The creation of three watches instead of two automatically called for three watch officers. Bligh decided that the watch officers would be Fryer, the Master, Christian, the Master's Mate, and Peckover, the Gunner. For a midshipman to have command of a watch was a powerful argument in his favour when he was considered for promotion to Lieutenant. On a long voyage the practical experience to be gained was invaluable. This is another instance of the help Bligh was giving to Christian in his career. More was to follow. Christian took over the watch on 11 January 1788, and seven weeks later Bligh issued a written order, read out to all hands, making Christian an Acting Lieutenant. This had been Bligh's own route to promotion and this action virtually assured Christian a similar endorsement on the ship's return.

Naturally Bligh expected Christian to justify his public and logged expression of faith in him, because any failures on Christian's part would reflect on Bligh's judgment. Christian's subsequent failure to meet

Bligh's standards goes some way to explaining the decline in their relationship.

Bligh's earlier problems concerned his relations with Fryer, who appeared to lose interest in the voyage from about this time and proved to be a sullen colleague. This may have been because Bligh interfered in Fryer's work as Master. Fryer was connected with some of the subsequent trouble on *Bounty*. Eight days after Christian's promotion (Log, 10 March 1788), Fryer quarrelled with a seaman, Matthew Quintal, and reported him to Bligh for 'insolence and contempt' (in Bligh's private Log this is described as 'insolence and mutinous behaviour'). Whether the altercation was trivial or serious, in the eighteenth-century Navy punishment was certain once a man had been reported to the Captain by the Master on such a charge. Quintal's behaviour contravened Articles 22 and 23 of the Articles of War and Bligh ordered the usual punishment: two dozen lashes. He wrote in the Log: 'until this Afternoon I had hopes I could have performed the Voyage without punishment to any One.'

The Surgeon brought his problems with him. Bligh's personal Log (23 January 1788) contains the following passage: 'I now find my Doctor to be a Drunken Sot he is constantly in liquor, having a private Stock by him which I assured him shall be taken away if he does not desist from Making himself such a beast.' Huggan's behaviour did not improve – his alcoholism was by then terminal – and to have a senior officer so conspicuously incapable was hardly conducive to respect for discipline.

From Tenerife *Bounty* set out for the Horn. Bligh informed the crew of the purpose of the voyage, its destination and its probable duration. He also committed himself to a public affirmation 'of the certainty of promotion to everyone whose endeavours should merit it' (Log, 11 February 1788). *Bounty* headed south for the hot weather and the equator. Since many of the crew had not crossed the line before, the traditional ceremony was held, but without the practice of ducking, for Bligh thought that 'of all Customs it was the most brutal' (Log, 9 February 1788). To make life more comfortable during the hot weather, Bligh ordered that whenever possible the men were to work under awnings. A daily programme of cleaning, drying and airing clothes was organised, and the hatches were opened to allow air into the ship. Bligh ordered the pumps to be used until the water coming out was as clean as the water going in; this not only cleared the air below decks of putrid smells, but also exercised the men (Log, 22 February 1788).

Once past the tropics, *Bounty* approached the colder southern regions, and Bligh prepared the crew and the ship for the rigours ahead. He was determined to double the Horn. On 22 March, the day before landfall, Bligh reported that the air was 'very sharp' and that some of the men were complaining of rheumatism. The next day they sighted Staten Island, of which he wrote: 'I am fortunate perhaps in seeing the Coast of terra del Fuego at a time when it is freeest of snow, however I cannot help remarking that at this time it has not shewn itself with the horrors mentioned by former Navigators' (Log, 23 March 1788).

Bligh had not been to the Horn before, and his knowledge of it came from the navigational journals he had brought with him, including an account of the ill-fated Anson expedition of 1740-1 (in which Anson lost seven ships and 1300 men but captured millions of pounds worth of Spanish bullion). Bligh regarded the passage round the Horn as the 'most difficult and grand part of our passage' (Log, 25 March 1788). He ordered hot breakfasts for the men, consisting of wheat with sugar and butter, and a few days later he ordered portable soup boiled in pease to be served with their hot dinners. By 29 March they had to batten down fore and aft as seas began to break over the ship. Bligh wrote that the seas at the Horn exceeded anything he had seen before, and his earlier scepticism about Anson's accounts abated under the weight of his own experience.

From 2 April the gales continued to batter the small ship. In his Log Bligh gives the impression of a man determined to perform his duty as he saw it. A lesser man might have succumbed to the first storm and turned away from the Horn under the cover of his discretionary orders. But Bligh kept *Bounty* hard at it, even though the gales kept blowing him back to where he started.

Bligh was worried about the privations that his attempts to fulfil the Admiralty's orders were causing for his men but was still confident his methods could overcome them. He wrote (Log, 22 April 1788):

> The Sails & Ropes were worked with much difficulty, and the few Men who were obliged to be aloft felt the Snow Squalls so severe as to render them almost incapable of getting below, and some of them sometimes for a While lost their Speech; but I took care to Nurse them when off duty with every comfort in my power. The Invalids I made attend and dry their Cloaths and Keep a good fire in every Night, so that no Man when he took his Watch had a Wet Rag on him. They were at three Watches, and When lying too, I would suffer two Men on Deck at a time. I gave them all additional Slop Cloaths, and I made their meal pleasant and wholesome as may be Observed in the different days Occurrences.

It was unfortunately necessary for the men to be aloft in these awful conditions. A sudden change of wind could have rent the sails or placed too great a strain on the rigging, and men were needed to take in or let out the sails. It was an appalling task, but none the less necessary if *Bounty* and her crew were to survive.

The ship leaked quite badly, and men had to work at the pumps every hour for most of the time. The damage was severe, but the toll on the men was as severe as on the ship. Day and night the gales blew, and what progress *Bounty* made it soon lost again as it was blown back. Even with fires and dry clothes, the damp got in everywhere. Bligh tried to help by moving some of the men to the great cabin to give them somewhere drier to sleep and to leave more room for their companions in the fo'c'sle. The hot breakfasts were supplemented with a concoction of diluted malt to strengthen resistance to colds.

On 13 April Bligh wrote: 'I cannot expect my Men and Officers to bear it much longer, [n]or will the object of my Voyage allow me to persist in it.' William Peckover, an officer of the watch, went down with rheumatism, along with Charles Norman, Carpenter's Mate. Thomas Hall, the crew's cook, fell and broke a rib, and the Surgeon fell and dislocated a shoulder (whether by the ship's motion or his drunkenness is not recorded). To keep himself steady on deck, Bligh had himself tied with a rope to the ship.

Casualties rose steadily. On 18 April two more men went down with colds, making five in all. Four days later this had risen to eight, which 'was much felt in the watches, the ropes being worked with much difficulty from the wet and the snow'. It was here that the shortage of genuine ABs was felt the most. The watches were turned out with men short, and while there is no record of it, with up to eight seamen off duty out of thirteen there must have been trouble in manning the ship, and some of the spare, but nominal, ABs were probably drafted in.

Years later, in 1831, the anonymous author of Peter Heywood's obituary claimed that Bligh had 'mastheaded' the 15-year-old boy by keeping him aloft for eight hours (two watches) in a snow storm at the Horn. Mastheading was a traditional punishment for errant midshipmen, but it is unlikely that Heywood would have survived such a punishment at the Horn, or that someone so concerned with his men's health as Bligh would have risked his father-in-law's protégé in this way. Heywood certainly never complained about this incident during his many criticisms of Bligh, nor did Fryer or Morrison. If Heywood and others were sent on deck to assist the few men available when 'ropes were worked with difficulty' it hardly reflects on Bligh. However, the story has gained credence through Sir John Barrow's repeating it and it was included by the imaginative scriptwriters in the 1960 MGM film.

On 17 April, despite having actually rounded Cape Horn, Bligh gave up the hopeless task and turned the helm for the Cape of Good Hope. But a turn in the wind changed his mind again and encouraged him, incredibly, to try once more. He battled on for a few more days until, on 22 April, he made a final decision to give up: 'I ordered the helm to be put round to the universal joy of all hands.'

# 6

# The First Rumbles of Discontent

*Bounty* anchored at False Bay at the Cape of Good Hope on 22 May and stayed for 38 days. The beating the ship had taken at the Horn necessitated considerable repairs, including the recaulking of the entire hull. The carpenter and his men were kept busy and needed help from local tradesmen. Bligh made courtesy calls on the Dutch officials in the local settlement and, as always, spent time on navigational observations. Everybody took the opportunity to rest and eat fresh food.

Bligh wrote about his 'Mode of Management' in the Log. He was clearly pleased about *Bounty*'s performance and proud, even boastful, of the fact that he had brought the ship thus far without loss of life. In a letter to Duncan Campbell he pointed out, in contrast to *Bounty*, 'a Dutch Ship came in to day having buried 30 Men & many are sent to the Hospital, altho they have only been out since the last of January' (ML Letters from False Bay, May 1788). He wrote:

> Perhaps a Voyage of five Months which I have now performed without touching at any one place but at Tenarif, has never been accomplished with so few accidents, and such health among Seamen in a like continuance of bad W[eather] ... Having never had a symptom of either Scurvy, Flux or Fever, and as such a fortunate event may be supposed to have been derived from some peculiar Mod of Management it is proper I should point out what I think has been the cause of it...We have it much in our power to act against the latter by taking care of the Men in their cloathing, and the rest will generally be prevented, by the timely distribution of the necessaries that Ships may be supplied with, and a strict regard to cleanliness. Seamen will seldom attend to themselves in any particular and simply to give directions that they are to keep themselves clean and dry as circumstances allow, is of little avail, they must be watched like Children, as the most recent danger has little effect to prevent them from the same fate. The Mode I have adopted has been a Strict adherence to the first grand point, cleanliness in their persons and bedding. Keeping them in dry Cloaths & and by constant cleaning and drying the Ship with Fires, to this I attribute their having kept free of Colds so wonderfully as they have done. A Great nuisance which is in general an attendant in ships in a long continuance of bad weather is dirty Hammocks and Bags, this I think I perfectly got the better of, by having two sets, one of which was in charge to be got cleaned and dryed as a general Stock of property whenever they were

done with, and by this Means I had it in my power to deliver Clean Hammocks and Bags as often as I saw necessary. One Person of a Watch was appointed to dry Cloaths by the Fire and a Man never came on Deck or went to sleep in wet apparel. No foul Cloaths were ever suffered to be kept without airing, and in cleaning Ship all dark holes and Corners the common receptacles of all filth were the first places attended to.

After all that can be done perhaps Ships may be subject to Fevers and Fluxes; but the Scurvy is rarely a disgrace to a Ship where it is at all common, provided they have it in their power to be supplied with Dryed Malt, Sour Krout, and Portable Soup. With these articles properly issued, I am firmly convinced no Scurvy will appear. Cheerfullness with exercise, and a sufficiency of rest are powerful preventatives to this dreadfull disease, a calamity which even at this present period destroys more men than is generally known. To assist in the first two particulars every opportunity I directed that the Evenings should be spent in dancing, and that I might be secure in my last I kept my few Men Constatnly at three Watches, even in the Worst of Weather, and I found them additionally alert on a call when their immediate Service was required...

Hot breakfasts are particularly prefered in Stormy and Wet weather to eating a Scrap of Salt Meat or a piece of biscuit, but very commonl[ly] Seamen do their duty without any breakfast at all, and this has a pernicious tendency.

I am thoroughly convinced that had I been a fortnight sooner there I could have made my passage round the Cape into the South Sea with the greatest of ease (24 May 1788).

Bligh's own perceptions of his almost parental good care of his men, the good results of which he was anxious for the Admiralty to credit to him, is supported in some measure by a letter written by Ledward, the Assistant Surgeon, describing the violent seas at the Horn: 'The Ship laboured so much that there was danger of rendering her unfit for the further prosecution of the Voyage. The Captain was therefore obliged to bear away, & I have no doubt will gain much credit for his resolution & perseverance & by the extreme care he took with the Ship's company' (*Notes & Queries*, 1903, 9th series, vol. xii, p. 501).

While at False Bay Bligh had time to make notes on the lack of humanity and compassion among the owners of slaves:

Slaves are a property here as well as in the West Indies, and the number imported by the French (to whom that Trade has been confined) from Madagascar, Musambique, Sumatra and Mallaca have been considerable, but it appears there is in some degree a Stop put to this trade, for the seller has now only permission to part with as many as can pay for the supplies he absolutely is in need of. To this if the Police could oblige the owners of these Poor Wretches consigned to constant drudgery, to cloath and feed them properly it would be much to their honour and humanity, for it is distressing to see some of them carrying Weighty burdens naked, or what is worse in such rags that one would imagine could not fail to reproach the owners of a want of decency and compassion in not relieving such a degree of wretchedness of which they were the cause, and had every call on their humanity to remove. Some of these poor wretches I have seen pick up the most offensive offals and claim them for food (Log, Remarks at False Bay, 1788).

With the repairs to the ship nearing completion, Bligh made arrangements for the 6,000-mile voyage to Adventure Bay in Van Diemen's Land (Tasmania). From here on *Bounty* was on its own. While at the Cape Bligh notes reports of the wrecking of the East Indiaman *Grosvenor* on the coast, not far from a Dutch settlement, but too far to effect a rescue of the European survivors who were taken by local tribes. *Bounty* was going out across an enormous ocean and past a whole continent up into the Pacific to a tiny island not visited for a decade. Disaster on any scale here was final. If authority crumbled, support was distant and retribution uncertain.

Two days before he left False Bay, Bligh wrote a final report to Sir Joseph Banks:

> I am now ready for sea with my little ship once more in most excellent order and every man on board in very good health. I flatter myself with a speedy passage to Otaheite as I apprehend there will be no want of wind. I might well wood & water at Botany Bay with very little loss of time and it may be imagined I will do so, but I cannot think of putting it in the power of chance to prevent my accomplishing the object of the Voyage. I shall therefore pass our Friends there but could I have taken a considerable supply it would have been for the good of the service for me to have done it and I should – In the present case I can render them no service, and Government will hear of them before any accounts could be brought home by me. Should any unforseen accident drive me there I have a great many seeds and some fruit plants which I shall leave them…I wish you to enjoy the most perfect health & happiness and to see you satisfyed with my conduct on my return will give (ML Bligh to Banks, 28 June 1788).

The 'friends' at Botany Bay were the first British settlers sent there in 1787 under the command of Captain Phillip. No news had been received from the new prison colony. A visit might have had a useful psychological effect on *Bounty*, particularly on the troublemakers. The new prison colony would have been a reminder that while Britain was far away, its reach stretched round the world. Interestingly, while still in Cape Town, Bligh did meet and have dinner with Lachlan Macquarrie, then 27, and en route to India. It was Macquarrie, twenty-one years later, who superseded Bligh as Governor of New South Wales in 1809.

Bligh set out on 1 July for the southern tip of New Holland (Australia), with the intention of sailing further south round New Zealand. The passage was uneventful. The routine of cleaning below, drying clothes, inspecting the hands and serving 'hot breakfasts', malt extract, flour and raisins, was strictly adhered to. The Log monotonously records this routine. The weather did not change much for the better; squalls and rain were interspersed with gales. The strong winds pushed *Bounty* along at a fair rate and seas occasionally broke over the ship, causing more discomfort than danger, though the man at the wheel on one occasion was knocked off his feet and 'much bruized' (Log, 22 July 1788).

Bligh was a fastidious navigator. The small ship, with what would be regarded today as primitive navigational aids, aimed for a small rocky island, St Paul, a month out from the Cape. Bligh wanted to fix the position of St Paul accurately. After St Paul, he sailed for the Mewstone Rock off the coast of Tasmania, where he made landfall. With cold weeks at sea, the compulsory keep-fit regime imposed by Bligh and the monotony of the diet, everyone probably yearned for a spell ashore.

On 20 August 1788 *Bounty* neared Adventure Bay and the next day anchored there. Having secured the ship, Bligh went ashore to look around. It was eleven years since he had been there with Captain Cook (who had named the bay after his ship *Adventure*). Nelson and Peckover were no strangers to the bay either, and for the three of them it must have been an exciting day – the more so because the bay was practically as they had left it. Work parties were organised to get wood, collect water, make some alterations in the cabin and hunt and fish for food. Nelson and Brown set to work to collect botanical specimens. The shore party was placed under the command of Fletcher Christian, assisted by Peckover. Fryer was left in command of the ship to supervise the loading of supplies. One man was directed to wash clothes. Everybody had a job to do, and all co-operated with the work programme, except for Purcell, the Carpenter.

Purcell was the centre of a serious incident at Adventure Bay, which made him obstructive. What exactly caused it is not known. Bligh hints at what happened but does not give further details in his Log and makes no reference to it in his published *Voyage* (1792). From the Log it appears that Bligh found some reason for criticising the way Purcell was carrying out his orders and that Purcell was imprudent enough to reply. Captains did not expect anybody on their ships to answer them back. Normally a warrant officer who was disrespectful or disobedient would have been confined to his cabin and brought before a court martial. But *Bounty* was not due home for fifteen months, and to confine Purcell for that long was impractical. Bligh's version states:

> My Carpenter on my expresing my disapprobation of his Conduct with respect to orders he had received from me concerning the Mode of working with the Wooding Party behaved in a most insolent and reprehensible Manner, I therefore ordered him on board, there to assist in the general duty of the ship, as I could not bear the loss of an able Working and healthy Man; otherwise I should have committed him to close confinement untill I could have tryed him, the prospect of which appears to be of so long a date made me determine to keep him at his duty, giving him a Chance by his future Conduct to make up in some degree for his behaviour at this place (Log, 23 August 1788).

Purcell was a warrant officer not a seaman and so was immune from corporal punishment without the authority of a court martial. As he could not be punished and could not be confined, he was effectively not intimidated by the captain's authority. If Purcell chose to argue with the captain, what could Bligh do about it? Hence, while Bligh had the authority of the King's commission, he had no means of enforcing it. This incident on Saturday 23 August was the first rumble of dissent and a sign that all was not well between Bligh and his officers.

Next day being a Sunday, no work took place, but on Monday everybody was back to their tasks – three work parties ashore, plus one party cutting wood and one party on board, under Fryer, loading supplies. Bligh wrote: 'I repeated my injunctions to the Comm[andin]g Officer Mr Fryer that he would take care to keep all Officers employed as well as Men' (Log, 26 August 1778). When Fryer carried out Bligh's instructions and tried to set Purcell to work alongside himself, William Elphinstone, Master's Mate, and one of the Quartermasters (not identified in the Log) 'he was opposed by the Carpenter who refused to assist in hoisting Water into the Hold…On my coming on board Mr Fryer acquainted me of this circumstance, but my directions and my presence had as little effect.' This was outright refusal of duty, the most serious offence, just short of mutiny, on a ship. It is arguable whether hoisting water was technically a carpenter's duty but, being under punishment for some failing in his official duties, it is also a moot point whether he had a right to refuse any duty ordered by his captain 'for the good of the service', especially one involving stowing water supplies for the ship. Barrack-room lawyers could probably debate this endlessly, but in the small society of a ship in the midst of a voyage it was essential that the captain's authority remain intact.

Purcell's challenge to the captain's authority must have been the main topic of conversation that evening and, as there could be no question of the incident passing unnoticed, all eyes must have centred on Bligh to see what he would do. Bligh took attested evidence of Purcell's conduct, with a view to his court martial on *Bounty*'s return, and also applied a stratagem: 'he who does not work neither shall he eat':

> I therefore Ordered the different Persons evidence to be drawn out and attested, and then gave Orders that untill he Worked he should have no provisions, and promised faithfully severe Punishment to any Man that dared to Assist him, which immediatly brought him to his senses.

Purcell, nevertheless, had struck a blow against Bligh's authority. He knew that the 'few I have even in the good State of health I keep them, are but barely sufficient to carry on the duty of the ship' and that 'it could then answer no good purpose to lose the use of a healthy Strong Young Man in my situation'. Making Purcell a prisoner would do more harm to the voyage than to Purcell (whatever the terrors of his possible punishment on his return to Britain), but Bligh's assertion that though he had 'laid aside my power' in Purcell's case, 'it continued in force with equal effect' was a sad illusion. Apart from two dozen lashes on the ABs, Bligh was limited in the punishment he could offer to errant junior officers, and without the power of punishment, immediate, certain and awful, Bligh's authority could not 'continue in force with equal effect'.

Nelson's leadership qualities have often been romanticised, but even Nelson, who at periods in his career had men scrambling to fight alongside him, was a severe disciplinarian. Cook was never loath to order a flogging, and other great seamen were the same or worse. Also, there were the floggers, the men who ruled by sheer terror, and if ever tyranny meant anything their ships were floating exhibitions of it at its worst. But Bligh was never a flogger in anything remotely like that sense. He expected discipline as a manifestation of duty. Perhaps another captain would have left the Carpenter to his own devices in command of the wooding party, but that was not Bligh's way: whatever happened to his authority he still had responsibility for whatever was done by anyone on *Bounty*. Perhaps another captain would have flouted the rules, flogged Purcell and risked a court martial on his return. But the rules forbade flogging, and that was that. Vancouver, in his voyage to the Pacific, had a midshipman flogged who complained about it on his return. It marred Vancouver's reputation.

Bligh applied his superior intelligence against Purcell, and won the issue. But in winning he also lost something he could not recover: immunity for Purcell was immunity for everybody else.

# 7

# Fryer's Refusal of Duty

*Bounty*, wooded and watered, sailed from Adventure Bay on 4 September 1788, intending to go southward past New Zealand, out into the east Pacific, and then northward to Tahiti, approaching it from the east. This roundabout route was necessary to catch the prevailing winds. After two weeks at sea, Bligh discovered a group of rocky islands south-east of New Zealand which he named, after the ship, Bounty Isles, a name they have to this day. The weather was again wet and uncomfortable and the Bligh routine of fires, cleaning and healthy food was resumed. But with every day's sail warmer weather was approaching. The men were put through regular exercises with the small arms. Bligh was taking no chances. He had no reason to think that the Tahitians would not welcome him as they had done when he was last there, but he had been scarred by the events in Hawaii and had no intention of being caught off guard or ill-prepared.

The situation on *Bounty* was by no means happy. Bligh was still smarting after the Purcell incident. It is worth quoting Morrison's version of the situation, although we must remember that he was writing long after the voyage while attempting to exculpate himself as a pardoned mutineer. He wrote: 'Here also were sown the seeds of eternal discord between Lieut. Bligh and some of his Officers. He confined the Carpenter and found fault with the inattention of the rest, to their duty, which produced continual disputes every one trying to thwart the others in their duty, this made the men exert themselves to divert the storm from falling on them by a strict attention to their duty and in this way they found their account and rejoyced in private at their good success' (ML MS Safe 1/42).

It is possible that, after Purcell's challenge to his authority, Bligh sought many opportunities to exercise his authority over others, and that this caused friction between him and the officers and a wholly laudable strict attention to duty among the seamen. That the one sure way to 'divert the storm' was to excel in one's duty was unlikely to persuade the Admiralty of Bligh's tyranny.

Fryer's reaction to the tauter supervision of the ship's officers constituted the second challenge to Bligh's authority. The Fryer episode has received more attention than Purcell's insubordination, yet it parallels the altercation between Bligh and Purcell.

On 9 October 1788 Bligh was presented with the Boatswain's and Carpenter's expense books. By signing them he approved their contents, and when these were counter-signed by the Master, John Fryer, it was formally established to the Admiralty's satisfaction that the books were correct. Upon this authority, and only upon this authority, at the end of the voyage the Admiralty would make allowances for any expenses claimed. This routine was replicated on all ships every month or so, and by involving several officers, except in the unlikely event that they were all corrupt, the Admiralty ensured that moneys claimed, either against stores, or against purchases on the voyage, were not falsified. Bligh wrote in the Log (9 October 1788):

> The Clerk was then returned with a Certificate for me to Sign, before the Books could, the Purport of which was that he [Fryer] had done nothing amiss during his time on board. As I did not approve of his doing his duty conditionally I sent for him and told him the Consequence when he left me abrup[t]ly saying he would not sign the Books upon such conditions. I now ordered the Hands to be turned up. Read the Articles of War, with the particular parts of the Instructions relative to the Matter, when this troublesome Man saw his error & before the whole Ships Company signed the books. [Bligh added in his Journal: 'Here I forgave him.']

Why should Fryer feel he needed a certificate of his good behaviour? Most authors have ignored this question and asked why he would not sign the books, implying something corrupt in Bligh's ledgers. It is worth going back three days before this incident to 6 October for enlightenment on Fryer's odd conduct.

In Bligh's Journal, but not included in the Log, we find details of a furious row he had with Huggan, the drunken Surgeon:

> Mr Elphinstone, one of the Mates of the Ship came and told me this morning that Jas. Valentine (who had an inflamed arm after some blood being take from him some time since) was delirious and had every appearance of being in a dying state. This shock was scarce equal to my astonishment, as the Surgeon told me he was getting better, and had never expressed the least uneasyness about him. I therefore sent for the Surgeon and was perhaps severe for his remissness – However, all I could get out of him was that he intended to have told me of it last night ... that he must now inform me that he had not many hours to live. – The strangeness of this declaration, as the Man had been daily fed from our Table and he not knowing the tendency of his symptoms gave me very unfavourable ideas.

When Bligh admits he was 'perhaps severe' he probably understated his 'heiva-like' reaction to the news of Valentine's imminent death. This meant that his much-vaunted 'mode of management', which highlighted the means to keep a crew healthy, was undermined by the incompetence

of the ship's surgeon. To lose a man through scurvy was unthinkable –
Bligh called it a disgrace – but to lose a man through blood-poisoning
brought about by the surgeon himself was even worse. It certainly
mocked Bligh's claims at the Cape. The fact that it was Elphinstone who
broke the news, and not the Surgeon, or the Assistant Surgeon, or the
Acting Lieutenant, or the Master, implicated them all in the neglect.
Bligh was probably extremely 'severe'; he would not be slow to tell the
officers concerned what he thought of them.

As Fryer was the other member, with Huggan, of Bligh's mess, he
would be a particular butt of Bligh's temper. Fryer was already in trouble
over the Purcell affair (and perhaps also reminded of his altercation with
Quintal eight months earlier), because Bligh had found it necessary to
give him a written reminder of his orders that everybody was on duty at
Adventure Bay. As a Warrant Officer himself, Fryer probably
sympathised with Purcell in the matter of refusing a seaman's duty of
hoisting water. Bligh perhaps sensed a sullen support in this matter
(after all he had felt it necessary to warn 'everybody' not to slip food to
Purcell). Whether because of this earlier occasion, or others not recorded,
or because of Bligh's outbursts over the Valentine affair, and his need to
rely on junior mates for information, or a combination of everything,
Fryer apparently felt threatened by Bligh's opinion of him.

The Log records the death of Valentine on 9 October, the same day that
Fryer refused to sign the books. This suggests that the row originating in
Valentine's death was connected with Fryer's desperate conduct. The
only lever he had on Bligh was to refuse duty in the sensitive area of the
ship's finance where a whisper would spread scandal. But his gambit
could only succeed if there had been some irregularities which Bligh
would fear being brought into the open. The penalty for signing false
books was 'to be cashiered, and rendered incapable of further
employment in His Majesty's naval service' (Articles of War, XXXI). If it
was a game of bluff, and Fryer had something on Bligh, the bluff was
called by Bligh entering the incident in the official Log. In doing so he
drew it to the attention of the Admiralty (Log, 9 October 1788, p. 344). It
was a case of put up or shut up. Fryer's action can only be seen as an
ill-judged emotional outburst. The intensity of feelings on a small
overcrowded ship, with irritable men in close contact, and the pettiness
this can cause are not unknown phenomena.

Morrison's version of what happened hints that Bligh had falsified the
accounts:

> Previous to making Taheiti, a dispute happened between Mr. Bligh and the
> Master Mr. Fryer relative to signing some books, which the Master had
> refused to sign, for reasons best known to himself, Upon which all Hands
> were calld aft, and the Articles of War, and some part of the Printed
> Instructions, after Which the books and papers were produced with a Pen
> and ink and Mr. Bligh said Now Sir Sign the Books. The Master took the Pen

and said 'I sign in obedience to your Orders, but this may be Cancelled hereafter.' The books being signed the People were dismiss'd to return to their duty (ML Morrison, Journal, p. 17a).

Bligh referred to this incident in his 'Remarks on Morrison's Journal' (which, in fact, was a comment on Morrison's Memorandum) written in 1793. Bligh claims that he gave Fryer the opportunity to record his complaint: 'Captain Bligh ordered the Master to sign the Books, or to express his reasons (for not complying) at full length at the bottom of the Page where his signature was to be made – The Master thought proper to sign the Books' (ML Safe 1/43, p. 48). The balance of probability is that Fryer had nothing of substance to charge Bligh with (though he had a 'friendly' witness against Bligh in the person of Purcell, who kept one of the books). If Bligh had fiddled Purcell's books he had chosen a most unreliable ally to prove his innocence, given that Purcell was under the threat of a court martial at this time. William Cole, Boatswain, kept the other book, and his Mate was James Morrison; yet Morrison added nothing to his vague hints, even though he was under sentence of death when he wrote his Memorandum in 1792.

The books Fryer refused to sign were for the months of August and September. The ship's accounts system worked like this: all provisions and stores and their values were listed at departure and adjusted for usage and losses and for purchases en route. At the end of a voyage, the stock remaining would equal the original amount plus purchases less losses and usage. Captains were always concerned about losses, as the Admiralty took a dim view of discrepancies. To fiddle the books the captain required the collusion of the warrant officers, two of whom he did not get on with and one of whom he court-martialled. Is it likely that Bligh overlooked the thin ice he stood on? By making the matter public – the Log and the general muster – the balance of probability is that he felt he had nothing to hide.

Two officers, Purcell and Fryer, had now clashed publicly with Bligh, and a third, Huggan, had been responsible for a seaman's death. Nothing was, or could be, done about the warrant officers' behaviour. Indeed Huggan's public inebriation was a daily insurbordination against the captain. Within a few weeks the entire crew had seen three men challenge the captain and suffer no punishment, an extraordinary state of affairs on a British naval vessel. More was to follow.

# 8

# The Drunken Sot

As *Bounty* approached a warmer climate, Huggan became increasingly incapable through drunkenness. After nine months at sea it was inevitable that some men would report sick. The prolonged periods of sea duty had an effect on the crew's health. Captain Cook's reforms in health and hygiene were primitive by modern standards, though they were revolutionary in the eighteenth century. Bligh was completely committed to Cook's reforms and he took a special interest in any illness in his men, especially after the Valentine affair. It was at this time that Huggan listed three men as suffering from scurvy.

Nothing was more likely to enrage Bligh than the charge of scurvy on his ship. He had declared it to be a 'disgrace' and had no doubt informed Huggan time and again of his views on the matter. Huggan was still smarting under the lash of Bligh's tongue over the neglect of Valentine, and he struck back by claiming that the much-vaunted reforms had failed. Taking one look at three seamen complaining of 'rheumatism' on 14 October 1788, he seized his chance to rubbish Bligh, and diagnosed them as suffering from scurvy, and then promptly joined them on the sick list.

Bligh was predictably furious, but he did not automatically reject Huggan's diagnosis. He promptly put the men on a concentrated diet of 'the decoction of Essence of Malt' (Log, 14 October 1788). Over the next few days the battle of wills between Bligh and Huggan continued. Unlike Purcell or Fryer, Huggan did not have his soberest wits about him. His personal disintegration allowed Bligh to take over the treatment of the men complaining of rheumatism. He issued the declining stocks of malt and sweet-wort to the three sick men. On 18 October he 'Served decoction of Malt as Yesterday and on examining the Men who the Doctor supposed had a taint of the Scurvy, it appeared to be nothing more than the prickly heat. – However their decoction I desired to be continued.'

He personally supervised his health programme with renewed vigour. Diet, cleanliness and exercise, the three main ingredients of his campaign, were enforced rigorously over the following days. Any man claiming to have rheumatism was to be given decoction of essence of malt, 'the Doctor to issue it himself' (his Journal adds, perhaps sarcastically: 'if able') (Log, 19 October 1788).

Bligh supervised the dancing session that evening. He had 'always directed the Evenings from 5 to 8 O'Clock to be spent in dancing & that every Man should be Obliged to dance as I considered it conducive to their Health'. Two men, John Mills and William Brown, took the extraordinary step of refusing to dance. Bligh immediately ordered 'their Grog to be Stopt with a promise of further punishment on a Second Refusal'.

William Brown was David Nelson's assistant and a supernumerary on the ship's books. He was technically a civilian, though he had been a midshipman previously and was Acting Lieutenant in HMS *Resolution*, Captain Lord Robert Manners, at Rodney's action of 12 April 1782. Why he abandoned a naval career for botany is not known. Brown complained that he had been suffering rheumatic pains in his legs for three weeks. Huggan backed him up and declared that Brown had the scurvy. Bligh reports that he could 'discover no Symptoms to lead me to be apprehensive' (Log, 19 October 1788). In his Journal Bligh expressed his doubts about Huggan's professional competence in diagnosing scurvy in Brown: 'The doctor's opinion likewise to me, is of little value as he has been constantly drunk these last four days and is ever so when he can get liquor. I do my endeavour to prevent it, but all has no effect' (Journal, 19 October). In contradiction of Huggan's judgment, he gave his own medical opinion that 'I think I never saw a more healthy set of Men and so decent looking in my life' (Log, 19 October 1788)

The next day he entered in the official Log similar thoughts about Huggan: 'The Doctors Intoxication has given me much trouble these last five days having been obliged to be attentive with much anxiety to the complaints of four Men who complain of the Rheumatism – with some difficulty I got a Sick list from him to day with only Jno. McIntosh in it under a Rheumatic complaint – the others he now seems to think nothing about' (Log, 20 October 1788). Significantly, Brown's name was not on the sick list. Perhaps he had been trying it on, taking advantage of the public discord between the Surgeon and Bligh. Also, losing his grog was a severe blow.

Huggan's drunkenness was reaching embarrassing proportions. He was in public breach of the Articles of War, which prohibited 'profane oaths, cursings, execrations, drunkenness, uncleanliness, or other scandalous actions, in derogation of God's honour, and corruption of good manners'. While persons in home waters risked 'such punishment as a court martial shall think fit to impose', Huggan in the Pacific risked little more than Bligh's impotent wrath.

Bligh tried a softer approach. He sent for Huggan on 21 October 'and in a most friendly manner requested him to leave off drinking, but he seemed not sensible of any thing I said to him and it had little effect' (Journal). Thomas Ledward, the assistant surgeon, took over several of

Huggan's official duties, and Huggan went onto the sick list, only to get permanently drunk in his cabin.

The sick list for 22 October had McIntosh, Milward and Huggan on it under rheumatism, and some others complained of a 'feebleness & Pain in their Bones'. Bligh ordered the issue of portable soup, barley and malt to the complainants and for the entire crew he ordered, after consulting the surgeon, a medicine of elixir of vitriol in water to be taken half an hour before breakfast. Some of the crew objected, including Purcell, but they were threatened with loss of grog and thought it better to comply (Journal, 22 October 1788).

Bligh was of the opinion that the warmer weather was causing much of the reported discomforts. For much of the voyage they had been in cooler climates, and the fact that he received complaints from men of a 'faintness towards Mid Day' fully confirmed him in his judgment. He also stopped serving salt meat and substituted portable soup thickened with pearl barley, plus the equivalent amount of salt meat in flour and raisins (Log, 23 October 1788).

On 24 October he was optimistic about his men's medical condition:

It is with much pleasure I find the few Invalids recovering very fast. The faintness which they complained of is totally gone away and their Spirits and looks are good, but the most of them still complain of the Rheumatism and they all say it is particularly troublesome when they go to bed. This with their having no eruptions or swellings, convinces me that their complaint is not scorbutic. Their Gums also are as sound as any can be expected after such a length of Salt Diet and their breath is not offensive neither is their teeth the least loose.

With the sick men on the mend, Bligh ordered Huggan's cabin to be cleaned out and his liquor store removed. He blamed the need for this on the Assistant Surgeon, Ledward, who had been 'deceiving me with respect of the Surgeon's illness. It was now over four days since he had seen light and in bed all this time intoxicated' (Log, 24 October 1788). Bligh was implying to the Admiralty that he had believed the Surgeon's indisposition was due to rheumatism because that is how his absence from duty had been explained by Ledward's sick list. But we know from his Journal, written several days earlier, 21 October, that Bligh knew what was wrong with Huggan:

The Surgeon kept his Bed all this day and always drunk, without eating an ounce of food. If it is ever necessary this should be publicly known, I may be blamed for not searching his Cabbin and taking all liquor from him; but my motive is that, altho Every person on board is acquainted with his ebriety, yet hoping every day will produce a change in him, I forebear making a publick matter of My disapprobation of his conduct, in expectation as he has done many times this Voyage, he may turn sober again.

How candid was Bligh in this matter? It may be that Huggan's latest bout of drunkenness made it easier for Bligh to gain control over the medication of the men on the sick list. The more drunk Huggan became, the more discredited his diagnoses of scurvy. But Bligh's excuse was thin. Hence poor Ledward took the blame, and Bligh did what he should perhaps have done earlier: confiscated Huggan's private liquor store.

The drunken surgeon was naturally disturbed by the commotion in his cabin (an operation 'not only troublesome but offensive in the highest degree': Log, 24 October 1788), and when he was sober enough to understand what had happened he tried to get his own back on the source of his torment. He put himself down on the sick list as suffering from a 'Paralytic Affection' – a diagnosis occasioned by having 'lost the use of one side' of the body, as Bligh described it. Huggan also rediagnosed McIntosh and Milward as having the scurvy and Matthew Thompson as having 'lumbago'. Bligh was furious and demanded to know why the diagnosis had been altered when 'every Man was recovering and almost well' but he got no sense out of Huggan, who had been out of his bed searching for liquor despite his 'paralytic' state.

*Bounty* passed Maitea, the first of Tahitian group, on 25 October 1788. The voyage out was almost over. The sick men were even fitter, according to Bligh, and even the Surgeon came on deck, having lost his paralytic disorder, which Bligh noted 'has been perfectly cured in 48 hours by giving him not Spirits to make use of, and only a little Wine and water'. Bligh ordered Huggan to make a very meticulous inspection of everybody on board for venereal disease. He believed that nobody else had visited Tahiti since Captain Cook and he did not want to be tainted with any 'illfounded suppositions that we might renew the Complaint'.

Huggan reported 'every person totally free from the Venereal complaint' (Log, 25 October 1788). This contradicts the evidence of *Bounty*'s Sick List. If the men were clear of VD on arrival, some of them had been treated for it during the voyage. As 'cures' cost 15s. a time, it was no trivial matter to report for a cure during the voyage. Huggan had dispensed to seven men. Huggan's patients were William Cole, Bo's'n; John Swan, AB; Alexander Smith, AB; Fletcher Christian, Master's Mate; James Valentine, AB; Matthew Quintal, AB (twice); and William Brown, Assistant Gardener (twice). Ledward treated fourteen, including two on Huggan's list, Quintal and Brown, as well as Peter Heywood. In fact, nearly half the ship's company had been treated for venereal disease by the time *Bounty* left Tahiti.

How many of these cures were given before *Bounty* arrived at Tahiti? Two at least were treated before 9 October; this was the day Valentine died, and Swan deserted *Bounty* at Portsmouth on 27 November 1787. Huggan was to die on 9 December 1788 at Tahiti. Hence five men on his list had the disease some time between their signing on and Huggan's death. The question is complicated by Bligh's Log recording that five unnamed people were treated for VD by the surgeons between 26 October and 9 December. Some, if not all, of the five men treated at Tahiti were Ledward's patients. This inescapably means that some, if not all, of Huggan's patients were treated before *Bounty* arrived at Tahiti.

With Huggan's assurance that nobody had VD before landfall on 26 October, Bligh could assert that any of his men treated for VD after landfall must have caught it from the Tahitians. But if they brought it with them, as some of them undoubtedly did, this was no defence against 'ill-founded suppositions'.

# 9

# Landfall at Tahiti

On his first visit to the Pacific with Captain Cook, Bligh had seen at close hand the fragility of relationships between islanders and Europeans. On this visit he hoped to prevent incidents that might disturb the collection of breadfruit trees, and before *Bounty* reached Tahiti he had made some arrangements to ensure the security of the mission.

One of the main sources of trouble was the proclivity of islanders to steal anything they could lay their hands on. Cook called them 'the arrantest thieves upon the face of the earth' (Barrow, 1961, p. 28). It does not matter that this behaviour was not regarded in the same light by Tahitian society as it was in Europe. Cook noted that 'an Indian among penny knives and beads, and even nails and broken glass, is in the same state of mind with the meanest servant in Europe among unlocked coffers of jewels and gold'. Property is a culturally defined phenomenon, and the two societies that met in the Pacific had very different cultures. But it was theft that led indirectly to Cook's death, and theft in European eyes was endemic among Polynesians. Attempts to recover stolen property or, its converse, to confiscate the property of the islanders always led to trouble.

On the other hand, sexual relations between seamen and island women were not the source of conflict they would have been if visitors had behaved this way in Europe. The Tahitian women, or rather some of them, were always willing to have sex with European men, and their menfolk did not seem to care. Trade was the other source of potential trouble. Food could only be acquired by trading petty items of European manufacture that were popular among islanders – iron objects, adzes, axes, nails, mirrors, beads and cloth. *Bounty* had brought a large stock of such items. The main problem was in the incidental depreciation of the currency as time went by and as seamen engaged in unofficial trade for personal purposes.

Captain Cook had faced similar problems and had developed a sensible policy to deal with them. He enforced rules of conduct to govern the relationships between seamen and islanders, and Bligh had learned the benefits of such rules from experience. He copied Cook's policies. He posted 'Rules of Conduct for the Officers and Men of the *Bounty*' the day before landfall. They aimed at 'better establishing a trade for supplies of provisions, and good intercourse with the natives of the South Seas, wherever the ship may call at'. In some respects they were more lenient than Cook's.

The first rule was that 'no person whatever is to intimate that Captain Cook was killed by Indians; or that he is dead'. Disclosure could undermine the awe in which European power was held by the Tahitians. But Bligh did not know that a ship, *Lady Penrhyn*, returning to Britain after transporting convicts to Botany Bay, had called at Tahiti before him and that Lieutenant Watts had disclosed the fact, but not the manner, of Cook's death (Watts had been a midshipman with Bligh on *Resolution* and had been at Kealakekua Bay). Bligh's fiction that Cook was alive was accepted by the Tahitians for a while.

Bligh also insisted that 'no person is ever to speak, or give the least hint, that we have come on purpose to get the breadfruit plant, until I have made my plan known to the chiefs'. Careless talk might raise the 'price' of breadfruit trees.

The third rule specified that 'every person is to study to gain the good will and esteem of the natives; to treat them with all kindness; and not to take from them, by violent means, any thing that they may have stolen; and no one is ever to fire, but in defence of his life'. The best policy to deal with theft was to prevent it by locking loose property away from prying eyes. Ship's property left carelessly about, either on board or on shore, was an avoidable temptation to the islanders. The men must look after the equipment in their charge and so 'every person employed on service, is to take care that no arms, or implements of any kind under their charge, are stolen; the value of such things being lost shall be charged against their wages'. And to close the circle to unauthorised thefts Bligh required that 'no man is to embezzel, or offer for sale, directly, or indirectly, any part of the King's stores, of what nature soever'. In contrast to Cook, he did not threaten delinquents with court martial for these offences.

Like Cook, Bligh appointed an official trader to 'regulate trade, and barter with the natives'. William Peckover, the Gunner, was the choice. He was the most experienced man on board in dealings with islanders – he had been to the Pacific three times with Cook – and spoke Tahitian. In support of the ship's trading monopoly, Bligh ordered that 'no officer or seaman, or other person belonging to the ship, is to trade for any kind of provisions or curiosities; but if such officer or seaman wishes to purchase any particular thing he is to apply to the provider to do it for him'. Bligh's intentions were to avoid 'all disputes which otherwise will happen with the natives'.

*Bounty* entered Matavai Bay, Tahiti, on Sunday 26 October 1788. Their welcome was tumultuous even by Tahitian standards. As the ship swung inside the reef and into the calmer water off Point Venus (named by Cook after his observatory was set up here to watch the transit of Venus), hundreds of canoes put off from the shore towards her, and within minutes *Bounty*'s deck was covered with smiling and laughing near-naked islanders. It must have been a bewildering experience for the seamen who were visiting Tahiti for the first time. Some impression of the atmosphere can be gleaned from the 1983 film version of the mutiny, 'HMS *Bounty*', which captures brilliantly the excitement of *Bounty*'s entrance into the bay. Unfortunately the ship was endangered by this exuberant welcome, as the anchor was not clear and the sails were not reefed. Bligh noted that 'in less than ten minutes the deck was so full that I could scarce find my own people'. He shouted his orders to stop the ship drifting aimlessly towards the shore, and *Bounty* dropped anchor safely at the end of its 27,000-mile journey.

The Tahitians quickly established that the ship was from Britain – 'Pretanee', as they called it – and many of them claimed to recognise Peckover, Nelson and Bligh. They asked eagerly after the others they remembered. Bligh wrote: 'Captn. Cook was the first person asked after, and they said a Ship had been here who had told them he was dead ... ' The situation was saved by David Nelson, who in a fit of over-enthusiasm declared loudly, pointing at Bligh, 'This is the Son of Captain Cook'; as Bligh noted, 'It seemed to please them very much' (Log, 26 October 1788). They also asked after Sir Joseph Banks (who had been intimate with several of the women and had been Cook's official trader on *Endeavour*), and also after Dr Solander (also from *Endeavour*). Bligh also mentions that Lieutenant Williamson (who had disgraced himself at Hawaii) and Sergeant Gibson, of the Marines, were among those asked after.

Bligh asked after Omai, the Tahitian taken by Cook to Britain on his second voyage who had returned with Cook on his third. Omai had been a great favourite at the Court (where he shocked some of the women by his blatant invitations to sex). He also asked about the two Maori boys brought to Tahiti from New Zealand by Cook, but the news about all three was depressing: they were all dead, apparently from natural causes.

Bligh asked for the Chief, Otoo, because it was only through Otoo that Bligh could get on with his business. He was away, but on hearing that Bligh had returned he sent on ahead some presents with a message that he would arrive at Matavai next day. When he arrived, with his family and retinue of servants, he told Bligh that he had a new name, Tinah. As chiefs often changed their names it could be confusing. He had sent ahead of him a framed portrait of Captain Cook, which Webber, the official artist of the third voyage, had painted for him, as a symbol of friendship towards other ships visiting Tahiti.

Bligh went ashore the day he arrived with another chief, Poeeno, and inspected the site of Cook's 1777 shore camp with a view to using it for *Bounty*'s shore party. During this visit ashore a Tahitian was caught trying to steal a pot. The thefts had begun.

When Tinah arrived the celebrations got underway and lasted two days. Tinah was not quite the powerful personage that Bligh had been led to believe from his previous visit, as much had happened in the intervening Tahitian game of politics in the intervening years. But Tinah knew how to carry himself in style. While other chiefs took their own canoes out to meet *Bounty*, Tinah demanded and received one of *Bounty*'s boats to carry him over the water. Bligh became very attached to Tinah and apparently enjoyed his company.

Nothing was said about the purposes of the visit until the appropriate moment arrived. From Bligh's Logs and his 1790 and 1792 accounts we can reconstruct the interview. Tinah asked Bligh how long he intended to stay at Matavai and was told he would stay a while and then move on to other islands. Tinah's own kingdom had been plundered by rivals from across the island, but the arrival of the Europeans gave him an opportunity to reassert himself. He expressed horror at the thought of his European friends leaving Matavai. 'Here,' said Tinah, 'you shall be supplied plentifully with everything you want. All here are your friends, and friends of King George: if you go to the other islands you will have everything stolen from you.' This was the opening Bligh was looking for and pointed out that King George knew of Tinah's friendship and had sent out valuable presents for him. Having got Tinah to state how much he wanted Bligh to stay at Matavai and having introduced the subject of presents from King George to Tinah, it only remained to finesse an offer of presents from Tinah for King George. Bligh asked Tinah: 'Will not you, Tinah, send something to King George in return?' Tinah said yes and immediately began listing everything he could think of which was in his gift. Among these he mentioned the breadfruit. Bligh pounced:

> This was the exact point at which I wished to bring the conversation; and seizing an opportunity, which had every appearance of being undesigned and accidental, I told him the Bread Fruit trees were what King George would like; upon which he promised me a great many should be put on board, and seemed much delighted to find it so easily in his power to send anything that could be received by King George (Bligh, 1792).

Tinah had reason to be pleased with his negotiation. He had ensured the presence of the Europeans for the cost of a plant that grew in abundance on the island. Bligh also had reason for being 'much delighted'. Without commitment to any of Tinah's plans to chastise his enemies, he had secured the peaceful purpose of his visit. And so were the crew, for the ship's rules allowed Tahitian women to stay on ship for the night; only the Tahitian men had to go ashore.

Bligh made the necessary arrangements for the stay at Tahiti. He had decided, on David Nelson's recommendation, not to bring breadfruit plants on board until they had demonstrated that they had taken root in the small pots brought for that purpose. Also, by arriving in October instead of March he had missed the easterly winds that would take him through the Endeavour Straits. These were not due until March or April, according to the Admiralty's instructions. These circumstances could mean a stay of some months.

The shore party was commanded by Fletcher Christian and consisted of William Peckover, gunner and official trader, the botanists David Nelson and William Brown, midshipman Peter Heywood and four seamen. Fryer was left in command of *Bounty* for the duration of the stay. Bligh spent his time supervising everything and conducting the mainly diplomatic relationships with the Tahitians. He made copious notes of everything he saw and his accounts are often a testimony of his scientific objectivity. His Log, Journal and published Narratives, plus the Journals of Morrison, who lived among the Tahitians after the mutiny, constitute almost unadorned eyewitness anthropological studies of life in Tahiti in its heyday, at the point where the seeds of fatal contamination were sown by the European visitors.

# 10

# Troubles Ashore and Afloat

Inevitably the first troubles were associated with a spate of thefts. The first row was on Thursday, 30 October 1788. Bligh made an issue of the theft of hooks and thimbles cut from their gun mountings. He 'ordered every Man except the Cheifs Attendants out of the ship' (Log, 30 October 1788). This exercise was accomplished with some difficulty (who was, or was not, a chief's attendant 'was not an easy matter to distinguish'), and there were many rows and recriminations, probably due to the roughness with which the seamen carried out the order and their scanty knowledge of Tahitian. In one of these rows a Tahitian attacked with his club an armed sentry who, according to the Rules of Conduct, was not permitted to open fire. The incident caused such a commotion that Bligh was brought to the scene, but the Tahitian 'escaped narrowly with his life among the Crowd where I did not choose to fire lest an innocent person might suffer'. Bligh was happy that 'Every one was excessively alarmed at my determination, and I hope it will be the last provocation I may meet with among them' (Log, 30 October 1788).

Chastisement of the Tahitians for their thefts proved an insufficient deterrent, so Bligh adopted the alternative policy of chastisement of the seamen responsible for losing ship's property. On 4 November Alexander Smith was punished with 12 lashes for negligence in allowing a Tahitian to steal the gudgeon from the large cutter 'without knowing it'. When the chiefs and their wives saw the preparations for the punishment (which followed a specific drill) they attempted to intercede on Smith's behalf and pleaded with Bligh to cancel the punishment. Bligh was deeply moved by the reactions of the Tahitians, but did not cancel the flogging. He noted that the 'women in general showed every degree of Sympathy which marked them to be the most humane and affectionate creatures in the World'.

Punishing Smith did not stop the thefts. With a constant stream of visitors to the ship and the shore camp it was impossible to police everything and conduct the necessary work of the voyage, yet thefts could not normally be ignored. 'Frequent disputes with Indians have a dangerous tendency, as all altercations produce threats on our side without being able, or perhaps not convenient, to put them in execution, it is therefore better to put up with trifling losses unless the Offender can be detected' (Log, 1 December 1788). The theft which prompted these remarks was the 'remissness of my Officers & People at the Tent, they suffered the Boats Rudder to be stolen'. While this was the only theft 'of consequence' since the shore camp was set up, Christian, the officer in charge, had done somewhat better than Fryer on board ship in keeping thefts down. Punishment was not ordered because Bligh did not know who was responsible (suggesting that in Smith's case he had direct evidence of his negligence). We can assume that Christian, Peckover and Heywood were reprimanded for the incident, with Bligh, no doubt, covering the main points he wrote in the Log about the dangers of 'disputes with Indians'. The discriminatory treatment of the officers compared with that of seamen such as Smith was a feature of eighteenth-century naval life. He got 12 lashes for losing a gudgeon, and they got a telling off for losing a boat's rudder. This was rubbed in a few days later when an (unnamed) 'Gentleman' (probably Christian) had a pair of sheets stolen from his hammock.

Next day, Friday, Bligh was asked by one of the Tahitians if he could have a stone to sharpen the hatchets they had received as presents. He agreed immediately, and ordered Purcell to prepare a stone for that purpose. To his astonishment, Purcell refused, saying: 'I will not cut the stone for it will spoil my Chissls and tho there is law to take away my cloaths there is none to take away my Tools' (Log, 5 December 1788). Purcell was standing on his rights as a tradesman: the carpenter provided his own tools; they were not Navy property. Bligh was embarrassed, but there was nothing he could do except fulminate about Purcell in the official Log. He wrote: 'This Man having before shewen his Mutinous and insolent behaviour, I was under the necessity to confine him to his Cabbin. Altho I can but ill spare the loss of a Single Man, but I do not intend to lose the use of him but to remitt him to his duty to Morrow.' The same day, Matthew Thompson, a seaman, received 12 lashes for 'insolence and disobedience of Orders'. Again the contrast was probably a talking point below decks: Purcell got confined to his cabin for insolence and disobedience, Thompson got 12 lashes.

The next day the carpenter was returned to duty (though he was ordered to consider himself still a prisoner). The reason for his release to work was the sudden storm that struck the bay. The Tahitians informed Bligh that storms often hit the bay at this time of year, and he decided to move *Bounty* to somewhere safer. It blew hard for several days, mounting concern being expressed by the Tahitians. Chief Poeeno's wife displayed such an 'excess of Greif for the danger the Ship had been in, that would have affected the most dispassionate creature existing' (Log, 8 December 1788). It was not possible to move *Bounty* immediately, but Bligh ordered the men on shore and on board to make the necessary preparations.

During the preparations, a young Tahitian playing near a ship's boat, which was being run up on shore, fell under one of the wooden rollers and was injured. Some Tahitians present immediately set off in their canoes to appraise Bligh of what had happened. He hurriedly summoned medical assistance for the boy, only to find Huggan once again drunk in his cabin and incapable of moving. He then called Ledward out, but he was unable to find 'instruments or any thing necessary for some time'. Fortunately the boy had no broken limbs.

Later that day Ledward reported that Huggan was in a deep alcoholic coma and he recommended that he be moved to the main cabin to get fresh air. Fryer and some seamen went off to attend to this task, only to find Huggan already on deck though unconscious (how he got there is a mystery). Huggan was put into the main cabin (set aside for the breadfruit trees) and offered some coconut milk. He died at 9 pm. This was the second death on *Bounty*. Bligh reports:

> This unfortunate Man died owing to drunkeness and indolence. Exercise was a thing he could not bear an Idea of, or could I ever bring him to take a half dozen turns on deck at a time in the course of the whole Voyage. Sleeping was the way he spent his time, and he accustomed himself to breath so little fresh Air and was so filthy in his person that he became latterly a nuisance ... In the Morning the News of the Surgeons death became known to all the Natives. Most of them particularly the Cheifs knew him very well and without hesitating a moment pronounced his death owing to his 'not working and drinking to much Ava no Pretanee' [liquor of Britain] for this was the literal meaning and they had Often remarked before that every person was imployed but himself.

The Surgeon was buried at Point Venus, and Ledward was promoted from AB to Acting Surgeon. Huggan's effects were 'disposed of' by auction among the crew, excepting those Bligh held back because 'not one half of the Value was Offered for them' (they were probably too soiled). Ledward purchased Huggan's instruments and medicines at Bligh's valuation less 5, and could look forward to confirmation of his promotion by the Admiralty on *Bounty*'s return.

Throughout the following week the men were busy bringing out sails, stowing stores and picking the foul bits out of the ship's bread. Tinah tried to persuade Bligh not to depart from his little kingdom, and he suggested an alternative anchorage just along the coast at Oparre. To the delight of Tinah and the other chiefs, Bligh agreed. This drew *Bounty* closer into the society of Matavai. Tinah's people were not interfering with the collection and nursing of breadfruit plants at the shore camp, and were also proving helpful in other respects. Many of the men had formed temporary liaisons with local women and the arguments against moving to another district entirely included the risks attached to making new arrangements with different inhabitants.

Joseph Coleman, Armourer, set up a forge to make iron parts for the ship and by accident Bligh discovered a popular way to please the Tahitians. They were bringing Coleman pieces of iron to fashion into something useful, which he gladly did (in contrast to Purcell). Some of the iron pieces dated from Cook's visits. Bligh told Coleman to continue with his excellent efforts at public relations.

On Christmas Eve Fryer was sent to sound the channel from Matavai to Oparre. He reported a depth of 16 to 17 fathoms (about 100 feet) all the way. The plant pots were brought on board under Bligh's supervision by late afternoon (somebody unnamed had estimated that it would take nearly two days), and *Bounty* was ready to sail.

The ship's launch, commanded by Christian, had been sent to Oparre to land the tents and stores from the shore camp. It was ordered to return to the reef and await the arrival of *Bounty*. Fryer was sent aloft to the Foreyard to 'acquaint me of what danger might be in our way as from thence it might be seen'.

As *Bounty* approached the opening in the reef to the harbour at Oparre, the launch instead of keeping ahead let the ship get between it and the wind. This becalmed the launch and allowed *Bounty* to slip past unattended. This has to be put down as a mistake of Christian in command of the launch. Bligh ordered the anchor dropped and called the men aloft to shorten sails. The ship slowed to a stop, which Bligh attributed to action he had taken, but Fryer came down from the foremast and told him that the ship had grounded (in the channel Fryer had personally surveyed). Bligh was astonished:

> I have been in many situations of this Nature much more hazardous and I thought my precautions were abundant to carry me safe. A Lead in the Chains, a Boat sent to be ahead, and the Master on the Fore Yard to look out. Yet with all the Ship went on shore (Log, 25 December 1788).

Bligh took command of the launch (his remarks to Christian are not reported) and took the bower anchor astern with a view to hauling on it to move *Bounty* off the obstacle holding it forward of midship. He also sent Fryer to place a kedge anchor astern on the port side. Fryer and Christian were on board hauling in the kedge line but nobody was ordered to haul in the bower anchor line. The inevitable happened: the lines got entangled and one of them fouled a rock on the sea bed. It took thirty minutes to refloat *Bounty* and several hours to clear the entangled lines. Bligh's temper had been provoked by this incident and characteristically he no doubt gave vent to his feelings on the luckless ears of Fryer and Christian.

The next day the plants were taken ashore and the shore party reassembled under Christian. Peckover set up his trading post. Christmas Day was celebrated on Sunday 28 December instead of 25 December (a working day). The new anchorage was 'a delightful situation' and safe from sudden storms. Everything not needed was stowed below, including the rigging and booms. *Bounty* remained at Oparre for another three months.

Two days after Fryer and Christian had been publicly criticised but otherwise not punished for neglect of their duty, William Musprat, seaman, received a dozen lashes for 'neglect of duty', and on 29 December, Robert Lamb, butcher, was considered negligent in respect of the theft of his cleaver, and received twelve lashes in front of the chiefs, who were warned that 'any of their people would receive the same punishment if they were detected'. Bligh was sceptical about the effect of his message: 'It is however much more our fault than theirs, and I am certain that with the same kind of intercourse with a like number of Europeans more Acts of roguery would be committed' (Log, 29 December 1788). Tinah promised to get the cleaver back, and, much to Bligh's surprise ('I have no hope that it is in his power to get it'), he returned it a few days later.

# 11

# Desertion, Dissent and Departure

The *Bounty*'s first week at Oparre passed uneventfully. Coleman set up his forge again and was inundated with work both from the ship and from Tahitians. Purcell was busy repairing the small cutter, and Peckover opened his trading post and had increasing difficulty in getting supplies. On New Year's Day double grog was issued to all hands, and, as on all working days, two seamen were rostered ashore free of all duties for 'their own amusement', while the rest were employed, at least nominally. As with much military activity, we can assume that some of this work was not really necessary, but the men still had to look busy when an officer, especially the Lieutenant, looked their way. Nominal work can be even more irksome than hard labour, especially when there are other more pleasurable diversions to hand.

Sunday, 4 January 1789, was a day of rest for everybody. In the early hours of Monday morning three men deserted the ship: Charles Churchill, the ship's corporal; William Musprat, who had been flogged for neglect the previous week, and John Milward. Desertion from European ships was fairly common in the Pacific in the eighteenth and nineteenth centuries. It did not always indicate harsh treatment on board. It could as easily be motivated by the sheer contrast between life on a ship and the idyllic splendours apparently available on a Pacific island. The pleasant climate, the little need for work, an abundance of food, obliging women – the islands were certainly different from the cold and crowded ports of Europe. Desertions were attempted in Cook's ships, and the London Missionary Society reported seamen shipwrecked and refusing rescue.

The fact that it was easy to desert presented the Navy with a problem. Ships were often manned with society's misfits. To deter all but the most determined, punishment for desertion was extreme: 'Death, or such other punishment as the circumstances of the offence shall deserve' (Article XVI).

Bligh reported:

a.m. at 4 on the relief of the Watch found the small cutter missing. Mustered the Ships Company, when Charles Churchill, the Ships Corporal, Willm

55

Muspratt and Jno. Milward, Ab. were found absent, the latter being the
Centinel from 12 to 2 O'Clock in the Morning – Also eight Stand of Arms
and Ammunition were taken away by them all owing to the Mate of the
Watch being asleep on deck.

It was not untill a half past four that the above circumstance was found
out and I acquainted of it. Not the least knowledge had we of which way the
Boat had gone, I therefore went on shore to the Cheifs who soon got me
information that they had proceeded to Matavai, and were sailed for
Tetturoah in a Sailing Cannoe. – As the Boat was the most of my concern, I
returned to the Ship with Tynah, Oreepyah & Moannah and sent them
away with the Master to search for her. – They had but just got to One Tree
Hill when the Boat was rowing towards them with five Natives who were
bringing her to the Ship, and as a thorough knowledge of the Deserters plan
was with certainty known, they returned to the Ship and I rewarded the
Men for their fidelity.

As the object now was to adopt means to get the people I told Tynah and
other Cheifs I looked to them for that Service, and that therefore without
delay they must proceed to Tetturoah and get them taken and brought back
to me – that I would not quit the Country without them, and that as they
had always been my Friends, I expected they would show it in this instance,
and that unless they did I should proceed with such violence as would make
them repent it. It was therefore agreed that in the morning Oreepyah and
Moannah should set off in two Cannoes and take the Deserters, but they
appeared afraid on account of the Arms. – This however I was obliged to get
the better of describing to them for the Natives to collect round them as
friends, and then to seize on them and their Arms, and bind them with
Cords, and to show no mercy to them if they made resistance. Oreepyah was
very desirous to know if they had Pocket Pistols like mine, for with such he
said they might kill him while they were held, but as I assured him they had
only musquets, all fears and doubts were laid aside but one, which was
whether I would not serve them as Capt Cook had done Tootahah; confine
them on board, however they laughed when they asked this question, and I
showed them they had no reason to fear, the Boat being manned to carry
them on shore when they liked.-

As I have never shown any violence of Anger at the trifling Thefts that
have been committed, because it was our own faults, and having lived
among them with so much harmony and good will, they place every
confidence in my word and are faithfull in return to me – I have therefore no
doubt but they will bring the Deserters back, but in case of failure I shall
proceed to no extremities untill I have the Plants on board.-

Had the Mate of the Watch been awake no trouble of this kind would have
happened I have therefore disrated and turned him before the Mast. Such
neglectfull and worthless petty Officers I believe never was in a Ship as are
in this – No Orders for a few hours together are Obeyed by them, and their
conduct in general is so bad, that no confidence or trust can be reposed in
them – in short they have drove me to everything but Corporal punishment
and that must follow if they do not improve.

Morrison's account of the incident says that a search was made of the
possessions of the deserters, and a paper was found in Churchill's chest
'Containing his own Name & that of three of the Party on shore, which

Churchill had written, on which Lieut. Bligh went on Shore to the House & informd Mr. Christian of the Business and calling the men and challenging them with being concerned with Churchill and intending to disert. They persisted in their Innocence, and denyd it so firmly, that He was inclined from Circumstances to believe them and said no more to them about it' (Morrison, Journal, pp. 26-7). Christian's name was among the names on the sheet and Bligh accepted his denial of any knowledge of what this meant.

Bligh's main attention was centred on the plants. At this time they were 'of more Value than the Men', but he was prepared to use the stratagem of holding the chiefs hostage to secure the return of the deserters if they did not show sufficient efforts to do this voluntarily (Log, 6 January 1789). Meanwhile Fryer reported that another 1,754 pounds of ship's bread were unfit to eat and they were condemned.

The next problem arose with the shore party. One of the officers – again not named by Bligh – had plucked a branch of the Tutuee tree and had taken it into the tent. At the sight of the branch the Tahitians got up and left the area, as this tree was taboo to Tahitians and was associated with one of their religious festivals. Notwithstanding this reaction, the tree was tied to one of the posts in the camp, thus keeping the Tahitians away from the area altogether. This was a severe affront to the Tahitians, and Peckover's trading activities ceased altogether. Bligh was called to the camp, probably by Peckover, who had more sense than to indulge in a petty prank. After discovering the cause of the problem, Bligh persuaded Tinah to remove the taboo; the Tahitians returned to the camp and trading recommenced. Whoever did ignore Tahitian sensibilities in this manner was behaving extremely provocatively, yet Bligh does not name him.

Two weeks later it was Fryer's turn to cause trouble. Bligh was ashore making observations to check the rate of the time-keeper. Fryer was on board and sent a message to Bligh that the islander who had canoed the deserters from Matavai to Tetturoah was on board and wanted advice as to what he should do. Bligh was furious: 'As he knew perfectly my determination in punishing this Man if ever he could be caught, it was an unnecessary delay in confining him, but what was still worse, while the Mesenger was absent, which was about 10 Minutes, he [Fryer] suffered this Offender to jump overboard and escape without hoisting the Cutter out which was on deck, so that I now lost an Opportunity of securing the return of the Deserters without disturbing my friendly intercourse with the Chiefs' (Log, 16 January 1789).

It is possible that the Tahitian concerned got wind of what Fryer was doing and chose to escape. He may have visited *Bounty* to make contact with somebody on behalf of Churchill (the other men on the list?), and they may have encouraged him to leave to avoid their own discovery (and certain punishment).

The next day Bligh exploded into rage with Fryer, this time over a serious example of incompetence. The sailroom was ordered to be cleared so that all sails could go ashore for an airing. While this was underway it was discovered that the new and spare sails for the topsail, foresail, main topmast sail, staff sail and main staysail were mildewed and rotten. Without spare sails *Bounty* was at the mercy of the weather. Direct responsibility for this lay with Fryer and the bo's'n, William Cole. According to Bligh both men had reported to him on several occasions that the sails had been taken out and aired and that they were all in good order. 'Scarce any neglect of duty,' writes Bligh, 'can equal the criminality of this, for it appears that altho the Sails have been taken out twice since I have been in the Island, which I thought fully sufficient and I had trusted to their reports, Yet these New sails never were brought out, or is it certain whether they have been out since we left England, yet notwithstanding as often as Sails were taken to air by my Orders they were reported to me to be in good Order' (Log, 17 January 1789).

That Bligh would have liked to sack Fryer and Cole for their neglect of the ship's sails, and the kind of statements he might have made while expressing his views on their competence, is clear from his Log: 'If I had any Officer to supersede the Master and Boatswain, or was capable of doing without them, considering them as common Seamen, they should no longer occupy their respective Stations.' But the central problem of *Bounty*, that it was overcrowded and undermanned, remained. All Bligh could do was lavish increasingly pointed criticism on his officers in tones that were becoming more desperate with each incident (from confinement to their cabins, he went through disrating, considering corporal punishment, and now sacking them) and take on more work himself. He set Lawrence Lebogue, his sailmaker, to salvage what he could of the sails.

For the next week life returned to normal. Then news of the deserters arrived – they were only five miles from the ship. Bligh decided to arrest them himself and set off at dusk on Friday 23 January 1789 with an armed party. He walked along the beach and his boat party pulled along the shore. During the walk 'some fellows' approached him with a view to rob him but he 'dispersed them by threatening to destroy them, and clearing the beach with my Pistol'. He approached the house where the deserters were resting and they came out and surrendered without resistance.

On returning to *Bounty*, Bligh found that Fryer had let the ship's time-keeper go down; he had forgotten to wind it during the night he was in command. The time-keeper was crucial to Bligh's charting of new discoveries, which Fryer knew, of course, but he appears to have lost all interest in what he was doing.

By contemporary naval standards the punishment was lenient (though still excessive to modern readers). From records of Naval Courts Martial during the period 1750-1783 there were 170 cases of desertion tried. Mostly the men were sentenced to death, with a few sentenced to 500 lashes. The lowest sentence was 50 lashes. The men were ordered into irons: Milward and Musprat received two dozen lashes and Churchill a dozen and the punishment was repeated on 4 February. Milward, the sentinel on the night of the desertion, was regarded as particularly blameworthy, while Musprat had already been punished for neglect of duty. But why did Churchill receive only half the punishment of his companions? He was noted as a violent man, even a bully, which was probably regarded as a virtue in a Ship's Corporal responsible for keeping the men in order below decks. Neither Bligh, nor Morrison, nor anybody else has explained this matter.

The prisoners wrote a letter to Bligh on January 26:

> Sir, We should think ourselves wholly inexcuseable if we ommitted taking this earliest opportunity of returning our thanks for your goodness in delivering us from a trial by Court Martial, the fatal consequences of which are obvious, and although we cannot possibly lay any claim to so great a favour, yet we humbly beg you will be pleased to remit any further punishments and we trust our future conduct will fully demonstrate our deep sense of your clemency, and our steadfast resolution to behave better hereafter.

The 'fatal consequences' they mention were the death penalty, but the letter did not save them from further punishment. Unable to punish the officers, Bligh showed no compassion, whatever he might have felt, when punishing the seamen. And he still had Hayward, the officer of the watch who fell asleep, to deal with. Bligh blamed Hayward for the whole incident and publicly rebuked him during the two punishment musters when the deserters were flogged. In between times Hayward appears to have been kept below in irons. Short of flogging Hayward, this was the most Bligh could do. It was, however, of little value as a deterrent: Hayward fell asleep during the crucial watch when Christian led his mutiny a few weeks later.

Bligh's speech to the punishment muster gives an interesting insight into his attitude to the responsibilities of command:

> An Officer with Men under his care is at all times in some degree responsible for their conduct; but when from his neglect Men are brought to punishment while he only meets with a reprimand, because a publick conviction by Tryal will bring both into a more severe and dangerous situation, an alternative often laid aside through lenity, and sometimes necessity, as it now is in both cases; it is an unpleasant thing to remark that no feelings of honor, or sense of shame is Observed in such an Offender (Log, 24 January 1789).

Evidently Hayward displayed no remorse during the punishment muster, and this, perhaps, explains why Bligh sent him below to contemplate his different fate while he nursed his legs in irons and the deserters nursed their bloody backs in not a little agony. Hayward was 22 years old and as a midshipman had no excuse for his dangerous proneness to sleeping on his watches.

After Hayward's confinement, during the night of 6 February, the anchor cable was cut through. To ensure that it did not happen again, a stage walk was built so that sentries could inspect the cable from the deck. At the time nobody could say who had cut the cable. Bligh at first thought it was cut by a Tahitian, but after the mutiny he suggested it might have been cut by a mutineer hoping to stay in Tahiti if *Bounty* foundered. The truth came out when the mutineers returned to Tahiti. According to Morrison (Journal, p. 101a) a Tahitian friend (or two) of Hayward was so incensed at his punishment that he had the cable cut and was fully determined to murder Bligh if Hayward was flogged. Happily, the ship did not founder, and nor was Hayward flogged.

In the last few weeks before departure, thefts and trouble continued. Isaac Martin fought with a Tahitian whom he suspected of stealing an iron loop. Martin was sentenced to 24 lashes for breaching the rule about fighting with Tahitians (he was apparently the only person to do so). Such was the intercession of the chiefs on this occasion that Bligh commuted the sentence from 24 to 19 lashes. Still, the Catch-22 situation the seamen were in was a burden: they were flogged if they permitted a theft, and flogged when they prevented one; at least, we can surmise this was how it was put about below decks that night while they nursed Martin's back.

The activity for the voyage home increased. The ship was caulked, new planks were sawn and the spare rigging and booms got up from below. Cats were taken on board to chase out rats and cockroaches. Storms hit Tahiti and lasted for days on end, slowing down the work and, as always, threatening the breadfruit plants, which had been collected together in 774 pots.

On 2 March 1789 a thief stole an empty water cask, part of an azimuth compass and 'the Bedding out of Mr Peckover's Hammock while he had the look out'. The heavy rain gave sufficient cover for the thief to sneak past Peckover. When Bligh was informed in the morning he went ashore to berate the chiefs, who, sensing trouble, left Oparre to avoid him. They reappeared later, with the thief and the stolen items, and demanded that Bligh kill their guilty countryman. Bligh had no wish to impose capital punishment, or even the barbaric punishment imposed by Cook on an islander of cutting off his ear. He did impose the severest punishment of the voyage: 100 lashes. He had tried everything now short of hostage-taking. The Tahitian took his punishment almost without murmur and his skin did not break until the last few lashes.

The remaining days were spent by Bligh in rounds of diplomatic meetings with the chiefs and in making what observations he could in the appalling weather. During one of these rainy nights, George Stewart, mate of the watch, allowed the Tahitian who had been flogged to escape despite the fact he was in irons below. Bligh was angered by this latest display of sloppiness and connivance: 'I had given in Written orders,' he wrote, 'that the Mate of the Watch was to be answerable for the Prisoners and to visit and see that they were safe in his Watch, but I have such a neglectfull set about me that I believe nothing but condign punishment can alter their conduct. – Verbal orders in the course of a Month were so forgot that they impudently assert no such thing or directions were given, and I have been at last under the necessity to trouble myself with writing what by decent Young Officers would be complied with as the Common Rules of Service' (Log, 7 March 1789).

The rain eventually cleared, and preparations for departure were speeded up. The caulking was resumed and the masts and the rigging were checked over. Bligh noted that hogs were getting scarcer; Peckover was trying to buy them for curing and storing as well as for daily use. Thus his demands were increasing as supply was falling, partly due to the prolonged stay of *Bounty* in the area. Peckover was forced to go further into the island as supplies dried up. The men themselves added to these problems by trying to buy meat independently for their personal sea-stores. Bligh instructed that all pigs brought on board were to be registered by the watch, so that there would be no arguments later as to whose pig was which. Morrison later complained that this was an example of Bligh's harshness as a commander. He described how the men would go to considerable lengths to avoid detection by Bligh of their bringing personal sea-stores on board. From the individual seaman's limited point of view, Bligh's measures may have seemed oppressive, yet it is obvious that his concerns were with the whole ship and its food stores, which were for all hands, and that his measures were an example of good management not personal tyranny.

Peckover reported to Bligh that he had been warned by Tahitian friends not to go too far inland for fear that he would be beaten and stripped. Bligh got to the bottom of the problem through his good contacts with the Tahitian chiefs. The source of the trouble was Fryer. He had taken a mat and a piece of cloth from his Tahitian lover who had been staying with him on board. This was a 'misunderstanding', he claimed, when challenged by Bligh. Peckover's habit of wandering alone had given the woman's family the opportunity to plot revenge by attacking him when he was alone. Bligh's concern was to make peace, and he invited Fryer's ex-lover to the ship to receive her property from Fryer. Bligh's sentiments about the nature of the 'misunderstanding', and Fryer's ungallant conduct, were not recorded. Nor were Fryer's feelings about the humiliation he had suffered (entirely due to his own selfish and thoughtless actions).

In the final days of the ship's stay the main task was to get the men back into naval routine. All the men's spare time was spent with the many friends they had met, and in collecting local foods and curiosities. Such was the inflow of goods that orders had to be given to confine each man's collection to what he could store in his sea chest. By the day of its departure, *Bounty* was not just a floating greenhouse with the breadfruit plants, it was also a menagerie, literally stuffed to the gunwales with fresh fruit, coconuts and pens containing twenty-five hogs and seventeen goats.

The crew took their final farewells of their friends and their women, with whom some of them had formed deep attachments. Bligh entertained the chiefs and their families on the ship and made his parting presents to them. To Tinah he gave the most coveted of all gifts: two muskets and a thousand rounds of ammunition.

Departure was delayed until 4 April; then, to the accompaniment of the noisy population on the shore, and with three cheers for Tinah from the crew, *Bounty* slipped out of the anchorage and headed for the open sea. Bligh wrote: 'We bad farewell to Otaheite, where for 23 Weeks we were treated with the greatest kindness; fed with the best of Meat and finest Fruits in the World.'

# 12

# Passage to Mutiny

What happened on *Bounty* in the next three weeks is significant because of the clues it gives as to what caused the mutiny and why Christian led it. The main problem is the triviality of the events. It has been assumed that, as there is no smoke without fire, Bligh must have been unusually tyrannical for an eighteenth-century officer. Some authors have looked into the psychological dramas of people on board, including alleged sexual secrets of the protagonists.

The Admiralty's parsimony in the size of the ship, the inadequacies of the officers, Bligh's inability to cope with them, his temper and tantrums, the attractions of Tahiti, the remoteness of the Pacific, and the long train of incidents that started with Purcell's defiance of Bligh at Adventure Bay, all created a situation in which mutiny was possible. Aversion to duty had spread from the petty officers to the men and Bligh's attempts to deal with this – usually involving a bawling out of the officer or a flogging for the seaman – merely advertised his isolation. His own competence – much advertised by himself, if the Log is taken to be a sample of his remarks to all and sundry – only made matters worse; the more his officers wilted the angrier he became. Finally one of them broke.

The daily business of *Bounty*, in particular the food allowance, is recorded in the Log. Each man received rations of pork and plantain (yams), supplemented by private sea-stores they had brought on board. They ate better than they had on the first leg of the voyage. Additional food supplies were traded for at islands they called at. They had, however, lost the relatively free atmosphere of Tahiti, including the company of women.

*Bounty* passed close to Huaheine, where with Captain Cook Bligh had been present at the establishment of Omai's home. Out of sentiment Bligh steered close to the island to see if anything was left of Omai's house which had been built for him by the British. Nothing remained. Some canoes came off to the ship and an islander recognised Bligh, calling him by his name. Bligh was told that Omai was dead, his house was burnt down and only the mare remained of the animals left by Captain Cook. After a little trade, *Bounty* pulled away.

On 11 April 1789 an island was discovered, Aitutaki in the Cook group.
The next day John Sumner was punished with 12 lashes for 'Neglect of
duty'. It was the last flogging before the mutiny.

Throughout the next week *Bounty* was beset by squalls of rain and
occasional lightning. It was cloudy and overcast but the wind was fair,
and the ship was often under full sail. They passed Savage Island on 18
April and arrived at Annamooka on 23 April. An unnamed seaman had
been on the sick list since 8 April, suffering from 'a fall off Cape Horn' a
year earlier. It was either Thomas Hall, the cook, or Churchill, the
corporal, as both men had fallen at the Horn. Somebody else was on the
sick list as a 'venereal'.

Annamooka was the last stop before Endeavour Straits. What
happened there might have some bearing on the events to come. Bligh
wanted wood and water, and after settling on an anchorage on 24 April
(four days before the mutiny), he went ashore with David Nelson to find
suitable places for the working parties. While ashore, he met a man he
recognised from his previous visit with Cook in 1777. The man told him
that the friendly chiefs, Poulaho, Feenow and Tubow, were visiting
another island, and he promised to send for them. They did not arrive
before *Bounty* left, and this was unfortunate because it meant that the
islanders were less disciplined in the absence of the friendly chiefs.

While the ship was being anchored, Elphinstone, the Master's Mate,
through 'want of a little exertions', according to Bligh, allowed the bower
buoy to sink and it had to be replaced.

Bligh used Cook's wooding and watering places of 1777. The
water-casks had to be hauled 400 yards from a stream, and wood was
available 200 yards along the beach. Christian had eleven men in the
watering party and Elphinstone four in the wooding party. In case of
trouble arms were provided for the watering party, but none for the
wooding party. These were ordered to be left in the boats as there was no
spare man in Christian's party for sentry duties.

Within an hour a man lost his axe and another his adze, but fortunately
for them they 'cleared themselves of the Neglect as they could not comply
with every part of their duty and keep their Tools in their Hands, and
they therefore merit no punishment'. He reserved his bile for Christian
and Elphinstone: 'As to the Officers I have no resourse, nor do I ever feel
myself safe in the few instances I trust them.' The sojourn at Tahiti was
taking its toll in their attentiveness.

Morrison's version of the incident presents the problem somewhat
differently. He wrote that the islanders 'were very rude & attempted to
take the Casks from the Waterers and the axes from the Wooding party;
and if a Musquet was pointed at any of them [it] produced no other effect
than a return of the Compliment, by poising their Club or Spear with a
menacing look; and as it was Lieut. B.'s orders, that no person should
affront them on any occasion, they were emboldened by Meeting no

return for their Insolence, and became so troublesom that Mr. Christian who had the Command of the Watering party, found it difficult to carry on his duty, of this He informed Lt. Bligh of this [sic], who dam'd him for a Cowardly rascal, asking him if He was afraid of Naked Savages while He had arms; to which Mr. Christian answerd "the Arms are of no use while your orders prevent them from being used" ' (Journal, ML Safe 1/42, p. 33).

That Bligh well understood the difficulties in the task he had given Christian is seen by his remarks in the Log about the behaviour of the islanders who were a 'clever dextrous set of People, and would ever take advantages if they saw People Negligent, even before the Centinels when *Resolution* was here, if they ever caught them inattentive they took whatever they could lay hold of. We are therefore not to be surprised at those petty Violences as our Iron Utensils are Jewels of inestimable Value to them' (Log, 25 April 1789).

Who was right in this dispute? Bligh did not want trouble with the islanders, because he wanted wood and water. He gave orders for the firearms to be kept at the boat, not, as Morrison reveals, to be taken along the beach. He did not want them fired, except in defence of life, and thought Christian's excuse was weak. It was not the possession of firearms that prevented theft but the attention of everybody to duty. He believed that 'the Officers, contrary to my direct orders, suffered the Indians to crowd round them and amuse them, and by that means the Theft was committed'. Christian in explaining his difficulties with the islanders implied that he wanted to use the arms – they 'are of no use while your orders prevent them being used' – and Bligh abused him as a 'cowardly rascal'. Christian had no experience of hostile islanders; his only experience was of the tranquil and docile Tahitians. His first encounter with aggressive behaviour may have excited him, which Bligh mistook for fear (Bligh had seen frightened men before). Bligh might also have remarked about the unarmed men in Elphinstone's party not applying to him for help. We shall question again this character trait of Christian's in events after the mutiny. Notably, no more thefts took place from the watering or wooding parties that day. Bligh's intervention certainly had the appropriate effect on how Christian and Elphinstone performed their duties after the first hour, which is what being captain is all about.

The next day Bligh sent Fryer ashore to assist Christian in the supervision of the watering party. The stolen axe was returned and nothing else stolen from the work parties. But two other thefts took place. David Nelson, who was ashore searching for plants, had his spade stolen; Fryer had a grapnel stolen from his boat. Fryer claimed in his Journal (Rutter (ed.) 1934, p. 54) that his men disobeyed his order to hold the boat steady using their oars and instead used the grapnel for this purpose, whereupon it was within reach of a party of islanders playing around the boat.

Fryer's arrival at the watering place and the sight of the islanders harassing the work party, led, he claims, to his ordering Christian to quit the watering work and take the casks, empty or full, back to the boats, where he was appraised of the loss of the grapnel. He told Bligh of the loss, and remarked that it was not too serious, whereupon Bligh exclaimed: 'By God Sir, if it is not great to you it is great to me' (Fryer, Journal, p. 55). The Log simply records that the watering was completed in the morning and the wooding in the afternoon.

Bligh was undoubtedly furious at the losses. He was also aware of the potentially dangerous situation for his men on the beach. He wrote: 'As there were a Number of Cannoes from different Islands the Crowd of Natives became very great, it was therefore impossible to do any thing among such a throng without a principal Cheif who could command the whole which was not at present the Case' (Log, 26 April 1789).

Like Cook before him, Bligh attempted to get back the grapnel by taking some chiefs hostage for its prompt return. As this was planned to be the last opportunity to trade until *Bounty* reached Timor, trade was thrown open on an all-comers basis. Peckover was stood down as official trader and the men went at it with alacrity. This brought five chiefs on board among the crowd, and as the grapnel was not returned Bligh confined them below. In the event the grapnel was not returned by the time *Bounty* was some way off shore, so he had to let them go. He called their canoes alongside and gave them presents of a hatchet, a saw and several nails and knives each, and he claimed they parted friends. Morrison claimed that Bligh had insulted the chiefs by making them peel coconuts while below decks (Journal, p. 38), which implies a double standard when compared with his observation that the islanders on the beach became 'emboldened by Meeting no return to their Insolence'.

Bligh assembled the crew and addressed them. According to Morrison's account, he threatened them and said what he thought of them. He said that they were a 'parcel of lubberly rascals and that he would be one of five who with good sticks would disarm the whole of them, and presenting a Pistol at Wm. McCoy threatened to shoot him for not paying attention' (Journal, p. 38). The Log says nothing about this assembly (it was the night before the mutiny and Bligh had not finished the day's entries), though it would have been a natural time for one to be held, with the ship set to sail to the Endeavour Straits. An outburst like this suggests that Bligh had lost control of himself and the crew. He despised and distrusted his officers, and the men neither obeyed them nor honoured him.

What caused Christian to mutiny? His family identified a possible cause: a row over some missing coconuts! That he could commit the crime of mutiny over a row with his captain is not beyond belief – a trivial incident can spark off an emotional conflagration in which all reason and sense of proportion are lost for long enough to provoke horrendous acts of passion. Our courts often show petty dramas blowing up into blinding rows, which in the light of day, and under a court's scrutiny, have consequences for the participants, villain and victim alike, neither intended to be, nor defended as, examples of humankind at its best. One such clash, between Bligh and Christian, was over an incident so trivial that Hollywood scriptwriters have had to substitute in its place fictional horrors that are a libel on the men concerned. The myths of Bligh the tyrannical commander etc. are born out of, and sustained by, the over-reaction of Christian to Bligh's abusive tongue. Of all the mutinies in the history of the Royal Navy, *Bounty*'s is as petty as it was tragic for all concerned. It was not caused by keel-hauling, or incessant floggings, or monstrous cruelty, or any similar crimes that sparked off other mutinies. It was just a thief in the night making off with some of the ship's nuts, and an officer shocked at being accused of the lesser crime of theft reacting by committing the grosser crime of mutiny!

There are four versions of what happened over the coconuts: Morrison's, Fryer's, Edward Christian's and Bligh's. I shall examine them in the order in which they were written, and highlight the striking fact that with each version the incident was subtly transformed and elaborated in order to make it more plausible that the coconut incident should have driven anybody to snap.

First, Fryer's version, written in 1790:

> In the morning when Mr Bligh came on deck he sent for me and said Mr Fryer dont you think those Cocoa Nuts are shrunk since last Night. I told him that they were not so high as they were last night as I had them stowd up to the Rail but that the people might have put them down in walking over them in the Night – he said No, that they had been taken away and that he would find out who had taken them and immediately ordered the Master at Arms to see every nut that was below on Deck. Every Body's he repeated several times – after all the nuts was on deck that was found below every body was on Deck that ownd them – when Mr Bligh began, whose are these when the owner Answerd which was Mr Young – how many Nuts did you buy. So many Sir! And how many did you eat? he did not know but there was the remainder which he had not counted – then all the other Gentlemen were called and likewise the People – when Mr Bligh had examined as far as he thought proper, he told the Master at Arms that they might take their nuts down again and told Every body that he allowed them a pound and a half of Yams which was more than their Allowance, but if he did not find out who took the Nuts that he would put them on 3/4 of a pound of Yams and said I take care of you now for my own good, but when I get you through the Straits you may all got to hell and if they did not look out sharp that he would do for one half of them; many times in the Voyage have he told his young Gentlemen that he would leave them at Jamaica – that they should not go home with him (Journal, pp. 55-6).

First, some points from this, the earliest written account. There is no mention of Christian by name at all, only Young. In fact this is the only mention of Edward Young in all the surviving documentary evidence from the *Bounty*. Whatever Bligh said to his officers, Fryer only thought it

remarkable to report his interchange with Young, the first officer
questioned. Secondly, Bligh's 'abuse' was confined to his remarks about
the forthcoming passage through the straits. Thirdly, Bligh only
threatened to cut the yam allowance to three-quarters of a pound (i.e. half
of it) if he did not find the thief by the next day. Compare these points
with the next version, written by James Morrison in late 1792, three
years after the incident:

> In the Afternoon of the 27th Mr. Bligh Came up, and taking a turn about the
> Quarter Deck when he missed some of the Cocoa Nuts which were piled up
> between the Guns upon which he said that they were stolen and Could not
> go without the knowledge of the Officers, who were all Calld and declared
> that they had not seen a Man touch them, to which Mr. Bligh replied then
> you must have taken them yourselves, and orderd Mr. Elphinstone to go &
> fetch evry Cocoa Nut in the Ship aft, which He obeyd. He then questioned
> evry Officer in turn concerning the Number they had brought, & Coming to
> Mr. Christian askd Him, Mr. Christian answerd 'I do not know Sir, but I
> hope you don't think me so mean as to be Guilty of Stealing yours'. Mr. Bligh
> replied 'Yes you dam'd Hound I do – You must have stolen them from me or
> you could give a better account of them – God damn you you Scoundrels you
> are all thieves alike, and combine with the Men to rob me – I suppose you'll
> Steal my Yams next, but I'll sweat you for it you rascals I'll make half of you
> Jump overboard before you get through Endeavour Streights' – He then
> Calld Mr. Samuel and said 'Stop these Villians Grog, and Give them but
> Half a Pound of Yams tomorrow, and if they steal then, I reduce them to a
> quarter.' The Cocoa Nuts were Carried aft, & He went below, the officers
> then got together and were hurd to murmur much at such treatment, and it
> was talked among the Men that the Yams would be next seized, as Lieut.
> Bligh knew that they had purchased large quantitys of them and set about
> secreting as many as they Could (Journal, pp. 40-1).

Morrison did not know what Fryer had written two years earlier and
the discrepancies are therefore useful evidence on the reliability of the
author as a witness. First, he places the incident in the afternoon of the
27th while Fryer claims it was in the morning, which makes sense of
Fryer's suggestion that the piles were trod down during the night.
Secondly, Morrison claims it was Elphinstone, the Master's Mate, who
collected the nuts from below, and not Charles Churchill, the
Master-at-Arms. If Morrison is right, Fryer did not know the difference
between his own Mate and Churchill, which is unlikely. Thirdly,
Christian appears as the butt of Bligh's abuse and not Young.
Interestingly, Morrison's Memorandum, written a few months earlier in
1792, only refers to 'all the Officers' being called and does not single out
Christian in the text. A footnote at the bottom of the manuscript states:
'He particularly called Christian a Thief and a Villain and challenged him
with the Theft of the Nuts' (Memorandum, 1792, ML Safe 1/33, pp. 32-3).
As the Memorandum in the Mitchell Library is a copy of Morrison's
manuscript, the original of which is not available for study, we do not

know whether this was inserted at the time it was written or later (or even by somebody else). It supports the view that Christian began to assume a more central role in the coconuts row the further the authors were from its occurrence, suggesting an attempt to increase the row's significance as the cause of Christian's subsequent behaviour. We do know that what was not mentioned as being important in 1790, and was a mere footnote in October 1792, had become a major role in the incident a month or so later. Christian's rewritten role certainly improves the credibility of the assertion that he was driven to mutiny by Bligh's direct, public and personal aspersions on his character.

By 1794, Edward Christian, Fletcher's brother, a professor of law at Cambridge, published a criticism of Bligh based on interviews with the surviving crew, including Fryer, and by correspondence with Morrison, in 1793. In this version, various details are changed, and Christian moves from the anonymity of Fryer's 1790 and Morrison's October 1792 accounts to the centre of the stage:

> At this island [Annamooka] the Captain and the ship's company had bought quantities of cocoa nuts, at the rate of 20 for a nail; the Captain's heap lay upon the deck, and in the morning of the 27th, Captain Bligh fancied that the number was diminished, but the master, Mr. Fryer, told him he supposed they were pressed closer from being run over by the men in the night. The Captain then ordered the Officer of the morning Watch, Mr Christian, to be called; when he came, the Captain accosted him thus, 'Dam your blood, you have stolen my cocoa nuts'; Christian answered, 'I was dry, and I thought it of no consequence, I took one only, and I am sure no one touched another.' Captain Bligh then replied, 'You lie, you scoundrel, you have stolen one half.' Christian appeared much hurt and agitated, and said, 'Why do you treat me thus, Captain Bligh?' Captain Bligh then shook his hand in his face and said, 'No reply'; and called him a 'thief', and other abusive names. He then ordered the quarter masters to go down and bring all the cocoa nuts both from man and officer, and put them upon the quarter deck. They were brought. The Captain then called all hands upon deck, and desired 'the people to look after the officers and the officers to look after the people, for there never were such a set of damned thieving rascals under any man's command in the world before'. And he told the men, 'You are allowed a pound and a half of yams today, but tomorrow I shall reduce you to three quarters of a pound' (Edward Christian, 1794, pp. 63-4).

This version reverses the sequence of events by having Christian and the officers abused before the coconuts were brought on deck instead of after. The nut collectors also change identity: they are neither Churchill nor Elphinstone, but the quartermasters, John Norton, George Simpson and Peter Linkletter. Memory fades during the passage of time, but in this case, as the memory fades on the sequence of events and who was doing what, so the successive accounts get more and more specific about Christian's role, even to the point of supplying verbatim accounts of the speeches of Bligh and Christian to each other. From Fryer's 1790 vagueness of what happened to 'the officers', we have Christian's brother, who was not present, reproducing in 1794 the exact words used in the exchange.

What of Bligh's version? He wrote nothing about it in the Log, nor in his published accounts. He did make reference to it in some notes he wrote in 1793 for Sir Joseph Banks, who had received the substance of Edward Christian's charges which he was about to publish:

> When the ship sailed from Anamooka [...] A heap of Cocoa Nuts were between the guns under the charge of the officer of the Watch, with orders for no one to touch them until the ship was clear of the land, when they would be issued equally and considered highly refreshing, without which caution some would have & waste one half, & others would have none. In one Night (the first) the Officers permitted the whole within a score to be taken away. As this was evidently done through design Captain Bligh ordered all Cocoa Nutts to be replaced – The officers of the Watch declared they were taken away by stelth – Here was publick theft, a contumacy, & direct disobedience of orders – the particular offenders could not be found out, any more than had been effected in private thefts which had been frequently committed; could therefore either the epithet Thief or Villain, had it been used, have justified their taking the Ship next day (Bligh, Remárks on Morrison's Journal, ML Safe 1/43, pp. 50-1).

Bligh's failure to comment publicly on the rows he had with the officers before the mutiny leaves him open to the suspicion that he was embarrassed by them. It could also be that he never thought that these rows, and the coconut row the day before the mutiny, had the significance credited to them by others. Like Fryer, who did not single out Christian, he was unaware of what Edward Christian, the talented and litigious advocate, could make of an incident once it had been rewritten to recast his brother in the central role.

In all versions, Bligh came on deck on 27 April and thought the coconuts were reduced in number from the night before. Fryer, according to himself and Morrison, agreed that this appeared to be so but, to avoid another row, opined that they had been trodden down in the night. Fryer's apparent indifference, or his facile explanation, annoyed Bligh enough for him to make an issue of what he was convinced was only the latest theft and blatant example of a disobedience of orders. He sent for Christian, as the Officer of the previous Watch, who exhibited the same lack of concern about the issue, which Bligh took to mean that he was careless of his charge of the ship's stores. The scene was set for another row, Bligh indignant and exasperated with his officers, the officers indignant and exasperated with their captain's foul moods. The ordering up of the coconuts and the hope of finding a 'thief' by this method was forlorn from the start. Probably several men were involved in casually replenishing themselves rather than outright thieving of stores on a collusive basis (one man helping himself to a coconut is of no consequence, half the crew taking one or more each becomes a provocative outrage). Fryer's report of Young's answers suggests that they probably set the tone for everybody else: parry the captain's questions with vagueness. With no evidence, Bligh could not punish anybody, so he developed the theme that the officers were lax, if not involved in the crew's purloining of the nuts. This led to the blanket tirade about 'thiefs' and 'villains', and the empty threats about Endeavour Straits, where he was convinced that the incompetence of the useless among them would cause the lax and indifferent to see why only their captain's skills could get them through safely, though he suspected (being sarcastic as well as caustic) that they were also cowards and that half of them would jump overboard with fright. He ended his diatribe with the hardly tyrannical threat that the yam allowance would be cut unless the thieves owned up.

What then can we make of this otherwise trivial incident? We have examined it in gross detail precisely because so much has been made of it.

Purcell contributed to the rewrite with the report that Fletcher and Bligh had another row that afternoon, but he does not report what it was about. He said that Christian's distress was so severe that he came away from Bligh with 'tears running fast from his eyes in big drops'. Other witnesses interviewed by Edward Christian quoted Fletcher as saying: 'I would rather die ten thousand deaths, than bear this treatment: I always do my duty as an officer and as a man ought to do, yet I receive this scandalous usage', and that 'flesh and blood cannot bear this treatment' (Edward Christian, 1794, pp. 64-5).

That we know now that Fletcher was indeed distressed that night, and that he blamed Bligh for his state, does not increase the significance of the coconut row. His brother needed a black finale to make sense of Fletcher's preference for a 'thousand deaths' to standing it a minute longer. But it is just as plausible that it was not the immensity of the burden imposed on him by Bligh's abuse so much as a weakness in himself that made his captain's irritable temper – to which he was no stranger, having sailed with him twice before – loom larger than it justified.

Of the two men in the unfolding drama, one was in an emotional, almost suicidal, state, of which the other, the alleged cause of the unbearable stress, remained completely unaware up to the moment of the mutiny. It is extraordinary that nobody on board that evening should have had the slightest inkling of what the morning was to bring. Bligh certainly was genuinely surprised. He carried on as normal. He sent his servant, John Smith, to Christian with an invitation to join him as usual for dinner (at sea, taken just after noon). Now if Bligh had picked on Christian over the coconuts, this is an extremely odd invitation, unless you believe that Bligh was remorseful and was going to apologise, in which case it would have been best if Christian had not declined the invitation by pleading that he was unwell. Bligh accepted Christian's excuse and sent for one of the midshipmen (Hayward) to join him. From Bligh's point of view the incident that morning was over; it was a minor disciplinary matter, during which he had had an altercation with the officers and reminded them of their duty. As he believed that they could never be reminded of their duty enough, he thought nothing remiss, either in his conduct as captain or in Christian's as second-in-command.

We know just how normal Bligh regarded the evening's events. After supper, Bligh made his final rounds on deck, exchanged some small talk with Fryer, and went below to bed, unarmed, and unprepared for anything other than a night's sleep. The contrast between Christian on the verge of suicide and Bligh calmly going about ship's business is inexplicable unless the impulse to mutiny came from within Christian, with Bligh's behaviour the straw that broke the camel's back. Christian's sudden hatred of Bligh and Bligh's unalarmed behaviour suggest that the mutiny had more to do with the state of Christian's mind than with the customary treatment he received from Bligh.

# 13

# Fletcher Christian

Attention must now focus on the man who led the mutiny, Fletcher Christian, then 24. He was five foot nine inches tall, with a dark swarthy complexion and dark brown hair, and was tattooed in the Tahitian fashion with a star on his left breast and other tattoos on his back. His knees stood a little out, so that he gave the appearance of being slightly bow-legged. He also sweated profusely, so that he soiled everything he handled. This at least is how Bligh described him in 1789 (ML Safe 1/43, p. 1).

Of his background, much more has recently come to light with Glynn Christian's masterly, balanced and well-written account of his ancestor's life (*Fragile Paradise: the discovery of Fletcher Christian, Bounty Mutineer*, 1982). He was born on 25 September 1764, the seventh of ten children. His father, Charles, died when Fletcher was 4, leaving his mother, Ann, to fend for her family out of the income from her farm, Moorland Close, near Cockermouth in Cumberland. Two of his three elder brothers, John and Edward, were educated at St John's College, Cambridge and both had legal careers. Whatever hopes Fletcher and Charles, two years his senior, may have entertained of following their elder brothers through Cambridge into the professions, they were rudely terminated by the bankruptcy of their mother's estate. It is not clear what this was due to, though Glynn Christian thinks that the drain of financing the careers of John and Edward, plus some risky investments made by John, frittered away Fletcher's inheritance. She had to remove herself and the family to the Isle of Man to avoid her creditors and was bailed out by other members of the Christian family (Glynn Christian, pp. 34-7).

This puts an entirely new perspective on the statements made by Edward Christian, after the mutiny, that Fletcher 'stayed at school longer than men generally do who enter the Navy, and being allowed by all to possess extraordinary abilities, is an excellent scholar'. Fletcher was set for an academic career until circumstances forced him to seek another. The Royal Navy was not his first choice (as it had been Bligh's), but a distant second (or even third?).

His family was in the Isle of Man at the time Bligh returned from

Cook's Third Voyage, but Fletcher may still have been at St Bede's, a boarding school near Whitehaven. After leaving school, probably some time between 1779 and 1782, he had to find a living. A member of the 'nouveaux pauvres', his mother could not afford to maintain him any longer. His elder brother Charles, at 18, ceased to be an expense on his mother when he left home for a two-and-a-half year spell (May 1780 to mid-1783) in the West Riding of Yorkshire militia, followed by a two-year course at Edinburgh University, where he graduated as a surgeon in mid-1785. He then found employment on board *Middlesex*, Captain John Rogers, of the East India fleet in February 1786, as the ship's surgeon. When Fletcher reached 18, he too had to seek a living, in view of his mother's circumstances. He signed on as a midshipman in the Royal Navy on 25 April 1783. His more scholarly plans thwarted, which his brother Edward testified that he was excellently qualified to pursue, and his family circumstances reduced, he was forced to seek his fortune in a service where talent, hard work and a little luck could still take determined survivors to senior rank.

To date no letters or journals of Fletcher Christian are known to have survived. Everything we know about him has come second-hand. This forces us to judge him by his behaviour; though this is a risky resort, for thereby he has no chance to speak in his own defence.

'I am in Hell', Christian is said to have cried during the mutiny. And so he probably was. But what put him into that private hell? There can be no doubt that he believed his captain's behaviour to be the prime cause. To what extent his perception of his private hell was due to a fatal weakness in his own character is conjecture. His altercations with Bligh, particularly after *Bounty* left Tahiti, drained him of his reserves of self-restraint. He first bent under the storms of Bligh's invective, and then he broke. The change from their mutual trust, going back to the voyages in *Britannia*, was doubly painful for the favoured protégé: it undermined his self-confidence and, with the injury of his lost inheritance, rankled. The resultant stress may have made him less efficient by Bligh's martinet standards – brooding is no help when carrying out one's duty with alacrity – and Bligh's tetchiness may have increased Christian's mental torment.

Bligh's behaviour, notorious during his lifetime, tipped the balance. Christian snapped, and overturned everything an officer was supposed to abide by in all circumstances, namely, the absolute, uncompromising and resolute adherence to duty (in this case, to bringing *Bounty* home after completing the King's mission to transfer the breadfruit). The Royal Navy could not function without its all-pervasive code of duty, irrespective of how unfair it was to the individual and the torments of his private hell. Men faced appalling difficulties in carrying out their duty – witness the dreadful experiences of *Bounty* at Cape Horn, or the acrid smog of the gun deck receiving an enemy's broadside – and no wavering was permitted by the Admiralty in any circumstances. The one crime for which there was no palliative, no excuse and, almost universally, no mercy was mutiny.

It is in this context that we should note just how brief was Christian's naval experience. He had gone to sea first in 1783 in HMS *Eurydice*, a sixth-rater (24 nine-pound guns), where he served for 2 years and 2 months, during which he was Mate of a Watch on the return journey. He was ashore for nine months (and was therefore keen to find a berth) from June 1785 to around November 1786, when he made the first of two passages with Bligh in Duncan Campbell's merchant ship *Britannia* to the West Indies. He was paid off from *Britannia* in August 1787 and rejoined Bligh on *Bounty* in September. His service before the mutiny lasted 1 year and 7 months (7 September 1787 to 28 April 1789). In all, then, he had 4 years 6 months actual sea experience in his six years (April 1783 to April 1789) in the Royal Navy. Moreover during his 4 years 6 months actual sea duty he spent at least 14 months on shore duties of one kind or another, five of them at Tahiti, 1788-9, thus reducing his actual sea-duty experience to 3 years 4 months. Bligh, by the time of the mutiny, had spent 19 years in the Royal Navy.

Christian had served in only three ships and under only two captains, George Courtney in *Eurydice*, and William Bligh in *Britannia* and *Bounty*; Bligh had served in eight ships under eight captains (including Captain Cook) and had commanded four ships, three in the merchant navy, *Lynx*, *Cambrian*, *Britannia* and *Bounty*. Bligh's obsessive attention to duty arose from the effects of his long experience. Christian's apprenticeship was not yet complete; he was immature, and though a promising candidate he had not yet been passed fit for command.

His crumbling on *Bounty*, under Bligh's rough and vulgar tongue-lashing, when others, as badly abused, took it as a disagreeable, though not exceptional, part of service in the Navy (there were captains of every disposition in the service, and Bligh though difficult was by no means the worst), exposed Christian's claim to command in that most cruel of ways, a self-inflicted wound.

With more time on sea-duty, and with more experience of other ships and their irascible commanders (though few were alternately as irascible and friendly as Bligh), Christian might have grown wiser; but, as the next and last few years of his life were to show, he demonstrated an instinct first to run from unpopular responsibility and then to resort too hastily to violence. He could not cope with 'difficult' islanders – the scenes at Annamooka had shown Bligh something of his former friend's reactions, though the epithet 'cowardly rascal' was probably (and typically) too strong a chastisement – and he later acted appallingly, and thoughtlessly, particularly in respect of women. His relatives rightly remembered him as a model young gentleman, 'adorned with every virtue', and so he might have remained if John and Edward had not squandered his inheritance. In the two and a half years of his absence from home (November 1786 to April 1789) a great deal had happened to change him. Soon, removed from the restraints of naval discipline, encouraged by the need to keep the peace between a few evil and dangerous men and given the power of life and death over others, he failed to live up to his family's memories of him.

Before we describe Fletcher's mutiny, there is another piece of the jigsaw to complete: his brother Charles, who was also cheated of his birthright, and who had embarked on a naval career, albeit as a surgeon for the East India Company, had been confined by his captain for mutiny on 5 September 1787, three months before *Bounty* sailed from Spithead! And, significantly, Fletcher almost certainly knew the circumstances of the mutiny from a conversation with his brother in September 1787 before *Bounty* sailed.

The facts are sparse, but interesting. At 6 pm on 5 September 1787, Captain Rogers wrote in his Log that he had confined W. Greace in irons for presenting a loaded pistol at his captain's breast. Rogers also dismissed the first officer, G. Aitken, for aiding and assisting the mutineer, and three hours later the second officer, D. Fell, was dismissed for 'drunkenness, Insolent Language and striking at his captain on the Quarter Deck'. 'At this time,' Rogers wrote, 'I also dismissed the Surgeon [Charles Christian], also in the conspiracy.' The East India Company directors were furious with Rogers for not reporting to them on his return to Spithead the mutiny and 'the several transactions relating to the behaviour of his officers in September'. From service with the East India Company they banned Aitken for three years, Fell and Christian for two years and Greace for ever, and for failing to report the mutiny they fined Rogers £500 and suspended him from trading and profiting for one year.

In the Royal Navy, of course, the officers would have been court-martialled and, if found guilty, hanged. Fortunately for Fletcher's brother, *Middlesex* was a merchant vessel and thus absolved from the iron laws of naval discipline. But two mutineers in one family hardly suggest an accident of circumstance.

It is not reported by Glynn Christian (ch. 10) what the grievances of the officers on *Middlesex* were, but it is interesting that they concerned their captain's behaviour. Charles Christian wrote about the mutiny in his unpublished autobiography in 1811, though Glynn Christian reports that the facts were mentioned in Captain Rogers' personal Log (Archives of the India Office, Whitehall). Charles's account of the mutiny must have featured in his all-night talk with Fletcher on shore at Spithead in September 1787, where *Bounty* was waiting for sailing orders, and where *Middlesex* was anchored. There is a poignant irony in Charles's own mutiny, given the mood that Fletcher was in, 19 months later on the morning of April 28. Charles wrote:

> I am persuaded that few men had a stronger propensity to Beneficence or possessed a greater share of Benevolence, or a more anxious Disposition to be

pleasing and serviceable to all Classes of the Community until a chagrined Turn of Thought arose, the offspring of the Middlesex East Indiaman Voyage. In that Ship, as well as in every other Ship or in every House … it might be a peace-serving Mean to have the following Mottoes always placed conspicuously … 'Beware of whom you speak, to whom, of what and where', 'Give every Man thine Ear, but few thy Voice', 'Take each Man's censure, but reserve judgement.'

It is a pity that Fletcher in *Bounty* (only his third ship) was no more able than Charles in *Middlesex* (his first), to abide by this sound advice. Charles continues:

The Precepts and Doctrine of our Religious circulate the Forgiveness of Injuries, but when Men are cooped up for a long time in the Interior of a Ship, there oft prevails such a jarring Discordancy of Tempers and Conduct that it is enough on many Occasions by repeated Acts of Irritation and Offence to change the Disposition of a Lamb into that of an Animal fierce and resentful – What can not the Power of Provocation bring to pass on Land, where there is a free Range for Separation (Glyn Christian, p. 69).

Both Charles and Fletcher (for the above could have been written of how each saw the cause of his own mutiny) appear to have been changed from their 'normal disposition of a Lamb into that of an animal fierce and resentful' by the 'jarring Discordancy of Tempers and Conduct' and 'repeated Acts of Irritation' inflicted on them by their captains. It is singular that they both reacted the same way: one fortuitously escaping further punishment, the other destroying not only himself, but many other innocent people.

Before describing the events that night we should dispose of another explanation of Christian's actions – the theory that Bligh and Christian were homosexual lovers (Richard Hough, *Captain Bligh and Mr Christian*, 1972), or, in its original Freudian format, that Christian became demented when he realised that he loved Bligh and not 'Isabella', his Tahitian lover (Madge Darby, *Who Caused the Mutiny on the Bounty?*, 1965). The homosexual thesis claims that Bligh and Christian quarrelled when Christian took up a heterosexual liaison at Tahiti, and later when Bligh wished to resume their illicit (and highly dangerous) relationship when they set off for home. Christian's refusal to resume their affair drove Bligh to behave tyrannically, and this in turn drove Christian to mutiny.

The problem for the hypothesis lies in the paucity of evidence to support it. It relies virtually entirely on a single ambiguous statement of Peter Heywood's in 1830, a year before his death: namely, that Christian had confided a 'secret' to him just before *Bounty* sailed from Tahiti for the last time. Heywood advertised this secret, both as an explanation by Christian of his infamous conduct and as something so sensitive that he did not know whether he would ever make it public.

Heywood wrote: 'At that last interview with Christian he also communicated to me, for the satisfaction of his relations, other circumstances connected with that unfortunate disaster, which, after their deaths, may or may not be laid before the public. And although they can implicate none but himself either living or dead, they may extenuate but will contain not a word of his in defence of the crime he committed against the laws of his country' (Barrow, 1831, p. 90).

It is likely that Christian disclosed to Heywood the extent of his personal disappointment when he was told that his elder brothers had squandered his mother's finances and that in consequence he had to seek another, less personally rewarding, career. This circumstance alone, he might have told Heywood (who, following a reverse in his father's fortunes, was on *Bounty* for a similar reason), left him with little incentive to return home and explained his willingness to act 'against the laws of his country', without, of course, justifying what he had done. It is wholly plausible that the 'other circumstances connected' with his leading the mutiny were family matters, and that Christian's reaction to what had happened 'implicated' him and nobody else. This conclusion is given credence by the fact that Heywood disclosed that Christian's message was communicated to him for 'the satisfaction of his relations'. That Heywood was unsure whether to make the contents of the message public 'after their deaths' supports this interpretation. It was not so much a case of embarrassing Christian's memory, as of embarrassing those of his relatives who had caused him to be on *Bounty* in the first place.

Though the existence of this message had been known since 1830, nobody writing on the mutiny speculated on its contents until 1936, and even then it was assumed to be that Christian had venereal disease (D. Bonner Smith, 'Some Remarks about the Mutiny of the *Bounty*', *The Mariner's Mirror*, vol. 22, no. 2, April 1936, pp. 200-37). A case of VD in the eighteenth-century Navy may not have amounted to much (we know Christian was on the Surgeon's VD list), but it might have had some significance for Peter Heywood (who had also been on the VD list). His step-daughter, Lady Belcher, had been embroiled in a stormy court case against her husband, Captain Belcher, whom she accused of giving her VD on her wedding night.

The circumstantial evidence for the homosexuality thesis depends solely on Bligh's clear favouritism in respect of Christian. Bligh wined and dined with Christian regularly, gave him access to his private liquor cabinet and went to some lengths to help his promotion. But he also separated himself from his alleged lover by giving him command of the shore camp. Hough suggests that he was also attracted to young Heywood, and also favoured him. But Bligh also posted Heywood to the shore camp, putting both his alleged lovers out of reach.

The most telling objection to the theory is partly practical: on a ship the size of *Bounty* an affair of this nature would have been impossible to hide.

And, given the intense and bitter feelings between Bligh and his men, such a scandal, or even the hint of it, would have done more to destroy their tormentor than anything else they managed to allege. Sodomy was punished by a mandatory death sentence (Articles of War, XXIX). Of course, it could be argued that Christian's family would have been distressed to have their relative branded not only as a mutineer but as a sodomite as the price of destroying Bligh, and that Heywood would have been well aware of this likely reaction, so that he suppressed the secret message. It could be that he was protecting his own reputation, but none of this applied to anybody else. For these reasons, the homosexuality hypothesis must be rejected unless written evidence from an hitherto unknown source comes to light.

In the meantime we must accept the simpler explanation for the mutiny: namely, that Fletcher Christian mutinied because he believed he could no longer take verbal abuse from Captain Bligh. In stating that he ought not to have mutinied, for this or any other reason, we are not asserting that Bligh was correct in verbally abusing him, or anybody else, only that in the personality of Fletcher Christian there was a inability to take the kind of abuse his captain inflicted on everybody under his command throughout his entire career. It is not a matter of apportioning guilt, for Christian's guilt is unchallengable, or of whether Bligh was to blame, or Christian was at fault, but of observing that at that time and place, and in that ship, Fletcher Christian, Bligh's second-in-command, could no longer cope with what his more experienced companions managed to shrug off.

# 14

# Bligh's First Mutiny

What happened on the night of the mutiny has been documented in several primary sources and reported in hundreds of secondary accounts. Bligh's own reports naturally seek to exonerate him. After all it was he who lost command of the ship, and he had to clear himself of culpable blame for this event before a court martial. Everybody else who had anything to say also had a stake in presenting his own views of what happened. All sources therefore have to be treated with care.

Whatever version we rely on, Christian's behaviour during the night exhibited signs of severe mental distress; he was behaving irrationally and to some extent suicidally. From several reports he appears to have decided to quit the ship during the night by jumping overboard with some food stolen from his messmates and, with a makeshift raft, making for the nearest island, Tofoa. What he intended to do there, assuming he survived the shark-infested waters, is not clear. Judging by Bligh's experiences there after the mutiny, it seems likely that Christian would have been killed by the islanders (if only for his clothes, which were prizes to islanders at that time). At the very least he would have been used badly. Bligh dismissed the whole notion of Christian acting in this way, as it was reported to him in Morrison's account, as too ridiculous for any man in his senses to contemplate (ML Safe 1/43, p. 51). But Christian was not in his senses.

Christian apparently involved others in his scheme. He asked Purcell, the carpenter, for some planks, rope and nails, and Purcell provided these. This was made public by Edward Christian in 1794 (*Appendix*, p. 65), which was a damaging revelation for someone in Purcell's position. Fletcher also told George Stewart, midshipman, of his plan, though this could have been at 4 am when he was wakened by Stewart for his watch (*Appendix*, p. 71) and not the night before.

According to Morrison, he also told William Cole, the boatswain, and midshipman Thomas Hayward. This last is almost beyond belief, for Hayward was disliked by Christian and others for being too much of a toady to Bligh. In fact not a few lines further on in his account Morrison, in referring to Christian's finding Hayward asleep at the start of the

mutiny, adds in brackets: 'with whom he [Christian] refused to discourse.'
The only explanation for this direct contradiction is that Morrison had
misheard Christian's speech and thought he had said 'Hayward' when in
fact he said 'Heywood'. This confusion in names between the two
midshipmen is common in *Bounty* manuscripts, with one name crossed
out and the other entered, even by those who knew them well, such as
Bligh, Morrison and Captain Edwards. If Morrison made a slip here, it
destroys Heywood's later claim to have been totally innocent of the affair.

Christian also collected some extra nails and some beads for barter
with islanders, and stole some roast pig from his messmates, which he
put in a bag he allegedly got from Hayward. A mess was a group of men
who combined their rations, which they drew and prepared jointly; in
Christian's mess were Robert Tinkler, Fryer's brother-in-law, George
Stewart and Peter Heywood. In removing the roast pig he was taking his
messmates' rations – odd behaviour for a man running away from a
captain who called him a thief. Robert Tinkler, feeling hungry that night,
went below to get some of the roast pig, only to find it missing. He thought
somebody from another mess had hidden it for a lark (for them to have
stolen it would have been a crime indeed). Later, according to Fryer, he
found the bag with the roast pig in it hidden behind a sea-chest while he
was looking for his hat, though he did not query why it was there. In the
various accounts of this incident of Tinkler's the pig moves about:
Morrison says that Tinkler found it in the clue of his hammock; Edward
Christian says it was found with some breadfruit in Christian's own cot.

Christian did not go through with his plan. Edward Christian claims
that this was because there were too many people on deck during the
night who were not in his confidence, some because of the heat, others
watching a volcano on the horizon. But jumping overboard would hardly
pass unnoticed however many or few were on deck.

These reports of the evening's events are strange. They assert that
Christian planned some time during the night, perhaps during his 4 am
watch, to swim thirty miles to Tofoa; that he had involved at least four
other people, one of whom he disliked; that he gave away his personal
possessions, including some Tahitian curios, and tore up all his private
letters and notebooks; and that the men concerned no more remarked
about this lunacy than attempted to dissuade him, but all went to sleep in
the knowledge that the Acting Lieutenant was acting very strangely
indeed. It is remarkable that Fletcher did not inform Peter Heywood, his
close friend, of his plans. (Or did Morrison and Edward Christian know
differently but keep quiet in order not to compromise Heywood's
strenuous efforts to project his innocence?)

If Christian had informed these men and others of his intentions, he
now had the problem of how to avoid looking silly the next morning. He
had created a dilemma for himself, and his watch was due to commence
at 4 am. In most accounts he slept fitfully.

At this point George Stewart, midshipman – none too popular, incidentally, with the crew as a disciplinarian – enters the story. Morrison states that Stewart and Christian were seen 'several times up and down the Fore Cock pit where the Boatswain's and Carpenter's Cabbins were, and where Mr. C. seldom or ever went' (Journal, p. 47). The fore cockpit was on the deck below Christian's berth. Edward Christian reported that his brother had been in conversation with Purcell at 4 pm in the early evening, having had another row with Bligh:

> Christian came forward [i.e. to the fore part of the ship] from Captain Bligh, crying, 'tears were running fast from his eyes in big drops.' Purcell, the Carpenter, said to him, 'What is the matter Mr. Christian?' He said 'Can you ask me, and hear the treatment I receive?' Purcell replied, 'Do not I receive as bad as you do?' Christian said, 'you have something [his status as a Warrant officer] to protect you, and can speak again; but if I should speak to him as you do, he would probably break me, turn me before the mast, and perhaps flog me; and if he did, it would be the death for us both, for I am sure I should take him in my arms, and jump overboard with him' (*Appendix*, p. 64).

This would have brought Christian near to the forecockpit, and when he asked Purcell for the planks, nails and rope he would have had to visit the area to collect them from the carpenter's stores.

Morrison reported that Christian 'went to sleep about half past three in the Morning. When Mr Stuart calld him to relive the Watch he had not Slept long, and was much out of order, when Stuart begd him not to attempt swimming away, saying "The people are ripe for any thing", this made a forcible impression on his mind' (Morrison, Journal, p. 46). Thirty-three years later in 1825 much the same story was told to Captain Beechey on Pitcairn Island, by Alexander Smith (John Adams), the last of the mutineers:

> His plan, strange as it must appear for a young officer to adopt who was fairly advanced in an honourable profession, was to set himself adrift upon a raft, and make his way to the island [Tofoa] then in sight. As quick in the execution as in the design, the raft was soon constructed, various useful articles were got together, and he was on the point of launching it, when a young officer, who afterwards perished in the Pandora, [George Stewart] to whom Christian communicated his intention, recommended him, rather than risk his life on so hazardous an expedition, to endeavour to take possession of the ship, which he thought would not be very difficult, as many of the ship's company were not well-disposed towards their commander, and would be very glad to return to Otaheite, and reside among their friends in that island. This daring proposition is even more extraordinary than the premeditated scheme of his companion, and if true, certainly relieves Christian from part of the odium which has hitherto attached to him as the sole instigator of the mutiny (Beechey, 1831, vol. 1, pp. 71-2).

Both Morrison and Adams, separated in time and space, made the same point about Stewart's role, but it did not suit Peter Heywood. His defence at his court martial was that both he and Stewart were kept below by the mutineers and had no chance to make their innocence known to Captain Bligh; hence they were listed incorrectly among the mutineers. Now if Stewart helped push Christian to mutiny, this compromised Heywood's protestations of their joint innocence.

As it was, the account of Stewart's conduct in Morrison's Journal was not published until 1820, when it was paraphrased by Samuel Greathead as follows: '[Christian] proposed to have privately made a raft, and to have escaped in it from the ship; but, on hinting his design to a brother midshipman, named Stewart, he derived encouragement to draw a party on his side' ('Authentic History of the Mutineers of the *Bounty*', *The Sailor's Magazine and Naval Miscellany*, 1820, vol. 1, p. 404). In 1825 some extracts from Morrison's Journal were edited into a biography of Peter Heywood by Marshall in his *Royal Naval Biography* (1823-30, vol. 2, part 2). The editor's hand was heavier here, for Heywood's entry, which refers generously to Morrison's account in most matters, drops the reference to Stewart's saying that the men were 'ready for anything' and gives the impression that Stewart only tried to dissuade Christian from going into the water.

When Beechey returned from Pitcairn, he noticed the discrepancy in what he had been told by Adams and what was published in Marshall and he wrote to Heywood asking for an explanation (Beechey had not seen Morrison's Journal). Heywood replied that the remark attributed to Stewart by Adams was 'entirely at variance with the whole character and conduct of [Stewart], both before and after the mutiny; as well as with the assurances of Christian himself, the very night he quitted Taheite, the idea of attempting to take the ship had never entered his distracted mind, until the moment he relieved the deck and found his mate [Hayward again!] and midshipman asleep' (quoted in Barrow, 1831, p. 90).

Heywood did not inform Beechey that Adams's story had been corroborated by Morrison's account written in 1792, nor did he remind him that Edward Christian's account of 1794 had attributed similar words to Stewart: 'It is agreed that Christian was the first to propose mutiny, and the project of turning the Captain on shore at Tofoa, to the people in his watch; but he declared afterwards in the ship, he never should have thought of it, if it had not been suggested to his mind by an expression of Mr. Stewart, who knowing his intention of leaving the ship upon the raft, told him, "When you go, Christian, we are ripe for anything"' (Edward Christian, *Appendix*, p. 71). In this version Stewart refers to the men as 'ripe for anything' after Christian went, not if he stayed. The issue, of course, centres on how these words were interpreted by Christian and not on how they were meant. As Heywood was a party to Edward Christian's *Appendix*, and had at least one copy of Morrison's Journal among his private papers, and was on *Bounty* after the mutiny, I think he was prevaricating on the issue of Stewart's role in prompting Christian to mutiny.

We do know that Stewart said something to Christian, which his listener interpreted either as an invitation to stay on board and mutiny or, equally likely, as a warning that, if Christian left the ship as he intended, the men might mutiny in his absence. Either of these remarks, the one a criminal act, the other a personal plea for Christian to stay and avert a mutiny (Du Reitz, *The Causes of the Bounty Mutiny*, 1965, p. 13), is consistent with all the accounts, including Christian's reported speech to the crew after the mutiny.

Morrison and Heywood agree on Christian's mental state at the time of the mutiny. Heywood quotes Christian as saying that he 'had a distracted mind' and Morrison reports him as 'being much out of order'. And Stewart had given him a way out of his torment: instead of a desperate act, which in his saner moments he must have known amounted to suicide, why not set his tormentor adrift off Tofoa, while he, Christian, remained in the comparative safety of the ship?

Morrison gives us Christian's own version of what happened after he relieved Stewart for the 4 am watch:

> [Christian] finding that Mr. Hayward the Mate of his Watch (with whom he refused to discourse) soon went to sleep on the Arms Chest which stood between the Guns, and mr. Hallet (the midshipman of his Watch) not making his appearance, He at once resolved to Seize the Ship (Journal, p. 46).

Much the same story was told to Beechey by Adams in 1825.

Having made his decision, his first job was to recruit help. This was the point of no return; the bare suggestion of mutiny to anybody put his life, and also his listener's, at risk under the Articles of War:

> If any person in the fleet shall conceal any traitorous or mutinous practice, or design, being convicted thereof by the sentence of a court martial, he shall suffer death, or other such punishment as a court martial shall think fit (Article XX).

The Articles of War were read out in their entirety at Sunday musters on board every ship in the Navy, and nobody joined a mutiny ignorant of the penalty of being caught:

> If any person in or belonging to the Fleet shall make, or endeavour to make, any mutinous assembly, upon any pretence whatsoever, every person offending herein, and being convicted thereof by the sentence of the court martial shall suffer death (Article XIX).

The exact sequence of events that followed varies slightly in the accounts, though the events are fairly well known and accepted.

Christian's first choice was a near-disaster. He spoke to Isaac Martin and Quintal. Martin refused to join the mutiny. If he had cried the alarm, Christian was in trouble. Christian had tied a heavy weight round his neck and hidden it under his shirt in readiness for such a contingency. He intended to jump overboard and drown if his personal plans misfired.

Some accounts have Martin refusing to join, and Quintal agreeing. As Martin, in Bligh's view, certainly dithered and changed sides, it seems more likely that he at first refused Christian's attempt to recruit him. He was an American from Philadelphia, aged about 32, and had little love for Bligh. He might have surmised that as an American his chances of being charged for mutiny a few years after the American War of Independence (itself no trivial mutiny) were not good.

Quintal undertook to recruit two more men and he went below and brought back the two most violent men on board, Charles Churchill and Matthew Thompson. There were now four men in the conspiracy, and Martin, fortuitously keeping silent about their intentions. Alexander Smith (now known to be John Adams), William McKoy and John Williams joined in the first half-hour. Christian needed to arm his men if he was to thwart resistance, and his leadership qualities came to the fore.

In the Navy arms were not left lying about for anybody to pick up at will. They were secured and issued only on lawful authority. John Fryer was responsible for them and was supposed to keep the keys by his person. But Fryer preferred his sleep to being disturbed by requests from the watch officers for a musket (to shoot at sharks). He had made the informal, and fatal, arrangement with the armourer, Joseph Coleman, that he should keep the keys and hand them out at night. Thus, to get the keys, Christian had no need to disturb Fryer (whose cabin was opposite Bligh's). He went to Coleman and demanded them. Coleman gave them over without hesitation and went back to sleep. He had no reason to question the Acting Lieutenant.

The next problem was the two midshipmen, Hayward and Hallet, neither of whom had come up for his watch. Hayward was sleeping on a chest on deck, and Hallet was sleeping on the arms chest below; in the hot Pacific they made excellent berths. It was of course typical of what Bligh had been complaining about, that two midshipmen were sleeping through their watch; Hayward's punishment for sleeping through the desertions at Tahiti had not had much effect. Christian simply woke Hallet and ordered him on deck. In his concern for his fate if Bligh found out that he had been sleeping on watch, Hallet did not think to question why Christian was accompanied by several men, not all of them on his watch. Hayward, meanwhile, had been wakened by Norman, one of Christian's watch who had not yet been invited to join the mutiny, to tell him that there was a shark following the ship. They both repaired to the side to observe it.

Christian handed out the arms to his party from Hallet's irregular berth. Thomas Burkitt and Robert Lamb had joined the mutineers and were soon under arms along with the others. Thompson was left to guard the arms chest, while Christian went to the quarter deck to arrest

Hayward and Hallet. This was accomplished without trouble. The two lazy midshipmen were no match for the armed and desperate men who confronted them. Mutineers were posted about the deck to guard the hatchways and prisoners. In the hullaballoo young Ellison, the boy at the wheel, left his post and, picking up a cutlass, joined the mutineers. His thoughtless enthusiasm was to cost him his life.

*Bounty* was now effectively under Christian's command. It only remained to arrest the sleeping and unarmed Bligh. He had given his pistols to Fryer, who, in an exhibition of sloppiness similar to that concerning the keys to the arms chest, did not have them loaded (or so he later claimed, but Bligh never believed him). Christian selected his arrest party and proceeded to Bligh's cabin. This was the first Bligh knew of the mutiny.

# 15

# 'I am in hell'

Bligh's own account of what happened when he was wakened was that Fletcher Christian, Mate, accompanied by Charles Churchill, Ship's Corporal, John Mills, Gunner's Mate, and Thomas Burkitt, Seaman:

> came into my Cabbin while I was a Sleep and seizing me tyed my hands with a Cord behind my back and threatened me with instant death if I spoke or made the least noise. I however called so loud as to alarm everyone, but the officers found themselves secured by Centinels at their Doors. There were four men in my Cabbin and three outside Viz Alexr. Smith [John Adams], Jno. Summer and Matu. Quintall. Mr Christian had a cutlass in his hand, the others had Musquets and Bayonets. I was forced on Deck in my Shirt, suffering great pain from the Violence with which they had tied my hands. I demanded the reason for such a violent act but recieved no Answer but threats of instant death if I did not hold my tongue (Log, 28 April 1789).

John Sumner and Matthew Quintal arrested Fryer and kept him in his cabin. Churchill came down from the deck and looked into Fryer's cabin, saw Bligh's pistols and pocketed them. Apparently neither Fryer nor his guards had noticed them. From Fryer's cabin they could prevent David Nelson and William Peckover, confidants of Bligh, from coming up, as they had to climb past Fryer's cabin to get on deck.

Neither Nelson nor Peckover was expecting a mutiny. When Peckover heard that the ship had been taken, his first reaction was that it had been taken by islanders in a surprise attack (Edward Christian, *Appendix*, p. 67). The same applies to everybody else on board; only later did the 'inevitability' of a mutiny emerge as various participants sought to exculpate themselves or to excuse their conduct.

Bligh was brought on deck as daylight broke. Everybody on board was now aware of what had happened. Most were in the role of spectators, watching to see what would happen. The mutineers, always a minority of the ship's company, were armed and apparently determined, and this more than made up for their smaller numbers. Men such as Purcell, Cole, Lebogue, Elphinstone, Stewart, Heywood and Young came up on deck and wandered aimlessly around. During this time, Heywood, as he admitted at the court martial, picked up a cutlass, though with what intentions has never been clear. In contrast Edward Young clearly threw in his lot with Christian and joined the mutiny.

Christian's first plan was to put Bligh, Samuel, Hayward and Hallet, the most unpopular men on board, into the jolly-boat and set them adrift. Orders were given to this effect, but first the boat had to be emptied of its contents. Men were ordered to work, and James Morrison, who later claimed to have been against the mutiny, was one of those clearing the boat. George Stewart was 'dancing and clapping his hands in the Otaheite manner, and saying, It was the happiest day of his life' (Edward Christian, *Appendix*, p. 72). Incidentally this was yet another blow at Heywood's defence at his court martial.

Whatever problems Bligh's behaviour had created for Christian, his taking the ship was not greeted with universal approval. Experienced hands tried to get this across to him both before and during the mutiny. Purcell, the unlikeliest man to concede anything to Bligh, but who fully understood the wider tapestry of naval life, had cautioned the distraught Christian, who complained of his treatment the night before the mutiny, to 'Never mind it, it is but for a short time longer' (Edward Christian, *Appendix*, p. 64). Fryer, a man as experienced as anybody on board in the vagaries of naval life, told Christian 'that Mr Bligh and he not agreeing did not say that he should take the ship' (Fryer, Narrative, 1790, p. 31). Nor did the experienced hands countenance the thought of three men and a boy set adrift in the jolly-boat. It was a death sentence and everybody believed it (though, obviously, some cared less about it than others).

Meanwhile Bligh was exhorting anybody who would listen to 'knock Christian down' and retake the ship. Among those guarding him was Isaac Martin, though Bligh believed he had 'an inclination to assist me, as he fed me with shaddock, (my lips being quite parched) we explained our wishes to each other by looks; but this being observed, Martin was removed from me' (Bligh, *A Voyage to the South Seas*, 1792, p. 156). Confusion also increased as the contents of the boat spilled onto the deck in the hurry of the unloaders to clear it for use. Fryer pleaded with Christian to let Bligh have another boat as the one being prepared for him was badly wormed and hardly waterproof. A bigger boat meant that more troublesome people (i.e. those less disposed than others to Christian's mutiny) could be sent away. The original four nominated for the boat were joined by Nelson, Peckover and John Smith (Bligh's servant).

What degree of disappointment Christian felt at not being regarded as a saviour of the innocent from the despot we do not know, but his failure to carry the whole crew with him was a necessary result of righting a personal wrong and not a collective grievance. Those declaring against the mutiny (by the only test that mattered: their determination to collect a few possessions and get into the boat) were a larger party than Christian's by the time the second boat was emptied. This deserves some consideration. For a declaration to accompany Bligh in an open boat over three and a half thousand miles from the nearest European settlement, in preference to staying on board a much safer ship, albeit in the company of mutineers, was no idle gesture. The open boat with Captain Bligh meant an almost certain and early death; *Bounty* with Christian postponed that prospect, at least until the Navy caught up with them.

As a morale booster, and to avert a shift in allegiance, Christian ordered John Smith to issue rum from Bligh's cabin to all men under arms. Meanwhile the others were ordered to collect their possessions and join the boat party, including by now Purcell and Fryer. Byrne, the near-blind fiddler, elected to go with Bligh and was in fact sitting in the cutter waiting for it to be swung over the side.

The cutter was now found to be unseaworthy and Christian agreed that Bligh should have the launch, which was quickly put over the side, leaving the deck a shambles of food and stores. Two boats had been ready, in one of which Byrne was left sitting, alone and unheeded, as the men got into the other. Personal possessions were grabbed in the rush to get away (there being no telling how ugly the mood of the mutineers might become under the influence of their crime and the rum they were imbibing). Fryer had hoped that the undiluted rum would make it easier for a counter-action against the mutiny, but his plans were foiled by lack of support and by careless choice of places to brief co-conspirators. (He was overheard several times and reported to Christian, who decided to get rid of him.)

Purcell got his tool chest into the launch, against the protestations of some mutineers, and Smith and Samuel got Bligh's papers, including his all-important commission with which he could secure resources, on the authority and international creditworthiness of the Admiralty, at any place run by Europeans.

Bligh was still tied to the mizzen mast when Hayward and Hallet, amid their protests, were ordered into the launch. Fryer also, after an appeal to Christian, joined them. Others went in voluntarily and as each man joined the open boat party, the 23-foot launch sank deeper into the water. Incredibly, two mutineers, Isaac Martin and Robert Lamb, got into the launch. Churchill spotted Martin abandoning his weapon and briskly ordered him back on board at gunpoint. Lamb was ignored. Bligh declared that other men were 'also kept contrary to their inclinations', suggesting that he thought that Martin was not a mutineer (though he listed him as such). Among those he noted as being inclined to go with him he included Coleman, McIntosh, Norman and Byrne. He did not exculpate Stewart, Heywood or Morrison, which in truth is not surprising given that Stewart was dancing and clapping his hands, Heywood had lifted a cutlass and Morrison was busy emptying all three boats.

After three hours at the mast Bligh was hoarse with shouting. Nobody reacted to his exhortations except Christian, who continued to threaten

him with a bayonet pressed to his chest. According to Morrison, Bligh
made frantic appeals to Christian, swearing friendship and forgiveness.
But Christian could not be dissuaded, and it is doubtful if the mutineers
would have let him. Churchill and Thompson were appearing everywhere
and strengthening the resolve of any waverers (such as Martin). They
wanted Bligh off the ship and intervened ruthlessly at every turn. They
stopped the boat party taking anything except the most meagre of
possessions, and they decided who came on deck and who went into the
boat. With Young under arms, Christian's party was intimidating in the
extreme, given the reputation and visible propensity to violence of
Churchill and the armed determination of Thompson, Adams, McKoy and
Brown. Bligh's group, such as it was, was divided, unarmed and
disorganised.

Only when the men who might support him were in the boat and the
deck was completely dominated by armed mutineers did Christian untie
Bligh's cords. Then, with muskets pressed into his back, cutlasses within
striking distance and a bayonet pressing into his chest, Christian ordered
him into the boat. 'Come, captain Bligh, your officers and men are now in
the boat, and you must go with them; if you attempt to make the least
resistance you will instantly be put to death,' said Christian (Bligh,
*Voyage*, p. 158). According to Bligh, though disputed by some,
'notwithstanding the roughness with which I was treated, the
remembrance of past kindnesses produced some signs of remorse in
Christian. When they were forcing me out of the ship, I asked him, if this
treatment was a proper return for the many instances he had received of
my friendship? he appeared disturbed at my question, and answered with
much emotion, "That, – captain Bligh, – that is the thing; – I am in hell – I
am in hell" ' (Bligh, *Voyage*, p. 161). The boat was now dangerously low in
the water and Bligh, to prevent anybody else joining them, told some of
those left on board, 'Never fear my lads you cant all go with me, but I'll do
you justice if ever I reach England' (Morrison, Journal, p. 46).

With Bligh in the launch it was veered astern by paying out the rope
holding it. Some food and other necessities were passed or thrown to the
boat, but some pieces fell into the sea. Meanwhile on deck some of the
mutineers were getting drunker and more violently disposed. Death or
exile was their lot and it sharpened their attitude to the man they had
rebelled against. While Bligh lived he was a threat to their chances of
getting away with their crime. The shouting increased as people egged
each other on to shoot at Bligh. 'After having undergone a great deal of
ridicule, and been kept some time to make sport for these unfeeling
wretches, we were at length cast adrift in the open ocean' (Bligh, *Voyage*,
p. 158).

The sound of the shouts and laughter from *Bounty* grew fainter and
fainter until eventually the ship passed from view. None of the nineteen
men in the launch were ever to see Christian, or *Bounty*, again, and it was

three years before some of them saw a few of their tormentors of that morning at their court martial. The launch, 23 feet by 7 by 3, was to be their home and refuge as they set out on a 3,900-mile journey. It was to test them all and, in particular, their captain's seamanship and navigation as these had never been tested before. It is still the longest open boat voyage ever undertaken in such circumstances.

# 16

# Huzza for Otaheite!

In the hours following the mutiny there was too much confusion on board for anybody to think about the future. But the magnitude of the problems Christian had created for the men on the ship would dawn on everybody eventually. They were now fugitives from the Royal Navy. Without official papers, and the all-important commander's Commission in the name of the person purporting to be commanding the ship, they had no proof of their legitimacy. A captainless ship was difficult to explain, but one without a Commission was an impossibility in any European settlement. *Bounty* was exiled from Europe and anywhere that Europeans ruled.

By steering clear of European settlements, however, they only postponed the hue and cry. If Bligh survived, they would be hanged if they were caught for, whatever blame might be attached to him for his behaviour by drawing-room society, it was now dwarfed by the crimes of mutiny and piracy that they had committed. If Bligh perished (on that morning, a near certainty), the failure of *Bounty* to return to Portsmouth would prompt the Admiralty to send a ship to look for him and to complete the King's breadfruit mission. The mutineers' best chance lay in disappearing into the Pacific, a huge ocean indeed, but one rapidly reducing in mystery as more and more European ships entered it. If Bligh conveniently disappeared too, it might be assumed that *Bounty* had sunk without trace, and as long as nobody found them they could live out their lives in isolation. A number of problems, however, made this ideal solution difficult to put into practice.

First, and most obviously, it was outside their control whether Bligh survived in the open boat, though they had made it likely he would not. Secondly, and most tellingly, the men who remained on board *Bounty* were not of one mind; in fact, some were distinctly hostile to being associated with the mutiny. Coleman, Norman, Byrne and McIntosh, the men mentioned in Bligh's publications, and reported to the Admiralty and the Dutch authorities, were kept on board against their will. There was also another group, Stewart, Heywood and Morrison who, while not hostile to Christian individually, were conscious that their best chance of survival was to separate from the mutineers, and prove their loyalty to their lawful captain and their duty by returning to England at the first opportunity. Lastly, among the mutineers there was dissension, particularly from that troublesome pair, Churchill and Thompson.

The seamen who had joined Christian's mutiny did so each for his own reasons, and they shared neither Christian's motivations nor necessarily his plans for the future. The notion of taking these men out of reach of the Navy, to live in peace and security, was impracticable. While they were united to each other by their deeds, and by their need for the ship, they were bound to begin fragmenting into groups once the hopelessness of their situation became apparent, even to the most myopic.

The 'loyalists', numbering seven in all, might try to leave the ship or seize it at the first opportunity. If they were to seize the ship and sail it to Botany Bay they could clear themselves of complicity in Christian's mutiny. They were most vulnerable if Bligh's party perished, for then there would be no record of their captain's acquittal of their involvement in mutiny. Merely to be found on board the pirated *Bounty* would condemn them. Others might 'change sides' too (as Lamb and Martin had demonstrated) and the hard-core mutineers might end up outnumbered. Treachery promotes treachery, and while they were inhibited from the step of mutiny against their lawful commander the fact of a mutiny against him removed any restraints they might have had about conducting a mutiny against his usurpers. Indeed they had every incentive to do so, as it was their only chance of averting a hanging.

Contrary to the claims of Christian's relatives, he did not have the personal authority needed to keep his disparate band together. His inexperience had led him into the act of mutiny; it would now be stretched further when he tried to lead the mutineers, some of whom had no intention of swapping one captain for another.

There was also the problem of how to form a permanent settlement without women and help from friendly islanders. (Taking the former from anywhere but Tahiti might provoke the patience of the islanders.) As far as they knew, both were available only at Tahiti, but returning there would compromise the purpose of disappearing without trace, and would certainly disclose their crimes to any ships which came after them.

In Bligh's view it was the attractions of life on Tahiti, especially the women, that was the inspiration of the mutiny. He claimed in his *Narrative* (1790, p. 7) that he heard cries from the mutineers of 'Huzza for Otaheite' echoing round *Bounty*. Edward Christian challenged this view on the basis of his interviews with survivors of the mutiny. He reported that those he interviewed 'neither heard nor observed any huzzaing whatever in the ship' (*Appendix*, p. 69). John Adams, however, the last surviving mutineer, reported to Captain Beechey (without benefit of prompting) that the men did indeed 'huzza' as Bligh had reported. Moreover in Heywood's journal he reports a conversation he had with

Churchill during the mutiny: 'He [Churchill] told me that he [Bligh] and those who chose to accompany him were to take the launch and go on shore where they thought it proper after which the ship was to be taken back to Otaheiti and those in her settle there' (Captain Edwards's personal papers, Admiralty Library, Fulham).

On balance it seems reasonable to believe that most of the seamen left on *Bounty* considered it certain that they were going back to Tahiti, even if one does not accept Bligh's assertion (he was, after all, naturally looking for some cause of the mutiny that did not reflect on himself) that the seamen mutinied solely in order to get there. But whether this was the premeditated motivation to mutiny, it certainly rapidly became its inevitable consequence: Morrison reports that by 9 o'clock that morning, not long after the launch passed out of sight, the mutineers agreed to steer for Tahiti (Journal, p. 47).

Some confusion in the mutineers' intentions has been caused by the necessity for *Bounty* to steer in a deep southern loop rather than directly for Tahiti because of the prevailing easterlies (which had brought them more directly to Tofoa). The stop-off at Tubuai, about 450 miles south of Tahiti, is entirely consistent with Morrison's disclosure that Tahiti was their chosen destination within a few hours of Christian's captaincy.

Certainly Churchill and Thompson were strongly in favour of Tahiti. Churchill had, of course, deserted at Tahiti. He told Heywood within the opening moments of the mutiny that the plan was to return to Tahiti, and he and Thompson voted against Christian in favour of settling at Tahiti over Tubuai.

# 17

# Christian in Command

Four weeks after the mutiny, on 25 May 1789, *Bounty* arrived off the island of Tubuai. Christian decided that Tubuai would be suitable for the mutineers' settlement. It had a pleasant climate, if slightly cooler than that of Tahiti, was away from the main shipping lanes and had an anchorage of sorts inside the reef. Tubuai had been visited and mapped by Captain Cook, and was therefore an obvious place to look for the mutineers when the hunt began in earnest. Christian's belief that it was too far off normal sea routes to be visited accidentally was disproved even while he was there, when Captain Cox in *Mercury* passed within two miles of the island and reported seeing camp fires. Had he passed during daylight he would certainly have seen *Bounty*, and would probably have attempted to make contact. What dangers for him and his crew that could have created, when he realised the truth behind *Bounty's* presence, can only be conjectured.

Morrison disagreed with Christian's choice: 'I cannot say that I ever agreed in Oppinion With Mr. Christian with respect to the plan he had formd nor did I ever form a favourable Idea of the Natives of Toobouai whose savage aspect & behaviour could not gain favour in the Eyes of any Man in his senses, but was fully capable of Creating a distaste in any one' (Journal, p. 56). But Christian, in or out of his senses, decided to settle there.

The 'savage aspect' of the inhabitants was demonstrated on the first day. George Stewart was sent ahead in the ship's boat to survey the entrance through the reef and was attacked by islanders in their canoes. He fired a pistol and wounded one of the islanders, and they wounded a seamen with a spear (Heywood, Journal, p. 2). Later the islanders attacked *Bounty* in force and were driven off by the ship's guns firing grapeshot at close range. Eleven men and women were killed and many others were wounded before they fled in terror. They named the anchorage 'Bloody Bay', a prelude to the violent relations between Christian's party and the inhabitants of Tubuai from the beginning to the last day of their settlement.

Another aspect of Christian's command that remains in stark contrast to his brother's defence of him is his relationships with the men he commanded. Edward Christian reported the following testimony from an unidentified seaman: 'One of the seamen being asked, if they never mutinied afterwards in the ship, and told Christian, they had as good a right to the command as he had, said, "No, no man would ever have mutinied against Mr. Christian, no one ever thought of resisting his authority" ' (*Appendix*, p. 75). If this absurd eulogy had been true, it would have condemned the loyalists on board, for it was their duty to attempt to retake the ship at the first opportunity. We have, however, three sources that totally contradict this claim: Morrison's, Heywood's and Stewart's Journals, the latter two written contemporaneously with the events they describe and, because they were removed from them by Captain Edwards, therefore immune from judicious editing. These sources reveal that Christian was incapable of keeping control of his men, except by force, or of controlling his passions, and that his command was riddled with dissension, mutinous actions and outright refusals to comply with his orders.

Morrison's defence at his trial centred on his efforts to lead a counter-mutiny. These efforts, he claims, began soon after Christian's mutiny. Indeed he claimed that he remained on board instead of going with Bligh precisely in order to overthrow Christian. He writes:

> As I had reason to believe from the Countenance of Affairs that the Ship might yet be recovered if a party could be formd and as I knew that several on board were not at all pleased with their situation, I fixd on a Plan for that purpose and soon gaind several to back my opinion, when We purposed to take the Opportunity of the Night the ship should anchor at Taheite when we could easily get rid of those we did not like by putting them on shore, and that in all probability our design might be favoured by an extra allowance of Grog. These matters being settled I had no doubt but that evry one would stand to the test; and to prevent the others from knowing our design affected a shyness toward each other, but I soon found out to my unspeakable surprize that Mr. Christian was acquainted with our Intentions, some of his party overhearing some part of the Business – but as he was not positive how many were Concerned he took no further Notice then threatening Coleman that he should be left on shore at Toobouai till the Ship returnd from Taheite and Got the Arms Chest into the Cabbin taking the keys from Coleman who had always kept them, they were now given to Churchill who made his bed on the Chest and each of Mr. Christians party were Armd with a Brace of Pistols Mr. Christian himself never going without a Pistol in his pocket the same which Lieut. Bligh formerly used, and a sharp look out was kept by his party one of which took care to make a third when they saw any two in Conversation (Journal, p. 50a-1, crossed through in manuscript).

Christian's counter-mutiny measures of having everybody watching each other are ironical in view of criticism of Bligh's invitation for 'the people to look after the officers and the officers to look after the people' at Annamooka.

Captain Edwards's extracts from Heywood's journal mention mutinous murmurings on 5 July 1789 and include the following entry for 6 July: '2 of the men were put in Irons by a Majority of Votes – and drunkennes fighting and threatening each others life was so common that those abaft were obliged to Arm themselves wth pistols' (Journal, p. 2). By those 'abaft' Heywood would normally have meant the officers, but under Christian's command he was probably referring to the mutineers (it being too dangerous for Christian to arm the loyalists). Though George Stewart was made second-in-command by Christian (over the objections of the crew who pointed to his 'former severity') and Morrison and Coleman were given responsibilities, it is unlikely that they were armed unless Morrison's claims to be plotting a mutiny were untrue. But whatever the truth, it is clear that Christian armed himself and his closest cronies against threats from others on board.

In his extracts from Stewart's Journal Captain Edwards reports that on July 7 Christian made a vain attempt to end the atmosphere of crisis on *Bounty*: 'Articles were drawn up by Christian & Churchill specifying a mutual forgiveness of all past grievances which every Man was obliged to Swear to and sign. Matthew Thompson excepted who refused to comply.' The evidence is clear from these extracts, and from the events that followed, that Christian was far from being the charismatic commander his family sought to portray him as. Leadership is about more than being liked.

In spite of the bloody beginning to the settlement of Tubuai, Christian was determined to go through with it. Having surveyed part of the island, he took *Bounty* back to Tahiti to collect women and the stock his plans needed. He 'Gave orders that no man should tell the name of the Island, nor mention It to the Natives and if any person was found to mention the real name he would punish him severely and declared if any Man diserted he would shoot him as soon as he was brought back, which promise evry one knew he had in his power to perform' (Morrison, Journal, p. 56). No wonder 'no one ever thought of resisting his authority'. (It was also a convenient alibi for Morrison to excuse his and others' failures to desert at Tahiti.)

There is a typical piece of Morrison moaning at this point in his journal (a style we shall become familiar with when we examine his complaints against Bligh). The possessions of the men sent off with Bligh were divided by drawing lots among the people remaining on *Bounty*. This, of course, was theft, but having crossed the rubicon of mutiny minor peccadilloes were no longer of consequence. Morrison, however, was troubled with his share of his erstwhile shipmates' possessions: 'These were made out in lotts by Churchill, & were drawn for by tickets, but it always happend that Mr. Christians party were always better served than those who were thought to be disaffected, however, as they had different views No Notice was taken of it at present' (Journal, p. 56).

When *Bounty* returned to Tahiti, Christian told the Chiefs that Bligh had met Captain Cook and had gone off with him and that he had been sent back to get some stocks for a new settlement. The Chiefs' willingness to help Cook and Bligh exceeded their curiosity about the missing men and the plants, but to avert trouble Christian posted armed guards around the ship's deck. They were also a deterrent to would-be deserters. In the short time *Bounty* was at Matavai under Christian's command there were two shooting incidents (under Bligh in five months there were none). William McKoy fired at some Tahitians who 'did not get so fast out of His way as he thought proper' and Churchill fired at a canoe that did not respond to his challenge (Morrison, Journal, p. 58).

On 19 June 1789 *Bounty* sailed from Tahiti for the second time. It had on board 312 hogs, 38 goats, 96 fowls and the bull and the cow left by Cook, plus nine Tahitian women, eight men and ten boys. 'Most went voluntary', wrote Heywood, so some must have gone otherwise. The men were taken in order to smooth relationships with the Tubuai islanders, and the women for the usual purpose. Fletcher took Mauatea, or 'mainmast', after her figure and posture, later known as 'Isabella' (after his aunt): John Adams took 'Jenny', and McIntosh 'Mary'.

In moving out of the Matavai anchorage, it was necessary to cut a cable and lose an anchor to avoid a grounding. This suggests some sloppy seamanship. *Bounty* arrived off Tubuai on 26 June, and through the Tahitian intermediaries Christian established more peaceful relations with the inhabitants than he managed on his first visit.

Trouble within the crew soon broke out. John Sumner and Matthew Quintal went ashore without Christian's leave and stayed away all night, presumably with local women. Those without women had to risk finding their sexual comforts on shore, and the wrath of their captain when they returned. Next morning Christian 'enquired how they come to go on shore without his leave' (any seaman could have told him that an activated libido has no conscience!). They replied 'the ship is Moord and we are now our own Masters' (Morrison, Journal, p. 64). Christian's response (in which he must have been less than calmly disposed to them) was to clap 'the pistol he carried to the head of one, saying, "I'll let you know who is Master", and ordered them put into leg irons'. Glynn Christian, his descendant, quotes Fletcher's behaviour in this incident as an example of his resoluteness (*Fragile Paradise*, p. 139). Needless to say, if Bligh had behaved this way it would have been taken as further proof of his mindless 'tyranny'. Indeed in the incident where Bligh clapped his pistol (actually the very same pistol used by Christian) against William McKoy at Annamooka, Glynn refers to this act as a 'mindless tirade' (p. 110), which serves to illustrate how 'other authors colour events to favour or denigrate a character'.

The next person to fall foul of Christian was Tom Ellison. He was accused of stealing a red feather from Christian, which was an item of great value in trading ashore. Ellison was brought on deck and stripped, ready for a flogging, but after loudly protesting his innocence, and in the absence of positive proof, he was let off (Morrison, Journal, p. 65).

Christian's ideas for the settlement included an ambitious plan to build a large fort, to be known as Fort George. With the ship's guns mounted on it the mutineers would have protection from the local inhabitants and, perhaps, from a lightly armed naval landing party. But as the Navy would not give up, having found the mutineers' lair, it is unlikely that the fort would have protected them from the full retribution of a warship. Christian planned to build the fort, and strip and then fire the ship.

Morrison claims that the imminent removal of *Bounty*'s masts for conveyance ashore prompted him to revise his plans for escape, for once the masts were out *Bounty* would be a useless hulk. 'I spoke to G. Stuart,' says Morrison, 'on the affair, who told me that He and P. Heywood had formed the same plan' (Journal, p. 72). He determined on sabotaging the blocks and tackle, to prevent the masts being put back into *Bounty*, and escaping to Tahiti in the the ship's boat. Fortunately for Morrison and his friends, the plan was made redundant by yet another crisis over women among the mutineers.

As mentioned, men without women had to find their comforts ashore. After the absence without leave of Quintal and Sumner, Christian followed Bligh's policy of allowing two men ashore each day and as many as wanted on Sunday. This meant something like one sexual liaison ashore every fortnight. Meanwhile those who had Tahitian women (Christian included) had a woman for company each night. Any settlement on Tubuai meant a permanent acceptance of this unequal arrangement. Heywood reports:

> On 1 August a party went on shore to get wives by force but they met with some opposition from the Natives, one of whom was shot and another run through with a Bayonet. The natives propos'd peace & requested that their goods might be restored that had been taken out of the house that was burnt, but Christian refused to accept it unless the Men were provided with Wives – however women were not got & on 24th those that were without them were heard to declare that the place wd not do & that the Masts shd not be got out until Women were procured & that the ship shd be carried where they could be had – on 30th the discontented party proposed to make slaves of the Otaheitians Men Women & boys and to cast lots for them & destroy the Natives to procure Women by force, but Christian wd not agree to either Scheeme & and work on the fort was now discontinued (Journal, p. 3).

This is quite the most appalling evidence of the brutality of the men Christian had allied himself with. Procuring women by force meant, of course, removing them from their families and raping them repeatedly. Even Glynn Christian feels obliged to slide over this revealing admission of the mutineers' mood (*Fragile Paradise*, p. 144). Heywood's testimony, written on Tubuai, is corroborated by Morrison, when he reports that the

men in Christian's party 'began to Murmur, and Insisted that Mr.
Christian would head them, and bring the Weomen in to live with them
by force and refused to do any more work till evry man had a Wife'
(Journal, p. 75).

Christian proposed that a meeting be held to discuss the situation, and
this was agreed to, though some of the more difficult among them
demanded grog while they debated the issue. Christian did not like the
way things were developing, especially the proposal to put his Isabella
into a lottery along with the other Tahitians, and in an effort to keep the
debate reasonably rational he refused to issue grog. The men, who
according to his brother 'did their duty at a look from Mr. Christian'
(*Appendix*, p. 76), broke into *Bounty*'s spirit room and helped themselves.
Ever resolute when faced with a challenge to his authority, Christian
changed tack smartly and ordered a double allowance of grog to
everybody.

The meeting lasted three days and in the end they decided to abandon
Tubuai and return to Tahiti. The proposal to quit the settlement was
opposed by Christian, but he was now in a minority and he accepted that
he had to return to Tahiti and disembark the dissidents. The vote to
return was carried by 16 votes to 8. (Apparently Christian did not vote,
though no doubt he expressed his views.) The voters for Tahiti were
Coleman, McIntosh, Byrne, Norman, Heywood, Stewart, Morrison,
Churchill, Thompson, Hillbrant, Ellison, Sumner, Milward, Musprat,
Skinner and Burkitt. The nine voting to stick with the settlement were
Young, Mills, Brown, Martin, Adams, McKoy, Williams and Quintal.
Some of the men who voted against Christian later made statements to
his brother that they would 'wade up to the arm-pits in blood to serve
him', 'go without wages in search of him' and 'go through fire and water
for him'. The one thing they would not do, apparently, was stay with him.

After the vote *Bounty* sprang to life again as the ship was prepared for
the voyage to Tahiti. But, before leaving, Christian authorised and led
what can only be described as a punitive expedition whose bloody
consequences are inexcusable (though Glynn Christian does in fact
excuse them). According to Heywood, on 23 July 1789 'Christian's party'
had already killed an islander in an altercation over some coconuts
(shades of the night before the mutiny when Bligh saw fit to abuse
everybody, not kill them over the missing coconuts!), and they had beaten
up islanders while searching for stolen property. On 31 July 'they
plundered & burnt a house'. Against Bligh's futile attempt at confining
the chiefs at Annamooka, Christian's actions to recover stolen property
border on the criminally inept. (What chance would Europeans
shipwrecked on this shore have after 'Christian's party' wreaked their
vengeance?)

In the deliberately provoked massacre that followed, well inland and away from the ship, between fifty and sixty men and six women were killed and scores more wounded. The islanders were no match for the military prowess of the Europeans armed with muskets and bayonets. Though the islanders numbered about 700, gunfire is a ruthless equaliser. This unnecessary massacre may have satisfied the frustrations of Christian's party at having to leave their settlement, outvoted by their colleagues, but it is one of the burdens of command to resist such pressures and it is symptomatic of inexperience and immaturity to succumb to them.

*Bounty* left Tubuai on 14 September 1789, leaving behind bloody memories of their presence, a half-finished fort (whose workings were still visible when Glynn Christian visited Tubuai in 1981) and venereal disease and dysentery, which conspired with other European visitations to reduce the population from 3,000 to 300 by 1823.

They arrived at Tahiti on 22 September 1789. It was no longer possible to pretend that they were working for Captain Cook. The islanders with them would tell the Tahitians the truth, and the Europeans he was to disembark exposed Christian's deception that he was on a mission for Captain Cook. The disclosures of the truth had no obvious repercussions. The possessions of those going ashore were unloaded with their share of the ship's stores. This was completed by early evening, and the shore party left for their friends' homes. *Bounty* departed that night, and this surprised those left on shore. Christian had intimated that he would stay at Tahiti for a few days and even asked the men ashore to help him load fresh water the next day after organising a drunken party that night. Morrison wrote in 1792 that he was surprised at *Bounty*'s abrupt departure:

> In the night we found the Ship under way, standing out of the Bay, but it proving Calm in the morning She was not out of Sight till Noon ... We were all much surprized to find the Ship gone, as Mr. Christian had proposed staying a day or two to give us time to get on shore what things we might want or had forgot to take on Shore; this Gave us reason to suppose that He either was afraid of a Surprize or had done it to prevent His Companions from Changing their mind (Journal, p. 102).

For those left on Tahiti the prospect was bleak. It was the first place the Navy would look for *Bounty*, and to stay there meant a hanging, unless Bligh had perished and they had no witnesses against them, in which case they could plead that they had been the innocent victims of Christian's mutiny and had managed to escape from his band of criminals. Christian chose to 'Cruize for some Uninhabited Island where he would land his Stock ... and set fire to the Ship, and where he hoped to live the remainder of His days without seeing the face of a European but those who were already with him' (Morrison, Journal, p. 100). Having been dispossessed of his inheritance, forced into a naval career for which he was manifestly not suited and now abandoned by the majority of the men he led into mutiny, his wish not to see 'the face of a European' except those who stood by him is understandable. It was not, however, a sound basis on which to 'live the remainder of his days' in peace.

# 18

# The Death of Fletcher Christian

From the night of 22 September 1789, when Fletcher Christian sailed away from Tahiti for the last time, his fate was to remain a mystery for nineteen years. Nothing was heard of him again until the Captain of the American whaler *Topaz*, Mayhew Folger, out of Nantucket, informed Lieutenant Fitzmaurice of the Royal Navy in Valparaiso about what he had found on a remote island, marked on the charts as Pitcairn Island, in February 1808. The report reached the Admiralty on 14 May 1809. Folger reported that there was one European, Alexander Smith, eight middle-aged Polynesian women and twenty-six boys and girls of various ages. These were all that remained of the *Bounty* mutineers who had settled on Pitcairn in 1790. The story of what happened to the other *Bounty* men, and the Tahitian males who accompanied them, was a dreadful catalogue of racism, betrayal and murder.

With Fletcher Christian on board *Bounty* as she cut away from Tahiti (losing yet another anchor in the process), were William Brown, Matthew Quintal, William McKoy, John Adams (a.k.a. Alexander Smith), John Mills, Edward Young, John Williams and Isaac Martin, together with six male islanders and nineteen females, plus a baby girl. The women he simply kidnapped – few would have gone voluntarily – and one, when she realised what was happening, jumped overboard and swam back (apparently not wanting to go through 'fire and water' for Christian). After sharing out the women that were tolerable to the use to which they were to be put (a form of forced marriage), six 'rather ancient' women were put ashore on a neighbouring island next day, though it might have been better for Christian's ultimate purposes if he and his men had been less squeamish and had kept them on board, as they would have helped to reduce the sexual tensions of the island prison of Pitcairn.

Christian did not know where he and the mutineers were headed in the first months out of Tahiti. *Bounty* sailed westwards searching for an island suitable for their needs. The ship was grossly undermanned, having only nine experienced men on board. Christian navigated *Bounty* to within a hundred miles of Tofoa, discovering some new islands, including Rarotonga in the Cook Group. The celebration of this discovery by recent historians is somewhat blemished by what can only be described as a murder. Christian gave his midshipman's jacket to an islander, who promptly showed it off to his friends. His triumph and pleasure were cut short when a mutineer shot him dead. Christian's authority had reached such a low ebb, and his ship was so undermanned, that he could only reprimand the killer. (In contrast he had been prepared to flog young Ellison for stealing a red feather at Tubuai.)

It is hardly unfair to consider this incident as but one of several deplorable examples of Christian's command. Bligh is judged a tyrant for upsetting Christian's sensibilities, but Christian is praised, by such distinguished historians as Professor Maude, for his discoveries during *Bounty*'s voyage under his command; yet his part in upsetting the islanders of Rarotonga, when one of his party cold-bloodedly murdered one of their people, apparently warrants no personal criticism. Glynn Christian's apologia for this incident, for example, is a striking example of double-standards (*Fragile Paradise*, p. 153), the anguish of a white man being of more concern than that of a Polynesian. It is notable that the Tahitian woman 'Jenny', who witnessed the murder, and who was among those taken to Pitcairn, where she lived until she secured a passage off the island in 1818, had no doubts thirty years after the murder that while Christian was indignant 'he could do nothing more, having lost all authority, than reprimand the murderer severely'.

It was at the most westerly reach of this stage of *Bounty*'s final voyage that Christian found in Bligh's copy of Hawkesworth's *Voyages*, a description of Carteret's discovery of Pitcairn Island in HMS *Swallow* in 1767. Carteret named it after one of his midshipmen, who was the son of Major Pitcairn of the Royal Marines, killed at the Battle of Bunker Hill in the American War of Independence. *Bounty* was swung round near the Lau group (Fiji) and began a long southern detour in search of Pitcairn. It took them two months. For the escaping mutineers Pitcairn had much to recommend it: it was uninhabited, fertile, difficult to land on, and mis-charted by 3½ degrees of longitude.

The story of what happened on Pitcairn in its early bloody years has been pieced together from the contradictory and unreliable accounts of John Adams, as he told them to various visiting seamen between 1808 and 1828, and from the testimony of 'Jenny', as reported by Captain Peter Dillon of the *Research* in 1819. There are also various other sources, such as the Pitcairn Island register book, indifferently kept during the early years, a journal attributed to Edward Young, and other reports of the survivors' oral traditions, some of which are as unreliable as Adams's.

The basic problem of Pitcairn was its isolation. For the European mutineers it was a sanctuary from a hanging, but for the islanders it was a prison. There was also a dangerously unequal share-out of the women, each European having his own wife, and the six male islanders having to take what turns they could arrange among themselves to have sex with the remaining three. That the women involved in these male-decided arrangements were never happy with their lot is demonstrated, not surprisingly, by their subsequent behaviour.

The fugitives landed on 21 January 1790. They stripped *Bounty* of everything movable. It was no mean task in the heavy surf to manhandle stores ashore and then take them up the steep cliff face to the tiny settlement where they built their small houses. They intended to break *Bounty* up and salvage its timbers, but before this could be accomplished Matthew Quintal set her on fire. Why is not known for certain. It may have been to prevent anybody from leaving the island. Their security depended on there being no leakage of their whereabouts, but the only person who could navigate the distances involved was Christian, and the act, if this was the unlikely motive, must have been directed at him. The burning hulk sank in what is known today as Bounty Bay (its remains were found in 1957 by Luis Marden for *National Geographic Magazine*: Marden, 1957), and with it sank all hope of escape. Only the worm-eaten boats were left.

Christian divided the land, leaving nothing for the islanders. Their role in life was to be slaves of the Europeans, and it was in the treatment of the islanders, male and female, that are to be found the roots of the civil strife that afflicted the community in the early years.

Within a few months John Williams's wife slipped and fell to her death on the cliffs while looking for birds' eggs. Williams managed for a while as a widower, but then grew restless. He demanded that one of the three women currently servicing the sexual needs of the six islanders should be handed over to him. At first the Europeans refused to support his demands, which were accompanied by a wild threat to leave Pitcairn in the ship's cutter, until Christian ('adorned with every virtue' according to his brother) gave in and organised an armed party to take one of the islanders' women away from them. It was the worst decision he could have taken.

The six islanders now had only two women between them (what the women thought about any of this is not recorded, they being treated as mere chattels, or worse, by the men). The inevitable consequence was that the islanders plotted to kill the Europeans. They did not get very far in their conspiracy because the women informed the Europeans of what they were plotting (or, as likely, cooked up the story in the age-old tradition of turning one gullible man against another). The seamen armed themselves and marched on the islanders, two of whom ran off into the hills. They terrorised the remaining four into saving their own lives by agreeing to kill their colleagues. This they managed to do none too gently, leaving the seamen more secure and the four surviving islanders with the two unattached women.

The peace lasted for two years. Fletcher Christian and 'Isabella' had had a son, named Thursday October Christian in October 1790, and other seamen's wives had produced children, sons to Quintal and McKoy and a daughter to Mills (though no Tahitian children were born, or rather, survived beyond conception or birth, abortion and infanticide being a common practice among islanders as a measure of population control).

The treatment of the islanders grew worse. The community was riven by inter-family and racial tensions. In the end the men who had been turned into murderers by their European masters rounded on them with a view to murdering them. They had been trained in the use of muskets by the lazy Europeans so that they could use them to hunt for game. The Europeans were separated on their 'estates', tending their fields.

Towards late September 1793 the islanders met, checked their arms and set out to kill their masters one by one. Surprise and speed were the deciding factors. The first man to die was Williams, the original cause of the outbreak of violence. The next was Fletcher Christian, shot while tending his yams. McKoy and Quintal heard the shots and, stumbling upon one of the attackers, took off to the woods. Mills fell next, and after him Martin and Brown. With all the noise of the shooting, it is a wonder that the Europeans did not present too much of a challenge. For most killings it was a cold-blooded affair: the islanders just went up to their unsuspecting victims and shot them at close range, finishing off the job with a good battering around the skull.

One 'lucky' escapee was John Adams. His story is strange and raises suspicions that we have been left with a highly edited version, hiding perhaps a dark secret. According to Adams's story years later, he got away from the murderers at first but foolishly returned and was shot in the upper shoulder for his pains. He warded off blows from the musket stock and in doing so had two of his fingers broken. The musket misfired twice and in the confusion he roused himself and outran his pursuers. Then followed an unbelievable deal between him and his attackers: they offered him sanctuary if he returned with them, and, more remarkably, he accepted their offer at face value and they all went back to Christian's house.

Remarkably too, Edward Young does not feature in the massacre at all, nor did he seek sanctuary in the woods. In fact nothing is known of where he was while his companions were being butchered. It is assumed that he was protected by the Tahitian women, some of whom appeared to know what was afoot, and one of whom, Quintal's wife, is alleged to have warned Adams (though not her husband). Young and Adams were left in the village with the wives of their compatriots, a situation that was not altogether disagreeable for them.

After their victory over the hated white men, the Tahitians soon fell out over the sharing of the spoils. One islander shot another, and the perpetrator, Menalee, ran off to join McKoy and Quintal in the hills. Adams was sent by Young to arrange for McKoy and Quintal to murder Menalee and return to the village. This is circumstantial evidence that

Young and Adams were behind the massacre, for if they were innocent they would have welcomed McKoy and Quintal back before the Menalee incident. Indeed, having got their hands on muskets, it might be asked why they did not exact retribution for the murders of Christian, Mills, Brown, Williams and Martin. True, by all accounts Quintal was not popular, either with the women or the Tahitian men – he treated them like slaves and was no doubt brutal in his love-making, which perhaps explains his wife's duplicity. But when it is considered that the bodies of the Europeans were left to rot where they lay, it is hard to explain why the two surviving Europeans, Young and Adams, made no moves to exact revenge, if only on behalf of the murdered man who had led them in mutiny.

Adams has it that Menalee ran away after killing Temua, but it is just as likely that he ran away after seeing Adams or Young kill his countryman. In this context it is also possible that Adams was wounded while assisting in the original massacre rather than being one of its victims. Whatever the truth, Quintal and McKoy shot Menalee but still would not return to the village, allegedly because they did not trust the two islanders, but perhaps because they did not trust their own two countrymen, either from what they saw happen, or from what Menalee told them about the real instigators of the massacre. Instead of two frightened men in the bush there may have been two men bent on revenge.

Perhaps Young and Adams therefore wanted Menalee dead before he talked too much. Perhaps he was tracked down and killed by Adams before he could make his peace with the fugitives, and it was after this act that Adams made contact with them. Anyway it is unexplained why Menalee should seek refuge with Quintal and McKoy, whom he had tried to kill during the massacre, and why they should offer sanctuary to the murderer of their shipmates. Surely neither man was so naive as to trust Menalee – who played a major role in the massacre and in the earlier killings of the two Tahitians. According to Adams it was Quintal and McKoy who insisted that the remaining two male islanders must be killed before they returned to their houses. This neatly puts the blame for their murders onto the fugitives.

The first remaining islander was murdered by the women, who used an axe to despatch him, and this must have been at the instigation of the two Europeans. Next, Young shot the second islander dead at close range. The hands and heads of the two victims were taken to the bush and displayed to McKoy and Quintal. We may note that Adams's accounts leave him out of this transaction. As the sole survivor in later years, he could rewrite history in any way he liked (we know that he was terrified of European visitors speaking to the older women, perhaps less in the interests of protecting their virtue than in protecting his life).

By 3 October 1793 Young, McKoy, Quintal and Adams, plus ten

Tahitian women and the mixed-blood children, had the island to themselves. This did not make for peace. The major problem appears to have been that the women grew dissatisfied with their lot. The relatively settled family lives of the seamen had been destroyed by the bloodshed, and the new extended family that replaced them solved some problems – jealousy for one – but exacerbated others. Some of the women had lost their European husbands but now had to share four men. McKoy and Quintal were rough seamen, with a reputation for harsh treatment; they now extended that behaviour to all the women. Everybody lived together promiscuously.

First the women tried to build a boat to sail back to Tahiti, but it sank on its first flotation. Next, according to Adams, they conspired to murder the men. It took vigilance and judiciously timed interventions to break up the conspiracies, and life could hardly be described as relaxed.

McKoy died first, from falling off a cliff when drunk. He had been making a form of alcohol, using his knowledge of the distillation of Scotch. It is not beyond belief that he was pushed. Certainly Quintal was murdered in 1799. It was the only recorded confession of violence after the massacre. Adams declared that Quintal had become a threat to the community after demanding to sleep with his and Young's wives (Young had moved in with Christian's widow), and they killed him with an axe while he slept. The two men, suspected of being the original conspirators of the 1793 massacre, now ruled Pitcairn. A year later Young died from natural causes, according to Adams. He had an asthmatic complaint.

By 1800 Adams was the only survivor of *Bounty*'s mutineers left on Pitcairn. The scene was set for what can be described as its remarkable and, to some extent, questionable 'moral regeneration'. Adams claimed that he abandoned his wicked ways after a drunken bout and nightmare vision of the Archangel Gabriel, which motivated him to institute a version of what he could remember about Christianity, using the *Bounty*'s prayer book and Bible. The Tahitians adopted the new strictures laid down for them by Adams, and their evident sincerity in saying grace before meals and being scrupulously polite impressed the visiting naval officers, who in different circumstances might have been of a mind to arrest Adams as a mutineer and pirate.

Several ships are recorded as appearing off Pitcairn before *Topaz* put a boat ashore in 1808. The first of these appeared on 27 December 1795, but it did not stop; another appeared 'sometime later', and a third came close enough to see the settlement. One ship is known to have managed to land a boat, but its crew did not explore; they simply cut some plants and left. Other ships may have sighted Pitcairn but not been seen in return, or they were not recorded by the inhabitants. Captain Folger was the first to make contact with the community. Adams was afraid to meet him on board *Topaz*, in case he was arrested for mutiny, and insisted on Folger's coming ashore. Folger in return was worried that he would be detained on

Pitcairn to prevent news being forwarded to the Admiralty. Eventually his curiosity overcame his caution, and he went ashore and met the man still calling himself by his alias, Alexander Smith. He stayed a few hours. On his return voyage to the United States, news of his discovery was forwarded to the Admiralty by Admiral Sir Sydney Smith in Rio de Janeiro. He offered as proof of his claims two important pieces of evidence. The first was the name of the surviving mutineer, 'Alexander Smith', which could be checked against *Bounty*'s muster roll and Bligh's post-mutiny statements. The second was more convincing: Smith had given him *Bounty*'s time-keeper made by Larcum Kendall. This instrument had been used by Captain Phipps on the 1773 voyage in search of the North-West Passage, and subsequently on the North American station until 1787. It was Kendall's second time-keeper (hence known as Kendall's K2, for which he was paid £200 in 1771; there is a complete description of K2 in *Horological Journal*, by Peter Amis, vol. 99, no. 1191, December 1957, pp. 760-70). Unfortunately Folger was deprived of K2 in a dispute over money at Juan Fernandez.

In May 1809 the Admiralty received the following report from Sir Sydney Smith in Rio:

Captain Folger, of the American ship Topaz, of Boston, relates that, upon landing at Pitcairn Island, in lat. 25° 2′S, long. 130° 0′W, he found there an Englishman of the name of Alexander Smith, the only person remaining of nine that escaped in his Majesty's late ship Bounty, Captain W. Bligh. Smith relates that, after putting Captain Bligh in the boat, Christian, the leader of the mutiny, took command of the ship and went to Otaheite, where great part of the crew left her, except Christian, Smith and seven others, who each took wives and six Otaheitan men servants, and shortly after arrived at the island (Pitcairn), where they ran the ship on shore, and broke her up; this event took place in the year 1790. About four years after their arrival (a great jealousy existing), the Otaheiteans secretly revolted and killed every Englishman except himself, who they severely wounded in the neck with a pistol ball. The same night, the widows of the deceased Englishmen arose and put to death the whole of the Otaheiteans, leaving Smith the only man alive upon the island, with eight or nine women and several small children. On his recovery he applied himself to tilling the ground, so that it now produces plenty of yams, cocoanuts, bananas and plantains; hogs and poultry in abundance. There are now some grown men and women, children of the mutineers, on the island, the whole population amounting to about thirty-five, who acknowledge Smith as father and commander of them all; they all speak English and have been educated by him (Captain Folger represents) in a religious and moral way. The second mate of the Topaz asserts that Christian the ringleader became insane shortly after their arrival on the island, and threw himself off the rocks into the sea; another died of a fever before the massacre of the remaining six took place. The island is badly supplied with water, sufficient only for the present inhabitants, and no anchorage (quoted in Barrow, 1961, pp. 256-7).

Captain Folger wrote directly to the Admiralty on 1 March 1813, enclosing with his letter an azimuth compass Adams had given him. His letter repeats the account given to Admiral Smith, namely that after about six years (1796) all the Europeans except Smith were killed by the Tahitians and the same night the widows killed the Tahitians. Folger also corresponded with his friend Amasa Delano who wrote: 'Captain Folger was very explicit in his statement that Alex Smith told him Christian got sick and died a natural death' (Delano, *A Narrative of Voyages and Travels*, Boston, Mass. 1817, p. 140). This account, based on what Adams told Folger, has a charming simplicity about it. Since the guilty men had paid their debt by their violent deaths, and Adams had atoned for his smaller sins by moral regeneration, he should be left alone having brought the small community to respectability. The missionaries were to love this hymn to repentance. Adams had a sound sense of what would appeal to the otherwise stony-faced men of the Admiralty.

In 1814 two British frigates, *Briton*, Captain Sir Thomas Staines, and *Tagus*, Captain Pipon, searching the Pacific for the American ship *Essex* which was attacking unarmed British whalers, visited Pitcairn. They sent reports to the Admiralty of their conversation with Adams (who had ceased to pose under the alias of Smith). In them Adams's story begins to shift slightly. Captain Staines's letter from Valparaiso reads:

> I fell in with an island where none is laid down in the Admiralty or other charts, according to the several chronometers of the *Briton* and *Tagus*. I therefore hove to until day-light, and then closed to ascertain whether it was inhabited, which I soon discovered it to be, and, to my great astonishment, found that every individual on the island (forty in number) spoke very good English as well as Otaheitan. They prove to be the deluded crew of the Bounty, which from Otaheite, proceeded to the above-mentioned island, where the ship was burnt.
>
> Christian appears to have been the leader and sole cause of the mutiny in that ship. A venerable old man, named John Adams, is the only surviving Englishman of those who (then) left Otaheite in her; and whose exemplary conduct and fatherly care of the whole of the little colony cannot but command admiration. The pious manner in which all those born on the island have been reared, the correct sense of religion which has been instilled into their young minds by this old man, has given him pre-eminence over the whole of them, to whom they look up as the father of the whole and one family.
>
> A son of Christian was the first born on the island, now about twenty-five years of age, named Thursday October Christian; the leader Christian fell a sacrifice to the jealousy of an Otaheitan man, within three or four years after their arrival in the island. The mutineers were accompanied thither by six Otaheitan men and twelve women: the former were all swept away by desperate contentions between them and the Englishmen, and five of the latter died at different periods, leaving at present only one man (Adams) and seven women of the original settlers.
>
> [Pitcairn] is abundant in yams, plantain, hogs, goats, and fowls, but affords no shelter for a ship or vessel of any description; neither could a ship water there without great difficulty.

Smith had not only dropped his alias; he had also changed some of the details of the death of Christian. In particular the date of his death is moved from 1796 back to 1793. The cause of his death is alleged to be 'jealousy'. Also the sequence of events in the massacre has been altered. Instead of all the white men dying at one go and then their widows murdering the Tahitians, it is the Tahitians who are 'swept away' in one go and the five whites who die at various dates afterwards. The deaths of three Europeans are left unaccounted for in this version.

Captain Pipon also wrote an account of what Adams told him and of the little community he led. It differs in some material aspects from his colleague's account and gives much more detail of Christian's fate, and of his behaviour on the island:

I next come to the interesting narrative of Fletcher Christian. It appears that this unfortunate & ill fated young Man, was never happy after the rash & inconsiderate step he had taken, but always sullen & morose, a circumstance which will not surprise any one, this moroseness however led him to many acts of cruelty & inhumanity, which soon was the cause of his incurring the hatred & detestation of his Companions here: One cannot avoid expressing astonishment, when you consider that the very crime he was guilty of towards his Companions (who assisted him in the Mutiny) was the very same they so loudly accused their Captain B-- of. It is indeed very singular this circumstance should not have been a serious lesson to him, for his guidance in his future treatment of his Shipmates in error. This miserable young man having left Otaheite the last time (for he had visited Anamooka one of the Friendly Islands, after his desertion from his duty & obedience to his Captain, not finding the reception he expected there, or rather that his Plans could not be carried into execution without fear of detection) returnd to Otaheite with a feigned Story, which the Islanders readily gave ear to; of having met Captain Cook, who had sent him (Fletcher) for a supply of Provisions; his wishes were readily complied with, Capt. Cook being a great favourite there; & having filled the Bounty with Hogs, & such other Articles as he thought necessary, he sailed away suddenly in the night, on or about 22nd Sept. 1789 & never since been heard of: this was the period when 16 of his crew left him & went on shore: his object was to find an uninhabited Island, where he could establish a settlement, & hither he at last arrivd, tho with a very reduced Crew, & finding no Anchorage round the Island, & that the operation of landing the stores of the Bounty as well as his live stock, &c., was tedious & laborious, he ran the ship against the Rocks, a little to the southward of the place we landed at, & having cleared her of everything he thought necessary, set her on fire: this certainly was a wise plan on his part to avoid detection, for as Pitcairn is mentioned in the Charts & in all the accounts I have seen of it, as uninhabited, it is not probable that any one would seek refreshments there: whereas had the wreck ever been observed by any vessel passing that way, humanity if not curiosity would have led them to enquire, if some fellow creature in distress, might not have been cast away there; again, had the ship been preserved, there might have been a possibility that some of the dissatisfied would sail away in her & give information of the retreat of the Mutineers of the Bounty. It is therefore an extraordinary circumstance, that chance & meer accident should have led us

hither, for had we been aware that Pitcairn Island was near us, we should
have avoided it. We considered ourselves nearly 200 miles from it, when
Land was discovered, & we verily believd that in Sight was some new
discovery. To the error therefore, in which it is laid down is to be chiefly
attributed this unexpected visit of ours to it; happy however that it is in our
power to communicate the fate of the wretched people who composed the
Crew of the Bounty, after their shameful Mutiny against their Captain. It is
impossible to describe the surprize we all felt when we heard the Natives the
descendants of Fletcher Christian speak the English language uncommonly
well, & that this should be the general language among them: the old women
who from Otaheite, retain the Mother tongue, tho as has been mentioned
before, they have picked up many English words & understand the English
language tolerably. The fate of Fletcher Christian himself was such as one
might have expected from his cruelty & extraordinary unfeeling behaviour:
from what we could learn he was shot by a black man whilst digging in his
field & almost instantaneously expired: this happened about eleven or ten
months after they were settled in the Island, but the exact dates I could not
learn: the black or Otaheite man that thus murdered him was himself
immediately assassinated: the cause of these disturbances & violence is thus
accounted for by John Adams; that as he has before related, Fletcher
Christian behavd with such cruelty & oppression towards his people, as soon
alienated them from him & in consequence they divided into parties which
ran very high, seeking every opportunity on both sides to put each other to
death: old John Adams himself was not without his enemies, having been
shot through the neck: as however the ball enterd the fleshy part, he was
enabled to make his escape, & avoid the fury of his pursuers, who sought his
life. Another circumstance had arisen which gave particularly the Otaheitan
men still more discontent & roused their fury to a degree not to be pacified:
Christian's wife had paid the debt of nature, & as we have every reason to
suppose sensuality & a passion for the females of Otaheite chiefly instigated
him to the rash step he had taken, so it is readily to be believed he would not
live long on the Island without a female companion, consequently after the
demise of his wife, he forcibly seized on one belonging to one of the Otaheitan
men & took her to live with him: this exasperated them to a degree of
madness, open war was declared & every opportunity sought to take away
his life, & it was effected whilst digging in his own field. It is surprizing he
should not have been more on his guard, for he was well aware of the hatred
& enmity of all the blacks or Otaheitan men. Thus terminated the miserable
existence of this deluded young man, whose connexions in Westmoreland
were extremely respectable & who did not want talents & capacity to have
become an ornament to his profession had he adopted another line of
conduct. We could not learn precisely the exact number of Blacks or Whites
who were killed whilst this kind of warfare continued, certainly however,
many must have perished by the hands of each other & only old John Adams
remains of the Men that landed on the island with Christian (ML MS A77).

On one thing Adams was fairly consistent in his early accounts: the
conduct of Christian. Naturally his visitors were curious about the fate of
the leader of the mutiny and his explanations had to be consistent with
his visitors' prejudices (nobody in any navy has ever been less than
hostile to mutiny at sea). That Christian was morose, bad-tempered and

moody is consistent with the view that his mutiny was a rash, ill-considered and soon much regretted action. Contemplating what he had done was probably self-revealing in its exposure of his unfitness for, and basic lack of interest in, a naval career.

Adams tended to be vague about what happened and who died at which time (or, alternatively, his listeners did not pay close attention to what he was saying). For Adams life in the colony began around 1800, when he converted his flock to a life of religious rectitude, and not in 1790 when the mutineers landed. The decade before 1800 is fogged over with vagueness and contradictions and, in view of suspicions as to his own role, he no doubt felt it best that the past should remain buried.

Some measure of his credibility (and a comment on the depth of his religious conversion) is illustrated by his own version of his role in the mutiny; in his account to Captain Beechey he claims he was ill in his hammock at the time of the mutiny (he may indeed have been on the sick list) and that he only became active in the mutiny after almost everything had been settled. The facts are that Adams was one of the early men to join the mutiny – some accounts make him the third recruit to Christian's cause – and he was also one of the most determined and militant of the mutineers. He was trusted enough by Christian to be in the party that went with him to arrest Bligh in his cabin, and was set as an armed guard over Bligh at the mizzen-mast (Isaac Martin, it may be recalled, was removed from this task when he appeared to be too disposed to Bligh). Any of Adams's visitors who had read Bligh's narrative of the mutiny would have been aware that Adams was being 'economical with the truth' on these points. Given that he edited his own role in the mutiny so conspicuously, it is not improbable that he also edited his role in the first ten years of the colony.

When Adams told his story to Captain Beechey in 1825, thirty years after Christian's death, and now secure in the knowledge that he was not going to be returned to Spithead for courtmartial, he had reversed the entire character of Christian to make him a model of cheerfulness and virtue, and an inspiration for the settlement (Beechey, 1831, pp. 68-9). Remorse at his own role in Christian's death, and the growing security of his own position, may have induced him to be more generous to Christian's memory. Twenty-five years of preaching forgiveness and charity towards others on the island may have worked on his earlier, more truthful, attitudes towards the man he had followed to Pitcairn.

This leaves one final mystery of Pitcairn. Did Fletcher Christian somehow get off the island and return to England? The evidence that he did is entirely circumstantial and, it must be agreed, following Glynn Christian's diligent search for the truth among his forebear's family, largely unconvincing. There is not a shred of direct evidence that Christian died anywhere else than on Pitcairn in the 1793 massacre.

Sir John Barrow, Second Secretary to the Admiralty, wrote an account of the mutiny, published anonymously in 1831. Describing himself modestly as 'editor' of the book's contents, Barrow included this footnote:

> As the manner of Christian's death has been differently reported to each different visitor, by Adams, the only evidence in existence, with the exception of three or four Otaheitan women, and a few infants, some singular circumstances may here be mentioned that happened at home, just at the time of Folger's visit, and which might render his death on Pitcairn's Island almost a matter of doubt.
>
> About the years 1808 and 1809, a very general opinion was prevalent in the neighbourhood of the lakes of Cumberland and Westmoreland, that Christian was in that part of the country, and made frequent private visits to an aunt who was living there. Being the near relative of Mr. Christian Curwen, long member of Parliament for Carlisle, and himself a native, he was well known in the neighbourhood. This, however, might be passed over as mere gossip, had not another circumstance happened just about the same time, for the truth of which the Editor does not hesitate to avouch.
>
> In Fore-Street, Plymouth Dock, Captain Heywood found himself one day walking behind a man, whose shape had so much the appearance of Christian's, that he involuntarily quickened his pace. Both were walking very fast, and the rapid steps behind him having aroused the stranger's attention, he suddenly turned his face, looked at Heywood, and immediately ran off. But the face was as much like Christian's as the back, and Heywood, exceedingly excited, ran also. Both ran as fast as they were able, but the stranger had the advantage, and, after making several short turns, disappeared.
>
> That Christian should be in England, Heywood considered as highly improbable, though not out of the scope of possibility; for at this time no account of him whatsoever had been received since they parted at Otaheite; at any rate the resemblance, the agitation, and the efforts of the stranger to elude him were circumstances too strong not to make a deep impression on his mind. At the moment, his first thought was to set about making some further inquiries, but on recollection of the pain and trouble such a discovery must occasion him, he considered it more prudent to let the matter drop; but the circumstance was frequently called to his memory for the remainder of his life (Barrow, 1831, pp. 309-10).

Barrow is the only source for this story. He avows that Heywood frequently recalled the incident in later life, yet it was not mentioned by his friend Admiral Smyth in his obituary of Heywood published in 1831, nor by his biographer, Edward Tagart, in 1832.

The report from Captain Folger reached the Admiralty on 14 May 1809 and it was in the same month that Heywood received command of HMS *Nereus*. Heywood could have heard about the discovery of Pitcairn as the mutineers' haven while visiting the Admiralty; it would have been a natural item of gossip between him and one of the clerks or senior officers. It was a year later that Folger's discovery was made public in the *Quarterly Review*, for February 1810 (pp. 23-4) (which inspired at least one major poetic effort: Mary Russell Mitford's 'Christina, the Maid of the South Seas', 1811).

Barrow dates the Fore Street incident vaguely as 'at the time of Folger's visit', which was in February 1808. According to Tagart, Heywood arrived in Britain in January 1808 and was superseded in the command of *Polyphemus* in May 1808. He was occupied ashore from May 1808 to 3 November 1808, preparing charts of the Indian Ocean for his friend James Horsburgh's 'East India Directory'. He joined *Donegal* on 4 November 1808, as a relief captain, and was engaged in blockade actions off the French coast until he returned to London on 11 March 1809. He was at the Admiralty on 18 March 1809, received command of a frigate in May 1809 and some time in June joined the Mediterranean fleet, where he was employed until March 1810. Thus Heywood was ashore in Britain from January to November 1808 and from March to June 1809. The incident in Fore Street, Plymouth, could have occurred during either of these times. The fact remains, however, that the stranger, whoever he was, took to his heels because he panicked when he saw a man in a Post-captain's uniform bearing down on him – who knows what terrors that had for him?

There are other slight, though indicative, supplementary items of evidence that give tenuous support to Heywood's intriguing story. One of these was the intervention of William Wordsworth, a near neighbour of Fletcher's who had attended the same school, in the public controversy following a book published in September 1796 (three years after the massacre on Pitcairn) purporting to have been written by Fletcher Christian: *Letters from Mr Fletcher Christian, containing a narrative of the transactions on board His Majesty's Ship Bounty, Before and After the mutiny, with his subsequent voyages and travels in South America*. This volume must be accepted as a clever forgery, for it does not fit any of the factual activities of the mutineers once they quit Tahiti for the last time. It is, however, a well-written and convincing tale that shows that the author, or authors, had considerable detailed knowledge of the west coast of South America and the customs, culture and political administration of the peoples there. It also presents an interesting opinion of the mutiny, especially in view of the public controversy it had occasioned the year before. In the *Letters*, written allegedly from Cadiz, Fletcher Christian praises Captain Bligh and apologises for the mutiny.

This last theme prompted the thought that the *Letters* originated from within the Bligh camp. This is unlikely given Bligh's reaction to the pamphlet when he was sent a copy. He wrote to Sir Joseph Banks:

Mr Nicol [Bligh's publisher] has been so good as to send me down a Pamphlet called Christian's Letters – is it possible that Wretch can be at Cadiz and that he has had intercourse with his Brother, that sixpenny Professor, who has more Law about him than honour. My Dear Sir, I can only say that I heartily dispise the praise of any of the family of Christian and I hope & trust yet that the Mutineer will meet his deserts (ML MS C218, p. 31).

Bligh did not know that Christian had got his 'deserts', just or otherwise, only a year before the *Letters* appeared (*The Letters of Fletcher Christian*, ed. Stephen Walters, Guildford 1984).

William Wordsworth now weighed in, with a letter to the *Weekly Entertainer* (7 November 1796), published from Sherborne, Dorset. The Wordsworths were staying at Racedown, Dorset in 1796. William wrote:

> There having appeared in your Entertainer (vide the 255th page of the present volume) an extract from a work purporting to be the production of Fletcher Christian, who headed the mutiny on board the Bounty, I think it proper to inform you, that I have the best authority for saying that this publication is spurious. Your regard for the truth will induce you to apprize your readers of this circumstance.

This is a tantalising piece of evidence, though ambiguous in the extreme. Was Wordsworth's 'best authority' for repudiating the *Letters* Fletcher Christian himself, or was it simply that Fletcher's family not having heard from him – which surely they would have done if he had been at Cadiz or anywhere else within letter-writing range of the Isle of Man and Cumberland – were convinced the *Letters* were a forgery? Frankly, I think we must incline to the latter interpretation, argued eloquently by Glynn Christian in *Fragile Paradise* (p. 192).

In 1797 William and Dorothy Wordsworth joined Samuel Taylor Coleridge on a walking tour, during which Coleridge wrote his 'Rime of the Ancient Mariner'. Several authors have seen this poem as an allegory for the *Bounty* mutiny and the return of Fletcher Christian to England. The argument of the poem, published in the 1798 edition, is as follows: 'How a Ship having passed the Line was driven by storms to the cold Country towards the South Pole; and how from thence she made her course to the tropical Latitude of the Great Pacific ocean; and of the strange things that befell; and in what manner the Ancyent Marinere came back to his own Country.'

There is no doubt that Wordsworth helped Coleridge in the thematic construction of the 'Ancient Mariner' (he claimed to have suggested the idea of the mariner's killing of an albatross as the crime which the Spirits sought to avenge), and it is perfectly reasonable to suppose that the idea of Christian's mysterious and, at that time, unknown fate provided a backdrop to the dramatic tensions of the poem, and that this was simply a case of two poets unable to let go of a workable yarn. That it was a case of Wordsworth knowing the true fate of Christian and of manipulating Coleridge into creating for posterity a memorial of a home town connection, then in hiding in his native land, is less plausible.

We know that Edward Christian dropped all public references to his brother after his exchange of pamphlets with Bligh in 1794-5, and that he and his family were always circumspect about associating themselves with, or reminding the public of, their disgraced relative. When Fletcher's mother died on 30 March 1820, her obituary in the local paper noted only that she was the mother of Charles Christian, without mentioning either Fletcher or Edward; when Charles died on 14 November 1822, the same newspaper only mentioned that he was the brother of Professor Edward Christian, Chief Justice of the Isle of Ely. No mention was made of his more famous, and notorious, brother. (Had Fletcher's true feelings about his brothers, passed to his relatives by Heywood, poisoned them against him?)

In addition, during 1814 to 1818, while Edward was Professor of Law at Cambridge, one of his students was John Macarthur's son. Macarthur at that time was in exile in Britain after his role in the arrest and detention of the Governor of the New South Wales Colony, one Captain Bligh. Yet though these two men had much in common in their antipathy to Bligh, I found no reference to Bligh in the Macarthur papers in the Mitchell Library. This seems strange, given that it was an obvious topic of conversation between them and a natural topic for correspondence between John Macarthur junior and his family in Sydney.

There is an outside possibility that the reason why Edward was so reticent about his brother was that he believed that any mention of him might provoke the authorities to look more closely into the reports of his return to England, mentioned by Barrow as common knowledge as early as 1808-9. On mature reflection, however, we must settle for the view that Fletcher Christian was killed in the massacre in 1793, or in some other circumstance buried with Adams. The odds against his being able to return home without considerable assistance, and the knowledge of those left behind on Pitcairn, were overwhelming. The chances of fit men in seaworthy boats perishing a few miles off the British coast were high enough (it happened to scores of them in fact), let alone the chances of disaster for a man in a worm-ridden boat thousands of miles from anywhere. If he had got back, somebody in the family would have known about it, and in time, when the memory of the mutineer was dimmed by the memory of the man, it would have got out. After all it would have been the most sensational sea story of all time.

If Glynn Christian could not find evidence of the return of his forebear, we must conclude that he did not return at all. Fletcher died on Pitcairn, some time in the early years of the settlement, by whose hand and over what issue we do not know for certain. It is ironic that the most reliable reports have Christian murdered by a Tahitian in his field while tending his yams (other reports have him shot dead by Adams as he tried to escape in a boat). Given that the mutiny arose partly over Bligh's threats to the crew's yam allowance, it is poignant that Fletcher should die while more concerned with his yams than with his own safety.

# 19

# The Long Arm of the Navy

The story of the mutineers' settlement at Tahiti, from the time Christian sailed away in *Bounty* in September 1789 until the arrival of Captain Edward Edwards in HMS *Pandora* in March 1791, is not a happy one. It is a story of brutality, theft, rape and murder. It is not surprising that the Tahitians were glad to see the back of most of the *Bounty* men when Edwards came to arrest them.

One interesting aspect of the settlement is the way the men divided into small groups to live with their island friends, making no effort to distinguish themselves into mutineers and non-mutineers. This was highly dangerous for them, given their precarious positions. The mutineers Musprat and Hillbrant lived with the loyalists McIntosh, Byrne and Norman at Oparre with Oreepiah, the brother of Chief Tinah; Morrison lived with the mutineer Milward and Chief Poeeno at Matavai. Stewart and Heywood lived together, the former with his wife 'Peggy' and Heywood with an unnamed 'wife', while the leading mutineer Thompson lived with the loyalist Coleman, the man warned off by Christian for plotting a mutiny against him. Sumner, Burkitt and Ellison, all three mutineers, lived together. Mutineers Skinner and Churchill lived separately.

According to Morrison, Churchill was a trouble-maker who caused problems with the Tahitians (while he himself was a pillar of moderation, goodwill and leadership). Both Morrison and Churchill, however, broke the most important rule for contact with people of another culture: non-interference in their domestic affairs. Cook and Bligh understood this. Bligh adamantly refused to intervene in local politics. He insisted on complete neutrality and even punished Isaac Martin for violence towards a Tahitian. By breaking this sensible rule, Churchill and Morrison brought death and misery to hundreds of islanders on an even larger scale than Christian at Tubuai. Peter Heywood fully participated in these bloody excesses, though from later descriptions of this misguided youth one would never guess that he could speak ill of anyone, let alone spill their blood.

Captain Cox in *Mercury* called at Tahiti while *Bounty* was at Tubuai.

He put ashore a troublesome seaman called Brown who had knifed a colleague. Thus merchantmen could rid themselves of trouble, whereas His Majesty's captains were constrained, by penalty of dismissal, from releasing any of their men, no matter how troublesome, except into the custody of the Admiralty. Brown was still on the island when *Bounty* returned for the last time, and he made himself known to the stranded mutineers. Brown does not seem to have been universally liked, but he took part in all the depredations of the mutineers and, indeed, may have instigated some of them.

Morrison claims that he conceived of the idea of building a boat to escape from Tahiti and return to Britain. The fact that several of the hard-line mutineers participated in the heavy work of construction suggests that they may have had other ideas about their eventual destination. In the absence of any notion of escape, the situation of the mutineers was truly pathetic. Morrison explains their help by claiming that he told them that they could visit other islands in the Tahiti group, which was the story he told also to the local chiefs. But boat-building was constantly interrupted by thefts, and to deal with them Morrison introduced summary punishment by flogging. As boatswain's mate, Morrison was no stranger to the art of flogging, for he was the man who flogged delinquents on *Bounty*. He ordered that any Tahitian caught thieving was to be flogged. (One received 100 lashes.)

When the boat was eventually built it measured 33 feeet by 9 feet. It was launched on 5 July 1790 and named *Resolution*. Its first use was in local wars. There was also an attempt to take it to Batavia, in the Dutch East Indies, but Coleman changed his mind, not trusting Morrison's navigating abilities, and insisted on returning to Tahiti. Heywood reports that a second attempt was to be made in the rainy season. David Renouard of *Pandora* reported that the mutineers intended to sail to the north-west coast of America, and that 'they had actually put to sea for that purpose' (*United Service Magazine*, 1842, part 3, pp. 1-3). If the two destinations were in such confusion, one being directly west and the other directly east, it is no surprise that Coleman was worried about the navigator! Perhaps Morrison hoped that the next attempt in the rainy season would preclude even the most ignorant of seamen from knowing which way he was headed?

Thompson caused problems for everybody's safety. He was set upon and beaten by a party of Tahitians after he had raped a woman. In view of the normally permissive sexual code of the Tahitians, it must have been a particularly brutal rape. He was lucky her compatriots were so restrained. Being a man of violent disposition, however, he returned home somewhat bruised and 'vowing revenge on the first that Offended him' (Morrison, Journal, p. 119). It so happened that a party of islanders from another part of Tahiti were visiting the area at the time, and they were curious about the ways of strangers in their midst. They paused to look at Thompson's house, and he, being in a fierce temper, ordered them away, speaking in English. The Tahitians, not understanding what he was saying and unalarmed by his strange behaviour – after all this is what they had come to see – they did not move away. Thompson produced his musket and fired at them. He shot dead a man and the child he was holding in his arms and also wounded a woman in the jaw and another man in the back. He fired at point blank range, adding murder to the crime of rape.

It is incredible that his fellows did not restrain him even though a war of revenge might have been sparked off (Tahitian wars were fought over less). Heywood tried to compensate the dead man's wife, mother of the dead baby, with a shirt. Christian's mutiny continued to exact its tragic toll. His own actions at Tubuai had set a standard for the likes of Thompson.

When Churchill heard about the two incidents involving Thompson – his beating up and the shooting – he planned to organise a punitive expedition to 'revenge' him! Morrison's group refused to support such a reckless and evil proposal, and in the recriminations that followed the seamen split into two parties. Churchill, Thompson and Brown went off to another part of Tahiti, feeling 'betrayed' by their fellows, while their erstwhile colleagues were no doubt glad to get rid of them. It is probable that Churchill and Thompson were the main supporters of the punitive attack on the Tubuaians to which Christian, to his eternal disgrace, acceded.

The separation of the Europeans did not lead to peace. Churchill shot two islanders 'for frightening away some ducks which he was about to fire at'. One of them died later from festering wounds (Morrison, Journal, p. 125a).

Churchill and Thompson soon quarrelled at their new residence, and during the row Thompson threatened to shoot Churchill. To protect himself, Churchill arranged with some Tahitians to have Thompson's muskets stolen. When Thompson discovered the theft he sought out Churchill and, being weaponless, agreed to make up their differences. Brown was blamed for causing the row between them. Churchill, assured of Thompson's peaceful intentions, pretended to find the stolen muskets and return them. Everything was amicable until a Tahitian, who had stolen the weapons for Churchill, had a row with him and in revenge informed Thompson of the truth. Thompson resolved to kill Churchill at the first opportunity, and this he did, shooting him in the back. Burkitt, who was staying nearby, rushed to the scene without a weapon and, seeing the enraged Thompson standing over the dead Churchill, promptly ran away. But Churchill's Tahitian friends were less fearful. They rushed Thompson and beat him to death with stones in the Polynesian manner. None of the *Bounty* men was upset at this news; Morrison told the leader of the men who had killed Thompson that he 'looked on Him as an instrument in the Hand of Providence' (Journal, p. 127). With these murders the worst of the hard-line mutineers were dead just after Bligh got back to Britain.

In September 1790 the *Bounty* men joined in a civil war between two Tahitian kingdoms, and they used their weapons to effect, for the issue was resolved 'with a great slaughter' (Morrison, Journal, p. 148). Their help given to one chief antagonised the others. Inter-kingdom warfare was common in Tahiti, but by introducing their fire-power the Europeans ensured that the mutual destruction was on a far greater scale than before. Personal ambition and aggrandisement were the common ingredients of these civil wars, which had the effect of containing Tahiti's population within the island's natural resources. But once the slaughter went beyond the culturally derived norm, the Tahitian social system was threatened. Tahiti's population began to decline after *Bounty*'s visits, and eventually the Tahitian economy collapsed; mutineers and loyalists alike must carry part of the responsibility for this tragic process.

Having won the opening round in the latest civil war, the victors planned an even more spectacular victory over their rivals. They decided on the stratagem of taking the boy-king Tu round the island accompanied by a Union Jack. Local chiefs and their subjects were to be compelled to show deference to the British flag on pain of violence. That Morrison and company were willing to permit the symbol of Britain to be used in this way says little for their sense of responsibility, for it would put at severe risk the welfare of British seamen calling at the island in future whose ships carried the same flag. Fortunately the planned tour was prevented by the arrival of HMS *Pandora* on 23 March 1791.

Before *Pandora* arrived there was another noteworthy and disgracefully violent incident, this time involving Coleman, Milward, McIntosh, Hillbrant and Morrison. Coleman was accused by a Tahitian of raping his wife, and the Tahitian remonstrated with him. In the course of their altercation the man ran off, obviously frightened. Morrison confesses forming an armed party, not to arrest and punish the rapist, but to hunt down the victim's husband. Morrison's view was that the rape charge was merely a ruse to get compensation from Coleman in the form of iron goods, and unless an example was made of the penalty for false charges the demands for compensation for every peccadillo, real or imaginary, would get out of hand. In the man-hunt that followed shots were fired by Morrison's party and two Tahitians were wounded, 'one in the Thigh & Body and the other in the Arm' (Journal, p. 158). Further violence was prevented by the arrest of the mutineers and their removal from Tahiti.

*Pandora* had left Britain in August 1790, and Captain Edwards had taken the Cape Horn route to Tahiti (which incidentally was the time of year that *Bounty* had been scheduled to sail this route). *Pandora* passed within a few hours' sailing of Pitcairn Island and Edwards missed his chance, if he had but known it, to seize the leader of the mutiny. Edwards had fought under Lord Howe and Sir Samuel Barrington, and the Admiralty were confident that he could accomplish his mission to seize the mutineers and return them to Britain for court martial. His Lieutenants on *Pandora* were Larkan, Corner and Thomas Hayward (the former *Bounty* midshipman prone to sleeping on his watch); he was promoted to Lieutenant because he knew all the mutineers by sight and also knew the area from his time in *Bounty*.

*Pandora* reached Matavai on 23 March 1791, but before it could anchor Coleman swam out to it and surrendered himself. He was followed by Stewart and Heywood soon afterwards. From them Edwards got full details of who was on the island and what had happened to them. They were put into irons and confined below, no distinction being made between mutineers and alleged loyalists. Meanwhile Morrison was on a voyage round Tahiti on *Resolution* to chastise some islanders in one of the local quarrels they had allowed themselves to be drawn into. His party were informed that a ship had arrived that day and that one of the officers was Hayward. This told them that at least one of Bligh's party in the open boat had got back to Britain, which meant that any hope of concealing their roles from the Admiralty was gone. From the point of view of the Navy they were fugitives. The mutineers knew they were dead men, but the loyalists had only a slim hope that Bligh had cleared their names. Morrison claims that his group agreed to surrender voluntarily to the ship in the hope of 'better treatment'. They then indulged in behaviour which magnified any suspicions that Edwards could have about them.

Burkitt, Sumner, Musprat, Hillbrant, Milward (all mutineers), McIntosh (cleared of mutiny by Bligh, though he did not know it) and Morrison were ashore. Morrison went to obtain coconuts for *Resolution*, leaving Norman and Ellison on board (itself interesting, as they were only a few hours at most from *Pandora*; did they see the nuts as a seastore for the voyage back to Britain or for a dash for freedom in *Resolution*?). The local chief, Tamari, knowing of the arrival of *Pandora*, and apparently its purpose, decided that discretion suited his future and confined Morrison (and later Norman and Ellison) as a gesture of goodwill to the new arrivals. He also ordered his people to seize *Resolution* and, taking advantage of its acquisition, ordered it to be plundered of all its possessions. Meanwhile the others had run off into the mountains to escape their fate.

Morrison and his two companions fled, with the help of a Tahitian and Brown (who was in the area and supplied them with hatchets for 'self defence'). The three men gave themselves up to a search party led by Lieutenant Corner, who later in the morning handed them over to Lieutenant Hayward (which must have made his day!). Their hands were tied behind their backs and when they boarded *Pandora* they were put in irons along with the men who had surrendered the previous day. All the prisoners were searched and their possessions examined for evidence that might lead Edwards to Christian. Edwards found some journals belonging to Heywood and Stewart in their sea chests, and he made notes from them (the originals were lost in the sinking of *Pandora*).

Within a short while all the *Bounty* men were arrested, either when they voluntarily gave themselves up (the half-blind Byrne stumbled his way back to Matavai), or with the connivance of Tahitians. There was no escape from their island prison. And no distinction was made between loyalists and mutineers, which is not altogether surprising. Though Bligh testified at his court martial and in print to the innocence of four of the men (Byrne, Coleman, Norman and McIntosh), Edwards had no way of knowing what had survived of their innocence in the intervening two years while they had been in the company of men the Navy regarded as mutineers and pirates (some of whom we know to have been extremely violent, even murderous).

Edwards was also technically correct: the men on Tahiti were not with their Captain and therefore they were in jeopardy of their lives. The Navy's fear and loathing of mutiny was unrestrained in its arbitrary treatment of anybody who ended up on the wrong side of the line between duty and mutiny. Hence their very presence on *Bounty* after the mutiny, whatever their role in it, placed them in the shadow of a criminal charge of piracy. It was Edwards's task to deliver them to the Admiralty for their fate to be decided by court martial. The loss of one of His Majesty's ships was not accompanied by a presumption of innocence on anybody's part – not even of the Captain and those who stood by him. Bligh, like other captains in the same predicament, had to clear his name by verdict of a court martial, not by protestations, or even manifest evidence, of innocence. In naval practice nobody was innocent until proved guilty in these matters. Quite the reverse: everybody was guilty until proved innocent. It is, therefore, somewhat precious of some commentators on this matter to expect Edwards, or any other captain, to indulge his personal judgment about who was, or who was not, likely to be found guilty at a court martial. He knew better than to trespass his opinions, even should they have been sympathetic to his prisoners' plight, which they were not, in place of the jealous prerogatives of his superiors in the Admiralty.

A wooden prison was built on deck, measuring 11 by 18 feet (known inevitably since as 'Pandora's Box'). The entrance was a small scuttle eighteen or twenty inches square, with two smaller scuttles nine inches square for air. At night, the prisoners were handcuffed, and they were under guard twenty-four hours a day. Edwards was taking no chances that they would infect his own crew with mutinous thoughts and he took measures to prevent contact between them. He has been heavily criticised for this treatment, as the conditions in the box were appalling.

For some, it became their coffin. In retrospect a ration of three-quarters of a yam a day may not have seemed such a burden – even Bligh might have appeared in a benign light while they were under the charge of a tyrant like Edwards.

In spite of his efforts, the prisoners managed to talk to members of the crew. The curiosity value of their mutiny would have ensured a ready interest, if only for gossip. Edwards noted that 'Lieutenant Corner reported that when the prisoners went forward they could not be prevented from conversing with the Ship's Company in defiance of the orders that had been given to prevent it' (Edwards Papers, 'Memo made at Otaheite'). The expression 'went forward' suggests that the prisoners were allowed out of the box to obey the calls of nature at the ship's 'heads'. As the crew quartered in that area and the passages were cramped, it was impossible to prevent them whispering to seamen who spoke to them. Edwards countered this breach of his orders with the simple, though for the prisoners uncomfortable, response: they could discharge their toilets in the box. Heywood described to his mother their plight, but did not mention the circumstances.

Corner also mentioned his belief that he 'suspected that they carried on a correspondence with some of the people by letter' (Edwards, ibid.), which seems extraordinary if true. Where they got the pen and ink from is not disclosed.

Heywood described his contacts with his former shipmate Hayward, which suggest that his treatment, while hardly that of a friend ('he, like all wordlings when raised a little in life, received us very cooly and pretended ignorance of our affairs'), was not that of an implacable enemy either. Hayward told Heywood that in his absence from Britain his father had died. Heywood 'naturally' assumed that it was 'Mr Bligh's ungenerous conduct' that had caused his father's death, though what Bligh had to be generous about in the circumstances he left unsaid. As it happened, Heywood senior died before news of the mutiny reached him.

The Tahitians were kept well away from the prisoners while the ship was at Tahiti. This provoked many tears and emotional scenes from the women friends of the prisoners, some of them mothers and others visibly pregnant. Edwards noted that there were rumours that some Tahitians planned to cut the ship's cables 'should the wind blow strong from the sea towards the shore'. Edwards took the threats seriously and kept the Tahitians away from the ship, thus denying his prisoners the comforts of talking with their lovers. The fact that the prisoners spoke Tahitian caused Edwards further qualms about their ability to converse unintelligibly and perhaps to conspire to commit further trouble. He ordered them to speak only English on pain of being shot. These measures, and the general treatment he meted out to them, have given Edwards an odious reputation, though in the circumstances he was merely being prudent.

Morrison described the conditions in the box thus:

The Heat of the place when it was calm was so intense that the Sweat ran in Streams to the Scuppers, and produced Maggots in a short time; the Hammocks being dirty when we got them, we found stored with Vermin of another kind, which we had no Method of erradicating but by lying on the Plank; and tho our Friends would have supplyd us with plenty of Cloth they were not permitted to do it, and our only remedy was to lay Naked, ... the roughness of the Work made our Habitation very leaky, and when any rain fell we were always wet. As the place was washd twice a week we were washd with it, there being no room to shift us from place to place and we had no other alternative but standing up till the Deck dried (which we could but very badly do when the ship had any motion), or lying down in the wet ... (Journal, pp. 181-4).

For those prisoners known to have been held on *Bounty* against their will (Byrne, Coleman, Norman and McIntosh), and those who claimed that they were also detained by force (Morrison, Heywood and Stewart), or seven out of the twelve seized by Edwards, such treatment must have been resented fiercely. For the five guilty mutineers (Ellison, Burkitt, Musprat, Milward, Skinner and Sumner) their treatment, while harsh, and not without precedent in eighteenth-century penal history, must have caused some resentment, if only from the fact that the leader of the mutiny and eight of their companions had escaped the horrors they were made to endure in the box. Two others, Churchill and Thompson, had also escaped the box and we may wonder which fate struck the men as worst.

*Pandora* left Tahiti on 8 May 1791, taking with it *Resolution*, which had been commandeered by Edwards, fitted with proper sails and given a small crew. They sailed for Wytootackee, which Edwards had heard was the island Christian intended to aim for, though why he thought Christian would go to an island discovered by Bligh is not explained. Finding nothing there, he went to Palmerston Island, arriving on 21 May. Here some pieces of *Bounty* were found – some spare spars and rigging lost by the mutineers at Tubuai and taken there by the tides. Having found part of *Bounty*, *Pandora* lost some of its crew. A midshipman, Mr Sivall, and four seamen in the jolly-boat disappeared in a storm while on an errand between the ship and the shore. They were never seen again and presumably were drowned or starved at sea. These were the first casualties on *Pandora*.

The search continued as *Pandora* sailed west, each day further from Pitcairn. The prisoners were on full rations, including grog, though they were hellishly cramped in the box. The islands they visited were a relief to the crew but only of nominal interest to the prisoners. Each day that took them from Tahiti took them nearer to Britain.

On 22 June 1791 *Resolution* became separated from *Pandora*. Edwards spent two days looking for it and then sailed for Annamooka. *Resolution*'s fate remained unknown until the survivors from *Pandora* arrived in Samarang in October. Its solitary voyage to the East Indies was an event in itself and a tribute to the solidity of its construction by Morrison's party.

Edwards continued to move from island to island. He had now lost fourteen of his crew – five in the jolly-boat and nine in *Resolution*. There were literally hundreds of islands for the mutineers to hide in, especially if they burnt *Bounty* and could not be seen from the sea. He passed Vanikoro (which he named Pitt Island) on 13 August 1791. He 'saw smoke very plain, from which it may be presumed that the island is inhabited' (Edwards and Hamilton, *Voyage of HMS Pandora*, edited by Basil Thompson, 1915, pp. 67-8). A month earlier they had visited 'Otutuelah', and George Hamilton, *Pandora*'s surgeon, reported in his Journal how they had 'found some of the French navigator's cloathing and buttons; and there is little doubt but they have murdered them' (ibid., p. 137). The 'French navigator' he refers to was Admiral de La Pérouse, who had disappeared while in the Pacific. The smoke could have been frantic signals from stranded survivors of the La Pérouse expedition, but Edwards did not stop to investigate. He appears to have lost heart by this time in the search for Christian.

*Pandora* was now heading for the Great Barrier Reef off Australia. These were the most dangerous waters in the Pacific, and Edwards failed to take his ship through them. On 28 August *Pandora* violently struck coral. It took in water – nine feet in fifteen minutes – and as the ship settled it heeled over enough to cause a gun to break loose and crush one seaman to death. The ship's boats were lowered and loaded with provisions and sent astern. By early next morning the end was near; orders were given to abandon ship.

Captain Edwards ignored the prisoners while *Pandora* was sinking and took no steps to ensure their safety. The prisoners were manacled in leg and wrist irons in the box, and the exit scuttle was kept locked. They were guarded by a sentry until the last moment. Three prisoners were let out to help man the ship's pumps in a futile bid to keep *Pandora* afloat. The others were left manacled in the box and ignored, until Edwards was told that some of them had broken their irons so as to save time when the scuttle was opened for them to make their escape into the water. Edwards sent the Armourer into the box to re-manacle the prisoners, and also gave orders to the Master-at-Arms to shoot any prisoner creating a disturbance.

Edwards's actions can be explained, if not justified. Morrison reports that 'We could hear the Officers busy getting their things into the boats which were hauled under the stern on purpose & heard some of the Men on Deck say "I'll be damnd if they shall go without us"'. According to Morrison, at this the prisoners began to clank their irons and join in the shouting. Edwards, who had already experienced a mutiny in one of his earlier commands, and undoubtedly under stress and with much to think about, may have reacted to the clamour with the thought that another mutiny was about to break out. Ordering his Master-at-Arms to 'fire upon the buggers' is more understandable in this context. Given that there was not enough room in the ship's boats for everybody (he had also lost the jolly-boat), occupancy was related to rank. The fact that the boats were astern, where the officers' cabins were, shows who had priority of a place. Booms were cut loose to act as rafts for the seamen unable to get into a boat, one of which fell on the deck and killed a seaman who got in the way.

In the confusion it is not unlikely that the prisoners had a different perspective from the officers. Edwards appeared to be concerned to get his officers into the boats first, and then accept seamen and prisoners into the boats in an orderly fashion. The prisoners thought he was deliberately trying to let them drown. Trapped inside the box, with only a small scuttle through which to see what was going on, their perceptions depended entirely on their imaginations and were somewhat influenced by their understandable anxieties and fears of the worst. They would have been superhuman to have remained calm and composed in the circumstances.

The ship was lurching badly and threw the Master-at-Arms over the side. Hodges, the Armourer's Mate, who was preparing the prisoners for release, was trapped inside the box with them. Whatever Edwards's plans for an orderly embarcation of the ship's boats, the end came quicker than expected. His First Lieutenant ended up clinging to the roof of the box, along with three prisoners, before he got to his boat.

Morrison's description of the sinking of *Pandora* is a moving account of survival in adversity and an excellent example of his prose style. It is written with the passion of an angry man:

> Most of the Officers being aft on the top of the Box, we observed that they were armd, and preparing to go into the Boats by the Stern ladders – We Beggd that we might not be forgot, when by Captain Edwards's Order Joseph Hodges, the Armourers Mate of the Pandora, was sent down to take the Irons of Muspratt & Skinner & send them & Byrn (who was then out of Irons) up, but Skinner being too eager to get out got hauld up with his handcuffs on, and the other two following him Close, the Scuttle was shut and Bar'd before Hodges could get to it and he in the Mean time knockd off my hand Irons & Stuarts. I beg'd of the Master at Arms to leave the Scuttle open when he answered 'Never fear my boys we'll all go to Hell together'. The words were scarcely out of his Mouth when the Ship took a Sally and a general cry of 'there She Goes' was heard, the Master at Arms and Corp. with the other Centinels rolld overboard, and at the same instant we saw through the Stern Ports Captain Edwards astern swimming to the Pinnace which was some distance astern, as were all the Boats who had shoved off on the first Appearance of a Motion in the Ship. Burkett and Heilbrandt were yet handcuffd and the Ship under Water as far as the Main Mast and it was now beginning to flow in upon us when the Devine providence directed Wm. Moulter (Boatsns Mate) to the place. He was scrambling up on the Box and hearing our Crys took out the Bolt and threw it and the Scuttle overboard, such was his presence of Mind tho He was forced to follow instantly himself

on this. We all got out except Heilbrandt and were rejoiced even in this trying scene to think that we had escaped from our prison – tho It was full as much as I could do to clear my self of the Driver boom before the Ship Sunk (Journal, pp. 186-91).

The men were in the water, though not yet saved. A sinking ship is a dangerous object both while it goes down and in the immediate period afterwards. Loose timbers and appurtenances sucked down in the initial moments are likely to surface quickly and cause danger to men swimming in the vicinity. Morrison was almost dragged down by the driver boom; a gangway that 'came up' killed some of the survivors; planks and objects galore littered the surface where the ship had been. Morrison described what happened next:

> The Boats were now so far off we could not distinguish one from the other, however observing one of the Gangways Come up I swam to it and had scarcely reached it before I perceived Muspratt on the other end of it having brought him up with it but it falling on the Heads of several others sent them to the Bottom, here I began to get ready for Swimming and the top of our Prison having floated I observed on it Mr. P Heywood, Burket & Coleman & the First Lieut. of the Ship, and seeing Mr. Heywood take a Short plank and Set off to one of the Boats, I resolved to Follow him and throwing away my trowsers, bound my loins up in a Sash or Marro after the Taheite Manner, got a short plank & followed and after having been about an hour and a half in the water, I reached the Blue Yawl and was taken up by Mr. Bowling, Mrs Mate, who had also taken up Mr. Heywood after taking up several others we were landed on a small Key on the Reef about 2½ or 3 miles from the Ship.

Thirty-four men drowned in the sinking, four of them prisoners. Stewart and Sumner were two of the men killed by the gangway. Hillbrant drowned while still manacled in the box, and Skinner probably as a result of being unable to swim as he was still handcuffed 'from being too eager to get out'. Edwards had now lost 44 of his crew and four prisoners and his homeward journey was not half completed.

For nineteen days the 102 survivors of the wreck stayed on a small key while the ship's boats were prepared for the long journey to Timor. The ten remaining prisoners were kept separate from the crew. They were given no shelter from the sun during the day, nor from the cold at night; they blistered in their nakedness from the hot sun and shivered at night in the cold. Their plight did not ease when the time came to move off.

Morrison was put into Edwards's boat with McIntosh and Ellison, and the other prisoners were divided into the other three boats. Morrison was not pleased at his treatment: 'On the 9th as I was laying on the Oars talking to McIntosh Captain Edwards ordered me aft, and without assigning any Cause ordered me to be pinnioned with Cord and lasshd down in the Boats Bottom, and Ellison, who was then asleep in the Boats Bottom, was ordered to the same punishment' (Journal, p. 197). One cannot help feeling that there was something more to this incident than the arbitrary tyranny of Edwards. Morrison remonstrated at his treatment 'but received for answer, "Silence, you Murdering Villain, are you not a Prisoner? You Piratical Dog what better treatment do you expect?"'. Morrison indiscreetly decided to tell him: 'that it was a disgrace to the Captain of a British Man of War to treat a prisoner in such an inhuman Manner upon which he started up in a Violent Rage & snatching a Pistol which lay in the Stern sheets, threatened to shoot me. I still attempted to speak, when he swore "by God if you speak another Word I'll heave the Log with You" and finding that he would hear no reason & my mouth being Parchd so, that I could not move my toungue, I was forced to be silent & submit; and was tyed down so that I could not move.' Morrison claims he was kept in this condition until the boat reached Timor, which seems extraordinarily harsh, but in the context of the eighteenth-century Navy it is remarkable that he had the courage, let alone the temerity, to answer back a Captain, especially one distressed at his misfortunes. To have spoken thus once, let alone persisted, as Morrison reports he did, to any officer in the Home Fleet, would have provoked an awesome punishment of several hundred lashes. That Morrison brought his difficulties on himself does not excuse Edwards's behaviour, though we should note that it appears to been one of empty threats and bluster: shooting bound prisoners, or heaving the log with them, i.e. throwing them overboard on the end of a log line, was hardly an everyday occurrence in the Royal Navy. Morrison, from his experience, knew that, and we can only surmise that he wrote up the incident this way in order to impress a less worldly reader than himself.

The only light that might be thrown on this incident is a mention by Hamilton, the ship's surgeon, in his Journal (1793 edition, p. 129) of some trouble with a prisoner in the pinnace. Hamilton, who was in the *Red Yawl*, wrote: 'In the Captain's boat, one of the prisoners took to praying, and they gathered round him with much attention and seeming devotion. But the Captain suspecting the purity of his doctrine, and unwilling he should make a monopoly of the business, gave the prayers himself.' If this was Morrison, we can surmise that his prayers strayed strictly off the course of seeking salvation, and that he made allusions to the distressed situation they were in, which Edwards took to be a thinly disguised form of criticism of his command.

At Timor the prisoners were put into a Dutch prison in stocks in a cell so disagreeable that the Dutch surgeon sent to look them over would not enter the cell until a slave washed it out. When they were eventually ready to depart, Lieutenant Larkan, the First Officer, personally supervised the binding of the prisoners. He used a cord and 'setting his foot against our back, and bracing our arms together so as almost to haul our arms out of their socketts; we were tyed two & two by the elbows, & having our Irons knockd off were Conducted to the Beach and put on board a long Boat to proceed to the Ship but before we reachd her some of us had fainted owing to the Circulation of the Blood being stopd by the lashings – When we got on board we were put both legs in Irons, and our lashings taken off' (Journal).

The passage from Coupang in Timor to Batavia was not without incident. *Rembang*, the Dutch ship carrying the prisoners and survivors of *Pandora*, was struck by a storm during which even the prisoners were let out to man the pumps. Morrison, by now almost reckless in public criticism of the officers, remonstrated with Lieutenant Larkan about the prisoners' state of health and their inability to work a full shift on the pumps. Larkan replied: 'You damn'd Villain, you have brought it on yourself and I'll make you stand it; if it was not for you were should not have been here nor have met with this trouble' (Journal, p. 200). The Dutch crew were apparently so frightened of the storm that they hid below and *Pandora*'s crew sailed the ship. This might be a bit of Jack Tar prejudice, as the Dutch were good sailors and regularly sailed these waters. Having survived one shipwreck, and in imminent danger of another, it is not surprising that Larkan was unsympathetic. It is also interesting that he held the *Bounty* men responsible for his being in danger.

*Rembang* reached Batavia on 7 November 1791. En route they picked up the missing *Resolution* at Samarang and heard the crew's tales of how they had brought the little ship to the Dutch settlement after losing touch with *Pandora* six months earlier. At Batavia the survivors were divided into groups to make the journey home in separate ships. The prisoners' treatment did not improve. ' ... our lodgings were none the Best,' writes Morrison, 'as we lay on rough logs of Timber, some of which lay Some inches above the rest and which our small portion of Cloathing would not bring to a level, the Deck also over us was very leaky, by which means we were continually wet being alternately drenched with Salt water, the Urine of the Hogs or the Rain which happend to fall' (Journal, p. 204).

When the party arrived at Cape Town they were transferred from the Dutch ship to HMS *Gorgon*. Once on a British ship they came under naval discipline, which had the singular advantage that they were no longer under the personal supervision of Captain Edwards and Lieutenant Larkan. They went onto full rations, had daily exercise and had only one leg in irons. McIntosh, Coleman and Norman were also regularly let out of their irons altogether, which favoured treatment owed much to Bligh having exonerated them of participation in the mutiny.

*Gorgon* reached Spithead on 18 June 1792, delivering its prisoners to HMS *Hector*. It was three and a half years since they had left Spithead in *Bounty*.

# 20

# The Court Martial

The court martial took place on HMS *Duke* from Wednesday 12 September to Tuesday 18 September 1792, under the presidency of Lord Hood, Commander-in-Chief of the Fleet at Spithead. Eleven Post-captains made up the court, namely: Sir Andrew Snape Hammond, John Colpoys, George Montagu, John Bazely, John Thomas Duckworth, John Knight, Richard Goodwin Keats, Sir Roger Curtis, Sir Andrew Douglas, John Nicholson Inglefield and Albermarle Bertie. The prisoners were charged with 'mutinously running away with the said armed vessel the "Bounty" and deserting from His Majesty's Service'.

The Court received a request, 'by the advice of my friends', from Peter Heywood to be tried separately. This it rejected, deciding that the 'whole of the prisoners must be tried together'. This had two consequences: first, it established, at least in the minds of the Court, the individual claim of Peter Heywood to be treated differently from the men who were publicly known to have actively participated in the mutiny; secondly, it created the legal technicality which was later to earn Musprat a pardon.

Heywood was in a dangerous position. As a midshipman, he was the senior by rank of those brought home for trial. If found guilty he could expect no lesser punishment than the able bodied seamen co-accused of mutiny. But, unlike ordinary seamen, Heywood had powerful friends. His family saw to it that his case was fully lobbied for in and around the Admiralty in the months before the trial.

Heywood's family had been warned to be reconciled to his predicament two years earlier, after Bligh and the survivors of his party reached England. The difficulties his family had in clearing him of the charges were formidable, though not insurmountable. The fact that Christian and the hard core of mutineers had separated from him and his companions was of some assistance. Here was a grey area in which his conduct shaded in and out of culpability. If testimony could be organised to narrow the area of his possible guilt and increase the area of doubt, he might yet be saved. This the family set out to achieve, in a campaign largely orchestrated by his younger sister Nessy. She had taken up her brother's cause soon after Bligh's return and his all but damning reports of his view of Heywood's conduct.

She gave a candid example of her objectivity in a letter she sent to Peter while he was incarcerated on *Hector*:

> I will not ask you, my beloved brother, whether you are innocent of the dreadful crime of mutiny; if the transactions of that day were as Mr. Bligh has represented them, such is my conviction of your worth and honour, that I will, without hesitation, stake my life on your innocence. If, on the contrary, you were concerned in such a conspiracy against your commander, I shall be as firmly persuaded *his* conduct was the occasion of it. But Alas! could any occasion justify so atrocious an attempt to destroy a number of our fellow-creatures? No, my ever dearest brother, nothing but conviction from your own mouth can possibly persuade me that you would commit an action in the smallest degree inconsistent with honour and duty; and the circumstance of your having swam off to the Pandora, on her arrival at Otaheite (which filled us with joy to which no words can do justice), is sufficient to convince all who know you, that you certainly staid behind either by force or from views of preservation (quoted in Tagart, 1832, p. 41).

Not surprisingly, from Nessy's point of view, Peter was innocent whatever he had or had not done (we expect no less from our family!), and she went on to assure him that the family was pulling all possible strings on his behalf:

> We are at present making all possible interest with every friend and connexion we have, to insure you a sufficient support and protection at your approaching trial; ... But, alas! while circumstances are against you, the generality of mankind will judge severely. Bligh's representations to the Admiralty are, I am told, very unfavourable, and hitherto the tide of public opinion has been greatly in his favour (ibid., p.43).

One of the instruments of family interest (a contemporary expression for using one's influence in high places) was Commodore Pasley, Peter Heywood's uncle, who at the time commanded *Vengeance*. He intervened with his friend Captain Morgan of *Hector* to see that Heywood received whatever assistance was available while he prepared his defence. Earlier Pasley had written to Nessie regarding his nephew's predicament:

> They have been most rigorously and closely confined since taken, and will continue so, I have no doubt, till Bligh's arrival ... I cannot conceal it from you, my dearest Nessy, neither is it proper I should – your brother appears by all accounts to be the greatest culprit of all, Christian alone excepted. Every exertion, you may rest assured, I shall use to save his life, but on trial I have no hope of his not being condemned. Three of the ten who are expected are mentioned in Bligh's narrative as men detained against their inclination. Would to God your brother had been one of that number! (ibid., pp. 46-7).

Former members of *Bounty* who might be called to give evidence were approached by the Heywoods. Their replies to letters enquiring of their views of Heywood's conduct during the mutiny identified the friendly witnesses. The fact that some witnesses were friendly gave the family hope. Young Hallet, for example, a witness likely to be called for the prosecution, was helpful: 'I shall begin with saying,' he wrote, 'that before the unfortunate period at which the mutiny in the Bounty took place, the conduct of your brother was such as to have procured him our universal esteem. But what were the unpropitious motives by which he was induced to side with the criminal party, I am totally ignorant of, nor can I (as you may readily conceive it was a time of great confusion among us) declare positively the part he acted in it' (ibid., p. 12). Thus, while assuming Heywood to be 'with the criminal party', he also confessed that he could not 'declare positively the part he acted'. It was a relief to know that a principal witness had nothing specific to charge Heywood with. This shifted the burden of a decision about his guilt from a judgment of the intentions of specific actions (for which there was little evidence) onto a judgment of his character (for which evidence could be marshalled to present him in a good light).

John Fryer, former Master of *Bounty*, was much more positive in support of Heywood: 'Keep up your spirits,' he wrote to the midshipman, 'for I am of the opinion, no one can say you had an active part in the mutiny, and be assured of my doing you justice when called upon' (ibid., p. 62).

Commodore Pasley used his rank to effect. He personally interviewed John Fryer and William Cole, Boatswain, and travelling up to Woolwich and Deptford he also interviewed William Peckover, Gunner, and William Purcell, Carpenter. He pronounced all four 'favourable witnesses' (a mistake in Purcell's case).

Pasley also went to the Admiralty, and 'read over all the depositions taken and sent home by Bligh and his officers from Batavia, plus the minutes of Bligh's own court martial. In none of these papers did anything specific appear regarding Peter Heywood's role in the mutiny. This was crucial information. It meant that Heywood could be condemned on direct evidence only if somebody testified to that effect during the trial. Apart from the unexpected testimony of Purcell, which the Heywoods could not know about, only Bligh was likely to carry the court with testimony to that effect. They had reason to suspect that Bligh would be hostile to Heywood's defence, but Bligh was away in the Pacific at the time (on *Providence*), which meant that his views on Heywood, expressed privately in private letters, and perhaps oral statements, only, were entirely unsupported in his official papers. Everything pointed to the benefits of an early trial of Heywood before Bligh returned.

Pasley despatched a legal adviser to *Hector* who advised Heywood 'to write a petition to the Lords Commissioners of the Admiralty to grant me

a speedy trial'. This gentleman, a Mr Delafons, obligingly provided
Heywood with the appropriate form of a letter of petition for him to sign,
which was delivered to the Admiralty in July 1792. Following the visit
from Delafons, Pasley sent Aaron Graham to act as Heywood's legal
counsel. Graham had experience of being a secretary at various
Admiralty courts martial and could be expected to use that knowledge to
effect on Heywood's behalf by advising him what to say, what to omit,
how to present himself and what sorts of things had the most influence on
Post-captains at courts martial. The presence of an experienced naval
lawyer certainly enhanced Heywood's chances of acquittal or a pardon.

The Heywood interest did not stop there, however. Captain Albermarle
Bertie, one of the trial captains, was related to Heywood by marriage. In
command of a ship at Spithead, he was likely to be called to sit on the
court martial (a routine task for Post-captains in ports). Bertie's
friendliness was assured when Pasley asked him to advance Heywood
some money, at which Bertie informed him that he was already obliging
his relative in this respect.

When the court opened its deliberations, it entered into the records,
Bligh's letter to Secretary Stephens of the Admiralty, dated 18 August
1789, and an extract from his published *Narrative* (1790). Protocol
required that an official record, such as a ship's Logbook or a deposition,
was presumed to be true in a legal sense. The letter was the first official
account of the mutiny, written by the commander, and as such was
admissible as evidence in the absence of its author. As neither document
mentioned Heywood, the defence had no objections to their status.

The case against Peter Heywood was largely based on his neutrality
during the mutiny. But neutrality was as much a crime as active
participation for, as Pasley had informed Nessy Heywood, 'the man who
stands neuter is equally guilty with him who lifts his arm against his
captain'. His defence was that he was not neutral, that only through his
extreme youth and confusion did he not know what to do, and that his
intention was to leave the ship with his captain but that he was
prevented from doing so by force (Churchill on the gangway).

Fryer testified that he had not seen Heywood during the mutiny. This
was supported by Peckover; but then he slipped up and stated that he had
supposed everybody who remained in the ship, except those mentioned by
Bligh (Coleman, Norman, McIntosh and Byrne), to be in Christian's
party. Heywood's defence tried to get him to correct this damaging
presumption during their cross-examination. William Cole helped
tremendously by testifying that he thought Heywood was on Bligh's side
and he did not see him armed. He indirectly corroborated Heywood's
claim that he was held by force by telling the court how he heard
Churchill shout to somebody below to keep someone down there, but he
did not know to whom Churchill was referring. When pressed by the
court, he agreed that it could have been Heywood. Then Purcell came on

and, while confirming that somebody had been held below by force, he sank Heywood's defence by testifying that he had seen him on deck armed with a cutlass (Rutter (ed.) 1931, pp. 100-12). This was the sort of evidence that could hang Heywood.

When Hayward and Hallet, since both promoted to Lieutenants, came to give evidence the case against Heywood took a further turn for the worse. Hayward reported that he had told Heywood to get into the boat and that 'I should rather suppose after my having told him to go into the Boat, and he not joining us, to be on the side of the Mutineers' (ibid., p. 121). Hallet turned the knife: 'Captain Bligh said something to him [Heywood], but what I did not hear, upon which he laughed, turned round and walked away' (ibid., p. 126).

In his defence, Heywood asked the court leave, which was granted, to have a written statement read to the court by Mr Const, one of his advisers. (According to Bligh's description of the mutineers, Heywood still had a strong Manx accent and this may have prompted him to have his defence read out.) It is a verbose treatment of the mutiny, somewhat flowery in expression, and may have been written for Heywood. His defence was that he was asleep when the mutiny occurred and that he knew nothing of it. When he went on deck and saw his captain a prisoner he was 'benumbed' and 'did not recover the power of recollection until called to by somebody to take hold of the tackle fall and assist to get out the launch'. In this state of 'absolute stupor' he may have handled a cutlass, but innocently. He had not realised, owing to his 'extreme youth and inexperience', that he had to make a choice between the boat and the ship, and he was also influenced by the behaviour of his seniors, Hayward and Hallet, who when ordered to get into the boat by Christian entreated him not to send them away; Hayward even burst into tears at the prospect. He went on to plead that if he had got into the boat it might have sunk with his extra weight, so close was the gunwale to the water. He denied he had spoken to Captain Bligh, much less laughed at anything he said. He also categorically denied that he had ever engaged in activities inimical to Captain Bligh: 'Indeed,' his deposition stated, 'from his attention to and very kind treatment of me personally, I should have been a Monster of depravity to have betray'd him – the Idea alone is sufficient to disturb a mind where humanity and gratitude have, I hope, ever been noticed as its Characteristic features' (ibid., p. 137-43).

James Morrison, the Boatswain's Mate, was another prisoner in the grey area between innocence and culpability. He had much less interest than Heywood to call upon. Fortunately Fryer was able to testify that he had not seen Morrison under arms, but though Cole was able to corroborate this important detail he also made the telling point that he had not heard Morrison express any desire to get into the boat with Captain Bligh, nor, to his knowledge, did anything prevent him from doing so. Purcell supported Fryer in his assessment of Morrison's loyalties. Hayward came close to charging Morrison with complicity in the mutiny, but this was based on his interpretation of Morrison's countenance compared with those of others like McIntosh, who was clearly innocent, rather than anything substantial. Hallet alleged that Morrison had been under arms when the boat had been veered astern and that he had called out in a 'jeering manner': 'If my friends enquire of me, tell them I am somewhere in the South Seas' (ibid., pp. 126-7). Cole confirmed that he had heard something like that said, but Fryer claimed that he had not seen Morrison at the taffrail (stern) at all.

Like Heywood, Morrison prepared a written statement in 'vindication of my conduct', which was read to the court by the judge-advocate. Accused of showing a rejoicing countenance during the mutiny, he replied:

> My countenance has also been compared with that of another employ'd on the same business. This Honourable Court knows that all Men do not bear their misfortunes with the same fortitude or equanimity of Mind, and that the face is too often a bad index to the Heart. If there were No Sorrow mark'd in my Countenance, it was to deceive those whose Act I abhorred, that I might be at liberty to seize the first Opportunity that might appear favourable, to the retaking of the ship (ibid., p. 166).

Interestingly, Heywood's deposition used a similar expression about his countenance not being 'an index to the Heart' (ibid., p. 146)

Morrison next tried to convince the court that his not joining Bligh in the boat was a rational decision and one that they would have taken in the same circumstances:

> Let the members of this Honourable Court Suppose themselves in my then unfortunate situation, and it will appear doubtful even to them, Which alternative they would have taken. A Boat alongside already crowded, those who were in her Crying Out she would sink, and Captain Bligh desiring no more might go in, with a slender stock of Provisions; what hope could there be to reach any Friendly Shore, or withstand the boisterous attacks of Hostile Elements? The Perils those underwent who reached the Island of Timor, and whom Nothing but the Apparent Interference of Divine Providence could have saved, fully Justify my fears, and prove beyond a Doubt, that they rested on a solid foundation; for by staying in the Ship an opportunity might offer of escaping, but by going in the Boat nothing but Death appeared, either from the lingering torments of Thirst and Hunger, or from the Murderous Weapons of Cruel Savages, or being Swallowed up by the Deep (ibid., p. 167).

He denied the charge that he was under arms at the taffrail, pleading that in the press somebody next to him with a weapon could have been mistaken for him, and he made the same claim about the words that Hayward had testified to him saying about being 'somewhere in the South Seas'. He asked the court to wonder why he should have taken up arms at the last moment after Bligh and his companions were already astern in the boat.

Of the others, Norman, Coleman and McIntosh had been cleared by Bligh of mutiny by their 'being detained against their inclination'. For them the trial was a formality as a prelude to an acquittal. Nobody contradicted Bligh's assumptions in evidence to the court. Likewise with Michael Byrne, the near-blind fiddler. He was in no physical condition to have participated in the mutiny and his affliction was a good enough reason for not going into the boat (though he had got into the jolly boat which was hauled off deck and placed in the water on the wrong side of the *Bounty*, as a result of which he was later overlooked).

This left four prisoners for whom no real plea of innocence was convincing. Ellison had been named by several witnesses as being under arms, acting as a sentry and obeying Christian's orders. Also, despite his youth at the time (a plea made several times on behalf of Heywood), he had little chance of a recommendation for mercy, especially as he had no powerful interest to speak on his behalf.

Thomas Burkitt was one of the armed men who entered Bligh's cabin. His defence that he was under threat of death from Christian, Churchill and McKoy was unconvincing to the court. Milward's defence was even weaker than Burkitt's. He was seen under arms and had acted as a sentry.

Musprat's case was slightly more convincing. Some witnesses did not see him under arms, and neither Fryer nor Hallet remembered seeing him at all. Hayward and Cole claimed they had seen him under arms, but Musprat counter-claimed that he had armed himself to help Fryer retake the ship. This plan of Fryer's to retake the ship had been mentioned several times to the court and Musprat hung his defence on it. As Fryer had not actually made a public move to carry out his alleged plan, Musprat did not need to demonstrate his intentions with deeds. Musprat's lawyer, Stephen Barney, was resourceful enough to concoct a legal defence that worked for his client. He alleged that he wanted to call Norman and Byrne as witnesses in support of Musprat's defence. The court, however, refused to allow prisoners to testify in favour of each other, even though both Norman and Byrne were likely to be acquitted. By refusing to acquit them before all the evidence was given (presumably in case something turned up which contradicted Bligh's evidence), the court created a loophole through which Musprat secured his life. As a civil court would have permitted these witnesses, who were not guilty of mutiny on Bligh's public testimony, Barney put in an appeal against Musprat's subsequent conviction. The effect of the appeal was to postpone his hanging until the Judges on the King's Bench decided his fate.

The court's decision, given on Tuesday 18 September 1792, was that 'the Charges had been proved against the said Peter Heywood, James

Morrison, Thomas Ellison, Thomas Burkitt, John Millward and William Musprat' and it 'did adjudge them and each of them to suffer Death by being hanged by the Neck, on board such of His Majesty's Ship or Ships of War, at such Time or Times and at such Place or Places, as the Commissioners for executing the Office of Lord High Admiral of Great Britain and Ireland etc. or any three of them, for the Time being, should in Writing, under their Hands direct; but the Court, in Consideration of various Circumstances, did humbly and most earnestly recommend the said Peter Heywood and James Morrison to His Majesty's Royal Mercy – and the Court further agreed That the Charges had not been proved against the said Charles Norman, Joseph Coleman, Thomas McIntosh and Michael Byrne, and did adjudge them and each of them to be acquitted' (ibid., pp. 198-9).

Musprat immediately lodged his appeal with the court. It took until 1 February 1793 for the appeal to be decided in his favour. Byrne's success cost money and he later worked with Fletcher Christian's brother Edward on a publicly circulated transcript of the court martial from which no doubt they financed the appeal. The four seamen acquitted by the court, Norman, McIntosh, Cole and Byrne, were released immediately and resumed their service in the Royal Navy. Less fortunate were the three seamen found guilty of mutiny and desertion, Ellison, Milward and Burkitt. They were hanged in public on 29 October 1792 on board HMS *Brunswick*. The hangings, as was the custom, were watched by a party of seamen from each ship in harbour. The gruesome business of execution was meant to be both a punishment to the men involved and a deterrent to anybody foolish enough to contemplate similar misbehaviour. A few days before the hangings, on 24 October 1792, Heywood and Morrison received their royal pardons.

Thus, of the 44 men who sailed on *Bounty*, and of the 24 who joined Christian's mutiny, only three somewhat pathetic ordinary seamen were left to face the full fury of the Royal Navy's wrath for the crime of mutiny. Whatever else Heywood and Morrison thought about their release from the same fate, they might have pondered the unfairness of it all. They – Heywood with interest (including a relative among the judges) and Morrison with ingenuity (his deposition was a masterly piece of advocacy) – escaped a hanging, though at the very least they were somewhat culpable; and the cost to Heywood's family was great, due to the early death of Nessy. The three seamen, no more or less guilty than the other mutineers, but with neither Heywood's interest nor even Musprat's cunning, were hanged. Their fellow mutineers were beyond the jurisdiction of the court, and remained so – some were already dead. In short their main mistake was to get caught and, having been caught, to fail (like Musprat) to get off.

# 21

# Tofoa's Silent Horror

As *Bounty* sailed from view, the full extent of their plight must have become apparent to the men with Bligh in the launch. They were alone in a largely uncharted ocean, with very little food and water, and thirty miles from the nearest landfall, the inhabitants of which had an unknown disposition towards strangers, and they were a long way from the nearest European settlements. If Endeavour Straits was a danger to a ship the size of *Bounty*, it would be perilous in a small boat. Botany Bay was only a dot on the map, and for all they knew it might already have been abandoned as a penal colony by Captain Phillip. But to seek refuge on an island, and await rescue, was also an unlikely objective. Few European ships visited the Pacific, let alone were likely to call at any island Bligh's party chose to remain on.

*Pandora* visited the area in 1791, looking for Christian, but if Bligh had not survived and caused the *Pandora* to be commissioned for its search mission in the first place, the vessel sent in search of the missing expedition might not have reached these waters until 1794. *Bounty*, under Christian, passed by Tofoa six months later, but they made no effort whatsoever to seek out the men they sent away in the open boat, nailing the excuse that they set them adrift with a realistic expectation that they could be rescued from a passing European ship. The fact that they made no attempt themselves to look for any survivors of the boat party, suggests that they were totally indifferent to the fate of all the men they put into the open boat. Thus the basic truth about the mutineers, Christian included, remains that their actions in sending Bligh away were an act of gross inhumanity. Attempts to whitewash their behaviour in this matter are unworthy. That anybody survived the ordeal at all was an extraordinary feat, and a tribute to Bligh's capabilities, which, except for that certain flaw in his conduct, ranks his seamanship, if not his leadership, among the very best.

Bligh's immediate intention was to get to Tofoa, the volcanic island which had fascinated some of the crew the night before. If the inhabitants proved friendly they might get enough assistance to reach Tongataboo, an island further south; Bligh had been there with Captain Cook, who had

139

made friends among the Chiefs. If, however, the Tofoans proved to be unfriendly, Bligh and his men had only four cutlasses with which to defend themselves.

The launch made for the smoke of the volcano, visible just above the horizon, and with an easterly wind on the sail they made good time. On nearing the island they could see that the shore was too rocky to attempt a landing before daybreak, so they spent the night huddled in the launch out in the open sea, using the oars to keep it steady. The launch had too many men in it for anybody to lie down, and with a light meal of a morsel of bread, washed down with some wine and grog, they had to make the best of it. Their fare on the ship from which they had been forcibly ejected must have seemed sumptuous in comparison – three-quarters, a half pound, or even a couple of ounces, of yams, the ostensible cause of people joining Christian's mutiny, were absolute affluence compared with the rations they were to suffer in the next month.

At dawn Bligh took the launch along the coast looking for a place to land. They found a small cove and Bligh sent Samuel with a small party to forage for food and water. The rest of the party waited at the cove, with three men, including Fryer, attending to the boat off shore. In the afternoon the forage party returned with a little water and Bligh decided to try further along the coast. They spotted some coconut trees on a cliff, and though the surf was very rough another party went ashore and climbed the cliff. They brought back twenty nuts, hauling them by rope through the surf. Bligh took the launch back to the cove they had discovered that morning and served each man with a coconut. They spent another night in the cramped conditions of the boat.

According to Fryer, Bligh set out next morning for 'Annamooka or Tongataboo' (Narrative, p. 61). Bligh only says he 'attempted to put to sea', but whatever the destination, the weather was too fierce for a sea voyage and they put back to the cove. Here, after a 'morsel of bread and a spoonful of rum' (Bligh, *Voyage*, p. 167), another expedition in search of food was undertaken, this time led by Bligh, with Fryer and Thomas Hall left in charge of the boat. They did not find much food – only three small bunches of plantains – but they did collect nine gallons of water. Bligh's plan was to live off the island and not to touch their boat stocks at all. He hoped to supplement their food stocks by foraging, or from the assistance of friendly islanders, so as to give them a better chance for the voyage ahead. They returned to the boat with their fare, but not before Bligh had an attack of vertigo on the way back down the cliff to the cove and had to be helped down by Nelson and others. The meal that day was a virtual feast – an ounce of pork, two plantains and a sip of wine.

It was obvious that the island was not going to provide enough for their survival. The stony cove they were in was on the north-west of the island – Bligh placed it at Latitude 19° 41′ south – and could be approached only by sea or by descending a steep cliff. This provided some means of averting a surprise attack, not that they had much with which to defend themselves. That afternoon another party set out but returned with less than the morning's party. Fryer and his group in the boat were told to look for fish or anything in the rocks, but they had no success either. To make things more comfortable in the boat, Bligh and some others slept in a small cave at the head of the cove – lighting a fire according to Fryer (Narrative, p. 57), who watched from the open boat, apparently slighted, not for the last time, by Bligh's distribution of duties and, by implication, selfish choice of comforts. Bligh's explanation for the 'good fire' was the nuisance caused by 'flies and mosquitoes' (*Voyage*, p. 169), which is a wholly convincing one to anybody who has ever slept close to nature.

On 1 May 1789 the first contact with the inhabitants was made. One of the foraging parties came across some Tofoans and brought them back to the cove, where John Norton shouted down from the cliff top, 'Good news. Good news', to announce their arrival (Fryer, Narrative, p. 69). The islanders' party consisted on two men, a woman and a child. Bligh attempted to trade with them and sent them away to collect some breadfruit, plantains and water. Other islanders arrived at the cove – the news was spreading – and soon there were thirty of them. Bligh and his men traded their uniform buttons and beads for food. Naturally the islanders wanted to know where his ship was, and Bligh ordered the men to say it had been sunk. It was a dangerous gamble: although food supplies were increasing, without a ship and unarmed the Europeans were at the mercy of events and the notorious fickleness of the islanders.

Next day canoes began to arrive at the cove. Some brought food, but always in small amounts, confirming the view that the island was poorly provisioned. Bligh remarked that he was 'pleased to find that every one's spirits a little revived, and that they no longer regarded me with those anxious looks, which had constantly been directed towards me since we lost sight of the ship: every countenance appeared to have a degree of cheerfulness, and they all seemed determined to do their best' (*Voyage*, p. 171).

Bligh interpreted the looks of his men as an expression of their anxiety about what was to happen to them in their new-found predicament; others have interpreted them as being a non-verbal sign of their private feelings about the man who had placed them in the predicament through his intimidation of Christian. Fryer alludes to the latter view in his Narrative by reporting a remark made by 'poor Mr Nelson who Mr Bligh always made his confidant'. According to Fryer, Nelson said: 'Our Captns Oeconomy have upset our voyage', to which Fryer replied: 'Never mind Mr Nelson have a good heart we shall See old England tell them our grievances.' Nelson agreed: 'Aye Mr Fryer Sir Jos. Banks will ask me a number of Questions and be assured that I will speak the truth if ever I live to see him.' This is probably representative of the gossip of the men out of earshot of Bligh; but it is naive to think that any group of men placed in their position would not debate who was to blame for their fate, and the (unanimous) selection of Bligh, rather than Christian, as the cause of their troubles is hardly remarkable – a man who worries someone into wild passions, which eventually causes an outbreak of violence, is more likely to be blamed than the too sensitive man himself.

New arrivals at the cove included some chiefs, Macca-ackavow and Eefow, and a young man known to Bligh, Nageete, who had been at Annamooka during the incidents with Christian's watering party. Bligh enquired of two chiefs he knew, Poulaho and Feenow, and was assured that they were at Tongataboo, to which island Eefow agreed to accompany the launch when the weather moderated. The relief at such a friendly response soon dissipated. Trouble was about to begin.

Eefow, Bligh's new friend on the shore, was viewed differently by Fryer in the boat. 'This man,' writes Fryer, 'was very inquisitive – we had a chest in the boat which he much wanted to look into, but I told him in the Otaheite language the contents was fire arms ... there was a saw in the boat – which he was very desirous of having, as he could not get it he went away rather displeased' (Narrative, pp. 71-3). Fryer thought it was 'a wrong scheme to admit such a man as that to come near the boat' and he only let him do so because of Bligh's orders. Some of the islanders on shore attempted to haul the boat in, but once the shore party discovered what they were trying to do they desisted, though not before Bligh had brandished his cutlass and called on Eefow to intervene.

Bligh's party was split into three: a group foraging in the countryside away from the cove; the shore party he commanded; and the men in the boat (Fryer, Hayward and Tinkler). He had good cause for alarm; the number of islanders kept increasing and some of them were getting bolder and noisier. His problem was how to get away without provoking a mass attack. Having been at Kealakekua, where Captain Cook died, he well knew the dangers and how little it would take to start a murderous riot.

Nothing could be done until the foraging party returned. When it did, he told the men to get ready to leave the beach. This he hoped to accomplish at sunset to give them cover for an escape to sea. He kept buying breadfruit in small quantities, and also purchased two spears to supplement the two cutlasses he had on shore (the other two were in the boat). The scene at the tiny cove moved to its climax. Ominously the crowd began to knock stones together. Both Peckover and Bligh knew what that meant – they had heard this traditional Polynesian signal for an impending attack at Kealakekua while guarding the *Resolution*'s mast.

Diplomatically, Bligh ate with the chiefs. It was a tense meal, eaten in silence, with Bligh refusing to sit down and holding his cutlass in his hand. The islanders were eyeing the property of the seamen, the seamen the weapons of the islanders and everybody the distance between the shore and the boat. Quietly Bligh ordered the men to move their possessions to the boat, and Tinkler, being the youngest and not noticed too much by the islanders, went back and forth through the surf carrying things. Peckover took Bligh's Log and fended off an attempt to snatch it.

The islanders showed signs of settling down at the cove for the night. They lit fires as yet more islanders arrived and the general air of excitement increased. Bligh sent orders to Fryer to bring the boat in a little closer when he saw Bligh walking down to the water's edge. As the sun set, the seamen took up their things and walked down to the water. The islanders enquired if Bligh was not sleeping on shore and he told them, 'No, I never sleep out of my boat; but in the morning, we will again trade with you, and I shall remain till the weather is moderate, that we may go, as we have agreed, to see Poulaho, at Tongataboo.' The elderly chief, Macca-ackavow, said: 'You will not sleep on shore? then Mattie', which meant 'death' (Christian had used the same word when guarding Bligh at the mast) (*Voyage*, p. 173). Eefow followed Macca-ackavow into the crowd, and Nageete stayed with Bligh only to encourage the men around them to attack, for which treachery Bligh decided that, if he was attacked, Nageete would be the first to die.

Fryer hauled in on the beach rope to bring the boat's stern near to the shore. The islanders began to haul on the rope to get the boat out of the sea. John Norton ran along the beach to clear the rope. Bligh ordered Purcell to remain by his side and be last off with him (Fryer claimed that Purcell stood by him voluntarily 'longer than one in twenty would have done'). Bligh, holding Nageete's hand, walked with Purcell to the water's edge. Everybody on the beach was on their feet, clicking stones. The scene and the tension was a 'silent kind of horror'. As Bligh entered the surf the stones began to fly.

The boat was still held by the line on shore, which Norton, unaware of the danger he was in, was trying to free. The islanders charged, some at the boat and some towards their own canoes. Stones flew through the air; many of them weighed about two pounds. Norton was pounced on and knocked out, his skull being quickly fractured, and died before the eyes of his crewmates. He was the first victim of Christian's mutiny. Nobody in the boat had any illusion about their fate after this. Bligh, with some difficulty according to Fryer, was hauled aboard, and Purcell was left half in and half out, his legs dangling over the stern. Bligh cut the line holding the boat to the shore and the men pulled on the rope to the grapnel lying further out from the shore to move the boat through the surf. Luckily, the grapnel's fluke broke as they neared it, which released the boat towards the open sea, and the men pulled on their oars. Canoes followed them, with islanders aiming large stones across the water, causing severe bruising to those they struck. Bligh and Fryer, in the boat's stern, were struck several times by stones, their bodies acting as a shield for the men on the oars. If the men were struck and lost their stroke everybody was in peril. To slow down the attackers, Bligh and Nelson hove several clothes overboard, including, according to Fryer, the provisions they had purchased from the islanders at the cove. As intended, the pursuers stopped to pick up these easy prizes and in doing so allowed the launch to pull away from them to sea. With the sea running high, the launch gathered speed and, under sail, moved to the relative safety of the open sea.

The experience had terrified everybody. Norton had been lost, but once he went along the beach nothing could be done for him. Bligh was very touched by this man's death and publicly acknowledged his good character. He wrote: 'The poor man killed by the natives was John Norton: this was his second voyage with me as a quarter-master, and his worthy character made me lament his loss very much. He has left an aged parent, I am told, whom he supported' (*Voyage*, p. 175). Bligh's uncle noted in his copy of Bligh's *Narrative* (1790) that he had heard him remark that Norton's death was, from the selfish point of view of the boat's crew, 'a fortunate circumstance, for he was the stoutest man in the ship, which circumstance wd very materially have interfered with the boat's progress and the allowance of provisions' (quoted in Mackaness, 1951, p. 141).

Had events been a little different – the attack beginning while the party was divided into three groups, or while the shore party were trapped against the cave a hundred yards or so up the beach, or the boat failing to clear the vicinity of the shore – the intentions of some of the mutineers would have been realised within a few days of the mutiny. It was a remarkable example of Bligh's better, though rarer, style of leadership. He acted resolutely and on this occasion it saved their lives.

The alternatives they faced now were limited. Tongataboo was an unpopular destination in view of Norton's fate. While his 'mind was thus anxiously employed to consider what was best to be done', Bligh sailed the launch along the west coast of Tofoa, away from Tongataboo, under a fresh easterly wind. It was now dark and they needed to settle on where they were going.

Fryer states that Bligh for a while still wanted to try Tongataboo and that he, Fryer, supported by Cole, persuaded him otherwise. Enquiring of Bligh whether, when he was at Tongataboo with Captain Cook, he had 'had any words with the natives', Bligh told him that 'they had several of them in confinement for theft', to which Fryer opined that the islanders down there would 'play us some trick'. This assessment coincides with Bligh's own view that the Tofoa experience was 'a sample of the disposition of the natives' and 'there was but little reason to expect much benefit by persevering in the intention of visiting Poulaho; for I considered their good behaviour formerly to have proceeded from a dread of fire-arms, and which, therefore, was likely to cease, as they know we were now destitute of them: and, even supposing our lives not in danger, the boat and everything we had, would most probably be taken from us, and thereby all hopes precluded of ever being able to return to our native country' (*Voyage*, pp. 175-6).

Bligh certainly notes how all hands solicited him to 'take them towards home', which meant giving Tongataboo a miss, but whether his mind was set on them making for Tongataboo, or whether he was merely rehearsing the pros and cons of securing supplies there and was persuaded by Fryer's arguments, is less clear. From Bligh's notebook, which he kept during the boat voyage and which became public only in 1977 (a facsimile was published in 1986 by the Australian National Library), it appears that on 3 May 1789, in the hours following the attack on Tofoa, he contemplated sailing the boat back to Tahiti, but his calculations of the days required for the passage – 55 to Tahiti against 46 to Timor – forced him to settle on the latter (following a suggestion from Peckover who had been there with Cook), in consideration, presumably, of the food situation in the boat. The fact that Bligh was calculating the distances and time to both destinations, but not to Tongataboo, suggests that Fryer exaggerated his own role in the final decision.

They had only 150 lbs of ship's biscuit, 28 gallons of water, 20 lbs of pork, 5 quarts of rum, 3 bottles of wine, some coconuts and breadfruit, much of the latter made useless from being trampled in the flight from Tofoa. On normal rations this was a few days supply, and the minimum distance they would have to travel would take several weeks. Fear and necessity, however, are powerful persuaders. Bligh made each man individually swear in front of everybody else that he would accept the strictest of rationing ('One Ounce of Bread Pr. day and One Jill of Water') and he enjoined them, separately and together, to agree that he as Captain would not alter the ration under any circumstance whatsoever. Everybody swore and agreed: anything was preferable to what had happened to Norton.

With these oaths all sworn and regarded 'as a sacred promise for ever to their memory', Bligh 'bore away across a sea, where the navigation is but little known, and in a small boat, twenty-three feet long from stem to stern, deep loaded with eighteen men; without a chart, and nothing but my own recollection and general knowledge of the situation of places, assisted by a book of latitudes and longitudes, to guide us. I was happy, however, to see every one better satisfied with our situation in this particular than myself' (Log, 3 May 1789).

A minor controversy persists as to exactly what navigational equipment Bligh had with him in the boat, the implication being that it suited Bligh to exaggerate his limited tools in order to blacken the mutineers (as if that was necessary) and to enhance his own reputation. In a sense it depends on his audience: the Admiralty was unlikely to be fooled by his lying about his navigation, which from the Log and the Notebook clearly showed that he was using a sextant, even if the public were falsely impressed. The facts remain that Bligh did remarkably well with the limited but sufficient tools he had, and that any competent navigator would have done similarly. Fryer, for example, as a qualified and experienced Master, was capable of conducting the navigation of the launch (a point he makes bitterly in his Narrative, p. 63); whether he was capable of the stern leadership required to hold the increasingly distressed men together is another question.

According to Morrison's account (Journal, p. 60), Bligh was handed Christian's own sextant, 'which commonly stood on the dripstone case' just before the boat was veered astern of the *Bounty*. John Bach, editor of the facsimile edition of Bligh's Notebook, identifies the sextant as a 10-inch 'Ramsden B', Bligh's own instrument, and one of three he took with him for the voyage, which he refers to in his Log (p. 4). His daily calculations in the Notebook show that he was using data obtained from a sextant. His published accounts (the *Narrative*, 1790, and the fuller version, the *Voyage*, 1792, edited in his absence by Captain Burney) often refer to his noon observations. While these could be obtained using the quadrant he had with him – and Fryer states that he made observations with it – the evidence is conclusive that Bligh had a sextant and some appropriate nautical tables. Who Bligh was meant to be fooling is not obvious.

It was the totality of his seamanship, not just his navigational skills, that marked out the boat voyage. This voyage was to be difficult enough. The recognition for overcoming the difficulties was more than enough to earn Bligh praise, even from his sternest critics, and he needed no additional honours from pretending to be a navigational genius.

William Bligh, Midshipman. Oil portrait attributed to John Webber RA, c. 1775/6. Private collection

Elizabeth Bligh, née Betham. Signed and dated oil portrait by John Webber, 1782. Private collection

Sir Joseph Banks, President of the Royal Society and lifetime friend and benefactor of Bligh. Oil portrait by an unknown artist. Australian National Library – Dixson Collection

John Fryer in Master's uniform. Oil portrait by Gaetano Calleyo, Australian National Library – Mitchell Collection

Robert Tinkler, 'Midshipman', brother-in-law to John Fryer. Oval water-colour miniature by an unknown artist. Recently stolen from a private collection

Peter Heywood, Captain. Oil portrait by J. Simpson. National Maritime Museum, Greenwich

The crew of the *Bounty* loading breadfruit at Tahiti. Nineteenth-century steel engraving from a weekly subscription magazine retelling the *Bounty* story. Private collection

'Collecting the breadfruit'. Coloured mezzotint by Thomas Gosse from his own painting to commemorate the safe return in 1793 of HMS *Providence* and HMS *Assistant* under Bligh. Private collection

William Bligh. Engraving by
H. Adlard from J. A. Russell's
crayon portrait. Later used as
the frontispiece to Bligh's
1792 edition of *A Voyage to
the South Sea* . . . Private
collection

John Adams, sole surviving
*Bounty* mutineer on Pitcairn
Island. Pencil and wash sketch by
R. Beechey, 1826-8. Private
collection

William Bligh. Medallion
portrait, later engraved for the
Camperdown action
commemorative plate by
J. Smart, 1797. National
Portrait Gallery

William Bligh. Unusual miniature
three-quarter-length coloured
silhouette painted between 1790
and 1805, when Bligh held
Captain's rank. Private collection

Harriet, Bligh's eldest surviving
daughter. Oil portrait by an
unknown artist. Private collection

John Macarthur. Oil
portrait by an unknown
artist. Australian
National Library –
Dixson Collection

George Johnston, Lieutenant-Colonel, New South Wales Corps. Oil portrait by Henry Robinson Smith. Australian National Library – Mitchell Collection

William Bligh, Vice-Admiral of the Blue. Fine miniature portrait by an unknown artist showing his Camperdown medal, of which he was justly proud. Private collection

# 22

# Voyage of the Open Boat

Once the decision to make for Timor been made, Fryer asked Bligh if he should 'put the helm up'. Bligh replied: 'Yes, in God's name.' The launch bore away from Tofoa into the open sea. It was between seven and eight o'clock at night, and once away from the island the sea ran high and the wind increased, so that the foresail had to be shortened (reefed). The men were put into two watches (two days later they were redivided into three watches, one each under Fryer, Cole and Peckover: *Notebook*, p. 10).

The launch, which became 'home' for the eighteen men desperately seeking to survive the elements, was 23 feet long, 6 feet 9 inches in beam and 2 feet 9 inches deep. It had two masts, one forward in the bows and one amidships, and both had yards for the sails. In addition it had six oars. It was very uncomfortable, and before long things got worse.

Next morning the sea, running so high, alternately becalmed the sail between each wave and threatened it on the crest. Water came in over the stern and the men had to bail constantly. This threatened to spoil the bread, then lying in bags about the boat. Bligh decided to rid the boat of anything surplus. The first things to go were any clothes beyond 'two suits' for each man, followed by spare sails and rope. This made the bailing easier. The carpenter's chest was emptied and its tools stowed in the bottom of the boat, and the bread was stuffed into it to prevent it getting wetter. Fryer noted, with sarcasm, that had everybody else 'thought as much about their books as Captn. Bligh and his Clerk did, the boat would have [been] turn[ed] adrift without oar or sail' (Narrative, p. 89).

A spoonful of rum was issued to all, plus some 'scarce eatable' breadfruit, for 'we were very wet & Cold'. Bligh was 'sacredly determined with my life to make what provisions I had to last Eight Weeks, let the daily proportion be ever so small' (Log, 3 May 1789).

They passed a 'Small flat Island' the next day but did not attempt a landing. Other islands were observed, which Bligh assumed to be part of the Fiji group. Five small coconuts were cut up and distributed for the daily allowance. Though the bread was found to be rotten, it was too precious to throw away. By now they had been on their reduced diet for a week. 'Our wants,' wrote Bligh, 'are now beginning to have a dreadful aspect which nothing but a firm and determined resolution can fight against, a situation particularly miserable on a Commander' (Log, 4 May 1789). The misery was only just beginning. 'It may readily be supposed that our Lodgings are very miserable and confined and I have it only in my power to remedy the last defect by putting ourselves at Watch and Watch so that half is sitting up while the other has no other Bed than the Bottom of the Boat or upon a Chest, and nothing to cover us but the Heavens. Our Limbs are dreadfully Cramped for we cannot Stretch them out, and the Nights are so cold and being generally very wet, we can scarce move ourselves after a few hours Sleep' (Log, 7 May 1789).

To assist with the boat's navigation, Bligh enlisted the men to cast a primitive log line and practise counting off the seconds. Once they were tolerably accurate at counting, this gave the speed of the launch every hour, which, with the compass bearing of the course she had followed, enabled the distance travelled to be calculated. The log line was passed over the side and the rate at which knots tied in it passed the counter gave the speed (in knots!) of the launch. Hence the count had to be accurate if the dead reckoning calculation was to be reliable.

The islands they passed were 'fruitfull and hilly' but they were 'afraid to land' (Bligh, Notebook, p. 17). They hooked a fish 'but were miserably disappointed' to lose it while trying to land it into the boat. This left them with the daily allowance of one ounce of bread each and a quarter of a pint of water.

On 7 May, without any warning from the state of the sea, the boat passed over a coral bank with only four feet to spare. It was a lucky escape. Then after breakfast, consisting of a spoonful of rum and a morsel of bread, two sailing canoes were spotted chasing them. After days without full rations of food they were weaker physically and less able to defend themselves if their reception was hostile. In spite of their hunger they raced away from the canoes as fast as they could, all oars manned. Fryer, while criticising instances of Bligh's steerage, reports that everybody, including Bligh and himself, 'was very much alarmed' when the canoes appeared to be catching up on them. Bligh said: 'Heave away lads if they come up with us they will cut us all to pieces.' At this, according to Fryer, Lawrence Lebogue, 'a fine old sailor', said, 'God damn my eyes Sir you frighten us all out of our wits let the theifs come and be damned if they will we will fight as long as we can.' In what Fryer described as a 'rather impertinent manner', Lebogue added that it was 'very pretty indeed by God that the Captn. is the first man frightened'. Fryer intervened and said, 'You old scoundrel if you speak another word I will come and heave you overboard' (*Narrative*, pp. 95-7). Given that Bligh was the second last man off the beach at Tofoa, I do not think the imputation against his personal courage needs be taken too seriously.

The chase went on most of the day until about 3 pm when the islanders gave up, unable to close the final two miles that separated them from the launch. Each man received an ounce and a half of pork, a teaspoonful of rum, half a pint of coconut milk and an ounce of bread. Some feast indeed.

On 9 May Bligh 'amused all hands with describing the Situation of New Guinea & New Holland, and I gave every information, that in case of any accident happened to me, those who survive might have some Idea of what they were about and arrive safe at Timor, which at present they know nothing of more than the Names' (Log) ('and some not that' was added in Bligh's *Narrative*). This action was meant as a morale booster. For all any of the seamen knew they could be lost and going round in circles.

Supper consisted of a quarter of a pint of water and half an ounce of bread. To cheer themselves up, they sang a song and went to sleep (Notebook, p. 21). For breakfast they received a quarter of a pint of coconut milk and another ounce of bread, for supper the insides of the coconuts and what remained of the rotten bread. These paltry rations were to become their standard fare until they neared Australia.

Bligh made a pair of scales out of two coconut shells to measure the daily rations instead of guessing them (they are in a private collection, along with the pistol balls, each weighing an ounce, which he used as weights). Clearly, if arguments broke out about the distribution of the scanty rations, this would be dangerous for everybody. At the end of Fryer's Narrative, he reports accusations that Bligh deliberately let some of the bread drop while serving it so that afterwards he could pick it up and eat it (pp. 165-7). This might have been a misunderstanding of Bligh's method of eating his rations. While reporting that some men make their bread more savoury by dipping it into salt water, he wrote: 'For my part I always break it into Small pieces and eat it in my allowance of Water in a Cocoa Nutt shell with a Spoon taking care never to take but a piece at a time so that I am as long at dinner as at a more plentiful Meal' (Log, 26 May 1789). Starving men, having finished their tiny ration, may have become unduly suspicious that their Captain was still making a meal of his food long after they had wolfed theirs down.

To make the boat more comfortable and provide some minimal protection from the wind and rain, they erected a canvas cloth round the boat and the carpenter nailed the wooden seats at the stern to give about nine additional inches of shelter. On 11 May the sea broke over the boat and the situation became 'highly dangerous'. The weather turned to thunder and lightning and heavy rain. Rain meant fresh water, which was always eagerly collected, but it also soaked them through. In consolation, 'Hot weather,' Bligh noted, 'would have caused us to have died raving Mad with thirst' (Log, 15 May 1789). Bailing out the rain water was also an onerous burden for men in poor physical condition. It rained for several days and the launch had to be steered before the waves without concern for their course to prevent it capsizing. 'The day showed to me a poor Miserable set of Beings full of Wants but nothing to relieve them. Some complained of great pains in their Bowels and all of having but little use of their Limbs. What Sleep we got was scarce refreshing, being covered with Sea and Rain, and two persons were always obliged to keep bailing' (Log, 12 May 1789). To help alleviate their sufferings, Bligh issued a spoonful of rum again, but stuck to the usual breakfast, supper and dinner allowance of a morsel of bread and some water.

Some of the men were shivering with cold and their wet clothes. There was no way they could dry their clothes, and Bligh recommended a strange but apparently comforting practice. Because the sea was warmer than the rain, he told the men to strip, wring their clothes with sea-water and then put them on again. By this means 'they received a Warmth', claimed Bligh, and avoided 'Catching Colds and violent Rheumatic complaints'. The extent of the rain during the boat voyage can be gauged from the Log, which records twenty-three days of rain and gales out of forty-four days spent in the open.

They passed by some fertile-looking islands which only increased their misery. Being so near possible relief, yet too wary to take the risks involved in landing, they could only pass by in private contemplation of the possibilities. It is in these circumstances that starving men can believe they are being cheated by whosoever is in charge of the food. The effects of this punishing endurance test began to tell on the men. An ounce of pork was issued, but there were incessant demands for more which Bligh, with characteristic firmness, refused. He considered it 'better to give it in ever so small quantities than use all at once or twice, which would be the case if I would allow it' (Log, 16 May 1789). The next day Bligh 'found every man complaining, and some of them soliciting extra allowance, but I positively refused it' (*Narrative*, p. 35). He did issue a 'teaspoonful or two' of the dwindling stock of rum to each person, and everybody was 'overjoyed whenever he announced this to be his intention'.

Sleep was no comfort because the nights were bitterly cold and wet. Mornings were accompanied by complaints about the 'severity of the weather', and Bligh was tempted to issue more rum allowance 'if it had not appeared to them that we were to suffer much more' and in future 'we might be less able to bear such hardships' (*Narrative*, 19 May 1789). He relented enough to issue an ounce of pork with the dinner allowance of bread and water. Next morning everybody got two teaspoonfuls of rum. The situation was 'truly miserable' and the pressure on him to relent persisted, for he 'could look no way but I caught the Eye of some one. Extreme hunger is now evident, but thirst no one suffers or have we an inclination to drink that desire being satisfied through our Skin – What little Sleep we get is in the midst of Water, and we wake with Severe Cramps and Pains in the Bones' (Log, 20 May 1789).

The voyage was in its worst phase since the beach at Tofoa. How long it would be before somebody succumbed to the deprivations, or the boat capsized from the sheer exhaustion of the bailers, or of the person steering, was an ever-present anxiety for those with enough strength to think about it. 'Our distresses are now extremely great we are so covered with Rain and Sea that we can scarce see each other or make use of our Eyes – Sleep altho we long for it is horrible – for my part I seem to live without it' (Log, 21 May 1789). That night they were hit by a deluge of rain which threatened the boat so much that everybody bailed frantically. Next morning Bligh served a 'large allowance of rum', but the rest of the meals that day were confined to the usual morsel of bread and some water.

The situation was now perilous. 'I presume to say,' wrote Bligh, 'our present situation would make the boldest Seaman tremble that ever lived.' They had to run before the sea with the 'utmost care, as the least error in the Helm would in a moment be our destruction'. This did not prevent Bligh 'being propped up' to make an observation.

The next night was worse. The sea broke over them so often that they bailed 'with horror and anxiety', and Bligh was worried that some would not last another night in these conditions. He gave out two teaspoonfuls of rum and the usual bread and water allowance. Then the weather began to moderate. It was still bitterly cold but they were no longer threatened with capsizing in the storm. For the first time in fifteen days they were warmed slightly by the sun. They washed out their clothes, so threadbare that 'they would not keep out either wet or cold' (*Narrative*, p. 40).

On 25 May 1789 Bligh took advantage of the fairer weather to check the store of bread and came to the dreadful conclusion that rations had to be cut still further to give them a margin of safety. 'I determined to proportion my Issues to 6 Weeks. I considered this would be ill received, it therefore demanded my most determined resolution to inforce it provided I was opposed, for small as the quantity was I intended to take away for our future good, yet it appeared like robbing them of life, and some who were particularly Voracious would not like it' (Log). The men, however, accepted the necessity of Bligh's decision, and the supper bread allowance was cut out.

Fortunately a noddy bird (about the size of a small pigeon) was caught which, though providing a minute ration of 1/18th per person (with the blood directed to the three weakest men), also confirmed that they were nearing land. The next day another bird was caught. These were divided, entrails and all, according to the naval custom of 'Who shall have this?' One man points to a piece of the cut-up bird at random, and another man, who cannot see which piece is being pointed to, calls out a name, and the raw piece goes to that person. Some would get flesh, others entrails and the few unlucky ones the feet and beak etc. It was a traditional way of ensuring impartiality in food distribution in desperate circumstances, the officers, Bligh included, taking their chances along with the rest. By now all eyes would be vigilant about the destination of even the smallest morsel of food. Bligh considered it made a 'good supper, compared with our usual fare', a view no doubt endorsed by all. With the birds came the sun and the new problem of heat exhaustion for the already weakened men.

On Wednesday 27 May Bligh announced that his calculations showed them to be near the 'reefs of New Holland' (the Great Barrier Reef). Fryer's account of the approach to the reef is curious. He appears to be peeved that Bligh's published *Narrative* ignores his role in handling the approach to the breakers. According to Fryer, he had taken over the watch from Peckover at midnight and an hour later he asked the man (not identified by Fryer) at the helm if he could 'hear a noise like the roaring of the sea against the rocks'. The man said he could. Fryer got up and stood against the mast and when he eventually saw the breakers ahead he immediately woke up Bligh. Fryer, being in charge of the watch, told the helmsman 'to port the helm'. He started to lower the mainsail and, assisted by several men (presumably those on watch), got the sails dipped. This slowed the forward motion of the boat towards the reef. He ordered the men to get their oars out and pull on them. 'In the height of this bustle,' says Fryer, Bligh intervened and shouted out: 'Pull away my lads [or] we shall be all swamped.' This Fryer considered to be a 'very pretty encouragement for people in distress', so he contradicted Bligh by shouting out, 'My lads pull there is no danger' (Narrative, pp. 97-9).

Bligh's only comment about the incident in his Log is to say that the man at the helm (he does not mention Fryer) heard the breakers at one o'clock and that when he was wakened he saw them 'close under our lee not more than ¼ mile from us. I now hauled the Wind to the NNE and in 10 minutes we could not see or hear them' (Log, 28 May 1789). In the Notebook he states that they cleared the reef with only a cable (200 yards) to spare (p. 54). What appears to have upset Fryer is that his role in averting the danger is not mentioned by Bligh, but the fact remains that a lee shore a few hundred yards away is always a dangerous situation for any ship, and more so for one in the condition of the launch and its crew. Shouting encouragement to the men on the oars in the manner adopted by Bligh (warning them of the consequences of giving in to their physical condition) is hardly an example of his lack of courage, or seamanship. At worst it was what we might describe today as 'backseat driving'!

On 28 May, a calendar month after the mutiny, the launch entered smooth water on the land side of the reef, having stood off the reef all night and then approached it at daybreak in search of a passage. It was necessary, in Bligh's view, to get to the smoother water and make a landing as soon as possible to keep the men's spirits up. The manouvre by which this was achieved is the subject of another observation by Fryer, but comparing both accounts it is not clear what he is hinting at. Bligh writes:

In the Morning at day light I bore away again for the Reefs and saw them by Nine O'Clock – The Sea broke furiously over every part and I had no sooner got near to them, than the Wind came at East and could only lie along the line of the breakers, within which we saw the Water so smooth that every person already anticipated the heartfelt Satisfaction he would receive as soon as we could accomplish my intention. – But I now found that we were embayed, and I could not lie clear without my Sails such a heavy Sea Setting in and the Wind having backed against us, so that our Situation was now become dangerous. I expected but little from the Oars because we had no Strength to pull them, and it was becoming every minute more and more probable that I should be obliged to take the Reef in case we could not pull off. – Even this I did not doubt of effecting with success, when happily we discovered a Break in the Reef about 1 mile from us (Log, 28 May 1789).

Fryer's account says much the same thing but accords to himself the credit – if that is a suitable word for a man doing his duty – for spotting the break in the reef. Both Bligh's Log and his published accounts refer to the break in the reef as something 'we discovered', and not 'I discovered', so this could hardly be the reason for Fryer's huffiness at Bligh's version.

Bligh's professional duty obliged him to keep close to the passage for a couple of hours to make a noon observation to fix its latitude as nearly as he could for the benefit of other seamen, and not make haste to the nearest landfall in search of food. Fryer notes that Bligh 'had his sextant' and he had an 'old Quadrant' (p. 105) for this task, confirming Morrison's account that Bligh was not totally bereft of navigational instruments.

That afternoon Bligh brought the launch to an island that appeared to suit their purposes. It was about ¼ of a mile from the mainland and was uninhabited (they were still cautious of meeting natives). Bligh named the island Restoration, in dual recognition of the fact that 29 May was the anniversary of the restoration of Charles II and of what landfall meant that day for his crew. Fryer says that 'on first landing we were like so many drunken men', which is not surprising considering they had been in a cramped boat in rough seas since they left Tofoa on May 3.

With landfall, and the prospect of replenishing their food supplies, the extremes of deprivation were relieved a little. This occasioned a relaxation in their self-discipline, as if some thought that their problems were over. In the boat they suffered dreadfully (and more was to come on the passage to Timor), not seeing beyond the next wave which might capsize them, and were in a state of lethargy brought about by hunger and lack of exercise; on land they added quarrelling to their miseries. As the men split up into work parties, out of sight of their commander, and able to talk more freely about the causes of their situation, they were easily irked by their irascible Captain, who was obviously proud of having brought everybody so far without loss. Here Fryer's and Bligh's accounts differ sharply on who was to blame and what the rows were about. I think it essential, however, to remember that these were men in a dreadful state of deprivation, that the success, such as it was, of the first leg of their voyage punctured the solidarity that is induced by a constant fear of disaster, and that men who believe they need each other less are likely to resort to gossiping factions. That they were irritable with each other is therefore not surprising. *Bounty*'s open boat voyage would probably have caused mischief among a party of saints, let alone a group of men with little in common and some scores to settle.

There were two work parties, one to search for oysters while the tide was out (the island still produces fine oysters and plentiful supplies of fish within its coral reef today), and the other to see to the boat, a gudgeon of which had come out of the rudder. Fryer, Peckover, Nelson and Cole and four or five others set off to search for food; Bligh and the remainder, presumably including Purcell, the carpenter, saw to the repairs to the rudder. Fryer says that he sent Cole and Peckover back to the boat with a load of oysters and when they returned he asked them how things were with Bligh. They reported that Bligh was in 'a sad passion calling every body' names and 'telling them that if it had not been for him they would not have been there'. This left Bligh open to the obvious debating point that what he said was only too true! Mr Nelson, whom Fryer claimed he 'very seldom heard swear', said: 'Yes damn his blood it is his oeconomy that brought us here' (Narrative, p. 109).

We know that Fryer had been worried seven months earlier, in the dispute over the signing of the expense books, about what Bligh was going to say to the Admiralty about his conduct. His motive in writing his version of the mutiny and the boat voyage was to defend himself against any sullying of his own reputation. His Narrative was written in 1790 after he had read Bligh's published *Narrative* of the mutiny and the boat voyage, and it follows Bligh's account closely. On the whole Fryer says that Bligh's *Narrative* is 'true and just except some few omittances, where Capt. Bligh should have wrote single he should have wrote plural', and he complains that Bligh refused to let him have a rough copy of the Log at Timor. This forced him in his 'own defence' to write his own Narrative, based on the 'the best' his 'memory will allow' (p. 63).

At Restoration Island Fryer observes that Bligh 'did nothing but make a great noise and write his remarks which made every one unhappy about him' and that he spent all day sitting under a tree writing. Hallet, the midshipman, frequently carried him things to eat, and Fryer supposed that Bligh was making sketches of the island and the nearby coast for future navigators, but on questioning Hallet he was told that Bligh was correcting a prayer book. After they sailed they 'had a new prayer night and morning' (pp. 109-11). Bligh and Fryer were now irritating each other beyond the point of reconciliation. Bligh's Log, though not always his published *Narrative*, begins to name Fryer in the context of his criticisms of the conduct of some, though not all, of the crew. It should be noted when judging the two men and their respective charges that there are several instances where Bligh gives credit to individuals without claiming it for himself; for example: 'By the presence of Mind of one of my People he brought away a Copper Pot'; and again: 'and what was still fortunate one of the Men among the few things he had thrown into the Boat and Saved was a piece of Brimstone and a Tinder Box, so that I secured Fire in future' (Log, 29 May 1789).

The first row between Fryer and Bligh was over the recipe for oyster stew. In the above-mentioned copper pot the oysters the men had collected, plus some ship's biscuit and a little pork, were made into a stew. To cook the stew, Bligh had managed to make a small fire, using for this purpose the magnifying glass he 'always carried ... to read of the divisions of my sextants'. Each person received 'a full pint'. He continues: 'In the distribution of it the Voraciousness of some and the moderation of others was very discernable to me. The Master began to be disatisfyed the first, because it was not made into a larger quantity by the addition of Water, and showed a turbulent disposition untill I laid my commands on him to be Silent' (Log, 29 May 1789).

The sun was so severe that Bligh ordered everybody to shade themselves under bushes or a tree and have a 'short repose'. He reports how David Nelson, the botanist, was a source of knowledge as to what plants were edible, and how he discovered some fern roots usable as a means to quench thirst. Bligh warned the men not to eat berries they found without being sure they were not poisoned, but 'they were no sooner away than every one was secretly plucking ... and eating without any reserve'. Some ate too much for their desperate conditions, and became alarmed that the symptoms they felt were the beginning of their deaths; others, who had eaten less, were anxious to watch what was soon to befall them. However, Bligh notes, their 'imprudence' ended well: 'Happily, the Fruit proved wholesome and good.'

That afternoon there was another dispute over food. Oyster stew was again made, and each person this time got a pint and a half. The soft tops of some palm trees were added to the stew, and they had found a nearby source of water (both as a result of Nelson's expertise, acknowledged by Bligh in the Log) to increase the amount. Bligh decided not to add bread to the supper, considering it prudent to save as much as he could of the boat's store for the sea journey to come. This decision 'occasioned some murmuring with the Master and Carpenter [Purcell], the former of whom wanted to prove a propriety of such an Expenditure, and was troublesomely ignorant, tending to create a disorder among those, if any were weak enough to listen to him' (Log, 30 May 1789). Battle was being joined, a foretaste of what was to come when they got safely home and the gossip began.

Their troubles were not over yet. Somebody had been pilfering the pork and they had only two pounds remaining. Bligh states that everybody 'most sacredly denied' he was a thief (to have confessed would have been dangerous in the circumstances). He decided to put the remaining pieces in the stew to move it out of temptation's way. He mentions this incident in his Notebook – the only reference in it to any dissent – suggesting that he felt strongly about 'the Wretch that did it', adding that 'it is a most unhappy situation to be in a Boat among such discontented People who dont know what to be at or what is best for them' (pp. 60-1).

Next morning he organised the men to fill the 60-gallon water barrel and proposed that some should go off and collect more oysters for the sea store. Some of the men openly opposed him, their 'full bellies' making them forget their necessities, while they protested that they were too physically weak to collect oysters. Bligh was also informed – by whom he does not say – that when the men were away from him some complained that they were staying on Restoration Island too long and should be pushing on instead to Timor. Bligh called the men together and gave them the benefit of his opinions of such reprehensible behaviour. 'These unthankful people,' he wrote, 'were no sooner saved from perishing with want and fatigue than they had forgot the mercies they had received' (Log, 30 May 1789). He omitted this incident from the published *Narrative*, no doubt considering it reflected badly on all concerned.

After eating they loaded the boat and pushed off. Soon they saw a large number of aborigines across the bay on the mainland, some of them armed. Prudence dictated that they should not make contact, especially as they could see another large body further back, perhaps ready to swoop down if the Europeans came ashore. Bligh, however, did not stop and sailed up the coast, eventually stopping at another island (he named it Sunday Island) which he considered safe to land upon.

On Sunday Island Bligh had his most serious altercation with Purcell and Fryer, and, regrettably, he lost his head with both of them. We have two accounts of the incident, Bligh's and Fryer's. Bligh's first:

> I now sent two parties out one to the Northward and the other to the Southward to see what could be got, and others I ordered to Stay by the boat. A muttering now began who had done the Most, and some declared they would rather go without their Dinner than go out. In short I found I had but little Command among a few if they had not feared I was yet able to enforce it by more than laying simply my Commands.
> The Carpenter [Purcell] began to be insolent to a high degree, and at last told me with a mutinous aspect he was as good a Man as I was. I did not just now see where this would end, I therefore determined to strike a final blow at it, and either to preserve my Command or die in the attempt, and taking hold of a Cutlass I ordered the Rascal to take hold of another and defend himself, when he called out that I was going to kill him, and began to make concessions. I was now only assisted by Mr. Nelson, and the Master [Fryer] very deliberately called out to the Boatswainn [Cole] to put me under an Arrest, and was stirring up a greater disturbance, when I declared if he interfered when I was in the execution of my duty to preserve Order and regularity, and that in consequence any tumult arose, I would certainly put him to death the first person. This had a proper effect on this Man, and he now assured me that on the Contrary I might rely on him to support my

Orders and directions for the future. This is the outlines of a tumult which lasted about a quarter of an hour. I saw there was no carrying command with any certainty or Order but by power, for some had totally forgot every degree of obedience. I saw no one openly scouting the Offenders altho they were known, and I was told that the Master and Carpenter at the last place were endeavouring to produce altercations and were the principal cause of the murmuring there (Log, 31 May 1789).

From this moment on Bligh determined to keep a cutlass beside him. Of the cause of the incident with Purcell he says nothing. We must be grateful to Fryer who supplies that missing detail; he also helps us to understand something about the factionalism prevalent in the boat.

Fryer, responding to the brief mention in Bligh's *Narrative* that 'one person in particular, went so far as to tell me, with a mutinous look, he was as good a man as myself ' (p. 55), gives his account of the incident so that 'the reader' may 'judge whether this man was mutinous or not' (pp. 111-13). I paraphrase his account only because the version from the Royal United Services Institute collection, which I am quoting from, is so badly punctuated that it is difficult to read in its original form.

Fryer confirms that there were 'murmurings' about 'idlers' in the parties sent to collect oysters, though everybody, idlers included, took a share of the common stew. He reveals that he was the man leading the murmuring! He suggested that in fairness, each man should keep and eat what he himself collected. Now this is a dangerous step for a starving party to take, for it divides them over the sensitive issue of food and, if pursued, reduces them to warring parties (not only between the fit and the less fit, but between the just and the unjust). Each man looking out for himself is contrary to sound survival practice. There is also the precedent of the boat voyage of the survivors of the sinking *Wager*, who abandoned discipline under their commanders for individual survival (the incident is known as the *Wager* mutiny). Once equality under naval discipline is breached the madness of each against all is the end result.

Fryer, the second-in-command, made his suggestion publicly before he disembarked from the boat in the morning. He chose not to take Bligh aside and speak to him privately, thus revealing to everybody his opinions of some of them as idlers. This could do nothing less than spark off a row, and confirms Bligh's criticisms of Fryer's general conduct as a stirrer of trouble during this part of the voyage. Bligh, as commander, and Fryer as his senior officer had a duty to get all the men back to Britain. They had to enforce naval discipline to ensure that everybody shared all burdens, and that those least fit to survive from their share of the pitifully small stocks received what extras were available. (Several times Bligh used the small stock of wine to revive the weakest.)

William Elphinstone, Master's Mate, and a member of Cole's watch, responded to Fryer's remarks angrily. He said he would rather stay in the boat than go after oysters. Apparently he was too sick to undertake the strenuous activity of oyster-gathering. Fryer would have none of it. He was willing to get oysters for a genuinely sick person but 'as every one was as able to go through the fatigue as I was, therefore it stood thus every man should provide for himself'. Fryer states that Bligh agreed with him but modified the proposal sufficiently to maintain some semblance of collective order. He suggested that the men divide themselves into three parties and what they collected should belong to that party. The principle of division was to be that what every man put into the kettle he should take the same quantity out. Fryer agreed to collect a sufficiency for himself and Bligh. Fryer divided the men into the parties and informed Purcell which party he was to join, though it is not clear whether this was Bligh's and Fryer's party or some other. The fact that Purcell was in Fryer's watch and closely associated with Fryer may well have been assumed by Bligh.

The parties set out in search of oysters which were 'found in greater quantity than we did at Restoration Isle'. Purcell was the first man to fill his bag and he set off toward the boat. This demonstrates the real cost of this mode of dividing provisions, for if Purcell had carried on he might have filled two or more bags, thus increasing the supply of food for everybody.

Finishing first, Purcell got back to the boat first, where Bligh was waiting. Fryer was some way behind Purcell and did not witness the altercation with Bligh. He certainly heard 'a great noise in the boat' and made out Bligh 'calling somebody a damn scoundrel' among other things. As he got closer he heard Bligh tell Purcell that if he had not been with the boat 'you would have all perished'. To this Purcell replied, in language and no doubt tones of sarcasm similar to those reported by Fryer when Bligh had berated Cole and Peckover in similar circumstances on Restoration Isle: 'Yes Sir! If it had not been for you we should not have been here.' Bligh reacted angrily to the imputation: 'What's that you say Sir?' To which Purcell replied: 'I sa[id] Sir, if it had not been for you we should not have been here.' 'You damn'd scoundrel, what do you mean?' demanded Bligh. 'I am not a scoundrel, Sir, I am as good a man as you in that respect.'

Now it is obvious that Purcell was goading Bligh. No reasonable reading of this exchange and Fryer's earlier reporting of what Nelson had said on Restoration Island can conclude otherwise. The petty dissent over Bligh's style of management was not private thoughts kept silent over; it was fairly public statements made whenever Fryer and Purcell were away from the boat, as evidenced by somebody (Hallet?) informing Bligh of what some of the men were saying, and identifying Fryer and Purcell as the main culprits. From this point Bligh's and Fryer's accounts converge. Bligh did snatch up a cutlass and went forward in the boat and told the carpenter to pick up another, to which the carpenter said: 'No Sir. You are my officer.'

Fryer meantime had reached the boat. He reports that the scene made him laugh. An action less likely to calm Bligh could hardly be imagined. 'No fighting here, I put you both under arrest,' said Fryer. 'By God, Sir,' responded Bligh, not considering that Fryer was joking as he claimed to be, 'If you offered to touch me I would cut you down!' 'Sir,' said Fryer, 'This is a very wrong time to talk of fighting.' Bligh, pointing at Purcell, said, 'This man told me that he was as good a man as I am.' Purcell said: 'When you called me a scoundrel, I told you I was not, but as good a man as you in this respect, and you said that you had brought us here [and] I told you that had it not been for you we should not have been here.' Purcell's tone had changed and he must have removed the sarcastic imputations ('began to make concessions' according to Bligh) for Bligh responded: 'Well then, if you had not any meaning in what you said I ask your pardon' (indicating that Bligh was sometimes polite).

Fryer says that the quarrel happened in consequence of Bligh ordering Purcell 'to hand his oysters aft', where he and Fryer messed, and Purcell telling him that 'they belonged to his party as agreed before they went out the boat'. This is perfectly possible, though Bligh may have assumed Purcell to have been in Fryer's party for reasons mentioned above.

Later Bligh took Fryer aside and said: 'Mr Fryer, I think that you have behaved very improper … in coming into the boat and saying that you would put us under arrest.' Fryer replied: 'Sir, you will give me leave to tell you how far I think you was wrong – you put yourself on a footing with the carpenter when you took up a cutlass and told him to take another. If he had done so and cut you down it is my opinion that he would have been justified in so doing.' He told Bligh that 'there were other methods in making people do as they were ordered without fighting them'. He added 'that he might be assured I would support him in that as far as it laid in my power' (Fryer, *Narrative*, pp. 113-25).

The altercation with Purcell clearly worried Bligh. He was not sure of the loyalty and sense of discipline of some of the men he was leading and went so far as to list in his Log (31 May 1789) the ten men who gave him 'no uneasyness' and were 'well disposed' to doing their duty: Nelson, Samuel, Hayward, Peckover, Ledward, Elphinstone, Hallet, Cole, Smith and Lebogue. By implication, the remaining men in the boat were 'troublesome': Fryer, Purcell, Lamb (the mutineer who had changed his mind), Tinkler, Hall, Linkletter and Simpson, seven men in all. Interestingly, Cole's watch contained no troublemakers, Peckover's two (Linkletter and Hall) and Fryer's five, including himself – only Ledward in this watch was listed by Bligh as 'well disposed' and he may have been Bligh's source of information about how Fryer and Purcell were stirring dissent (Notebook, p. 10). Fortunately the men 'well disposed' to doing their duty as Bligh interpreted it remained in a majority.

Bligh was anxious to avoid contact with any inhabitants of the area and for this reason preferred to hop along the uninhabited islands off the coast rather than make night camp on the mainland. He also wanted to avoid any aborigines coming off shore in canoes because of his crews' weakened physical condition and lack of arms, other than the cutlasses, and he went to some lengths to avoid advertising the boat party's presence, though since Restoration Island the local inhabitants were aware that strangers were in the vicinity.

It was in consequence of this policy that Fryer got himself into trouble again. The party were camped on a little key at the extremity of an island on 2 June, and to avoid the possibility of any aborigines spotting the camp from a distance Bligh 'cautioned everyone' to keep the camp fire damped down. Peckover and Samuel had been placed in charge of the fire, and Bligh went along the beach to check that the camp fire could not be seen. He had only just satisfied himself of this when 'on a sudden the Key appeared all on a blaze that might have been seen at a more considerable distance. I therefore ran to know the Cause of such an Open Violation of my orders when I found all the Grass set on fire owing to the Master [Fryer] while I was absent insisting on having a fire himself, notwithstanding Mr. Peckover an[d] Samuel had remonstrated with him and told him the Consequence, and he knew [my] very particular orders. This disobedience was of a very serious nature. I might have been seen by more Natives than at the last place as I past the Coast; and now being assured that we were on this Key it only rested with them to come after us and we must inevitably have fallen a sacrifice, for even when all were in health I had only 12 Men that had either the Spirit or resolution to Combat any difficulty' (Log, 2 June 1789). With his last comment on the men able and willing to 'Combat any difficulty', Bligh has written off five men who were unwilling to do so, and these presumably are from the seven men he omitted to list as reliable several days earlier (and presumably he had favourable doubts about two of the seven).

Fryer's version confirms that he had been sleeping, after helping the very sick Mr Nelson back to the camp, and that he had lit a small thicket 'that I might lay warm'. He denies he knew of Bligh's orders (he calls the suggestion that he did know 'like some other mean tricks that Capt. Bligh have committed'), claims that neither Peckover nor Samuel were present, and states that he went to collect material for the fire with Lamb and Hall (two of the men not 'well disposed' to duty in Bligh's view) (Fryer, Narrative, pp. 123-7). Fryer also rejects Bligh's view that the fire, and the noise associated with putting it out, frightened away the turtles that Peckover and Samuel tried to catch later that night. He 'did not recollect any body making a noise' but Bligh.

That same night Robert Lamb was sent bird-catching with two companions but, separating himself from them, he went on a private expedition during which he caught nine noddy birds and ate them raw on the spot. His personal selfishness not only meant nine less portions of food for the boat party – ten of whom were so ill they were unable to leave the camp that night – but in chasing the birds for himself he disturbed the remainder and reduced the catch of the other two men. Lamb, the ex-mutineer who changed his mind, was only taking his lead from Fryer, who favoured a policy of the 'idle' doing without and making it 'every man for himself'. Bligh, however, was furious and reports in his Log (2 June 1789) and his published *Narrative* (1790, p. 61) that he gave Lamb a 'good beating'.

The party left the key at dawn and pushed on northwards along the coast. It was not long before the boat was in the open sea again and Bligh was remarkably pleased with their acceptance of a return to the privations of the boat after their 'rest' along the coast of Australia. 'It seemed as if every one had only embarked with me to proceed to Timor, and were in a Vessel equally calculated for their Safety and convenience' (Log, 4 June 1789). He was also pleased to see that the men had 'so much confidence' for 'whoever had despaired would have been dead before I got to New Holland'. The fact that some of the men grouped around Fryer had no confidence in their commander and were 'murmuring' on occasions was partly a result of their own weaknesses and typical of the small-group madness that occasionally engulfs those pressed close to starvation. Only Bligh's indomitable will, and his inability to accept a doubt as to his moral superiority over those he regarded as 'troublesome wretches', stopped the boat party from disintegrating into a factious band. It was, nevertheless, a close-run thing, and there was more trouble over the horizon.

In the meantime Bligh spent most of his time entering details of the coast they were passing, the currents and the daily positions as well as he could fix them. Peckover's watch, which Bligh had used for navigation, stopped on June 2 and added uncertainty to the timing of daily events. He also wrongly placed Cape York, misled by the table of latitudes he had with him, and this alone caused other errors to creep into his account (in the Notebook he covered himself by writing 'if it is the Cape', p. 73). He remarks several times that he was unsure of certain places, but is evidently proud to note that he called a place Booby Island, on account of the number of birds there, and that Captain Cook had given it the same name. He was able to tell the men that within eight or ten days they should be at Timor.

The men had the usual diet of bread and water plus a portion of a noddy bird, and Nelson, 'who was now so far recovered as to require no other indulgence', received half a glass of wine. The next day he added some oysters to the rations. He also commented on the benefits of their 'rest' on the islands while they were off the coast of Australia:

> With these advantages every one has certainly prolonged his life, and poor as the Supply has been I am very sensible of the great good it has done, and has relieved my mind from many a distressing thought. It would have been about this time that human Nature would have no longer been able to defend itself

against hunger and extreme fatigue, several would have given up Struggling with life that only insured wretchedness and misery, and those possessed of more bodily Strength would on such a Sight soon have followed their miserable and unfortunate companions. Even in our present situation we are reduced to beings horrible to behold. Yet while any fortitude and Spirit remain we drag on, and I hope that the Idea of the End of our Misery being so near at hand will yet enable me to land every one safe at Timor (Log, 4 June 1789).

His next paragraph, or the part of it published in the *Narrative*, apparently enraged Fryer, for it is in reply to it that he made his charge, already alluded to, that Bligh was thieving rations by deliberately letting crumbs drop as he cut up the food: 'For my own part wonderful it is for me to relate, I feel no extreme hunger or thirst. My allowance satisfies me knowing I can have no more.' In writing this last sentence Bligh may have deliberately chosen to touch a nerve, for he mentions elsewhere in the Log that Fryer was one of the men complaining about their allowances. Rising to the hook, Fryer makes a debating point that Bligh did not need to complain if he was getting more than his share.

Bligh finishes off the day's remarks (not included in the *Narrative*) with an observation on the possibility of cannibalism among the boat party. He denies the possibility that they would be driven 'to the necessity of destroying one another for food' as he thought they would all accept 'death through famine' in the same manner that they would accept death from 'any violent disease' (Log, 4 June 1789).

With the return to the open sea, they had to resort to the daily bailing, and two men at a time were ordered to spend what energy they could on this duty. On Friday 5 June 1789, after receiving their rations, which included six oysters each per man, there was murmuring from some of the men who wanted the ration increased. Bligh names them in the Log as Fryer, Purcell, Linkletter and Simpson, and notes that he refused their requests because he was not yet sure exactly how far he had to go to reach Timor nor how fast the boat was travelling.

In the night somebody stole some clams that were being dried for sea stores, but as usual everybody denied he was the thief. There were 'heavy complaints of distress' and Bligh checked the stores of bread again. There was 19 days' supply at the reduced rate he had imposed before landfall off Australia, so he restored the rations from 1/25th to 1/24th of a pound three times a day, or from a tiny morsel to a slightly less tiny morsel (Log, 7 June 1789). They caught a small dolphin on June 9, which gave them three ounces of raw fish each.

The Surgeon, Ledward, and 'an Old Hardy seaman', Lawrence Lebogue, were slipping away fast. The men generally were showing a 'common inclination to Sleep, a Symptom of Nature being almost reduced to its last effort'. The only relief he had was a little wine, which was given to the sick men.

Next day Bligh himself was ill (he thought from the oily part of the stomach of the dolphin) and he considered that half his men were in a worse state than ever. He knew that unless relief came quickly many would succumb. Lawrence Lebogue and Ledward were unlikely to live a week longer if they did not get relief. Of the rest 'An extreme Weakness, Swelled legs, hollow and Ghastly countenances, great propensity to sleep and an apparent debility of Understanding give me melancholoy proofs of an approaching dissolution'. He tried to cheer up Cole, the Boatswain, who in response told Bligh that he looked the worst of all in the boat. This amused Bligh, who returned him a 'better compliment'. He saw his role as rallying those men nearest to giving up, reminding them of how close they were to relief. He told them that his calculations showed that they had only 33 leagues (less than a hundred miles) to go, and the news gave everybody 'a Universal joy and satisfaction' (Log, 11 June 1789). In actual fact he was thirty miles nearer than this because, unknown to him, he had lost a couple of degrees of longitude on the voyage (latitude being easier to find than longitude with the instruments and tables he had with him).

On the 12th they discovered Timor at 3 am, and this provoked 'an excess of joy' among all. 'It is not possible for me to describe the joy that the blessing of seeing the Land diffused among us – indeed, it is scarce within the scope of belief,' wrote Bligh, 'that in 41 days I could be on the Coast of Timor in which time we have run by our Log 3623 miles which on a Medium is 90 Miles a Day' (Log, 12 June 1789). Finding Timor was not an assurance of instant relief. They had to find the Dutch settlement first and nobody in the boat knew where it was on the island. Bligh believed it was on the south-west coast, which was fortuitous, for to look for it along the northern coast would have lost them precious days. That evening they caught a booby bird 'which I reserved for our Dinner,' writes Bligh, 'but I had some difficulty to stop the Masters [Fryer's] muttering because I would not serve it for Breakfast, for this ignorant Man conceived he was instantly to be in the midst of Plenty' (Log, ibid.; this incident is not mentioned in the published *Narrative*, so Fryer was unaware of the criticism). Ledward and Lebogue received a little wine with their rations, but the men remained on the usual allowance.

Another dispute arose between Bligh and Fryer over the course they should take along the coast. Bligh was concerned not to sail past the settlement they were looking for in the dark. Hence he was cautious and preferred to hove to at night. He was also unsure of exactly where they were and knew they could easily get diverted among islands off the coast of Timor. Fryer's obsession was with obtaining food, and as the lack of food induced impatience and irritability, so by now neither man's temper was conducive to peace between them. Bligh was not asking Fryer his opinion on anything, which Fryer naturally resented, and when Bligh mistook an island to the south-west of their course for part of the mainland of Timor, it provided Fryer with another example of Bligh's failings as a seaman. It might just as well be said that Bligh was being cautious, and justly so, for the consequences of error in these matters were too serious for risks to be taken over uncertain geography.

If the high land to the south-west was part of Timor, the boat on a westerly course was steering for the shore and in danger of becoming 'embayed' (trapped in a bay). He considered the weather too hazy to be sure that the high land was separated from the coast, a point flatly contradicted by Fryer: 'the weather was not so hazy but any body might see that this SW high land was larger islands by themselves six or seven leagues distant from Timor' (p. 129). Bligh took his own counsel and put the helm to port to clear the southern tip of the high land, just in case it was Timor. Events proved him wrong. It was an island (Roti) and he had to retrace his track back towards the shore, not however before Fryer had another opportunity to demonstrate to his readers how much more sensible he was than his captain.

Fryer was certain that they were islands from their first sighting. He quotes Peckover in support of his own view – Peckover having seen them when he was with Cook – and he said 'several times' (to whom he does not say) that they were islands. Bligh apparently did not ask his opinion, so he studiously avoided giving it. Some of the 'Gentlemen and people' joined Fryer at the bow of the boat to express their unease that Bligh was taking them 'after all our sufferings' away from Timor, and Fryer assured them that 'there was no danger' because Bligh would soon find out his error. Meanwhile Bligh was in the stern 'in conversation with Messrs Nelson and Peckover, the only two that he made his confidants'. One wonders why Peckover did not give Bligh the benefit of the opinion he offered Fryer.

Fryer's prediction was correct, for Bligh 'at last' asked him what he thought of 'the land ahead': 'Sir,' said Fryer, 'what I first thought it was, islands.' Bligh asked him: 'Why did you not give your opinion before?' 'You must have heard me say, Sir, that they were islands when we first saw them,' replied Fryer, 'but as you did not ask my opinion I did not think it proper to give it.' At this Bligh asked Fryer, as on previous occasions, 'What is best to do now?', and Fryer obliged, of course, with the benefit of his advice, which was to return towards the land.

While the boat made its way back towards the shore, Fryer and Bligh continued their quarrelling as the sea began to run high under the influence of a gale. Bligh, says Fryer, got into a 'great passion', riled by Fryer's saying that he had not been asked his opinion. During this Bligh said: 'Sir, I suppose that you will take the boat from me.' Fryer denied that this was his intention, saying: 'No Sir. I, despise [despite?] your ideas far from my intention to take the boat from you, but Sir give me leave to tell you that life for me is sweeter than it have been yet since I left the ship.' Bligh threatened in reply: 'I am not afraid that you would take the boat from me. I would soon cut you to pieces.' Fryer took this threat as an attempt by Bligh to provoke him to 'say something that he could take hold of – which he had done numbers of times in the course of the voyage' (p. 135).

None of this altercation was mentioned by Bligh in his Logs, nor in his publications, though he does account for his decision to check whether he was in a bay or a passage between an island and Timor. Fryer says that 'there was now as much danger in swamping the boat as any time since we were turned adrift' (p. 137); Bligh logs that there 'were Strong Gales' and 'a high dangerous breaking Sea' (Log, 14 June 1789). He makes no onerous comparisons with previous incidents of dangerous seas. Fryer's implication is that Bligh's not asking him his opinion endangered the boat far more than anything they had previously encountered.

Bligh does, however, refer to another incident that occurred a short while later, and this did appear in the published *Narrative*. Having brought the boat in shore, they could see several parts of the land smoking from fires, which Bligh took to be where natives were clearing the land for cultivation. He could not see any evidence of European occupation and was determined to press on. He remarks in the Notebook (p. 96) that 'every one was solicitous & clamorous to get into to get food, particularly the Master', and expands on this in his Log: 'the Master [Fryer] and Carpenter [Purcell] having been troublesome and asserted I kept them from getting supplies, I gave them leave to quit the Boat but the others who had ever been too obedient to disobey my Orders, I directed to remain, so that finding no One to be of their party they chose to be excused' (13 June 1789).

What Fryer read in the *Narrative* (p. 75) is a paraphrase of the Log entry: 'During the little time we remained here, the master and carpenter very much importuned me to let them go in search of supplies; to which, at length, I assented; but finding no one willing to be of their party, they did not chose to quit the boat.' It is this version that he criticises in his own Narrative. The boat was twenty or thirty yards from the shore and they could see smoke in a nearby valley. As Fryer could not swim, he said to Bligh: 'if those that can swim take the small line on shore I then will go overboard and haul myself on shore.' Purcell offered to join him. But because 'this was not a plan of Mr Bligh's he would not encourage it' (p. 137).

The question is: which version is the truth? Fryer does not deny that he and the carpenter wanted to go ashore – he suggests how this might be done – and seems to restrict his criticism to Bligh 'not encouraging' his proposal. Bearing in mind that Fryer is dependent on what appeared in Bligh's *Narrative* and confines himself to the suggestion that nobody wanted to join his trip ashore, he surely missed an opportunity to clobber Bligh with the far more telling point that not only did he not encourage anybody to join Fryer and Purcell but, according to his own Log, he positively ordered the men not to do so. Given that 'ordering' rather than not 'encouraging' puts Bligh in the worst light as a tyrannical commander, which Bligh admits to in his Log, why did Fryer not expose Bligh's tyranny at this point? It can only be because he believed he only needed to be sarcastic about its not being a plan of Bligh's that prevented the men joining the forage for food on shore. This, in my view, exposes Fryer to partiality in his selection of incidents and his role in them, putting him, of course, on a par with Bligh.

Linking this incident to Fryer's claims that Bligh demanded to know if he was trying to take command of the boat, it is probable that each is quoting different aspects of the same incident. This view is supported by Bligh's entry in his Private Journal (not seen by the Admiralty) where he refers to the incident in a way which echoes the assertion that he was 'not afraid' of Fryer. 'Having given the master a severe reprimand and telling him he would be dangerously troublesome if it was not for his ignorance and want of resolution', he offered him the opportunity of landing (13 June 1789). Thus Fryer reports Bligh's accusation and threat to 'cut him to pieces', which refers to one part of the row, while Bligh quotes his challenge to the men to follow him or Fryer, which refers to its latter part. In short, we have a typical case of two men, both near starvation, in fraught dispute and now bitterly arguing as only the irremediably irritable know how. What their starving, half-dead companions made of their officers rowing in such terms a few feet from where they sat, or more likely slumped, is left to our imagination.

A few hours later, sailing along the coast, they spotted a small settlement, and Cole and Peckover were sent ashore to get information about where the Dutch Governor had his residence. They returned with five 'Malays', one of whom, having been shown 'a parcel of dollars' by Bligh (his clerk, Samuel, obviously got more out of *Bounty* than he let on to the mutineers), agreed to conduct the boat the short distance they were from Coupang harbour (Notebook, 14 June 1789). Double allowance of bread and a little wine was issued to each man that night and again at 4 am.

At daylight on 14 June 1789 the boat entered Coupang harbour. Bligh had made a small union jack out of some signal flags that Cole had brought with him. He had the make-do jack hoisted in the main shrouds as a signal of distress (Bligh's two attempts to get the design right for the union flag are recorded on the last page of the Notebook). Ever a man conscious of protocol, Bligh decided not to land until he was given permission by the Dutch authorities. Fortunately a Dutch soldier invited him to land, which he did immediately, and he fortuitously met with an English sailor from a Dutch ship in the harbour. This man conducted Bligh to Captain Spikerman, who, hearing Bligh's reports of his distress, immediately offered food to his men and went off to report his presence to the Governor.

# 23

# Landfall at Coupang

The Governor, William Van Este, was seriously ill but agreed to see Bligh later that day. Meanwhile Bligh states that he ordered everybody to come ashore (*Narrative*, p. 79) 'which was as much as some of them could do, being scarce able to walk: they, however, got at last to the house, and found tea with bread and butter provided for their breakfast'. He then describes, in a tolerable literary style, the scene of his men coming on shore:

> The abilities of the most eminent Artists perhaps could never have been more brilliantly shone than in a delineation of two Groups of Figures that at this time presented themselves, and where one might be so much at a loss to know which most to admire, whether the Eyes of Famine, sparkling at immediate relief, or their Preservers horror struck at the Spectres of men. For any one to Conceive the picture of such poor Miserable Beings, let him fancy that in his House he is in the moment of giving relief to Eighteen Men whose ghastly countenances, but from the known Cause would be equally liable to affright as demand pity; let him view their limbs full of sores and their Bodies nothing but Skin and Bones habited in Rags, and at last let him conceive he sees the Tears of Joy and gratitude flowing O'er their cheeks at their Benefactors (Log, 14 June 1789).

Probably nothing else Bligh wrote caused such offence to Fryer, for, if what Fryer's claims is true, then Bligh treated him somewhat shamefully, though not without provocation. In effect Bligh used his command to make things uncomfortable for Fryer, not so much by direct order as by the consequences of giving, or not giving, orders which left Fryer to his own devices. There is also, to be fair, more than a touch of self-imposed 'martyrdom' in Fryer's reaction to this treatment.

Fryer claims that he was left in the boat for several hours and was ignored by Bligh even when he came ashore and went to Captain Spikerman's house. Apparently Bligh sent orders to Fryer to send the men ashore but to keep one behind with himself to guard the boat and its contents. Fryer kept John Smith, Bligh's servant (retaliation?). Some tea and cakes were delivered to the boat by a soldier (to whom Fryer spoke in Dutch). Bligh sent orders for the boat's contents to be placed on shore and for the boat to be hauled out to avoid a tidal flow in the harbour. Fryer did this and was left for several hours alone in the boat. He reports that several Dutch people were surprised that he was left in this way and they told Captain Spikerman, who expressed astonishment that Fryer was still with the boat, he too believing that everybody was ashore. Fryer was left to amuse himself, and he spent the time shaving himself and the Dutch soldier who brought him the refreshments. Tellingly, Fryer admits that he 'was determined to stay by the boat till I was ordered away', thus in his anger and indignation making a public show of Bligh's neglect.

The punishment, as such it must be described even if by omission rather than commission, did not end even when Fryer did get ashore and up to Captain Spikerman's house, for, though Bligh spoke to him in a 'friendly' way, he failed to introduce him as an officer to his Dutch hosts. They were surprised to learn that there was another officer besides Bligh in the boat. Bligh had obviously failed to mention Fryer, and Fryer, dressed in Norton's coat and as gaunt as the rest, probably did not look like a person of any rank (he had cut off the buttons of his own coat at Tofoa, where Norton was killed).

Fryer's anger overcame him, and at dinner, instead of eating, he broke down and cried for some time, drank a glass of wine and laid himself down on a sofa. Later he was invited up to the Assistant Governor's house for tea ('which I believe mortified Capt. Bligh very much', p. 157).

The war between them went on. Bligh had been assigned a house which he shared with his men. He says he hired it, which means he was able to claim it as an expense; Fryer denies that it was hired, implying that Bligh cheated the Admiralty. The Governor sent two beds down, one for Bligh, and one, according to what 'a black man' told Fryer, for him. Bligh assigned 'Fryer's' bed to David Nelson, who was very weak, and Fryer objected to Bligh's insult but offered to share the bed with Nelson, which he did. Was Bligh being spiteful to Fryer or humanitarian to his friend Nelson?

Notwithstanding the universal joy that their salvation had occasioned, the old quarrels were never far from the surface. The Dutch asked Bligh for some chalk (what for is not stated) and Bligh told Purcell to deliver the chalk, which he refused point-blank to do on the grounds that it was his own and not naval property! This was extraordinary behaviour from a man so dependent on Dutch hospitality. Without the relief they received at Timor the boat party would have perished unless they could have reached Java. They had only eleven days' allowance left in the boat when they reached Coupang. Purcell's behaviour exasperated Bligh and he sent him to Captain Spikerman's ship for confinement.

All the men were ill for some days after they arrived at Coupang. Bligh had severe headaches and fever. Some of the illness was caused by eating normally on stomachs that were not yet ready to digest too much. All the men had pains in the lower bowels, caused by their not having been able to defecate for several weeks. But recovery was underway once they got rest and gradually increased their intake of food.

When he was fit enough, Bligh made a formal statement to the Dutch authorities regarding the mutiny and the circumstances of his arrival. He provided them with detailed descriptions of the mutineers compiled from the reports of everybody in the boat party. He also used the authority of his Lieutenant's Commission to purchase a small schooner and supplies for the voyage to Batavia, where they expected to get passages home when the next Dutch fleet sailed. He paid for these expenses by signing bills drawn on the Admiralty in London; when these were presented in London, the bearer of the bill would be paid in gold, or by a bill drawn on Amsterdam. Bligh was quite capable of manipulating bills of exchange from his experience as an agent for his wife's uncle. The boat he bought, which he named His Majesty's Schooner *Resource*, cost 1,000 Rix dollars, or about £300.

As the men gradually recovered, the troubles with Fryer and Purcell erupted again in a long series of petty squabbles. To the Dutch this behaviour must have seemed undignified, to say the least. Bligh and Fryer were reduced to communicating with each other by letter. In one such squabble Bligh told Fryer to check on Purcell, who was preparing *Resource* for sea with the help of some Chinese labourers. The work was proceeding too slowly in Bligh's judgment. Fryer told Bligh he was not a carpenter and would not know whether Purcell was slacking or not, and in any case he could not undertake this task without a written order. Bligh wrote: 'This man's insolence and contumacy joined with extreme ignorance is always giving me some trouble. I have no immediate resource but severe reprimands, which bring him to order for a few days when he meanly conducts himself to endeavour to make me forget his bad behaviour. His being the only responsible person next to myself on board, has been the only reason for his not being a prisoner for the greatest part of the voyage' (Private Log, 6 July 1789).

Next day, while Bligh was in the company of the Acting Governor, Mr Wanjon, Fryer's brother-in-law, Robert Tinkler, had a row with William Cole, the Boatswain. Tinkler was impertinent to Cole and was chastised in return. For a young boy to be cheeky to a bo's'n was unusual, but when Fryer intervened, according to Bligh, he told Tinkler to stab Cole with a knife, creating a situation that was bizarre. Cole told Bligh what had happened and Bligh warned Fryer that he was responsible if any violence was committed by Tinkler (Log, 7 July 1789). Having logged the incident, which is excluded from the *Narrative*, Bligh was raising the stakes in the quarrel. The Log was naval property, and in logging anything he made it public as far as the attentions of the Admiralty were concerned.

David Nelson 'imprudently leaving off some Warm Cloathing caught a cold and had an Attack of a Fever' on 8 July, and he died ten days later, the second victim of Christian's mutiny. Bligh was upset at losing this man: 'it bears very heavy on my mind, his duty and integrity went hand in hand, and he had accomplished through great care and dilligence the object he was sent for, always forwarding every plan I had for the good of the Service we were on. He was equally serviceable in my Voyage here in the Course of which he always gave me pleasure by Conducting himself with Resolution and integrity' (18-20 July 1789). The funeral involved the town dignitaries, including the Assistant Governor and an honour party of twelve Dutch soldiers.

Meanwhile Fryer's war with Bligh reached new depths. Fryer and Purcell were staying on board Captain Spikerman's ship and were in close contact with the Captain and his wife, who was a sister of the Governor's wife. They apparently advised the Governor through this social contact to get another signature (Fryer's?) besides Bligh's on the bills he had signed on London. Van Este understood from this that there was some doubt about Bligh's authority to commit the Admiralty to such expenditure. (It was a silly thing for Fryer to do because, if Bligh's line of credit was cancelled, all of them would be stuck in Coupang.) The Assistant Governor, Wanjon, stepped into the debate and offered to provide funds from his own resources on Bligh's signature alone.

What Fryer and Purcell had alleged to their hosts to back their comments is not known, but it is in the murky area of Bligh's financial peccadilloes (the sport of everyone who is on expenses) and Fryer's insubordination that I suspect the two men eventually came to make their peace rather than face each other in a court martial, which would be damaging to both of them. Unknown to Bligh at this moment, Fryer was collecting copies of the prices he was actually paying to the Dutch for supplies and comparing them with the accounts he was obliged to sign as Master. These provided him with ammunition in his final showdown with Bligh at Sourabaya a month later.

From Bligh's Log it is clear that he was not idle at Coupang. Health permitting, he was as inquisitive as ever in finding out what could about the Dutch settlement. The contretemps with Fryer and Purcell tends to overshadow the detailed exploration he undertook during the five weeks they stayed at Coupang, as he rested and recuperated from the boat voyage. The Log is full of descriptions of the local people, their customs and their habits, as well as of the flora and methods of cultivation. These pages on Coupang, along with his descriptions of the then unspoilt society he found in Tahiti in *Bounty*, and its degeneration by the time he returned in *Providence*, making Bligh's journals useful source material for social anthropologists.

Among his other activities he compiled his accounts of the mutiny and the subsequent events of the boat voyage for the Admiralty, his family and Sir Joseph Banks. Perhaps the most moving letter he wrote on the voyage was the one to his wife dated 19 August 1789:

My dear Betsy,

I am now in a part of the world that I never expected, it is however, a place that has afforded me relief and saved my life, and I have the happiness to assure you I am now in perfect health. That the chance of this letter getting to you before others of a later date is so very small I shall only just give you a short account of the cause of my arrival here. What an emotion does my heart & soul feel that I have once more an opportunity of writing to you and my little Angels, and particularly as you have all been so near losing the best of friends – when you would have had no person to have regarded you as I do, and you must have spent the remainder of your days without knowing what was become of me, or what would have been still worse, to have known that I had been starved to Death at Sea or destroyed by Indians, – All these dreadful circumstances I have combatted with success and in the most extraordinary manner that ever happened, never dispairing from the first moment of my disaster but that I should overcome all my difficulties. Know then my own Dear Betsy, I have lost the *Bounty* ... (ML, Bligh Family Correspondence, Safe 1/45).

Convincing his loyal wife of his integrity was one thing: protecting his reputation with the Admiralty was another. He still had to make the journey home for that purpose and had some time to compose his thoughts on how to explain his loss of a King's ship.

Bligh was keen to get away from Coupang before the monsoon rains, and to this end he directed Fryer to take *Resource* out into the roads to be ready to catch the tides. Fryer had to stay on board for a couple of days. But 'by neglect he let the tide fall two feet and that means I am detained,' wrote Bligh (Log, 12 August 1789). Two days later he ordered Fryer to stay with *Resource* and not to come ashore, but Fryer told him boldly: 'When I am commanding officer, I shall come ashore when I please.' The fact that Bligh was recording all these remarks and incidents suggests that he was building a case against Fryer for trial.

In the last few days before he left he was busy drawing up his accounts for settlement, during which he refused to pay a 5 per cent tax imposed on him for the purchase of *Resource*, so this was imposed on the seller. The Governor, Van Este, was near to death, and Bligh spoke warmly of him and of his deputy, Wanjon. Of the latter, especially in view of his personal support during the crisis over Bligh's authority to commit the Admiralty to certain expenditures, Bligh appealed to the Lords Commissioners 'if it may appear to them worthy of their attention' to intercede on Wanjon's behalf with the Dutch government to see that he was promoted to show that his 'Zeal to assist His Majesty's subjects has not been forgot' (Log, 19-20 August 1789).

*Resource* left Coupang on 20 August 1789, with *Bounty*'s boat, and headed for Batavia, the capital of the Dutch East Indies.

# 24

# A Near Mutiny at Sourabaya

*Resource* reached Sourabaya on 12 September 1789. Here Bligh's troubles with Fryer came to a head, and miraculously were hidden in silence. Only in his own Log were any references made to the events that unfolded there: the Log sent to the Admiralty was completely vacant of any hint that Bligh faced what he believed to be another mutiny. In his own Log he records what happened under the title 'Particular Transactions at Sourabaya'. His *Narrative* (1790) has only two innocuous paragraphs about Sourabaya (p. 87), while his *Voyage* (1792), which he edited himself and from which, therefore, he had full knowledge of what he was omitting, devotes two pages to what he describes as 'one of the most pleasant places I ever saw' (pp. 249-50). Pleasant as it was to look at, it was nevertheless the scene of some pretty unpleasant events.

Why he kept quiet about the affair, and why he did not pursue his intention of trying Fryer for 'tumultuous' conduct, i.e. near mutiny, is a matter for speculation. Fryer certainly gives no clue as to why he finally got off, though he has things to say about what happened, and, in the absence of anything positive, lurid speculation, naturally damning to Bligh, has had a free run over the years.

Bligh anchored *Resource* a mile off shore on arrival, as it was too late to send a boat to announce his presence. Next morning three guard boats came out and warned him not to go ashore until he had permission. Apparently this was a precaution employed against all strange vessels approaching Sourabaya, owing to the prevalence of piracy in the area. At 9 o'clock that morning permission to land was sent to *Resource* and Bligh went ashore, where he met the Governor, M. Barkay, and the commandant of the troops, M. de Bose. He was treated with 'great civility and friendship' and advised to remain at Sourabaya until 16 September, when a number of vessels were due to go in convoy to Batavia. Bligh spent the time visiting the countryside, meeting people and, as he did at all places he visited, making descriptive notes of interesting customs, flora and commerce.

In making his farewells to de Bose, who accompanied him to *Resource* in a 'commodious boat' made ready for the purpose, Bligh noted that his

172

own boat had not followed his order to accompany the Dutch boat. It was still roped to the river bank, complete with the 'small bullock, some poultry and vegetables' given to Bligh by the Governor. The boat crew on this occasion consisted of Peckover, Purcell, Elphinstone, Hallet, Hayward and Linkletter. When Hayward chastised them for the delay and threatened to take the boat off without them, according to Bligh's version, 'They abused him and called him a lackay because he would not do as they did'.

Bligh said goodbye to the Commandant and ordered Fryer to weigh anchor. He says that he heard 'some of my people complain that there was someone below that would not work, and upon enquiry I found Wm Elphinstone, mate, and John Hallet, midshipman, ... beastly drunk'. This is probably what delayed the boat crew – most of them officers, because several seamen were too sick – coming off shore, though some evidently could take their liquor better than others. Fryer says that, after Bligh's order to weigh anchor, he called Elphinstone to come on deck, who shouted back that he was too ill to do so. Hallet also claimed that he was not well.

Bligh asked Fryer, as Master, 'what was the cause of his carrying on duty in such a manner and the reason why he did not see these officers on deck'. Fryer replied that he did not know. Bligh was not satisfied. 'Are they drunk or ill, or what is the matter with them?', he asked. To which Fryer replied, not a little sarcastically and in a manner likely to provoke Bligh further: 'Am I a doctor? Ask him what is the matter with them.'

'What do you mean by this insolence?' thundered Bligh. 'It is no insolence,' replied Fryer. 'You not only use me ill, but every man in the vessel, and every man will say the same.'

The men hauling on the cable joined in this public row. 'Yes, by God,' they shouted, 'we are used damned ill, nor have we any right to be used so.' Bearing in mind that this is Bligh's own report of the incident in his own Log, and that he makes no effort to gloss over their charges against him, we can take it that it is an authentic account of what they said. Certainly Fryer does not alter the gist of the men's remarks, and as neither Bligh nor Fryer saw each other's report of the incident we have a clear proof of Bligh's general veracity.

At this point Purcell intervened and 'became spokesman' and 'uttered the above expressions'. This led to 'every body on board' making 'an open tumult', some of them the worse for drink. Bligh faced the open anger of his men once again and was on the receiving end of much abuse and accusations. It could have turned ugly, even though one of their complaints was that they had to pay to bring some vegetables from the house, in which some of them were drinking, to the boat. As on *Bounty*, trivial incidents could turn the heads of bickering men who had spent too long together in too small a space.

Bligh seized a bayonet and ordered Fryer and Purcell below. He called out to the Commandant and the Master Attendant, Mr Bonza, to return to *Resource*, which they did. De Bose told Bligh that he believed he 'had some villains about me who I did not suspect, for that in their way to the shore their coxwain had told them my officers and men had spread a report that I should be hanged or blown from the mouth of a cannon as soon as I got home'. The Commandant told his coxswain to point out who had said such alarming things and he gestured towards everybody, but particularly to Purcell.

Hayward at this point became distraught at the thought that he was being charged with criticism of Bligh. He begged Bligh not to believe that he could be 'guilty of such infamy and ingratitude', even bursting into tears at the thought that Bligh would harbour such suspicions, and declared 'that he never, but when he was obliged, had any conversations with anyone on board, for he believed they had not good principals'. When Bligh assured him that he did not believe he was involved, his 'grief subsided'.

The Commandant was asked to hold an enquiry, and Bligh ordered anybody who had any charges to go ashore with the Dutch so that they could be heard by the Governor. Ledward, Hallet and Cole 'presented themselves and went into the boat'. Curiously these three were included in Bligh's list of people 'well disposed' towards their duty which he had entered in the Log after the incident with Purcell on Sunday Island. What complaints did they have? And why did nobody else join them from among the men engaged in a 'tumult' not minutes before?

Fryer says that Bligh's clerk, Samuel, was ordered to write down what he had said to Bligh about being 'ill used' etc., and further that Bligh announced that anybody who did not sign the statement as being a true account of what he, Fryer, had said would be sent ashore under arrest. Of the two explanations neither is convincing on its own, for Fryer's requires us to believe that Ledward, Hallet and Cole refused to sign a statement setting out what Fryer at no time denied that he had said, and Bligh's requires us to accept that nobody, including Purcell, chose to go ashore and state his complaints to the Dutch officials.

The three men who went ashore had been in the shore party, and at least one of them, Hallet, admitted that he had been drinking. They might have been confused and asserted that they could not sign because they had been below when Fryer had his outburst. But why did everybody else, including men normally associated with Fryer's party, sign the statement? Why did they keep quiet the instant the Dutch officials came on board to find their captain waving a bayonet at his second-in-command and the carpenter? Did they wisely consider it too risky to make complaints about the conduct of His Majesty's officers to foreigners?

Fryer and Purcell were also sent ashore, and Bligh noted that he 'no longer found my honour or person safe among these people'. He wrote to the Governor ('in the name of the King of Britain') requesting that he send Fryer and Purcell, 'under an arrest' for acting 'tumultuously', by separate ship to Batavia, and that the three others be examined so that he could 'prove his honour'. Bligh implies that at this moment he planned to have Fryer and Purcell court-martialled in Britain.

Next day the examination was conducted by the Commandant and the Master Attendant. It took the form of a series of questions put to each prisoner. Their answers were noted and they were required to sign the record of what they said. It appears that the Commandant interviewed the prisoners before the inquiry, and it may be that on the basis of what he heard from them, and perhaps from others, such as the coxswain, he informed Bligh of the likely areas of complaint or allegation. This may explain the wide-ranging questioning of the men, not just about their complaints against him, but also about his role in trying to prevent the mutiny.

Hallet was the first to be questioned by Bligh. His only complaint against his captain was that 'he beat me once at Otahieti' because he failed to get into a boat. He agreed he had received his share of provisions, except a short measure of 'arrack', which was to be made up at Batavia. If he had made any remarks about Bligh being blown up by a cannon for ill-treating everybody, he must have been drunk when he said it. He agreed that Bligh had done his duty, that he was not brutal or severe, that he had taken 'every pains to preserve the ship's company' and that it was not possible for Bligh to have retaken *Bounty* during the mutiny.

Ledward's only complaint was that Bligh had not let him go ashore (he does not say where) until he, Bligh, returned on board. He answered the other questions in exactly the same way as Hallet. Cole followed likewise, saying he 'had no particular complaint against you, God forbid'.

The Commandant and Master Attendant signed the statements and Bligh 'dismissed these wretches and ordered them on board. He did not, however, relent over Fryer and Purcell. But Fryer struck first. He showed the Commandant a paper signed by the late Governor at Coupang, Van Este, giving the prices of provisions and other things 'for which I had made extravagant charges to Government as this paper would prove and that I would be roughly handled for it on my return to England'.

Bligh thought the 'villainy' of Fryer was matched by the 'improper and unwarrantable conduct of Van Este in laying a plot with an inferior officer to entrap his commander'. He exposed the charges as false by showing the Commandant his 'papers, in which there were receipts and vouchers for all my transactions in Timor, signed by the master and boatswain and witnessed by two respectable residanters'. Without the actual accounts we cannot prove this one way or another, nor know how serious the alleged irregularity was. We do know that Bligh and Fryer came to an agreement of some sort, partly evidenced by two letters Bligh received from Fryer which he included in his Log:

Sir, I understand by what the Commandant says that matters can be settled. I wish to make everything agreeable as far as lay in my power, that nothing might happen when we come home. As I have done everything in my power, as far as I know, to do my duty, and would still wish to do it, therefore, if matters can be made up, I beg you will forward it.

Sir, I am, your most obedient humble servant,

Jno Fryer. Septr 16th, 1789

Does this letter hide, in the first two sentences, something that was only too obvious in meaning to Bligh? Was Fryer offering a deal – he would keep quiet about Van Este's price list if Bligh would drop any notion of a court martial?

In reply Bligh refused to see Fryer, claiming he was too busy. So Fryer tried again 'most humbly beg[ging] of you to grant me that favor if possible it can be done' and saying he would 'make every concession that you think proper'. This was a total surrender on Fryer's part, perhaps supplemented by verbal remarks to the Commandant too discreet to put into writing, and it certainly induced Bligh to agree to meet him.

He met Fryer, accompanied by his clerk, Samuel (to write up a formal contract?), the Commandant and the Master Attendant on the day they sailed from Sourabaya, 17 September 1789. Bligh is scathing of Fryer's demeanour: 'like a villain who had done every mischief he could, and going to receive punishment for it, he trembled, look'd pale and humbly asked to be forgiven, declaring he would make every concession and disavowal of the infamous reports that he spread. That he would give every reparation I pleased to ask, but I ordered him away on board the prow, telling him that he was to converse no other way with me but by writing and that all his concessions and disavowals of what he had already asserted must be by letter.'

No letters from Fryer on this subject have been found among Bligh's extensive collections of correspondence. Perhaps Fryer did not write any? Judging by the tone of his *Narrative* (1790), he did not grow to dislike Bligh any the less afterwards. If he did write any formal disavowal, perhaps this was exchanged for the original of Van Este's price list? The most logical time for an exchange to take place was after Bligh's court martial for the loss of *Bounty* in October 1790, during which Fryer stated that he had no complaints against Bligh, and at which Bligh made no attempts to court-martial Fryer, as he did Purcell.

Fryer 'bent' but did not 'break' at Sourabaya; he was made of stronger stuff than Christian. He had told Christian that he did not think an officer's disagreeing with his captain was a reason for mutiny (if it was, the Navy would have been riven with mutinies). He experienced during the awful conditions of the boat voyage much the same torments from Bligh that Christian had suffered from the Tahiti landing to the denouement at Tofoa. Whatever his irritating qualities, Fryer was a different man from the youthful and inexperienced Christian.

Fryer never made his opinions of Bligh known in public, though some of them crept out in his interviews with Christian's brother. His *Narrative* and *Journal* were only circulated privately. Some of Bligh's complaints about Fryer did creep into the public domain – some were in the Log used by Burney to prepare his edition of Bligh's *Narrative* – but the more explicit references, including the 'mutiny' at Sourabaya, were suppressed by Bligh, presumably in his own best interest.

# 25

# Batavia and Home

The party reached Samarang on 22 September 1789 and Batavia, at the east end of Java, on 1 October. Bligh says he was advised, on account of a violent fever which struck him within days of arrival at Batavia, to quit the place as soon as possible, and to this end a passage was assured him and two of his men on a Dutch packet, *Vlydte*, which left on 16 October. The rest of his men, he was assured by the Governor-General, would be embarked on the ships of the main fleet about to leave for Europe (*Narrative*, p. 87). Compared with other places Bligh visited, details of Batavia are sparse in his Journal, which suggests that he was sufficiently out of sorts to curb his insatiable appetite for discovery and observation.

To pay for passages for everybody, and issue them with a month's wages, he sold *Resource* and *Bounty*'s launch (the latter with much regret, for it had served him and his men well since they were cast adrift), realising the dismal price of only 295 Rix dollars, compared with the 1,000 Rix dollars paid at Timor. Bligh was the victim of a 'Dutch' auction: progressively lower prices are called until someone bids; the first to bid is the winner. It may have been some consolation that it was bought by an Englishman, Captain John Eddie, out from Bengal. Bligh does not mention who bought the launch (*Voyage*, pp. 256-7; four replicas have been built in recent years). Once again he refused to pay tax on the transaction, this time as the seller!

Bligh was not the only man ill. Thomas Hall, one of *Bounty*'s cooks, fell ill 'with a flux' and was removed to the local hospital. He died on 11 October 1789. He had not recovered from the boat voyage and was the third victim of Christian's mutiny. The Dutch authorities required affidavits regarding the mutiny, so that they might legally detain any of the mutineers who passed through Dutch territory. All *Bounty* men were publicly examined about the mutiny and the identities of the mutineers. An affidavit was also sworn before the Governor (this, with a translation, is in the Mitchell Library, Sydney, Bligh, Safe 1/43).

Specific instructions were left to Fryer to take charge of the men until their ships left in the next few weeks. He was ordered to pay everyone a month's wages ('to enable them to purchase clothing for their passage to

England'), and to close the victualling account out of the money Bligh raised from selling *Resource*. The men complained about the prices they were being charged by the local traders and Bligh intervened with the officials to get them reduced.

Money was a problem in Batavia, as it was in any port overseas in the early days of the international monetary system. The method adopted of supplying money, or goods, to people whose own money was in a foreign country was for the borrower to give the lender a bill which could be presented for exchange into cash at a subsequent date at the borrower's bank, or government department, from which the borrower was authorised to draw money. As there was likely to be a delay between the lending of the money and the first opportunity the lender had to recover his loan (the borrower might by then be thousands of miles away), the face value of the bill would exceed the money the borrower received. The amount of the difference was the 'discount' referred to by Bligh in his account of Batavia's money situation. He reported that bills on Europe were discounted over 49 per cent by the officials (a borrower writing a £100 bill would receive only £51 in exchange; the person presenting the bill for payment would receive its face value of £100, i.e. in theory a £49 profit), but this discount could be more than halved if they traded their bills privately (a £100 bill would produce £80 in exchange). Bligh notes: 'This discovery, I made somewhat too late to profit by it' (*Voyage*, p. 258).

The bill system worked as follows. Traders would sell the bills they had collected from borrowers to visiting traders, who in turn would present them for payment when they arrived in the countries where the borrower's money was held (or sell them on at a discount to somebody else). Subsequent purchasers required a discount for their trouble, and for their risk; perhaps the borrower had no money, or he was not authorised to commit his government to expenditure; if so, the holder of the bill lost whatever he paid for it, hence lenders dealt only in 'unexceptional Bills' written on well-known and reliable agents. Of course, if you could purchase bills at a large discount, and were certain of cashing them with credit-worthy holders of the borrower's money, you made a profit equal to the discount. Bligh, for instance, traded in some bills in this fashion at the Cape in *Bounty*, and sent them to Campbell, his wife's uncle and his agent, in a ship returning to England. For any he took with him on *Bounty* he would have lost the money he paid, the rule being 'no bill, no payment' (and: 'whoever presents the bill is paid, no questions asked').

The serious deflation in the value of money may have been behind the dispute Bligh had with Ledward over the terms for advancing him money. Ledward wrote to his Uncle: 'There is one thing I must mention which is of consequence; the captain denied me, as well as the rest of the gentlemen who had not agents, any money unless I would give him my power of attorney and also my will, in which I was to bequeath to him all my property, this he called by the name of proper security. This unless I did, I should have got no money, though I showed him a letter of credit from my uncle and offered to give him a bill of exchange upon him. In case of my death I hope this matter will be clearly pointed out to my Relations' (Denman papers, *Notes & Queries*, 1903, 9th series, vol. xii). Ledward's reference to 'the gentlemen who had not agents' indicates the nature of Bligh's apparently harsh, but in those days unexceptional, behaviour in the matter of bills and the lending of money to anybody. Officers had agents who administered their money affairs while they were away on service; their agents disbursed money against any bills they wrote while away, by whomsoever they were presented, collected pay and prize money on their behalf and met their debts if they died in service. This last gave a degree of assurance in the financial affairs of people they dealt with, whether at home or abroad and out of contact. Bligh was not willing to advance money against a bill on Ledward's relative, who might repudiate it, and Bligh would have no recourse, and as Ledward was new in the Navy he had not gone to the expense, or perhaps did not have the time, or yet the financial credibility, to secure an agent before his passage on *Bounty*. His attorney and his will secured the loan, that is all, and 'all my property' may have signified nothing more than that at that time in his young life he did not have any property worth more than the loan.

The seamen were quartered in the country hospital, a building Bligh approved of (he stayed in a house in the grounds) compared to the town hospital, which he thought was too dirty. The officers (Fryer, Cole, Hayward, Hallet) chose to remain in the hotel in town (another building Bligh criticised for dirt and 'lack of attendance').

*Vlydte* sailed on 16 October, with Samuel, the clerk, and Smith, a cook, accompanying Bligh. Typically, Bligh had comments about Dutch standards of navigation (he thought it sloppy) and seamanship (they did not carry enough sail). It is to be hoped that he kept his views to himself and did not behave as if he was on his own quarter-deck.

Before the remaining men got away, Elphinstone and Linkletter died, 'the hardships they had experienced having rendered them unequal to cope with so unhealthy a climate as that of Batavia' (*Voyage*, p. 264). Robert Lamb, the mutineer who changed his mind, died on his passage home, and Ledward was lost when his ship foundered en route to the Cape. It has been suggested that Bligh should have taken Elphinstone and Linkletter with him instead of Samuel and Smith. But this would have been uncharacteristic of Bligh. He had noted how often Elphinstone and Linkletter had joined in the general dissent of Fryer and Purcell during the boat voyage, while Samuel and Smith had remained loyal. On other occasions, particularly during the voyage he made to New South Wales as Governor in 1807, Bligh demonstrated his ability to punish (by neglect or active measures) those who opposed him publicly. In the cases of Elphinstone and Linkletter Bligh showed a streak of vindictiveness; for Samuel and Smith their early voyage home was their reward.

*Vlydte* anchored at Table Bay, Cape of Good Hope, on 16 December 1789. Bligh notes that HMS *Guardian*, commanded by Lieutenant Riou, had sailed from the Cape about eight days earlier on a voyage to the new penal colony in New South Wales with supplies. This was to be an ill-fated voyage, for *Guardian* hit an iceberg, and, in a triumph of endurance and determination, Riou brought the stricken ship back to port in February. By this time Fryer and the remaining *Bounty* people had arrived at the Cape and they assisted with the disembarkation of stores from *Guardian*. Riou, two years later, applied to Bligh for a character reference for Fryer, which Bligh refused to give. On his own voyage in *Providence*, Bligh picked up one of the *Guardian*'s anchors, left at the Cape for any British naval vessel that required a spare.

Bligh spent his time at the Cape preparing and despatching short accounts of *Bounty*'s voyage and the mutiny, plus descriptions of the mutineers. These were sent to Governor Phillips at Sydney and to Lord Cornwallis in India. He also secured permission to leave the Dutch East Indies ship in the Channel instead of going on to the Netherlands. Characteristically he also made his usual observations of the people and locality – a water-colour done by him for his wife still survives in private hands. They sailed from the Cape on 2 January, 1790, arriving off Portsmouth on 14 March, where Bligh and his two companions were put ashore in an Isle of Wight boat, arriving home to the very port from which they had sailed in *Bounty*, just over two years before. Bligh immediately set about salvaging his reputation.

# 26

# A Brittle Triumph

One of Bligh's earliest tasks was to explain his failure to transport the breadfruit to Sir Joseph Banks and the Admiralty. This was crucial, because though his leadership in bringing the survivors to safety at Timor was exceptional, and would please the Admiralty, it did not meet the interests of Sir Joseph Banks that the plants were still in the Pacific instead of in the West Indies. Bligh, therefore, constructed letters to Sir Joseph in which he attempted to look on the brighter side of his failure and, in so doing, to elicit continued support from so powerful a patron. One of these he sent soon after his return:

> It is peculiarly distressing that I am to be the person to inform you of the failure of an expedition in which I had the honor to have your confidence and regard; but Sir I undertook it zealously and I trust you will find I have executed faithfully, securing every object but my return with the wonderful success I had acquired.
>
> If there is any one disposed to look unfavorably on the unhappy circumstance, I see with pleasure it can only be the loss of the Ship; for the intention of the Voyage was completed – Your plants were secured in the highest perfection – every thing in that particular, even more than you could have imagined, and equal to that the world expected from your honoring the expedition with your countenance and direction, and in this rests the greatest satisfaction I am now possessed of.
>
> As an Officer and a Navigator I have ever looked with horror on neglect and Indolence, and I have never yet crossed the Seas without that foresight which is necesary to the well doing of the voyage; but in the present instance I must have been more than a human being to have foreseen what has happened.
>
> It is with a View that you may readily understand the whole of my misfortune that I present to you the following Sheets, where you will find a series of distresses that are not made the most of; but simply a recital of facts as they happened, and which I hope will show you that to the last I never lost that presence of mind, or professional skills, which you have been pleased to allow was the first cause of my being honoured me [sic] with your notice (ML, Safe 1/37).

Bligh's efforts to continue in Banks's favour were successful and Banks was instrumental in getting Bligh appointed to command a second breadfruit expedition in 1791.

Meanwhile, when he was fit enough in July, Bligh did a spot of relief command in HMS *Cumberland*, temporarily without its captain, though he remained posted as commander of *Bounty* until his court martial on 22 October 1790. He also requested that the Admiralty compensate him for the loss of his personal possessions left behind on *Bounty*. His claim came to £283 1s 6d and, like many claims made by officers paid under rigid expenses systems before and since, there is more than a hint of padding. He claimed £47 for his library, 24 guineas for two sextants (proving, incidentally, that he brought one home in the boat as he had three on *Bounty*), £59 for the port, brandy and wine he had bought at Tenerife, and even 18 shillings for a dozen nightcaps. The Admiralty, long-toothed in the expenses game, simply rejected the lot. Bligh was more fortunate in some of his claims for provisions he purchased at Tenerife, the Cape and Coupang; though his attempt to get compensation for his 'purchase' of pork at Tahiti was rejected (the wily victualling clerks no doubt pointing out to the Lords Commissioners that the Tahitians did not live in a monetary society!).

Bligh took time to write up his Log and Journal, with help from his friend from Cook's last voyage, James (later Admiral) Burney, into a best-selling book, given the typical eighteenth-century-style title: *A Narrative of the Mutiny on board His Majesty's Ship Bounty; and the subsequent voyage of part of the crew in the ship's boat from Tofoa, one of the Friendly islands, to Timor, a Dutch settlement in the East Indies, illustrated with charts.* This was published in 88 pages quarto by George Nicol, of Pall Mall, the King's bookseller. In its preface Bligh informs the reader that a more detailed account of the whole voyage would be published later (as it was, as the *Voyage*, in 1792, edited by James Burney). It has been republished several times, sometimes in facsimile.

Two points arise from the 1790 *Narrative*. First, it annoyed Fryer, both for some of the things it said and for what it left out, particularly in respect of him, which led to his compiling his own narrative, quoted above in my account of the boat voyage; secondly, it gives Bligh's first, and lasting, opinion of what caused the mutiny. This issue was of great importance to Bligh, for on it turned his career and public image. As he was manifestly not the harsh disciplinarian flogger of the kind usually regarded as the main cause of a mutiny (such as Captain Pigot of HMS *Hermione*), and as Bligh never accepted that his personal manner – as a foul-mouthed nagger – could provoke anybody to mutiny, he was left with little option but to find an explanation in the character and conduct of the mutineers. He found such an explanation in the charms of Tahitian women: he, Bligh, did not cause the men to mutiny; they mutinied for their own evil and pathetic ends. At least that is how he presented it on p. 9 of the *Narrative*:

It will very naturally be asked, what could be the reason for such a revolt? in answer to which, I can only conjecture that the mutineers had assured themselves of a more happy life amongst the Otaheiteans, than they could possibly have in England; which, joined to some female connections, have most probably been the principal cause of the whole transaction. The women of Otaheite are handsome, mild and chearful in their manners and conversation, possessed of great sensibility, and have sufficient delicacy to make them admired and beloved.

That this aspect might have been instrumental in the motivations of some of the men, either in leading them to mutiny, or in their not being over-zealous in putting the mutiny down, is more than plausible, but it need not have been a motivating factor in Christian's behaviour. That some of the men had female attachments at Tahiti is undisputed (Stewart, Heywood and Morrison, for example), as is the probability that some of the mutineers, while having no particular attachments, may have been seduced by the memory of willing Tahitian women into returning among them undeterrred by the Articles of War. But whether these or similar motivations affected Christian is not so easily settled. True, he did form a relationship with 'Mainmast', whom he called Isabella after his aunt, but that was after his return to Tahiti.

After the mutiny there was no going back for Christian, as there was for Fryer after his outburst at Sourabaya. In the hours leading to his final outburst, it may have occurred to him that there was nothing in Europe for him anyway – he had lost his inheritance, his scholarly ambitions were never to be realised, he was set for a career in the navy and what he knew of the navy (very little, as we have noted) may not have appeared to be all that attractive, especially if his future depended on the likes of Bligh. It was not necessary, therefore, for Christian to be swayed by the prospect of a life of ease in Tahiti, or to be specially attracted to any particular woman, at the moment when he could no longer contain his emotions over his Captain's behaviour towards him. That the stark alternative of criminal exile was not so awful to contemplate once he thought about life in Tahiti – probably after the mutiny – is plausible, especially if he could find land to farm on some isolated island. But conjecture of this kind only has relevance in Christian's case once he had committed the crime of mutiny; it does not need to be relevant before the event, because Christian's mutiny is fully explainable as being occasioned by his inability to take Bligh's tongue lashings. That others were to stumble, though not mutiny (Fryer, for example), over Bligh's occasional behaviour lends support to this hypothesis. Bligh's explanation is no doubt the truth as he saw it; others, including some of the men present at the mutiny, had different views.

Fryer, paraphrasing Bligh's exact words, states specifically that Christian before the mutiny did not have any particular woman at Tahiti (Narrative, p. 49). He wrote this as a direct contradiction of Bligh's explanation (though Bligh, it should be noted, did not ascribe this reason to anybody in particular; he only said that it was 'most probably' the cause of the mutiny and left the implications to the imagination of his readers). Fryer's own explanation of the cause of the mutiny was different from Bligh's. He wrote that 'from what they said I suppose that they did not like their Captain' (p. 51). This fundamental difference between Bligh's public explanation and his Master's was to play a large part in the subsequent unravelling of Bligh's reputation as a commander within the Admiralty.

The Admiralty's view in matters of mutiny was that men who mutinied must be punished (no matter what the provocation, it admitted no excuse for mutiny) and those whose conduct caused mutinies should be employed with care in future. However, for the moment Bligh's version of the cause of the mutiny had the widest circulation, both in public and in the Admiralty. And his explanation was accepted at face value, with the evidence of his success in the boat voyage sufficient proof in itself of his fitness for command. Not only that, for Bligh was able to claim truthfully in the *Narrative* that his overt behaviour in respect of his personal safety on the night of the mutiny indicated that he was innocent of any fears that trouble was threatening. If he had had marines at his cabin door, he muses, perhaps the mutiny might have been prevented, 'for I slept with the door always open, that the officer of the watch might have had access to me on all occasions' (p. 10). This does not, of course, establish that he was innocent of causing the mutiny, only that he had no idea that one was threatening.

As none of the men who were with him in the boat 'had ever observed any circumstance to give them suspicion of what was going on', the mutiny, he asserts, must have been a deeply held secret among its perpetrators. He had, he asserts, a 'mind free from any suspicions', and 'had their mutiny been occasioned by any grievances, either real or imaginary, I must have discovered symptoms of their discontent, which would have put me on my guard; but the case was far otherwise' (p. 11). With this statement, Bligh moves onto contentious ground. He makes no reference to the row over the coconuts, nor to any other rows he had with Christian. Indeed he asserts: 'Christian, in particular, I was on the most friendly terms with; that very day he was engaged to have dined with me; and the preceding night he excused himself from supping with me, on the pretence of being unwell; for which I felt concerned, having no suspicion of his integrity and honour.'

Thus Bligh published his version of events for public consumption. Without contrary views from the other survivors of the boat voyage, it was unchallengable. The relatives of Christian, and the others still 'somewhere in the South Seas', for example, had to accept Bligh's portrayal of the mutineers until, and unless, they heard something different from other witnesses. True, some of the men who returned with

him could have contradicted their Captain, but for one reason or another
they remained silent for a couple of years. And this was Bligh's
vulnerability: only for as long as his version monopolised the concerns of
anybody interested in the mutiny could his reputation remain intact, and
as he had no means of silencing everybody indefinitely his triumph was
brittle.

The loss of a King's ship for any reason occasions a court martial of the
commanding officer (and still does today – the captains of the ships lost in
the 1982 Falklands war were all court-martialled, even though the world
watched the events on TV). The loss of *Bounty* was no exception, and
Bligh's court martial took place on HMS *Royal William* at Spithead on 22
October 1790, under the Presidency of the Hon. Samuel Barrington,
Vice-Admiral of the Blue.

Protocol required Bligh to state whether he had any complaints against
any of his men, present in the court, in respect of the seizure of *Bounty*.
This was Bligh's chance to charge Fryer, whom he had complained
enough about in his Log. He did not do so; hence his compact with Fryer,
agreed in Sourabaya, held good. He may also have been advised to be
circumspect about charges against the Master by his patron, Sir Joseph
Banks, a man Bligh was most anxious to please. There was nothing in
respect of Fryer's behaviour during the mutiny itself that he could charge
him with, except the minor detail of Fryer's neglect to load Bligh's pistols,
a charge which might anyway rebound on Bligh. Purcell, the carpenter,
was less fortunate. Bligh intimated that he had some charges in his case.

Interestingly, each of the men, Purcell included, also swore on oath
that they had no 'objection or complaint' against Lieutenant Bligh. The
reason for their reticence, even if, like Purcell and those of the men who
complained of 'ill-usage' by Bligh at Sourabaya, they might have had
objections or complaints, was understandable. As well as being an inquiry
'into the cause and circumstances of the seizure of His Majesty's armed
vessel, the *Bounty*', this was also a court martial 'to try the officers and
seamen for their share in the affair'. Anything they said was potential
evidence upon which the court would assess the culpability of anybody
who did, or did not, carry out his duty that morning. Any hint of dissent or
complaint against Lieutenant Bligh, in the circumstances of the
inescapable fact that a mutiny had taken place, risked prejudicing the
three vice-admirals, six rear-admirals and three captains of the court
against them. The draconian Articles of War accepted nothing less than
the wholehearted and unquestioning obedience of their commanding
officers. Complaints about Bligh's food regime ('seamen were never happy
unless they could moan'), or his swearing at them ('it's all some of these
lazy rascals understand') would be unlikely to cut much ice with senior
officers, each of whom could probably name a score or more First
Lieutenants given to robust language in dealing with the kind of men
swept into the King's ships by the press gangs. It was in everybody's

interest, and most certainly their own, to maintain the strictest distance from any hint that they, or anybody else, had any complaint whatsoever about their Lieutenant. And so they did: unanimously, Purcell included.

Fryer testified that 'Bligh and the rest' had done everything in their power to recover the ship. He named the men who had arrested Bligh and those who were under arms. He mentioned that Christian had told him to shut up 'for he had been in hell for a week'. The court did not pursue the opportunity to find out if Fryer knew what had upset Christian enough to put him in hell for a week. Nor did the court enquire too deeply into what Midshipmen Hallet and Hayward had been doing immediately before the mutiny. There was no mention of their proclivity to sleep on their watches, especially significant in Hallet's case as he had been midshipman of the watch during the crucial early minutes of Christian's mutiny. Hallet was also a member of Christian's mess (each mess drew its rations and prepared its food together) and he swore that Christian had not been talking to anybody and that there was nothing unusual in his behaviour. Hayward, likewise, did not inform the court that he too had slept in. He gave an account of the events of the mutiny that added nothing to what Bligh told the court in his own accounts deposited at the Admiralty.

The court considered its verdict and speedily decided that Fletcher Christian and others had mutinously seized the ship, and Bligh and his party were acquitted of 'responsibility for her loss'. This enabled all of them to resume their careers in the Navy.

The court also tried Purcell on six charges that Bligh had submitted to the Admiralty on 7 October 1790. These covered the incidents at Adventure Bay, his refusal to take the anti-scurvy medicine, his refusal to produce a grinding stone at Tahiti, his provocation of the duel at Sunday Island, his refusal to give chalk to the Dutch Governor at Coupang and a general charge of disrespect during the voyage. After a short deliberation, the court decided that the charges had been 'in part proven' and he was reprimanded. To have declared them 'proven in full' would have merited more serious punishment, but little effort appears to have been made to secure a full conviction. Perhaps Bligh was advised not to push too hard against Purcell in case his motives were misunderstood.

After the acquittal Bligh was presented to King George III at a levée. The Admiralty responded to the near-hero status of the young Lieutenant, endorsed by the reading public when his *Narrative* was published, by promoting him from Lieutenant to Commander and making him Captain of *Falcon*, a 14-gun sloop. A month later, on 15 December 1790, he was made Post-captain, the most coveted prize sought by any officer, and was formally attached, without command, to HMS *Media*. The three-year qualifying period for this promotion was waived, a mark of his favour inside the Admiralty and the Court at this time.

The Admiralty was bound to react to news of a mutiny in one of its ships, irrespective of who was to blame or what was its cause. By August 1790 it had already appointed Captain Edward Edwards to command HMS *Pandora*, a 24-gun frigate. He was ordered to sail to the Pacific, arrest the mutineers and bring them back for trial. *Pandora* sailed immediately after the verdict of the court martial, and included the newly promoted Lieutenant Hayward among its officers.

Bligh went on half-pay from 8 January 1791. On 16 April 1791 he was appointed Captain of HMS *Providence* and ordered to return to Tahiti and complete his mission of transplanting the breadfruit to the West Indies. To encourage him in his endeavours on their behalf, the House of Assembly in Jamaica voted him a gratuity of 500 guineas, a not inconsiderable amount for a Lieutenant on £70 a year.

# 27

# Squalls on the Second Breadfruit Voyage

Despite the failure of *Bounty*'s mission, Sir Joseph Banks did not give up his object of transplanting the breadfruit from Tahiti to the West Indies. Due to his influence with the King, a second expedition was agreed upon, and if Bligh remained above suspicion he was a strong candidate to be chosen as its commander. He had an inkling of his appointment in February 1791, for he wrote to Lieutenant Francis Godolphin Bond, on the 8th, under the heading 'secret', informing him of this possibility and asking him if he was interested in joining the expedition as First Lieutenant (Mackaness, 1953, p. 15).

This time a great deal more notice was taken of Bligh's views as to what the expedition required. He had discoursed at length on the inadequate provision of *Bounty*, in particular the smallness of the ship, the absence of marines, the thinness of the command structure, the quality of the men sent as petty officers and the delay in the sailing instructions. In response the expedition was given a larger, newly built, 420-ton 98-foot ship, *Providence*, and a smaller 100-ton 51-foot brig, *Assistant*. *Providence* was to have a complement of 100 men, including 20 marines, while *Assistant* had 27, including 4 marines (Log of *Providence*, ML MS A564-2). Bligh was instrumental in selecting the ships, spending from 10 to 23 March 1791, while on half-pay as a Post-captain, examining potential purchases for the Navy. He did not receive his commission to command the expedition until 16 April, and *Providence* was not launched until 23 April 1791.

As before, two botanists were assigned to the expedition, James Wiles and Christopher Smith. A party of marines, commanded by Lieutenant Pearce, joined the ships; discipline was not being treated lightly on this occasion. Nathaniel Portlock was chosen to command *Assistant*. Portlock had sailed with Bligh on Cook's last expedition, being a Master's Mate on *Discovery* and then transferring on Cook's death to *Resolution* as Mate to Bligh. Unlike Bligh, he was promoted Lieutenant in 1780 on the return of the expedition. Like Bligh, who sailed in the merchant service, he was not idle on half-pay after the demobilisation of 1783, and he took a civilian post as commander of *King George* on a voyage to the north-west coast of America in 1785. Hence he knew something of the Pacific, as he did of Bligh.

Bligh's rank as Post-captain, and the size of the expedition, ensured that a quota of commissioned officers were appointed. This deepened the officer structure. Lieutenants Bond, Guthrie and Tobin joined *Providence*, as did a young midshipman, Matthew Flinders, on the recommendation of Peter Heywood's uncle, Captain Pasley. Flinders later became a distinguished chartmaker of the Australian coastline. To complete the lessons of the *Bounty* voyage, Bligh received permission to sail via the Cape of Good Hope to Tahiti rather than endure the distress of the Horn.

This then was Bligh's second attempt to complete a voyage as a commander in the service of his king and country. This time there were no extraneous factors in the ships, the men or the calendar, undermining the prospects for success. He had no excuses for failure; indeed he left Britain with the universal presumption that he would complete the voyage and continue his promising career.

To understand how he fared in this second chance to prove himself, we must consider his relationship with his First Lieutenant, Francis Godolphin Bond. This is particularly important, as Bond served under Bligh in *Providence* in an analogous position to the less experienced Fletcher Christian in *Bounty* (and, to a lesser extent, to that of the more experienced John Fryer in the open boat). Bond's experience, or rather his perceptions of it, are material evidence in our judgment of Bligh as a commander (as they must be of our judgment of Bond as a lieutenant).

Frank Bond was born in Bligh's house, a connection which indicates the extent of their intimacy as an extended family of Bligh-Bonds. He took the name Francis from Bligh's father. In personal correspondence, of which a great deal is preserved, Bligh addresses him as Frank. He was born on 23 January 1765, so that Bligh was eleven years his senior.

Frank Bond followed his uncle into a naval career. His was typically that of a young gentleman. He became a midshipman on 1 July 1779 and served on Bligh's old ship, *Crescent* (twice), as well as on *Dunkirk*, *Rattlesnake*, *Artois*, *Tartan* and *Minerva*. He passed his Lieutenant's examination on 2 May 1782, aged 17 (though claiming to be 21!). One of his referees was a 'Captain Bligh', though not of course William Bligh, who at this time was serving as a lowly Sixth Lieutenant on HMS *Cambridge*; it was another member of the Bligh family. Bond was more fortunate than Bligh, who spent three-and-a-half years on a Lieutenant's half-pay from 1783 to 1787, while Bond, during these years and to 1791, served as a Lieutenant on *Bristol*, *Hound*, *Orion*, *Hyaena* and *Inconstant*. By 1791 he had twelve years' continuous service in the Royal Navy, on twelve ships and under as many captains, against Bligh's fifteen years and nine ships (including *Bounty*). Certainly Bond had far more experience of sea life than Christian, and he no doubt brought with him to *Providence* a not entirely undeserved sense of his extensive experience and personal merit. However, he also came on board as Bligh's nephew, not only as his First Lieutenant, and in neither role was he comfortable.

My account of the voyage is based on Ida Lee, *Captain Bligh's Second Voyage to the South Sea*, 1920; the Log of the *Providence* (PRO Adm. 55/152, 153), George Tobin's Journal (ML Tobin A562) and Lieutenant F.G. Bond's Log (PRO Adm. 55/96). In addition I refer to the Bond materials, collected by George Mackaness in three publications, 1949, 1953 and 1960. These last are crucial evidence for the relationship between Bligh and Bond. Naturally, condensing the entire voyage into a single chapter limits the amount of material we can consider.

Bligh was not entirely convinced that Frank Bond ought to join him on *Providence*. He felt he had to offer his nephew the chance – not to have used his personal interest for a member of his family would have reflected badly on him. For example, on 11 March 1791, when Bligh knew he was to get the *Providence* command, he wrote to Bond in reply to a letter, which, from the context, suggests that Bond had made written application to him for preferment as First Lieutenant:

> I wish you to determine on the propriety of your going, but do not press you to it, for fear you may not get promotion on your return, which is all the advantage you can expect to gain by the Voyage. I however think it is a better chance than any you may get again, and that it appears valuable to many people, as I have numerous applications. You must rest your situation with respect to being first Lieut. to my interest, which I shall exert – if I am not successful, you must consider if you can feel happy as Second, and do not be too sanguine in your expectations. If you have any dislike to the Voyage, don't go, for I have no motive in it but your promotion, and it being in some degree in my power, I feel happy to give you the chance (Mackaness (ed.) *Fresh Light on Bligh*, 1953, pp. 15-16).

In the event Bligh's interest on behalf of Bond was successful, and on 23 April 1791 he joined *Providence* as First Lieutenant. But the moment he stepped on deck as Bligh's second-in-command he ceased to be addressed as Frank by Bligh, or to be treated as a nephew by a kindly uncle. He became one of Bligh's officers, in fact the one closest to the commander in authority.

The change is noticeable in their correspondence during the voyage (Bligh used his earlier forms of address only rarely during the voyage; he resumed them thereafter). Letters from Bligh are addressed to Lieutenant F. G. Bond and begin 'Sir'. They are all peremptory in tone when they deal with the ship's affairs. Bligh appears to have been living at home during much of the fitting out of the expedition, occasionally visiting *Providence*, usually in 'company' (that is, showing distinguished guests around), but generally attending to other affairs. He left Bond in charge and expected him to tackle his responsibilities with attention to detail and promptness. His stream of letters (some small extracts from which follow) remind Bond of what was expected:

'As soon as the Beef and Pork is stowed, send in time for more Water Butts, and other Casks that may be wanted – likewise some wood for stowing the casks, which will be much wanted' (17 May 1791); 'See how Iron Ballast would stow in the bottom of the Short Locker, and what quantity we might put down in the wreckage of the after Hold upon the anchor stock. Get the spirits on board in the most proper casks. Make the boatswain get off all his junk to fill up the buntlings of the casks in the Fore Hold ... Don't enter any but men you like, as Mr Stephens says it will not be right for me to apply to discharge any we dislike. If you want a sextant, let me know, they will cost 12 or 14 pounds, but you need not have one if you do not like observing' (n.d. 1791); 'I shall be glad if you will take off the liquor as they stand filled, rather than lose time and waste in starting and soakage of fresh casks ... Order Mr Impey on board, saying every person is now to attend and that you will expect no one will be absent, as I have given you orders about it ... The Carpenter will have his warrant soon. Let him be sure of having plank and stores enough. Hurry the boatswain on' (n.d); 'Go on with your painting as you can. Is the Magazine secured? Send the Clerk to get from Mr. Larkins a Bill for the Wood had from him ... Send me the Barge at London Bridge by nine o'clock Friday morning' (n.d); 'mind the pumps and the Magazine Passage that I may apply in time, and the Boatswain's canvass' (10 June 1791), (Mackaness, pp. 17-22).

This insight into the relationship is important, for it shows Bligh delegating everything to his First Lieutenant as well as chasing up the details. In this we can note Bligh's style of management: he delegated authority but not his ultimate responsibility for what happened. He did not think it enough for an officer to give an order for something to be done; he regarded it as essential for the officer to check that it had been done. In other words officers should take full responsibility for the actions of those they command, and not hide behind the mere fact that they gave the appropriate orders. He certainly operated this way and expected his officers, Bond included, to behave the same way: command and check. Much of the frustration exhibited by Bligh towards Bond comes down to his perception that Bond did not apply what to Bligh was the only system of management that got things done properly. How Bond saw it we shall see.

The expedition sailed from Spithead on 3 August 1791, almost four years after *Bounty* had sailed on its last voyage. The Log shows that Bligh immediately instituted a regime of management similar to the one he had established on *Bounty*. He put the ship on three watches 'as an encouragement to the People to be alert in the execution of their duty as well as considering it conducive to their health'. Instead of giving the Master, William Nicols, command of a watch, as he had with Fryer, he stated that Nichols should be free of all watches but 'be ready for all calls'. He ordered an officer for each watch to tend a fire to dry out the clothes of the watch, and also required regular cleaning and drying below, activity familiar to anybody reading *Bounty*'s Log.

At Tenerife Bligh became ill (from the effects of the boat voyage), and he remained on the sick list almost until the ships reached the Cape of Good Hope. His illness necessitated a temporary change in command, and provoked Bond's first recorded grievance. Apparently Bond resented Bligh's orders that he should transfer to *Assistant* and that Portlock should take over command of *Providence*. The issue is illustrative of Bond's personality. In his own Log he reports, with a touch of sarcasm, that Bligh ordered him to swap ships with Portlock because he thought that Portlock's attendance on *Providence* was 'necessary for the welfare of the Expedition'. In consequence of not receiving a written order for this change (Bligh was violently ill at the time), Bond decided to keep his journal as if he was still on *Providence* and thereby ignored his command of the brig. He was not happy with this change at all, though by the rules of the service it was unexceptional, as Lieutenant Portlock, not Lieutenant Bond, was second-in-command of the voyage and thus the obvious replacement for Bligh if he was too ill to function as commander.

Bond did manage to visit *Providence* on the way to the Cape and, according to his son, the Rev. F.H. Bond, he 'seized' the opportunity to do so and was 'kindly received by Cap. Bligh' (Mackaness, p. 30). According to his son, Bond was unhappy about his 'secluded life and the loss of his merry messmates' on *Assistant*. This is revealing; it is as if he thought that his role on the voyage was to suit his personal convenience and the company of his 'merry messmates', rather than that he was a naval lieutenant doing his duty 'for the good of the service' in whatever circumstances arose.

Portlock's views of the transfer seem to have been different from Bond's. His own Log records the progress of Bligh's illness towards recovery – to which event he seems to be very sympathetic: 'Capt. Bligh something better but still continues very poorly & weak' (3 September 1791); 'Captain much recover'd and I trust in God in a few days his health will be quite restor'd' (4 September); 'Captain Bligh much better and is daily gaining strength' (6 September) 'Captain Bligh has had a very Indifferent night, but thank God this morning he is much better' (8 September); 'Captain Bligh quite recovered from his late alarming fever' (25 September). By October Bligh was fit enough to resume command, but he kept Portlock with him on *Providence*, leaving Bond to stew in his personal miseries on *Assistant*. Bligh was probably convinced that he was doing his nephew a favour, for command of a ship – any ship – was always excellent evidence in support of promotion for an ambitious Lieutenant.

If Bond returned to *Providence* with regrets at being close to Bligh, now almost recovered, he did not express them at the time. His son wrote some additional comments to extracts he made from his father's Log many years later. Under the presumption that he was influenced by his father's most private opinions, perhaps expressed over several years, these comments have a degree of credibility in showing how Lieutenant Bond regarded his uncle as a commander, but strictly they must still be taken as hearsay. The son's use of his special position as public interpreter of his father's views is seen in his description of how Bond regarded his transfer back to *Providence*. He writes: 'Lieutenant Bond returned to the *Providence* and old discomforts from which the late change had relieved him' (Mackaness, p. 32). Yet Bond himself noted that their arrival at the Cape of Good Hope was for him 'a happy relief', and that when Bligh ordered Portlock and him to resume their proper postings it 'was immediately put into execution to the great satisfaction of both parties'. The father's actual words carry more weight than his son's hearsay, particularly as they directly contradict him.

Frederick Bond's version of his father's opinions of the voyage must be quoted here, for though they must be treated with caution, as shown above, they do have more than an echo of the opinions of others who had sailed with Bligh on *Bounty* (the two quotations are from Bond's notes, the rest of the text consists of summaries made by his son):

Hardly had the voyage commenced when Cap. Bligh's arbitrary disposition and exasperating language began again to render his ship a most unfortunate one for his officers and especially for his First Lieut, who from his position was brought into closer contact with him. Orders of an unusual nature were given with haste and in a manner so uncalled for and so devoid of feeling and tact as to occasion very great irritation. The short exchange with the Assistant was felt at the time quite a relief and his resumption of his duties as First of the Providence was attended with discomfort wh he speaks of as frightful. A dictatorial insistence on trifles, everlasting fault-finding, slights shown in matters of common courtesy, strong and passionate condemnation of little errors of judgment – all these things stung the hearts of his subordinates and worked them up to a state of wrath wh would probably have much surprised Bligh himself had he known it. In spite of the terrible lesson, wh he had already had in the Bounty, he appears by no means to have realised the state of wretchedness to which he reduced his officers. The extant notes show instances of his severity and hauteur. There possibly was error of judgment in a subordinate, but the captain's want of tact and violence of language are evident also. Instances are given of his want of courtesy. At a ceremonial to the Governor of the Cape, Bligh takes the opportunity of snubbing Lieuts Portlock and Bond by presenting them after a junior Lieut, and the Commander of the Assistant last, quite against the rules of etiquette. At Teneriffe he refused to present two of his officers to the Governor, who thereupon boldly corrected the intentional blunder and presented themselves. The Governor, it is added, received them well. Refusals of leave to land, apparently without cause, which annoyed at the Cape, were felt still more strongly at Otaheite, when frequent leave was naturally expected during their 3 months stay. There was a strange jealousy, too, shown of his officers' sketching, making memoranda and forming scientific collections, which could only be attributed to a wish to prevent their after interference with his own desire for publishing. One other point was very trying to Bligh's nephew, the great inconsistency of his conduct. He says that in prosperity Cap. Bligh was all arrogance and insult, despotic insistence without explanation, advice or show of kindness; often an hauteur and distance wh utterly ignored the nephew as well as the rank of his First Lieut. In a time of real danger what a change to cordiality and kindness! The Devil's Hole, for example! ' "Oh, Frank! What a situation; into what a danger I have brought you! God grant that we may get safe out of it." I replied, "No sir, we shall do very well: I don't see that there's any real danger to the ship." ' The event which called for this conversation is not given; but there is a hint that the danger was caused by the helm being put up the wrong way, through mistake. An application to him for leave after intensely hard work on deck continued voluntarily till midnight 'was received in such a manner that I shall think the Grand Turk complacency after this. No thanks – only abuse and insult' (Mackaness, pp. 32-5).

Plainly, Bligh irritated his nephew with his behaviour; as plainly, some of Bond's complaints are trivial, though this does not discount their impact on his mind.

We know that Bligh worked Bond hard in the fitting out of *Providence* and the preparations for the voyage. The constant stream of memoranda on what to do and criticism if it was not done probably surprised his nephew. It is more than likely that the torrents of instructions continued once the ships sailed. Bligh put Bond through what today would be dubbed a 'shake-down cruise', probably the best training he could get, though that is not how Bond perceived his treatment. Perhaps Bond had hoped that a voyage of exploration to the South Seas would be relaxing after his experiences before *Providence* (which included severe injury and permanent disfigurement from an explosion on *Crescent*), and found Bligh's taut regime as discomforting as it was, in his view, unnecessary in a peaceful cruise. But Bligh's main strength as a commander was to prepare for eventualities and to check details; his main weakness was to nag until he got his way, and to nag if he thought his officers were not sufficiently diligent while he got it. The lack of warmth from his uncle hurt Bond as much as his lack of respect for him as a First Lieutenant. Bligh cut corners when he wanted things done his way; he did not abide by the conventions nor the common courtesies, nor, indeed, by the somewhat pompous concepts of 'etiquette', except when he was dealing with people whose rank made them his superiors.

All of this we know about Bligh, having followed him through the *Bounty* mutiny and the boat voyage. He was irascible at the best of times. On *Providence*, in the journey to the Cape, he was also extremely ill. In his Log he often refers to being 'distracted with headache'; 'Head ache all day long'; 'I am never thoroughly clear of the Head Ache, but when these dreadfull fitts seize hold of me I am almost distracted'; 'the pain I suffer when these fits seize me is beyond all description'. There is no doubt that Bligh was very unwell. The ship's surgeon, Edward Harwood, had to write his correspondence. (He also spoke very highly of Bligh on his return to Britain.) Bligh was not really fit enough for this voyage, but his failure to complete the original mission meant that he had to succeed in this one, even if he risked killing himself in the attempt. Bad health plagued him throughout the voyage and he only picked up his old enthusiasm on the last lap home. In his Log we get the impression of a less exuberant, less confident man than the one who set out in *Bounty*. Such a man, distracted by severe headaches, was hardly good company for a First Lieutenant, perhaps a trifle too conscious of protocol and his rank, who considered his duty in *Assistant* an annoying distraction from his 'merry messmates'.

A week before landfall in Table Bay the Log records the first flogging of the voyage. John Letby, Quartermaster, refused orders from Mr Impey (Commander's Mate) and in an altercation knocked down F. Barber, the Boatswain's Mate, for which he was awarded thirty lashes. (There were only twelve floggings in the two-year voyage.)

At the Cape they helped Captain John Hunter, formerly of the *Sirius*, a First Fleet ship, which had sunk off Norfolk Island, near Australia, to bring in a Dutch ship, hired to the New South Wales government, which was in trouble in heavy seas outside the port. Hunter at that time was Deputy Governor of the new colony. Bligh suggested in a letter to Sir Joseph Banks that the British Government should send out some cattle to the colony to help manure the soil; 'until it is done there will be eternal discontent and little returns' (Bligh to Banks, 7 December 1791). He also gave Banks his assessment of Hunter as a deputy governor, saying that he 'is not blessed with a moderate share of good knowledge to give stability to the new settlement'.

While at the Cape, Bligh and Bond had a difference of opinion which is revealed in letters they exchanged. Bligh wrote to Bond:

> I am very sorry to find Boats sent away from the ship so negligently – after a considerable expense of hiring carts to carry wine &c. to the wharf. This is the second time they have come on shore without tackles and necessaries to receive stores. It is the Duty of the Commanding Officer to see that no Boats are sent away from the ship's side without every necessary Tackle and furniture, and particularly when they are receiving things from the shore and sending for water as you have done. It is not sufficient with me that an officer orders, but I insist he sees every thing executed as he shall answer at his peril.

To which Bond replied:

> I have just received a letter from you directed to the Commanding Officer, wherein you complain of his negligence in not sending Tackles &c. in the Boat. The orders I received were to send the Launch for Wine, when the weather became moderate and the Carpenter on shore to repair the Observatory. From the discretional judgement allowed me, I had determined not to risque sending for the Wine, as an accident might happen to a deep-laden Boat, tho it did not blow so hard as to totally preclude a passage from the shore. I conceived the Carpenter's going on shore a piece of necessary duty; and had not given the least intimation to the officer of the Boat of any wine coming on board, as I then thought it an improper time.

> That the Boat would be detained on shore the night, with a fair wind to
> bring her off, I acknowledge was a want of foresight (Mackaness, p. 25;
> Bond's reply is a draft only, whether he sent it to Bligh or not is unclear).

The claim by Bligh that this was the second occasion the boat had been
improperly equipped, and Bond's last sentence acknowledging a 'want of
foresight', sums up their different styles of command.

Just before the ships left Table Bay, Lieutenant George Tobin recorded
in his Journal a comment that might be a coded reference to Bligh as a
commander. It is worth noting here in view of the Bond materials. The
passage is tantalising in its possible double meaning: 'A few passing
squalls had taken us, within board as well as without, but by clewing up
in time, without any serious mischief.' Was he referring not just to the
weather but also to the occasional atmosphere on board when Bligh let
the world know his opinion of some slackness in duty? To 'clew up' means
to haul on a line to shorten sail; this is done quickly when a sudden gust
threatens to split the sails. It may be that jumping to it and correcting
whatever Bligh was annoyed about soon calmed the commander's
temper; being dilatory or defensive about it would certainly have
provoked him further.

Tobin goes on (he is writing his account after the voyage was completed
for his brother):

> For myself, James, I began to feel at home in the charge of a watch, nor
> without considering my appointment to the Providence as a very flattering
> one, particularly as she was the first ship in which I made my debut as a
> commissioned officer. In her commander I had to encounter the quickest
> sailor's eye, guided by a thorough knowledge of every branch of the
> profession necessary on such a voyage. He had been master with the
> persevering Cook in his last voyage in 1776, and as has already been
> noticed, commanded the Bounty, armed ship, when the first attempt was
> made to convey the bread fruit tree to the West Indies. It is easy of belief
> that on first joining a man of such experience my own youth and inferiority
> were rather busy visitors. They were, but we had by this time crossed the
> equinoctal and were about doubling the Cape together and I had courage to
> believe that my Captain was not dissatisfied with me. Of this surely enough
> – even to you (ML, Tobin's Journal).

Tobin was connected with Lord Nelson through Nelson's wife's family.
He appears to have approached his duty in *Providence* from a far more
helpful stance than the more experienced Bond. Nelson regarded him as a
'fine young man' and spoke of 'being exceedingly pleased with him' (Lee,
p. 224). As we shall see, his letter to Bond following Bligh's death in 1817
is probably the most sensible short summary of Bligh's character ever
written by anybody. Tobin was also an accomplished artist and drew or
painted scores of pictures of the voyage (they are held today at the
Mitchell Library under ML PX A565). While Bond accused Bligh of a
'strange jealousy' about his officers' sketching, Tobin got on with making
them.

# 28

# A Hollow Triumph

The ships left Table Bay on 23 December 1791 and headed into the Indian Ocean for the passage to Adventure Bay. The Log shows that Bligh conducted detailed surveys of everything within his reach that might be of value to the Royal Navy, and he continued this work throughout the voyage. This made for a leisurely pace. The ships reached Adventure Bay on 9 February 1792. The wooding and watering parties were sent ashore, and Bligh took the opportunity to explore the area with a little more thoroughness than on his previous two visits. His shore work precluded Bond from shore leave, and, as we know, Bond was very bitter about this (once again his inclinations conflicted with his duty). It was many years before mariners (one of them Matthew Flinders, a midshipman on *Providence*) discovered that Tasmania was not part of the Australian mainland; it was only three months later that D'Entrecasteaux discovered that Adventure Bay was on a small island, itself not part of the island of Tasmania.

The botanists, Wiles and Smith, were employed in collecting information on the area's flora and fauna. Bligh planted some more fruit trees in addition to those he had left when in the bay with *Bounty*. Somewhat rashly he commemorated his efforts with an inscription on a nearby tree which read: 'Near this tree captain William Bligh planted seven fruit trees 1792:– Messrs S. and W., botanists.' When Labillardière visited the site in February 1793 he remarked about 'the despotism which condemned men of science to initials and gave a sea captain a monopoly of fame' (Lee, p. 22). As a naturalist himself he was not entirely objective about seamen (his ship mutinied on the voyage home and was later captured by the Royal Navy).

A few days before the ships sailed a seaman by the name of Bennet went missing. After a thorough search he was found and returned to *Assistant*. Bligh's remarks are revealing: 'It is wonderful to relate that this unhappy creature has determined to Stay behind with a wish to perish & never return to his Native Country. I found that he was of creditable Parents, but had been a disgrace to them, therefore they had recommended him to go this Voyage, as the most elligible either to improve or send him to destruction. I had many of these impertinent or thoughtless recommendations. Our minds were now at ease – the Man was kindly taken care of, and I ordered the Ships to be towed further out of the Bay' (Log of the *Providence*, 20 February 1792). This account shows that Bligh could distinguish between criminal desertion (the three men on *Bounty*, for example) and human folly. Bennet was not flogged.

On 24 February the ships sailed for the southern sweep round New Zealand. Portlock came over from *Assistant* to dine with Bligh, which indicates that relationships had nowhere deteriorated to the extent that they had on *Bounty* at this time.

On 9 April 1791 *Providence* and *Assistant* entered Matavai Bay, Tahiti. They were met by a ship's boat which, it transpired, had come from the wrecked *Matilda*, a small vessel of 460 tons which had originally been a convict transport. It had left Sydney for Peru on 28 December 1791 and had been wrecked on a reef off Muroroa on 25 February 1792. The survivors had returned to Tahiti, where the Captain, Matthew Weatherhead, had got himself a passage in *Jenny*, from Bristol, leaving his crew to their own devices. Three of them had sailed that same day, 31 March, for Sydney in one of the wrecked ship's whaleboats, which says much for their courage and their desperation. It is unlikely that they made it back to Sydney. If they had waited a week they could have secured a passage in *Providence*.

Naturally Bligh was extremely interested in the fate of the mutineers. He had heard nothing of them since 28 April 1789. 'It may readily be believed that I found great satisfaction to hear of these men all being taken by Captain Edwards except two who were killed by the Indians' (Lee, p. 43). He also discovered that 'George Stewart, Thos. McIntosh and Richard Skinner each left a daughter by women here. Thos. Birkitt and John Millward each had a son' (Lee, p. 44). Such information was certain to impress further upon him the correctness of his first supposition that the men had mutinied for what Vancouver called the 'voluptuous gratifications of Otaheite' (Vancouver, 1798, vol. 1, p. 102). He was also convinced that Vancouver's men had been as little restrained as *Bounty*'s, for he reports that the Tahitians blamed them for the epidemic of venereal disease that afflicted their women not long after his men sailed (though it was more probably introduced earlier).

In contrast to Bligh's last visit, only a few canoes came off to welcome *Providence*. Such visits were becoming commonplace, where, with *Bounty*, they were unique. Also, the local people at Matavai were busy with a war over the spoils of the *Matilda*. Only a few of the people Bligh knew were present and he was concerned that the distractions of war would militate against his object of securing the breadfruit trees. Of those who were present 'nothing', he wrote, 'could exceed the joy of these people at seeing me' (Log, 10 April 1792). Otherwise it was as before. The trading post was set up at Point Venus, where preparations were made to receive the breadfruit plants.

Unlike Morrison and his party, Bligh studiously avoided getting involved in the local wars then in progress. He recorded what was going on in his Journal but made no attempt to interfere. Intervention in a local war required a political judgment as to British interests, and this was not a task that was within Bligh's mandate; he endeavoured only to preserve goodwill towards Britain on the part of the local Chiefs. It was the goodwill created by Cook, and later by Bligh, that ensured the physical safety, if not the security of their property, of British seamen shipwrecked near Tahiti. Intervention by Europeans, the *Bounty* men with Morrison in particular, who used firearms, and trained the Tahitians how to use them, contributed to the rapid degeneration of Tahitian society and its population decline.

The arrival of British sailors, in or out of their vessels, was not an unmixed blessing for the Tahitians. Bligh was certainly gloomy, on this his third visit to Tahiti, about the influence of seamen on the manners and customs of the islanders. He wrote: 'Our friends here have benefited little from their intercourse with Europeans. Our country men have taught them such vile expressions as are in the mouth of every Otaheitan, and I declare that I would rather forfeit anything than to have been in the list of ships that have touched here since April, 1789' (Log, 11 April 1792). For one thing, their mode of dress had deteriorated. 'The quantity of old clothes left among these people is considerable; they wear such rags as truly disgust us. It is rare to see a person dressed in a neat piece of cloth which formerly they had in abundance and wore with much elegance. Their general habiliments are now a dirty shirt and an old coat and waistcoat; they are no longer clean Otaheitans, but in appearance a set of ragamuffins with whom it is necessary to observe great caution.' Paradise, apparently, was degenerating into an island slum.

About this time Bligh heard reports that Captain Weatherhead had suffered a loss of money, among his other possessions, when the locals dispossessed him of everything except his shirt. Bligh made several attempts to recover the money, constrained however by a desire not to upset the Tahitians at risk of jeopardising the collection of the breadfruit. In the event Bligh recovered a token amount (172 dollars and three half crowns). He also tried to recover some of his books and papers left behind by (or stolen from) the *Bounty* men. He managed to rescue a few books, among them some he had claimed for from the Admiralty.

He reports what he found out about his former crew, not surprisingly emphasising Christian's unpopularity with the Tahitians (which caused him to leave with his party). His veracity is supported by his remark that he was told that Christian 'openly declared his intentions to look for some land where he could make a settlement and then haul the ship on shore and break her up' (Log, 2 May 1792). A woman, calling herself the wife of McIntosh, and with a 18-month-old child, told Bligh that McIntosh, Coleman, Hillbrant, Norman, Byrne and Ellison 'scarce ever spoke of

[him] without crying'. Ominously he adds that she told him that 'Stewart and Heywood were perfectly satisfied with their situation, and so were the rest of them'.

The acquisition of the breadfruit plants was a minor matter this time, swiftly arranged, not subtly finessed. The Tahitian social structure was declining rapidly; the respectful negotiations with a stable Chief which were carried out on *Bounty*'s visit were not needed this time. Thieves were flogged and put in irons, with less concern for the sensibilities of their rulers. Bligh records the thefts and who the victim was – Lieutenant Bond lost a sheet from his cabin, etc. (no doubt receiving an ear-bashing for his slackness) – and appears to have been more concerned in case a serious incident arose from a sentinel shooting a suspect: 'These people have become so troublesome on dark nights that it requires all our exertions to prevent them taking all we have. I fear some one will be shot for I have been under the necessity to give orders to deter them. One vicious fellow may destroy our plants and cut our ship adrift! Every one knows they must not come near the Post after dark' (Log, 11 June 1792). In another altercation between a seaman and a Tahitian, Bligh heard both sides and decided that the Tahitian was totally in the wrong, so he told the seaman 'to take his own satisfaction', which he did by striking 'a few strong blows'. Characteristically Bligh adds that in general he forbade any 'officer or man to strike a native on any pretence whatever' (Log, 20 May 1792).

What Bligh's relations were with his officers at Tahiti are almost unknowable (we need their perceptions of him, not his of them). However, we can note a singular entry in his Log referring to Lieutenant Portlock. Bligh was ill once again and Portlock took over some observations Bligh was conducting at the time. He wrote: 'I left the rest to be done by Lieutenant Portlock whose alertness and attention to duty makes me at all times think of him with regard and esteem' (Log, 20 June 1792). Now this is praise indeed! It is a rare – too rare, perhaps – recommendation of one of his officers; there is absolutely no chance that Bligh wrote this about Portlock if he did not mean it unreservedly. In judging Bligh's almost wholly negative relations with Christian, Fryer and Bond, we ought to ponder why he got on (or even why he thought it necessary to claim he got on) with the excellent Portlock. This can only be because he found in Portlock the dedication to duty, the minute attention to detail and the obedience to his instructions that set Portlock apart from others who acted as his second-in-command.

On 20 July 1792 the time for departure came, and with 2,634 plants on board (of which 2,126 were breadfruit) the ships left Matavai Bay. They also gave passage to thirteen of the stranded crew of *Matilda*, leaving behind five who expressed a desire to remain in Tahiti (Bligh had to accept their wishes as they were in the merchant service, but he accused them of 'desertion'). A couple of Tahitians came away too, one invited and the other a stowaway. Neither returned to Tahiti.

The description of Bligh's journey across the Pacific is highly technical. His Log and his charts establish his claims to be the European discoverer of hundreds of islands, including many in the Fiji group. *Assistant*, under Portlock, went ahead to guide the much larger *Providence* through the reef-studded seas. His working partnership with Portlock was an outstanding success; their skills blended superbly.

Bond's relationship with Bligh was not blessed with the same degree of warmth as Portlock's. On 27 August 1792 he wrote in his Journal that 'several affairs have lately occurred to prevent the cordiality wh should have existed between my commander and myself, and his remarks tended to deprive me of self confidence. I was, e.g., reproached and threatened because my men in the Fore Tops yard were beaten by Tobin's and Guthrie's, the carpenter was abused for acting on my orders and ordered to take the skippers out; the boatswain similarly treated. The usual etiquette in our respective positions was quite set aside' (Mackaness, 1960, pp. 56-7).

They visited Wytootackee, the last island Bligh discovered in *Bounty*, partly out of curiosity and partly seeking news of *Pandora*. They also kept a sharp eye out for anything that might solve the mystery of La Pérouse. George Watson, Portlock's Master, neglected to inform his captain that he had seen what appeared to be a white studding-sail boom pass the ship one morning. Portlock was sufficiently annoyed at this to record his criticism of Watson in his Log. He thought it might have been evidence of the fate of La Pérouse; they were not to know it, but in 1793 there were some survivors of this expedition on an island about 1,400 miles from *Assistant*.

There were two violent exchanges between the ships and local islanders. The first involved some manned canoes and a boat party commanded by Lieutenant Tobin. Several canoes appeared while Tobin was five miles from *Providence*, exploring near Darnley Island. His signals for assistance were not noticed immediately by *Providence*, though they were seen by Portlock on *Assistant*, nor apparently were they seen by one of the other boats on its way back to *Providence*. When Bligh saw Tobin's signal, he sent Guthrie, the Master, in the pinnace. He could not outsail the canoes and had to decide between rowing on, trusting the islanders' intentions or hoving to and fighting them. Sensibly he continued to row his boat towards the safety of the ships, while preparing his men to repel any aggressive actions from the canoes, now bearing down on him fast. When they drew abreast, one of the men in the leading canoe held up a coconut and gesticulated towards Tobin's men. Tobin declined to accept the coconut while trying to indicate that it should be taken to the ships; but in a 'moment the whole crew were busy about the enclosure furnishing themselves with bows and arrows, which had hitherto been concealed from view'. As they drew to within twenty yards of the stern of Tobin's boat, he decided that 'self preservation prompted me to fire a volley of musketry among them'. The canoes thought better of closing and pulled away towards one of the nearby islands. For Bligh, Tobin's experience was a disappointment: 'This was the most melancholy account I have received,' he wrote. 'All my hopes to have a friendly intercourse with the natives was now lost.'

Eight days later, after some friendly contacts with a different group of islanders, there was another violent exchange, this time involving a ship's gun. Portlock's men were attacked first, 'without the smallest provocation on our part', by islanders firing arrows from a canoe. He ordered his men to fire back, but not before three of his men were struck by arrows. One William Terry, a quartermaster, died on 24 September from his wound, and another did not recover the use of his arm. Portlock made a signal to Bligh who at that instant came under attack from a canoe near his starboard bow. The small-arms fire, and the four-pounder on *Providence*, soon drove the attackers away. Some of the islanders were killed and others were wounded. These waters remained dangerous for Europeans for many years. In 1793, for example, five stranded seamen were killed – their three companions escaping in their open boat and sailing it to Timor. A similar incident occurred as late as May 1814.

The passage from the Pacific to the Indian Ocean took nineteen days. Flinders was to write of this passage: 'Perhaps no space of 3½ [degrees] in length presents more dangers; but, with caution and perseverance, the Captains Bligh and Portlock proved them to be surmountable' (Flinders, 1814, p. xxix). This was Bligh at his best: applying superb seamanship against the elements, and blending his skills with the exceptional Portlock. This prompts the question why he could not do the same with Christian, Fryer and Bond. The only answer must lie in the difference in quality of these men compared with Portlock. In the Torres Strait there had to be a total understanding between Bligh on *Providence* and Portlock on *Assistant*.

A lack of similar standards in *Pandora* led to tragedy, and even in *Providence* the margin of safety was narrow, requiring constant vigilance and nothing left to chance. For instance, Bligh writes: 'I furled all sails and also came to anchor. To my horror when the half cable came out it had the dogstopper on, which although I cut it immediately and let go a second anchor I only had it just in my power to save the ship from the rocks. The men who had done this were no more faulty than the officer who was in command so I did not punish them' (Log, 17 September 1792).

While the safe passage was a triumph for Bligh and Portlock, it was a trying time for the crew. For some weeks there was a scarcity of water. The breadfruit plants needed water and, as they were the object of the expedition, they received priority. This made life difficult for the crew who, tried and stretched by the difficult passage and probably bored by the fastidious navigational work of Bligh the cartographer, went without water while the plants were fed. Even so 224 plants died. According to

Flinders the absence of sufficient water caused discontent and led the thirsty men to lick drops as they fell from the plants. There was not much Bligh could have done about it, except perhaps to hurry along his explorations so as to leave the drought area more quickly. But the discontent did not lead to mutiny! If Bligh had been aware of the discontent he might well have reminded the moaners of how he and his companions had sailed roughly the same track with only a mouthful of water and a morsel of bread a day.

On arrival at Coupang, Bligh was delighted to meet the new Governor, Timotheus Wanjon, who, as the previous Governor's Assistant, had been such a personal help to him when he had arrived in *Bounty*'s boat (and when Fryer caused doubts about his credit). Four of the other Dutch residents whom Bligh had met on his last visit were dead, which is some indication of the inhospitable character of the place (why the Dutch did not move south and colonise 'New Holland' is a wonder; by default it became New South Wales). Wanjon showed some papers to Bligh, including a copy of his original deposition to the Dutch authorities about the mutiny. Unfortunately Wanjon had mislaid Captain Edwards's account of the loss of *Pandora* and the fate of the prisoners. He was able to give Bligh some account of what had happened, but the absence of details was sorely trying.

Bligh took advantage of a ship at Coupang sailing for Batavia to send a letter to his wife which he thought would reach her before he did. In it he reports his 'low nervous disease which I have had more or less since I left Tenariffe'. He also promised her: 'This is the last voyage I will ever make if it pleases God to restore me safe to you.' He added that he hoped 'to live to see you & my Dear little Girls', as if concerned for his health and the dangers of the voyage to come. He also complained about Edwards not leaving him any report about the 'villains'. In his last paragraph we get a glimpse of Bligh as the family man, rather than as a quarter-deck tyrant:

Next June, my Dear Betsy, I hope you will have me home to protect you myself – I love you dearer than ever a Woman was loved – You are, nor have not been a moment out of mind – Every joy and blessing attend you my Life, and bless my Dear Harriet, My Dear Mary, My Dear Betsy, My Dear Fanny & my Dear Ann. I send you all many Kisses on this paper & ever pray to God to bless you – I will not say farewell to you now my Dear Betsy because I am homeward bound – I shall lose no time every happyness attend you my Dearest Life and ever remember me your best of Friends & and most affectionate Husband (ML, Bligh Family Correspondence, Safe 1/45).

They left Coupang on 10 October 1792, having taken on board two buffaloes and a large collection of plants, including some mangoes which Bligh took to the West Indies, where they flourished and are today regarded as a local fruit. Six men reported sick and Bligh regarded the ship's departure as fortuitous. On the voyage across the Indian Ocean, his concerns were divided between the health of the plants and some of his crew. He lost a Marine, Thomas Lickman, on 6 November, from an illness contracted in Timor. The botanists advised him not to put into Madagascar and put the plants at risk. By the time he approached St Helena, in the south Atlantic, another 272 plants had died.

They arrived at St Helena on 17 December 1792 and deposited some of the plants in accordance with his instructions. They remained at St Helena for ten days and then resumed the voyage to the West Indies.

Just before arriving at St Helena Bond wrote a letter to his brother, Thomas, a draft of part of which has survived and is in the National Maritime Museum, Greenwich. George Mackaness considered it 'one of the most illuminating ever written concerning the character of Bligh' (Mackaness, 1953, p. 80). It is also somewhat illuminating of the character of Frank Bond:

Pleased with the expectation of soon anchoring in an English port, I already anticipate the pleasure of sending you the proof of my affection. Indeed, it is no small satisfaction to me when I indulge in the hope of receiving a letter at St. Helena, for I am thoroughly convinced you are aware what a gratification the news of our friends will be to me after a tedious voyage, remote from the busy world, where the mind is only enlivened by the thoughts of future happiness. Among the various scenes of our late navigation, we have tolerably passed our time, – in some dissipations, much novelty, and a little danger. To say a southern voyage is quite delectable is also to say you have every domestic comfort; but on this score I must be silent for at present I mean to say but little of our Major Domo [Bligh]. I assure you that it is no small disappointment to my hopes that I have not gained so much information as expected; – an unsurmountable bar has always lain in my way, since my pride will not allow me to receive magisterial tuition, nor bow with servile flattery. Is it the fashion to begin or end a miscellaneous epistle with our own grievances? It is evident mine commences in that style, but my intention is to have no obstruction in the end; and to go on with my journal ad libitum. Before this enigma is cleared up, let me enjoin the strictest secrecy and insist on your not acquainting even your good wife, my mother, nor my dear sister with the circumstance. (Pray God they are all alive and well.) Yes Tom, our relation had the credit of being a tyrant in his last expedition, where his misfortunes and good fortune have elevated him to a situation he is incapable of supporting with decent modesty. The very high opinion he has of himself makes him hold every one of our profession with contempt, perhaps envy; nay the Navy is but [a] sphere for fops and lubbers to swarm in, without one gem to vie in brilliancy with himself. I dont mean to depretiate his extensive knowledge as a seaman and nautical astronomer, but condemn that want of modesty, in self-estimation. To be less prolix I will inform you that he has treated me (nay all on board) with the insolence and arrogance of a Jacobs: and not withstanding his passion is partly to be attributed to a nervous fever, with which he has been attacked most of the voyage, the chief part of his conduct must have arisen from the fury of an ungovernable temper. Soon after leaving England I wished to receive instruction from this imperious master, until I found he publickly exposed any deficiency on my part in the Nautical Art &c. A series of this conduct determined me to trust to myself, which I hope will in some measure repay me for the trouble of a disagreeable voyage – in itself pleasant, but made otherwise by being worried at every opportunity. His maxims are of that nature that at once pronounce him an enemy to the lovers of Natural Philosophy; for to make use of his own words, 'No person can do the duty of a 1st Lieut. who does more than write the day's work in his publick journal.' This is so inimical to the sentiments I always hope to retain, that I find the utmost difficulty in keeping on tolerable terms with him. The general orders which have been given me are to that purport – I am constantly to keep on my legs from 8 o'th'morning to 12, or noon, altho' I keep the usual watch. The Officer of the morning watch attends to the cleaning of the Decks; yet I am also to be present, not only to get it done, but be even menially active on those, and on all other occasions. He expects me to be acquainted with every transaction on board, notwithstanding he himself will give the necessary orders to the Warrant Officers before I can put it in execution. Every dogma of power and consequence has been taken from the Lieutenants, to establish as he thinks, his own reputation – what imbecility for a post Capn.! The inferior Warrants have had orders from the beginning of the expedition, not to issue the least article to a Lieut. without his orders; so that a cleat, fathom of log line, or indeed a hand swab, must have the commanders sanction. One of the last and most *beneficent* commands was, that the Carpenters Crew should not drive a nail for me without I would first ask his permission – but my heart is filled with the proper materials always to disdain this humiliation. Among many circumstances of envy and jealousy, he used to deride my keeping a private journal and would often ironically say he supposed I meant to publish. My messmates have remarked he never spoke of my possessing one virtue – tho by the bye he has never dared to say I have none. Every officer who has nautical information, a knowledge of natural History, a taste for drawing, or anything to constitute him proper for circumnavigating, becomes odious; for great as he is in his own good opinion, he must have entertained fears some of the ships company meant to submit spurious Narrative to the judgment and perusal of the publick. Among the many misunderstandings that have taken place, that of my *Observing* has given most offence, for since I have not made the least application to him for information on that head, he has at all times found illiberal means of abusing my pursuit; saying at the same time, what I absolutely knew was from him. Tired heartily with my present situation, and even the subject I am treating of, I will conclude it by inserting the most recent and illegal order. Every Officer is expected to deliver in their private Logs ere we anchor at St. Helena. As our expedition has not been on discoveries, should suppose this an arbitrary command, altho the words, *King's request; Good of the Country; Orders of the Admiralty; &c &c &c*, are frequently in his mouth – but unparrelled [sic] pride is the principal ingredient of his composition. The future will determine whether promotion will be the reward of this voyage: I still flatter myself it will notwithstanding what I have said. Consistent with self-respect, I still remain tolerably passive; and if nothing takes place very contrary to my feelings all may end well; but this will totally depend on circumstances; one of which is the secrecy requested on you concerning the tenor of this letter. My time is so effectually taken up by Duty, that to keep the peace I neglect all kind of study; yet the company of a set of well informed Messmates make my moments pass very agreeably, so that I am by no means in purgatory. 13th Decr. – In three days we expect to be at anchor, St. Helena bearing to the N.W., dis. 135 leagues. All hands feel animated at the thought, for we have many circumstances to interest us – the news of our friends, and of our country, the fate of the Bounty's people; and the particulars of the loss of the Pandora, who proceeded us in the Streights of New Holand and Guinea, and was less fortunate than ourselves. But it is high time I should begin my Journal. My letter dated at the Cape of Good Hope informed you of our transactions thus far, but least it should be miscarried I will recapitulate the dates of that part of the Voyage. The 2nd August we left England, and had pleasant w. to Teneriffe, where Captain B. was taken very ill, and from particular *traits* in his conduct believe he was insane at times. By his desire I took command of the Assistant, and Lieut. Portlock came into the Providence. As this gentleman had been twice round the world (the latter voyage commander of 2 fine vessels) and consequently supposed to have more experience, I felt happy that he could make himself easy by the ships being navigated by so able a hand; besides had the death of our commander taken place it was necessary for the good of the expedition before that catastrophe took place that the 2nd in Command should be near to receive every information. [The fragment of the MS ends here abruptly].

Bond's criticism of Bligh bears on his general behaviour: 'imperious', 'want of modesty', 'an ungovernable temper', 'envy and jealousy', and 'unparrelled pride'. This behaviour manifested itself in Bligh's holding everyone else in contempt, denying any praise to others, publicly exposing Bond's alleged deficiencies, expecting him to be too busy with his duty as a First Lieutenant to have time to keep a journal other than his official Log, keeping Bond on duty for the morning watch as well as his regular watch, requiring him to supervise the watch officer in the cleaning of the decks, expecting Bond to be acquainted with every transaction on board, requiring him to ask his captain's permission before giving any orders to the warrant officers, and giving an illegal order to hand his journal over for submission to the Admiralty at the end of the voyage. Whether Bond deserved any or all of these irritations, for such is what they are rather than serious charges of culpable tyranny on Bligh's part, we do not know. We do not know which were the consequences of earlier perceived lapses – a failure to be acquainted with what was being transacted on board leading to Bligh's demanding that Bond check with him (for he certainly made it his business to know such things) before he gave anybody orders, for example. We only have a list of Bond's grievances, which do not amount to much.

That Bond was grossly irritated with his uncle there is no doubting; that he probably understood clearly what had happened to the inexperienced Christian under the pressure of similar treatment is almost certain. But unlike Christian, he had a strong incentive to remain on 'tolerable' terms with Bligh so that at least he could salvage a promotion on Bligh's recommendation in some compensation for his miseries. Whether he really deserved promotion on his performance is another matter.

What does the draft letter (we have no evidence that he posted it at St

Helena) tell us of Bond? For one thing, Bond was a very proud person. Bligh 'never dared to say I have none', referring to his own virtues. He also admits to 'an unsurmountable bar' lying in his way 'since my pride will not allow me to receive magisterial tuition, nor bow with servile flattery'. And he accuses Bligh of 'unparrelled [sic] pride'! When a haughty man is stung to the quick by another haughty man, there is usually an explosion of trouble. But Bligh's 'haughteness' was such that he was unaware of the offence he gave to his proud nephew, and, as we shall see, he went to considerable lengths to get Bond promoted, unaware of what the object of his efforts actually thought of him.

The evidence of one of Bond's messmates, Lieutenant George Tobin, is relevant here, for he too wrote to his brother, though it was in an altogether different tone from Bond's:

> For myself, James, I began to feel at home in the charge of a watch, nor without considering my appointment to the Providence as a very flattering one, particularly as she was the first ship in which I made my debut as a commissioned officer. In her commander [Bligh] I had to encounter the quickest sailor's eye, guided by a thorough knowledge of every branch of the profession necessary on such a voyage ... It is easy of belief that on first joining a man of such experience my own youth and inferiority were rather busy visitors. They were, but we had by this time crossed the equinoctial and were about doubling the Cape together and I had courage to believe that my Captain was not dissatisfied with me' (Mackaness, 1951, p. 239).

And twenty years later Tobin in a letter to Bond, on the occasion of Bligh's death, said remarkably similar things about his first commander, suggesting that his first judgment was unchanged.

The ships anchored at St Vincent on 23 January 1793. They received a civic welcome, and about 500 plants were deposited in the care of the botanical gardens. Bligh was feted as a dignitary and presented with a hundred guineas' worth of plate by the government. They then sailed to Jamaica to deposit the last of the plants, whereupon Bligh received a thousand guineas from the Jamaican government, and Portlock received 500. But despite the congratulations, the breadfruit was never found to be palatable by the slaves and it never fulfilled the purpose intended by the King's advisers, though it took to its new habitat and still thrives there.

The two ships were delayed at Jamaica from 5 February to 15 June by the outbreak of war with France. The local naval commodore refused permission for the ships to leave while his port was so badly defended. Though this prevented an early return home, it did bring with it the prospect of prize money if any French ships were captured. Eventually help arrived and the ships were cleared to sail for Britain. They arrived home on 7 August 1793 and delivered a cargo of plants from the West Indies for Kew Gardens.

Bligh completed his Log with the following entry: 'This voyage has terminated with success, without accident or a moment's separation of the two ships. It gives the first and only satisfactory accounts of the pass between New Guinea and New Holland, if I except some vague accounts of Torres in 1606; other interesting discoveries will be found in it' (Log, 6 September 1793). But the Torres Strait had nothing to contribute either to the war with France or to the development of trade with the East. Well-drawn charts of almost impassable seas off an inhospitable and inaccessible part of the earth thousands of miles from the French were unlikely to excite rapturous applause among men who, in the absence of their author, had formed different opinions of his conduct on *Bounty*. For by the time of his return Bligh was out of favour, both with the Admiralty and with the public. The trial of the mutineers, and the subsequent leaking of gossip about Bligh, had tarnished his reputation. His earlier triumph appeared to be brittle. Even the success of transplanting the breadfruit was regarded as a triumph for Sir Joseph Banks, who had sponsored the expedition, rather than for Bligh.

Significantly, the expected promotions for the officers did not materialise. Tobin wrote to his brother James: 'Save the regret occasioned by quitting our friends and country, we were ful of hope and spirits. Our calculations on the Admiralty, in the event of accomplishing the expedition, were rather sanguine – We calculated erroneously' (ML Journal A562, p. 9). He was realistic enough to describe it as a gamble that did not come off. He explained the reasons for this change in their prospects:

> I fear that the popularity which attended the equipment of the expedition was considerably diminished towards its completion. You are perhaps unacquainted that, about a short twelvemonth previously to our return, a Court Martial had been held on the mutineers of the Bounty. It does not belong to me to judge the necessity of such a measure while Captain Bligh was absent. It was thought proper – and it was not difficult to discover on our arrival that impressions had been received by many in the service, by no means favourable to him. It is hard of belief that this could have extended to the officers of the succeeding voyage – Yet we certainly thought ourselves rather in the 'back ground' – but enough at present of this truly melancholy subject.

A year later, Edward Harwood, Surgeon on *Providence*, wrote to *The Times* in defence of Bligh's reputation:

> Capt. Bligh's general conduct during the late expedition, which was crowned with the most ample success, his affability to his Officers, and humane attention to his men, gained him their high esteem and admiration, and must eventually dissipate any unfavourable opinion, hastily adopted in his absence (16 July 1794).

And according to a report in the less renowned local paper, the *Kent Register*, when *Providence* was finally paid off the scene was 'highly gratifying to observe'. There was 'cordial unanimity amongst the officers', the crew looked 'healthy and and respectable' even after 'so long and perilous a voyage', and, in what was either an act of outright cynicism or a genuine display of good feeling, the entire crew lined up at the dock gates to cheer their Captain as he left them (6 September 1793).

# 29

# Out of Favour and Under Attack

The undermining of Bligh's reputation began during the court martial of the mutineers in September 1792. The decision to recommend a pardon for Heywood and Morrison 'in consideration of various circumstances' was based, in part, on what the members of the court heard informally, and outside the court, from the powerful interest being deployed on Heywood's behalf by Captains Pasley and Bertie.

James Morrison, boatswain's mate, denied implacably that he was involved in Christian's mutiny and, like Heywood, knew that there was no direct evidence to contradict his assertion of loyalty to his captain. There was, however, sufficient evidence to place him in jeopardy over his failure to be demonstrably active in opposing the mutineers – for the Articles of War admitted no haven in neutrality in these matters. Morrison's defence had to be that he was not guilty of support of the mutiny and, further, that he was no more guilty than any other petty officer of failing to exhibit resistance to the armed mutineers. This fitted in with Heywood's defence that he was guilty neither of mutiny nor of failing to resist it because he was kept below on Churchill's orders in respect of the first count and by being kept below, was unable to convey his opposition to Christian to the satisfaction of his captain.

While Heywood's defence was to be stage-managed by his advisors – it included the spreading of a story in the press that he had inherited £30,000 (*The Star*, London, 19 September 1792) and the sanitising of any critical remarks about Bligh's style of command which might prejudice the court against him – Morrison had to contrive his defence out of no more resources than his own capabilities. His literary abilities were his greatest resource, and by using them he made a lasting impression on the court, albeit behind the scenes.

Both Heywood and Morrison had an interest in drawing the attention of the men who composed the court, and those whom they had to influence if an acquittal or pardon was to be achieved, to the one glaring fact of the mutiny: specifically, that nobody, including the officers, made any public attempt to recover the ship in response to any of the exhortations of Bligh to do so while he was held prisoner at the mizzen mast. Fryer, Coleman and Morrison certainly claimed that they were trying at one time or another to form a party to recover the ship, but none of them did anything overtly (though Fryer claims that the discovery of his initial efforts was the cause of his being sent away in the boat). If Morrison could show that the reason why nobody led a counter-mutiny was that everybody was so disaffected by Bligh's behaviour during the voyage that they submitted to the armed minority without demur, he had a plausible enough case to constitute a basis for the 'consideration of various circumstances' in a friendly court. (In view of the relationship between at least one of its members and one of the prisoners, 'friendly' is an apt enough description.)

To this end, while a prisoner on *Hector*, Morrison wrote a 50-page 'Memorandum and Particulars Respecting the Bounty and Her Crew' (ML MS Safe 1/33), for private circulation among people in contact with the officers of the court. It consists of two parts, the first dealing with his charges against Bligh, and the second, a letter, dated 10 October 1792, to the Reverend William Howell, dealing with the conditions under which he and the others were kept by Captain Edwards as prisoners on the voyage home. Apart from any oral evidence given by Heywood and others to their visitors during their confinement on *Hector* as to the circumstances that caused the mutiny – after all it would have been an obvious question for them to be asked by the curious, and for them to disclose if they were not asked – Morrison's Memorandum was the first written evidence to circulate in and around the Navy that contradicted Bligh's version of the causes of the mutiny.

For Morrison and Heywood this was not a matter of satisfying the idle curiosity of history, it was a matter of life or death. They believed they were innocent of mutiny, but they had not been cleared by Bligh in his *Narrative* nor in his reports to the Admiralty. For this omission they faced a death sentence. Fortunately Bligh left the question of their guilt unstated; he wrote nothing directly implicating them in the mutiny, and though it is known that he was convinced, at least by the time he reached Batavia, that Heywood was guilty, apart from stating this in private letters and, probably in oral statements too, having omitted to make specific written charges and being unable by his absence to make oral charges to the Court, his case against Heywood and Morrison rested purely on how the court interpreted their behaviour. From the fact that they were not named among those deserving acquittal, the inference was that they were included among the guilty. It was a slim plank on which to build a case for a favourable verdict – for if Bligh had reported them to be guilty before he left in *Providence* the court's discretion might have been too limited even to secure a pardon.

Heywood, from being a protégé of Bligh's and a guest in his home and the recipient of his wife's hospitality, was mortified by his predicament when he learned that Bligh had not cleared him. It is not plain why Bligh had turned against him – perhaps Bligh's last frenzied visual impression of Heywood was of someone laughing at his torment at the mizzen mast – and Heywood was desperate to have this opinion changed, if changed it could be. He wrote to Mrs Bligh from *Hector* on 14 July 1792, offering first his congratulations on her husband's 'miraculous' survival after being 'deprived' of *Bounty* as a result of 'that unfortunate Mutiny'. 'I hope, ere this,' he continued, 'you have heard the cause of my determination to remain in the ship; which being unknown to Captain Bligh, who, unable to conjecture the reason, did, as I have reason to fear, (I must say naturally) conclude, or rather suspect me to have likewise been a coadjutor in that unhappy affair: but God only knows, how little I merited so unjust a suspicion (if such a suspicion ever entered his breast); but yet my thorough consciousness of not having ever merited it, makes me sometimes flatter myself that he could scarcely be so cruel; and, ere long, let me hope I shall have an equitable tribunal to plead at; before which (through God's assistance) I shall have it in my power to proclaim my innocence, and clear up my long injured character before the world' (Bligh, 1794, p. 14). What effect this letter had on Bligh, let alone on Mrs Bligh, is not known, though by the time Bligh returned in 1793 his condemnation of Heywood was total.

Heywood's reaction to what he regarded as Bligh's 'cruelty', coupled with his own conviction that he was innocent, and Morrison's equally determined, and completely understandable, efforts to avoid hanging for a crime he felt he did not commit, are the keys to the events that led to Bligh's disfavour by the time he returned in *Providence*.

Morrison, unlike Heywood, had no relatives among the captains who formed the court, nor did he have powerful interests working away behind the scenes. He was a talented man, of about 30. Physically he was of sallow complexion, about five feet eight inches tall, with long black hair and of slender build. He had lost the use of the upper joint of his right forefinger and had been wounded in one of his arms with a musket ball. Following others at Tahiti, he had been tattooed with a star under his left breast and with a garter round his left leg, including the motto 'Honi soit qui mal y pense'. Previously, in 1782, he had been a midshipman on HMS *Termagant*, sloop of war, but had not continued with his career as a junior officer. He certainly had the abilities to do so, as the quality of his *Journal* testifies, but he may not have had enough interest to continue as a midshipman and make Lieutenant.

The essential purpose of the Memorandum is to explain why 'the behaviour of the Officers on the Occasion was dastardly beyond description none of them ever making the least attempt to rescue the ship which would have been effected had any attempt been made by one of them … ' (ML MS Safe 1/42, Journal, p. 45). The explanation, in Morrison's view, had to do with Bligh's mode of command in *Bounty*. The means by which Morrison circulated his views among those able to influence the court was through the offices of the 28-year-old Reverend

William Howell, minister of St John's Chapel, Portsea. Howell's ministry brought him in close contact with seafarers at Spithead and his status put him into close touch with men of all ranks at the main naval port of Portsmouth. Armed with copies of the Memorandum, Howell knew which doors to knock on and whom to invite to read Morrison's revelations about the 'true' state of affairs on *Bounty* and the somewhat misleading impression left by Bligh's *Narrative* (1790) and *Voyage* (1792). Given also that Heywood's family were pushing his case, it is more than likely than Morrison's Memorandum was used by them also to penetrate informal channels to the conscience of the Establishment.

Having won themselves Royal pardons for their convictions as mutineers, Morrison and Heywood did not let go their campaign of vengeance on Bligh. Indeed, for a while, their pardons seemed to have led them to travel down the road of publicly exposing Bligh, not just as a bad commander, but as a blatant falsifier of the truth as expressed in his public writings.

Morrison, for example, spent the months after his pardon writing his Journal, a much larger 378-page account of the voyage of the *Bounty*, the aftermath of the mutiny and the customs and culture of Tahiti. While the two publications are often confused, they clearly serve two distinct purposes (which I am quoting from I shall indicate). The Journal was clearly intended for publication. Howell wrote to Captain Molesworth Phillips (none other than the dubious 'hero' of Kealakekua Bay, Hawaii, and the death of Captain Cook) on 25 November 1792 to report progress in Morrison's writings which were to be ready for publication 'in about six or seven weeks'. He assured Phillips, mainly for the comfort of Sir Joseph Banks for whom Phillips was working at this moment, that 'nothing however will be mentioned that may tend to any disturbance or reflect on any characters', i.e. Morrison would not blacken Bligh. This consequence, however, was bound to be the effect of Morrison's publication. Howell had certainly learned enough, from Morrison, Heywood and others, to change his mind about Bligh's character ('there was a time when no one could have an higher opinion of an officer than I had of him – so many circumstances however have arisen up against him attended with such striking marks of veracity That I have been compelled to change that idea of him into one of a very contrary nature') (ML Banks Papers, MS A78-4). Publication was intended for early February 1793.

The Phillips connection brought Morrison's Memorandum to the attention of Banks, who passed it, or a copy of it, to Bligh for his comments on his return in *Providence* (one of Bligh's descendants presented his copy to the Mitchell Library, Sydney). What stopped publication of the Journal? A reading of the Journal (also in the Mitchell Library) does not support Howell's contention that it did not 'tend to any disturbance or reflect on any character'. That may have been Howell's wish and intention when he commissioned Morrison to write it, and he may very well have been disappointed when he saw what Morrison had written, as it clearly conflicts with his own perceptions of how far it was appropriate for a pardoned mutineer to denigrate a serving officer, even one as ill-suited to command as Bligh. Hence Howell may have cancelled the idea of publication. On the other hand, it may have been Sir Joseph Banks who intervened on the basis of what he read in the shorter Memorandum. He may have warned Howell off from considering publication of anything remotely critical of Bligh, especially as Bligh was not in the country at the time.

Events did not conspire so markedly against Heywood's determination to secure public redress for his sufferings as a prisoner. His stage-managed contrition in the court switched to seething indignation once he was released from *Hector* under the King's pardon. In court he had stated in his defence: 'Captain Bligh, in his Narrative, acknowledges, that he had left some friends on board the Bounty; and no part of my conduct could have induced him to believe that I ought not to be reckoned of that number. Indeed, from his attention to, and very kind treatment of me personally, I should have been a monster of depravity to have betrayed him. The idea alone is sufficient to disturb a mind, where humanity and gratitude have, I hope, ever been noticed as its characteristic features' (Bligh, 1794, p. 15).

On his release Heywood travelled to London to the home of Aaron Graham in Great Russell Street. Here he composed a letter to Edward Christian, brother of Fletcher Christian, and Professor of Law at Cambridge:

> Sir, I am sorry to say that I have been informed you were inclined to judge too harshly of your truly unfortunate brother, and to think of him in such a manner, as I am conscious from the knowledge I had of his most worthy disposition and character, (both public and private) he merits not in the slightest degree: therefore, I think it my duty, Sir, to endeavour to undeceive you, and to re-kindle the flame of brotherly love (or pity now) towards him, which I fear the false reports of slander and vile suspicion may have nearly extinguished. Excuse my freedom, Sir: if it would not be disagreeable to you, I will myself have the pleasure of waiting upon you, and endeavour to prove that your brother was not the vile wretch void of all gratitude, which the world had the unkindness to think of him: but, on the contrary, a most worthy character: ruined only by having the misfortune, if it can be so called, of being a young man of strict honour, adorned with every virtue, and beloved by all (except one, whose ill report is his greatest praise) who had the pleasure of his acquaintance' (ML MS A78-4, p. 2; Bligh, 1794).

What a transformation this is from Heywood's public sentiments expressed at his trial! Nothing would have saved him if he had expressed them at the time. Indeed it was somewhat rash of him to commit himself in writing so soon after his pardon. If the letter truly expresses his feelings at the time of the mutiny it puts a new light on his protestations

of youthful innocence, and makes it plausible that he did display support
for Christian. However, I think it more likely that the motivation for
writing this blistering defence of Christian's character ('adorned with
every virtue') and blackening of Bligh's ('whose ill report is his greatest
praise') had everything to do with his anger at coming close to being
hanged as a result of Bligh's 'cruelty' in not clearing him in 1790.

Heywood wrote his letter to Edward Christian on Saturday 5
November 1792. On 20 November the *Cumberland Packet and
Whitehaven Advertiser* carried the following report, including the text of
Heywood's letter:

> The world will be astonished at the information which will shortly be
> communicated by a gentleman who attended the trial as an advocate: the
> public will then be enabled to correct the erroneous opinions, which from a
> false narrative [Bligh's] they have long entertained, and to distinguish
> between audacious and hardened depravity of the heart which no suffering
> can soften and the desperation of an ingenious mind torn and agonised by
> unprovoked and incorrect abuse and disgrace.
>
> Though there can be certain actions, which even the torture of extremity
> of provocation cannot justify, yet a sudden act of frenzy so circumstanced, is
> far removed in reason and mercy from the final deliberate contempt of every
> religious and virtuous sentiment and obligation. For the honour of this
> county we are happy to assure our readers, that one of its natives, Fletcher
> Christian, is not the detestable and horrid monster of wickedness which
> with extreme and perhaps unequalled injustice and barbarity to him and
> his relatives he has long been represented, but a character for whom every
> feeling heart must now fiercely grieve and lament.

The Bligh controversy was now in the public domain. It has remained
there ever since. The immediate impact of the public revelations
broadcast by Edward Christian, and the private revelations circulated by
Morrison, was to create a change in mood, similar to that experienced by
Howell from his direct contact with the prisoners, among the naval
Establishment. It was this change in mood which Tobin sensed and
others experienced. It stung Bligh sufficiently for him to spend the better
part of the 18 months after the *Providence* voyage engaged in controversy
both publicly with Edward Christian and privately with his critics in the
Admiralty.

Before examining exactly what Edward Christian did to publicise the
information he gained from Heywood, Morrison and others, it is
appropriate to review what Morrison wrote about Bligh in his
Memorandum and his larger Journal.

Morrison's charges vary from the trivial to the criminal. The tenor of
his more trivial charges can be seen in the first, and possibly the most
famous, one: that of the missing cheese which occurred a few days after
*Bounty* left Tenerife:

the weather being fine, the cheese was got up to the Air, when on opening the Casks, two Cheeses were declared to be stolen, the Cooper [Henry Hillbrant] affirmed, that the Cask had been opened by Mr. Samuels order, and the Cheese sent to Mr. Bligh's House, while the Ship was in the river. Mr. Bligh without enquiring any farther into the affair, ordered the Allowance of Cheese to be stoped from the Officers & Men, till the deficiency was made good, and at the same time told the Cooper he would give him a damned good flogging, if he heard him say any more.

These orders were punctually obeyed by Mr. Samuel who was both clerk & steward, and on the next serving, Butter only was issued, this the Seamen refused to take, alledging that their acceptance of it would be a tacit confession of the supposed Theft, and John Williams said, that he had carried the Cheese to Mr. Bligh's house, with some other things and a Cask of vinegar which were sent in the Boat (Memorandum, p.7)

The context of Morrison's allegation was that naval regulations required all casks to be opened in public and their contents counted. Deficiencies were recorded in the Log (as indeed can be seen in *Bounty*'s Log throughout the voyage). If men received a short allowance for any reason, they were compensated in their wages on their return. Morrison claims that Hillbrant (the cooper) had already opened this cask on Samuel's orders for the personal benefit of Bligh's household. In case this last seems extraordinary, we must note that for *Bounty*'s voyage, Bligh was to be both Commander and Purser (as he was on *Providence*). Pursers were not popular on any ship: they made their income by reducing victualling costs to a minimum and pocketing the savings. Indeed Bligh, on *Providence*, was assumed by the Admiralty to have made a quarter of his income from the pursery and they docked his pay accordingly (PRO Adm. 1/509 B 165). After much protest he won back 8 shillings a day, which was a precedent emulated by George Vancouver in 1797.

Was Bligh 'playing the rogue'? Sir John Barrow, reviewing this incident in 1831, thought it unlikely that he would place his commission in the hands of his cooper, a clerk and a seaman, for if he was found out it would certainly cost him that. It is possible that several issues are confused: Bligh did divert some cheese to his house – merely the fruits of his pursery – but this was a different cask, or so he believed, and that two cheeses had been stolen, in which case his punishment was unexceptional. This was certainly Bligh's view of the affair when he responded to the request from Sir Joseph Banks for his comments on Morrison's charges: 'Captain Bligh declares,' he wrote, 'that a cask of cheese having signs of geting into a bad state was brought on deck and when opened was found full and counted out. In the interval of dinner time two of the cheeses were stolen. Captain Bligh considered this an audacious theft and could not be committed with knowledge of most of the ship's company – he therefore in preference to charging the value of the cheese against their wages, orderd it to be stopped from each person until

the whole was repaid' (Bligh, Bounty Mutineers, Remarks, ML Safe 1/43).
Whatever the truth about the cheese, the fact that Morrison, Hillbrant,
Williams and, presumably, others believed that Bligh had treated them
unfairly is the only relevant issue in their perceptions of their
commander.

Interestingly, Morrison's complaints about food in both his Memorandum and his Journal are confined to the first leg of *Bounty's* voyage to the
Cape of Good Hope and the last leg from Tahiti to Tofoa. Morrison
complains that as *Bounty* approached the equator, 'Pumpions', which
were beginning to spoil, were issued in lieu of ship's biscuit (bread) in a
ratio of one pound of pumpion to two pounds of bread. When Bligh was
informed of this he 'came up in a violent passion' and dared anybody to
refuse the ration, saying: 'You damn'd Infernal scoundrels, I'll make you
eat Grass or any thing you catch before I have done with you' (Journal,
pp. 3-4). Bligh adamantly denied the implication of this charge. He
asserted that he had logged the fact that in the interests of covering
contingencies he had placed the crew on '2/3 allowance of Bread', and
that, far from imposing an unfair ratio of one for two, he had imposed a
ratio of two for one, the reverse of Morrison's claim, and this only 'to those
who liked' pumpions. He claimed that his actions in regard of the
pumpions 'as the only fruit that would keep', and that of providing two
large drip stones to 'give his People pure water', were 'certainly acts of
kindness, & not oppression' (Bligh, Remarks, p. 43). Again, whatever the
truth – and we might note that Cook flogged two seamen who refused to
eat fruit – it is the perceptions of the men that are important because
Morrison is trying to establish why they became disaffected.

His complaints continue with a claim that the opening of the casks of
meat was not accompanied by the weighing of the pieces as was the
normal custom, which left them suspicious that they were getting short
measures. Fryer told Bligh that he had received complaints to this effect
and Bligh 'ordered all hands aft, and informed them, that every thing
relative to the Provisions, was transacted by his orders, and it was
needless to complain, as they would get no redress and further added,
that he would flog the first severely who should attempt to make any
complaint' (Memorandum, p. 11). If Bligh did threaten anybody who
complained quietly about his food, then he was in breach of Article 21 of
the Articles of War. Bligh's response was vigorous. He told Sir Joseph
that an officer attended the opening of all casks of beef and pork and saw
'the whole weighed out and divided according to Navy Rules' and that this
was done publicly on *Bounty* (Remarks, p. 44). Morrison extended the
source of complaints about their food from the seamen to the officers for
there were 'frequent Murmurings' among the latter 'about the Smallness
of their Allowance'. But because the seamen were intimidated by Bligh's
threats into witholding from making further complaints (Memorandum,
p.11), the officers did likewise 'and did not appear in publick or private to

take any notice of it' (*Journal*, p. 5). Bligh took a contrary view: 'Nothing can mark the Villainy of this Morrison more, than the reason he gives for the People never afterwards complaining, by this at once to shew that the Peoples good behaviour was not a proof of my commanding equitably' (Remarks, p. 45).

Bligh denied that the 'prime pieces' of any cask were taken for the cabin, i.e. Bligh's, table, and said that such a practice was 'forbidden on any pretence whatsoever' (Remarks, p. 45). But because the men believed the contrary, Morrison says the practice drew 'forth heavy curses on the Author of it in private' (Journal, p. 5). Of course, Bligh would not be the only beneficiary of this alleged practice, as he shared his mess with Fryer and Huggan and regularly dined with the other officers during this stage of the voyage.

Bligh was clearly exasperated by the Morrison charges regarding the ship's food. He thought 'these low charges would clearly mark the character of Morrison' and that they were 'convenient at a remote period'. However, he went over the top in claiming that his 'treatment to them was such that songs were made on him extolling his kindess'; I suspect that there may have been a touch of irony in the songs composed by Byrne, the near-blind fiddler, and sung by the men and that, fortunately for all involved, Bligh missed out on the joke.

The disposal of two of the live animals taken on *Bounty* gave Morrison another target to criticise Bligh. A sheep died and Morrison claims it was issued 'in lieu of their Day's allowance of Pork & Pease', but once it was divided the 'most part of it was thrown overboard ... for it was no other than Skin & Bone' (Journal, p. 7). Next month (18 April 1788) a hog was killed and though 'scarce anything else but skin and bone was greedily devoured' in lieu of the daily allowance. Bligh rejected the charges by saying 'it would be extremely vicious in a Captain to put his men at less than full allowance unless from the prospect of being in want of supplies', and whenever this happened on any ship everybody received on their return to Britain 'short allowance money' in lieu of any food they had foregone. He declared to Sir Joseph Banks 'on his honour he never did or could permit his people to eat anything that was improper' (Remarks, p. 46).

Given Bligh's concentration on the health of his men, as recorded in his Log (unless the Log is a complete travesty of the truth), Morrison's charges must have been particularly hurtful, especially when he dismissed the much-heralded 'hot breakfasts' Bligh introduced. These, says Morrison, were so scanty in amount that 'it was no uncommon thing for four Men in a mess to draw lots for the Breakfast, and to divide their bread by the well known method of 'Who shall have this', nor was the Officers a hair behind the Men at it'. Moreover such was the frequency of scanty allowance that it caused fights in the galley. In one dispute somebody broke two of Thomas Hall's ribs and at another time Churchill 'got his Hand Scalded', and to maintain order the master's mate of the watch was sent below to superintend the division of food (Journal, p. 8). Bligh's Log records the cook, Thomas Hall, breaking one of his ribs, but assigns the cause to 'the violent motion of the ship' (Log, 13 April 1788). Otherwise he makes no comment on this charge.

From the Cape of Good Hope onwards, Morrison's charges switch to other, perhaps more serious, matters. He claims that there was false book-keeping by Bligh. The officers, he alleges, had 'been base enough to sign false Survey Books and papers to the prejudice of his Majesty & Government'. He goes on: 'That it may not be supposed, that this account has no foundation the Bills drawn at the Cape of Good Hope, will prove, that Wm. Muspratt and Thos. Hayward, both belonging to the Bounty have signed as respectable merchants of that place' (Memorandum, p. 39). Bligh was furious at this charge: 'Surely if any thing will confute this assertion, & show this Morrison, (who was the worst of the Mutineers next to Christian & Churchill, if not their adviser,) in the light he ought to be held, it is this – Musprat & Hayward signed only as witnesses in C. Bligh's behalf that He payed the Money to Mr C. Brandt due to him on an account with capt. Bligh to prevent by any accident his calling on Capt. Bligh for a second payment – These Papers are now to be seen at the Publick Boards' (Remarks, p. 52).

That Bligh did business with Brandt is known from a letter he wrote to Duncan Campbell announcing that he had made 'a little Cash' by buying an endorsed bill from Brandt for presentation to the victualling board for 1236 Rix dollars (ML Bligh Correspondence, 28 June 1788, MS Safe 1.40). What Bligh was doing was buying a bill from Brandt at a discount and making a small profit on presenting this to London. A British ship must have received victuals from Brandt and signed a bill in lieu of a cash payment; by selling the bill for cash to Bligh, Brandt got paid, albeit at a discount, and Bligh received the full amount from the victualling board when it was presented to them by Campbell. This bill system (see above) was essential if the Navy was to ensure that its ships should be able to acquire necessary supplies in distant ports without having to carry substantial amounts of cash with them. People like Bligh, who speculated in endorsed bills, were a respectable (and essential) part of the system.

Fortunately for Bligh, in view of the fate of *Bounty*, he sent the bill to Campbell from the Cape and in the course of making his profit left the evidence of his probity at the victualling office. His bills were available for inspection by whosoever was concerned that Bligh had behaved to the prejudice of 'his Majesty and government'. I think this disposes of Morrison's charges in this specific case, and casts doubt on some of the others. Interestingly, Morrison did not repeat this charge when he came to write his Journal.

Morrison's allegations continue with a claim that some of the men were ill with scurvy just before landfall at Tahiti. Bligh told Banks: 'Captain Bligh never had a symptom of scurvy on any ship he commanded.' He stood by his measures to combat scurvy – food, exercise and cleanliness – which he recorded in his Log.

He returns to the subject of food with a complaint that Bligh confiscated all pigs coming on board *Bounty* at Tahiti and issued them to the men as their allowance at a rate of 'one pound pr man pr Day' (Journal, p. 19). This is hardly a serious charge. The official market for pigs, administered by Peckover, slackened according to Morrison, which presumably means that demand outstripped supply. To ensure equitable distribution, Bligh instituted a policy of requisition to ensure that all shared in whatever was available. His motives were hardly tyrannical. They were, however, futile, as any study of administered markets shows – people find ways round rules that inconvenience them. The Tahitians created ingenious schemes to get pork to their friends and in doing so outwitted the vigilant Bligh (Journal, p. 20). That Bligh was right in his intentions is beside the point; the fact that the men believed him to be working against their personal interests (collective interests are less cherished in the main) fuelled their disenchantment with their captain.

Morrison concludes his Memorandum with a candid explanation for the failure of the majority on board to resist the mutiny:

> It will no doubt be wondered at, that a Ship with 44 Men on board, should be taken by so small a Number as 10 or 11 which were the whole that ever appeared in Arms; on that Day 10 muskets, 2 cutlasses and 2 Pistols were all that appeared to have been in use, when the Boat put off – But no resistance was made. It will be asked why? It may be answered, that the Officers were not on such good terms with their Commander, as to risk their Lives in his service, and the Service of their Country was not in their hearts (Memorandum, pp. 37-8).

His Memorandum was dedicated to establishing this one point. He was careful not to condone the mutiny itself, only to show the reason why nobody resisted, i.e. that Bligh was a disgraceful commander. These were the special circumstances that secured Morrison his pardon along with Heywood. No matter that Bligh was able to lament that 'among all these charges there is not one of cruelty or oppression', for that was not the charge against him (whatever fictional accounts have cobbled together to show otherwise). Bligh, Morrison was asserting, was not a fit commander.

While Morrison's criticism remained private, Edward Christian's was made public. His method was ingenious, as befitted an academic lawyer. He organised a 'court of inquiry' that heard 'evidence' from the *Bounty* men themselves. Whether Fletcher Christian was guilty of mutiny was not in dispute – his guilt on this charge was conceded, indeed affirmed, in advance. What was not conceded, but in fact strenuously challenged, was that Fletcher was driven to mutiny by something ignoble in his character. The questions raised were whether, in fact, his criminal act followed from a degree of abuse and dishonour from his captain, and whether his captain's behaviour in this respect went beyond acceptable norms of command. Christian was not on trial – his conviction for mutiny was inevitable – but Bligh's veracity, particularly in his published accounts, was on trial, and Edward Christian set out to make what was in effect a brilliant plea in mitigation on behalf of his absent brother with all the formidable skills of advocacy he could command.

Christian persuaded, and perhaps financed, Musprat's lawyer to publish the minutes he had taken at the court martial, to which he added an 'Appendix' reporting the findings of his inquiry. Altogether twelve survivors of the *Bounty* mutiny gave evidence to the panel of 'several respectable gentlemen' during 1793. These were John Fryer, William Purcell, Thomas Hayward, William Peckover, John Smith, Lawrence Lebogue, Joseph Coleman, Thomas McIntosh, Michael Byrne, Peter Heywood, William Musprat and James Morrison (the latter only by letter). Among the people not interviewed were John Samuel, George Simpson, John Hallet, Robert Tinkler and William Cole. Their absence may have been entirely innocent; it may, on the other hand, have been due to their testifying contrary to the image of his brother that Edward wanted to project.

The 'respectable gentlemen' Edward Christian collected together to hear the testimony were not all they seemed – they certainly were respectable and they were all gentlemen, but they were also close friends of the Christians, a fact not disclosed to the public. To appreciate the significance of their relationships we need only go back to Fletcher's boyhood in Cockermouth in Cumberland. Among his contemporaries were William and Dorothy Wordsworth. William went to the local grammar school and later had Edward Christian as a headmaster. He went to St John's College, Cambridge, as had his uncle, the Rev. Mr Cookson, Canon of Windsor and a member of the enquiry (the Wordsworths were his house guests during the months of the enquiry). His tutor at St John's was a Rev. Dr Frewen, another member of the enquiry, listed in the *Appendix* as from Colchester.

Wordsworth at the time of the enquiry was in the full flush of his unrestrained passion for the French Revolution, a connection he shared with several other of the 'respectable gentlemen'. France was not yet the mortal enemy it was to become a few years later.

Other members of the panel included the Rev. Mr Antrobus from Cockermouth, another graduate of St John's, and listed in the *Appendix* under the disarming title of 'Chaplain to the Bishop of London'; Captain John Wordsworth, William's relative (and also related to the Christians through Isabella Curwen), and an officer in the employ of the East India Company (under whose auspices Edward Christian held the professorship of Law at the East India College in Hertfordshire); the Rev. Dr

Fisher, an intimate friend of Edward Law and a first cousin of Fletcher Christian, who became Rector of Nether Stowey in Somerset (where the Wordsworths were house guests in 1795-6); James Losh, a legal contemporary of Edward and a friend of Fletcher Christian, deeply sympathetic to the French Revolution, being a member of the Society of Friends and a friend of Marat; Samuel Romilly, another legal contemporary and close friend of Edward Christian and William Wilberforce, and an honorary member of the French Revolutionary Convention; Mr Gilpin and John Atkinson, both from Cockermouth though listed as at The Strand and as Somerset Herald respectively. Two others, John Fairhill and John France, the latter a barrister, have no obvious connection with the Christians, but a relationship is inferred from what we know of the others.

The enquiry panel was hardly a random selection of respectable gentlemen; it was a collection of Edward Christian's and William Wordsworth's clique. The strong French Revolutionary interests of some of them no doubt prompted comparisons between Fletcher's mutiny and the storming of the Bastille. That is, if they attended more than one meeting of the enquiry. Only Edward Christian was present at all the meetings with the witnesses. Some members of the enquiry heard the evidence of only one of the witnesses, others heard more than one; none heard them all; all were predisposed in sympathy towards Fletcher Christian before they heard a word.

Two of the witnesses, Fryer and Purcell, can be identified by their statements (six each in all), but the rest cannot. Bearing in mind that Edward Christian was not averse to Bligh's suing him for libel – he seems almost disappointed that Bligh did not: 'Many gentlemen, besides myself, suppose that if any answer could be given, it would be attempted in a court of justice by some judicial proceeding' (Edward Christian, 1795) – his method of reporting what he had been told was a clever device to make any libel claim difficult to sustain. Bligh could not be sure who said what. Fryer and Purcell, however, were sound witnesses against Bligh and were unlikely to lose their nerve before him in a court. Both had recently had reason to oppose him: Purcell because he had been court-martialled by Bligh; Fryer because Bligh had 'refused to give' him 'a good Character' when Captain Riou (of *Guardian*) had asked for one (ML MS Safe 1/43, p. 49).

Fryer's testimony established that Fletcher had planned to get away from the ship the night before the mutiny, which was public evidence that all was not well between Christian and his captain. He also testified that two of the mutineers had told him that Christian and the mutineers had agreed not to commit murder (the normal occurrence in these affairs). Bligh is also shown to be in dispute with Fryer by the fact that they were no longer dining together (the cause of this breach between them is left unstated). Fryer also reports that Christian was in 'hell' from his sufferings under Bligh's command, and he states that it was the opinion 'of all those who came in the boat' that in spite of their 'sufferings and losses' they nevertheless spoke of Christian 'without resentment and with forgiveness' and, indeed, 'with a degree of rapture and enthusiasm'.

Purcell's contribution was no less damaging to Bligh's public persona. He told the panel about Christian's emotional state before the mutiny: 'tears were running fast from his eyes in big drops.' Christian, according to Purcell, told him that 'if I should speak to him as you do, he would probably break me, turn me before the mast, and perhaps flog me; and if he did, it would be the death of us both, for I am sure I should take him in my arms, and jump overboard with him' (Edward Christian, *Appendix*, p. 64). In Purcell's view those who went in the launch 'were sure of getting to shore, where they expected to live, until an European ship arrived, or until they could raise their boat or build a greater'. An objection that this expectation was soon frustrated at Tofoa was overturned by Edward's shifting the blame for the bad relations with the Tofoans onto Bligh who is accused of provoking the Chiefs unnecessarily at Annamooka. The idea that they could build a boat was encouraged by Purcell's quotation of a mutineer's reaction to his getting his tool chest into the boat: 'You might as well give him the ship as his tool chest.' As 'every person who went into the launch, went voluntarily' (*Appendix*, p. 66), and as they expected to get ashore, and as they had sufficient food for that purpose, any complaints about the consequences of their treatment were really Bligh's fault and not Christian's.

Bligh's explanations of the mutiny in his *Narrative* (1790) included the possibility that the mutineers – he did not specifically identify Christian in this context – were anxious to return to their female companions at Tahiti. The *Appendix* denied that this applied to Christian: 'The Officers who were with Christian upon the same duty declare, that he never had a female favourite at Otaheite, nor any attachment or particular connection among the women' (p. 75). We know, however, that he had some connections of an intimate kind with at least one woman (and in view of the wording of the denial he must have had relations with several) because he appeared on *Bounty*'s sick list as being prescribed a cure for venereal disease. But the *Appendix* is somewhat precious on the question of Christian and women. For example, it states loftily that the reason for taking Tahitian men and women with the mutineers to Tubuai was because 'the Otaheite men would be useful in introducing them to the friendship and good offices of the natives'. What use the women were to be put to is not, of course, mentioned. The fact that the Tubuai episode was not a homely jaunt across the ocean tarnishes this aspect of the *Appendix*. The bloody truth of Christian's attempt to settle there, including the man murdered for his coconuts and the bloody retribution of the last massacre, are in stark contrast to the portrait the *Appendix* was painting. Christian could only be sold as a clean-living young man, beloved by all in contrast to the odious Bligh, if the records of their dealings with the islanders they contacted are suppressed. If Bligh's row with the chiefs at Annamooka occasioned his distress at Tofoa, what effect did Christian's bloody murders at Tubuai have on any one luckless enough to be cast away after he left?

In summary, the main messages of the *Appendix* were that the mutiny was not premeditated or planned at Tahiti (pp. 65-6); nor was Christian involved with a woman (p. 75); nobody was 'huzzaing for Otaheite' (p. 63); nor did Christian seek the men in the boat's destruction (indeed he intended to tow them near to land and see them make landfall safely, p. 67). His mutiny was caused by Bligh's intolerable abuse (p. 63), by his impugning of Christian's honour over the coconuts (p. 64) and by the chance remark Stewart made to Christian about the men being 'ripe for any thing' (p. 71). The character of Christian was virtue personified, and some testimonials of the witnesses were quoted to show how loved he was (in contrast of course to their views of Bligh, which were less than warm where they were not bitterly critical): 'He was a gentleman, and a brave man; and every officer and seaman on board the ship would have gone through fire and water to have served him'; 'Every body under his command did their duty at a look from Mr. Christian, and I would still go through fire and water for him' etc. (p. 76). One witness added that he would 'wade up to his arm-pits in blood to serve him', a somewhat ironic comment in view of the events at Tubuai.

Edward Christian knew his profession well, for he ends the *Appendix* with a powerful example of the rhetoric of the advocate in full flight:

> The sufferings of Captain Bligh and his companions in the boat, however severe they may have been, are perhaps but a small portion of the torments occasioned by this dreadful event: and whilst these prove the melancholy and extensive consequences of the crime of Mutiny, the crime itself in this instance may afford an awful lesson to the Navy, and to mankind, that there is a degree of pressure, beyond which the best formed and principled mind must either break or recoil. And though public justice and the public safety can allow no vindication of any species of Mutiny, yet reason and humanity will distinguish the sudden unpremeditated act of desperation and phrenzy, from the foul deliberate contempt of every religious duty and honourable sentiment; and will deplore the uncertainty of human prospects, when they reflect that a young man is condemned to perpetual infamy, who, if he had served on board any other ship, or had perhaps been absent from the Bounty a single day, or one ill-fated hour, might still have been an honour to his country, and a glory and comfort to his friends (*Appendix*, p. 79).

The *Appendix* appeared in the first half of 1794. Bligh was at home on half-pay since he signed off *Providence*. Whatever private reports, including Morrison's Memorandum, had influenced the Admiralty about Bligh's fitness for command, the publication of the *Appendix* made his future a matter of public debate. London society buzzed with speculation and gossip; sympathies were generally in favour of Fletcher Christian, and the earlier post-mutiny glory draped on Bligh became tarnished. This left Bligh with the choice of quietly withdrawing, and seeking a career elsewhere, perhaps in the merchant service, or of grappling with the charges, in a spirit of do-or-die, and attempting to rescue his naval career. Answering them, as Edward Christian wanted, in a legal case would cost an unknown amount with uncertain prospect of success. He chose instead to publish an answer.

Bligh's *An Answer to Certain Assertions contained in the Appendix to a Pamphlet* ... appeared in December 1794. It was nowhere near being as polished a job as the *Appendix*. It merely presented some material that had the potential to form the basis of a proper reply. It had a short introduction and fifteen items of evidence, not all of them of obvious relevance to the charges in the *Appendix*, and all of them presented without comment (apart from the odd footnote). Where the *Appendix* is a brilliant polemic, *An Answer* ... is a mere skeleton of a legal brief, and one inadequate to destroy the credibility of the charges made against him.

Bligh, for example, shows how Peter Heywood changed his testimony in praise of Bligh to criticism, the implication being that Heywood was an unreliable witness, and probably also a mutineer. Surgeon Harwood's letter to *The Times* is quoted to show that Bligh had good relations with the officers on the *Providence*, the implication being that he was a good commander. Affidavits from Coleman, Smith and Lebogue denied that they made the assertions quoted in the *Appendix*, implying (perhaps?) that whoever else made them they were unreliable. One item of historical interest came from Edward Lamb, a former officer in *Britannia*, the merchant ship under Bligh's command in which Fletcher Christian sailed. He wrote: 'In the Appendix it is said, that Mr. Fletcher Christian had no attachment amongst the women of Otaheite; if that was the case, he must have been much altered since he was with you in Britannia; he was one of the most foolish young men I ever knew in regard to the sex' (*An Answer*, 1794, p. 30).

Bligh justified his restrictive method of defence in the introduction, where he stated: 'One of the hardest cases that can befall any man, is to be reduced to the necessity of defending his character by his own assertions only. As such, fortunately, is not my situation, I have rested my defence on the testimony of others; adding only, such of the written orders issued by me in the course of the voyage, as are connected with the matter in question: which orders being issued publicly in writing, may be offered as evidence of unquestionable credit. These testimonials, without further remark from me, I trust will be sufficient to do away any evil impression which the public may have imbibed, from reading Mr. Edward Christian's Defence of his brother.' In the last paragraph of the *Answer* he added: 'I submit these evidences to the judgment of the Public, without offering any comment. My only intention in this publication, is to clear my character from the effect of censures which I am conscious I have not merited: I have therefore avoided troubling the Public with more than what is necessary to that end; and have refrained from remark, lest I might have been led beyond my purpose, which I have wished to limit solely to defence' (p. 31).

The only result of Bligh's efforts to answer Edward Christian was that he provoked *A Short Reply to Capt. W. Bligh's Answer* (1795). It continues the polemics of the *Appendix* and attacks Lawrence Lebogue for his 'most wicked and perjured affidavit that ever was sworn before a magistrate, or published to the world; and it is perhaps a defect in the law that these voluntary affidavits are permitted to be made; or that, when they are false, the authors of them are subject to no punishment' (p. 7). Edward Christian's complaint was that Lebogue had said the things he denied, and he cited two witnesses, John Atkinson and James Losh, to confirm this.

Among Bligh's papers in the Mitchell Library is an interesting manuscript which is a draft reply to the charges made by Edward Christian, though from the format they appear to be answers to letters written by Edward to Sir Joseph Banks rather than to the *Appendix* itself. One of the letters is dated 1792 and the others merely 'December' (presumably December 1792 after Heywood had contacted Christian). We can surmise that when Bligh returned he was sent copies of the letters, along with Morrison's Memorandum, for his comments. His return, of course, prompted Edward to issue the *Appendix*.

In one of these letters Bligh gives his account of his treatment of Christian: 'Mr Christian asserts that his Brother has been driven to desperation [and] would have been a Glory to his Friends, had he not sailed with Captain Bligh.' In reply Bligh refers to Fletcher's three years' previous experience with him in the merchant service and how he was his only support. This presumably refers to financial support, for Fletcher had no other source of income following his family's misfortune, a circumstance Bligh must have learned about from him during this period. He added that 'to render him still further help, Captain Bligh took him with him into the Bounty where he made him Acting Lieutenant, & he would have received his Commission on his return to England. He occupied the same place of confidence & trust to the moment of his Horrid act of ingratitude' (ML MS Safe 1/43, pp. 19-24) This expresses Bligh's view of his relationship with Christian, implying that any criticism he made was on a professional plane, not a personal one, for had he not done so much for him over three years? This was not how Christian saw it, of course.

Bligh makes a good point about Heywood's letter to Edward Christian following his pardon: 'That Peter Heywood the Mutineer would write to Mr Christian a favourable account of His Brother, cannot be doubted; for by endeavouring to prove the Ringleader of the Mutiny not guilty; the rest of the party must in case he succeeded be surely free of any blame' (3rd letter, 17 December). He also attacks the credibility of Fryer ('in disgrace with Captain Bligh') and Purcell ('tried by Court Martial') because they brought no charges against him at his court martial for the loss of *Bounty*. They only spoke out when the mutineers were brought home to save them 'from being hung'. As to the credibility of the mutineers who escaped hanging (Heywood, Morrison and Musprat) he states: 'As all the Men & Officers who came home with Captain Bligh declare, that four Men were deserving of Mercy, & as such were recommended & acquitted: can a Mind open to conviction be more perfectly satisfied that it was their opinion that all else who remained on board were guilty' (pp. 21-2). This point was made in his *Answer* by producing the text of the statement made at Batavia and signed by everybody in the launch, including Fryer and Purcell, that twenty-five men had mutinied and, incidentally, that they had heard the mutineers say 'We shall in a short time return to the Society Islands' (*Answer*, pp. 7-8).

In short, Bligh accuses Edward Christian of 'tampering with witnesses', and the witnesses of wishing to 'paliate their own conduct' by pleading that 'their temptation arose from having been ill used' (pp. 23-4). It must be noted, however, that Bligh was not above a little 'tampering with witnesses', as his correspondence to Bond shows that he tried to solicit a statement from Michael Byrne, the half-blind fiddler from *Bounty*, who was serving at the Nore, along the same lines of the affidavits from Coleman, Smith and Lebogue (Letters, July 26, August 14, 1794; Mackaness, 1953). Byrne, in the event, did not do as he was asked, for which Bligh thought he deserved a flogging.

The public controversy between Christian and Bligh died down in 1795. Bligh spent 18 months on half-pay of £120 a year. This was not entirely a punishment, as some have asserted. He had promised his wife he would not undertake another voyage after *Providence* and needed time to recover from his illness. His letter to Bond on July 26 1794 shows the more likely cause of the delay in getting a command:

> I am employed in my own defence against Christian, the Mutineer's Brother, who has written a Pamphlet in order to show that the Mutiny was owing to my conduct. This has been making up ever since the Mutineers came home, and with all their Roguery and contrivance for more than 2 years amounts to nothing but that I damned and swore at them – that I would make them jump overboard in Endeavour Straits, and make them eat grass like cows. I cannot find out the Parties concerned, yet I attribute all their low malevolence to Heywood's Friends, who may work some way or another to Lord Ch. But this must terminate soon, and then when I have finished and given my statements I expect to be employed (Bligh to Bond, 24 July 1794, Mackaness, 1953, p. 56).

The 'Lord Ch.' was Lord Chatham at the Admiralty. He had been 'got at' by Heywood's friends (Captain Pasley etc.) in Bligh's view (i.e. he had been given accounts of Bligh's style of command on *Bounty*), and was prejudiced against him on this account. But Bligh's expectations that he would be employed again once he had made his 'statements' is interesting. It suggests that the purpose of his remarks on the letters from Edward Christian, making much the same cases against him as later appeared in the *Appendix*, was to prepare himself for some unofficial, perhaps private, account of his conduct within the Admiralty. The gist of his statements formed the basis of his published *Answer*, which appeared in December 1794.

His statements, both private and public, must have satisfied the Admiralty, for he tells Bond on 25 March 1795 that he been informed that he was 'to have a Fifty' (a 50-gun ship) and be 'employed in the North Sea' (Mackaness, 1953, p. 64). As all his letters to Bond during this period report on his efforts to get him made Post-captain, including the drafting of a personal memorial of his case for the Admiralty for Bond to copy out, it is interesting that he was totally unaware of Bond's attitude to him. This supports the view that Bligh never realised how much he antagonised his officers by his behaviour and how naive he was at times about their real feelings towards him. It is certain that he would have been mortified to read Bond's comments on the verso of the letter he wrote to him on 17 April 1796 from HMS *Director*, a 64-gun ship with a crew of 491 men which Bligh was commanding. Evidently, in order to help Bond get out of his ship, *Prompte*, which he had complained enough about, he had offered him the post of First Lieutenant on HMS *Calcutta*, some time in 1795. 'You have only yourself to blame,' writes Bligh, 'as you might have got out of the Prompte. You might have been free of that Tub, and been first Lieutenant of the Calcutta and after that of the Director, which would have strengthened your claim to anything more to be done.' Bond made a note on the rear of this letter: 'I impute no blame; as any situation would be preferable to that of first Lieut. with the blamer. I knew the choice I had. If I had acted contrary to my former sentiments, I should have been unworthy of the approbation of those who know the truth' (Mackaness, 1953, pp. 67-8). In other words, Bond preferred to stay in the 'tub' he was in than return under Bligh's command.

Bligh's expectations of employment were realised in April 1795. He took command of HMS *Warley*, 24 guns, on 29 April, which changed its name to HMS *Calcutta* the next day, and was placed under Admiral Duncan's command in the North Sea. He held this command until 7 January 1796 when he took over HMS *Director*, 64 guns. In this ship he faced his second experience of mutiny.

# 30

# The *Defiance* Mutiny

1795 was a bad year in Britain's war with France. In January the French marched into Amsterdam and proclaimed the Batavian Republic. By April the remnants of the British army were evacuated from Germany, leaving the northern coastline of continental Europe in the firm grip of the French. The Dutch navy, ice-bound in the Texel, was captured by jubilant French cavalry. In June Sweden sued for peace, followed by Spain in July. The disastrous landing of French Royalists and British regulars in Quiberon Bay, Britanny, in July ended hopes of a Royalist rising, and this, plus the virtual destruction, through pestilence and disease, of the British army in the West Indies – some 80,000 men in all – left the isolated islands of Britain with about 60,000 troops and the Royal Navy to continue the war. And continue they must, for the Establishment viewed the revolutionary events in France, and their spread across Europe, with an awe born of fear. The great French monarchy had 'crumbled into dust', as Edward Gibbon expressed it in a letter to Lord Sheffield, and he went on to state: 'If this tremendous warning has no effect on the men of property in England; if it does not open every eye and raise every arm, you will deserve your fate.'

Economically the situation was no better. Disastrous harvests in 1794 were followed by an extremely cold winter. Rising food prices squeezed an already desperate population; so desperate did it become that the magistrates at Speenhamland in England ordered the wages of farm labourers to be supplemented out of public funds.

A sense of crisis was reflected in the parade of radicals through the courts. Among these the Scottish 'martyrs' Thomas Muir and Thomas Palmer were sentenced to fourteen and seven years transportation to New South Wales respectively for advocating parliamentary reform. In October 1795 a London Corresponding Society meeting attracted 150,000 people, while for motives unknown someone threw stones at the King's coach. Parliament reacted with appropriate draconian legislation to deal with Treasonable Practices and Seditious Meetings. In England Habeas Corpus was suspended and those charged with sedition had little protection from the fury of magistrates who allowed their fear to overcome their decency.

The formation of the Batavian Republic added the formidable Dutch navy to that of the French. In response the Admiralty formed a North Sea Fleet to enforce a naval blockade along the Dutch coast. Adam Duncan (1731-1804), Admiral of the Blue, from Dundee, was chosen to command it. He was by all accounts a striking man, about six feet four in height, white-haired and handsome. He had a quiet but forceful personality, imbued with a tough no-nonsense charisma. He owed his appointment, as did most Admirals and their officers, to the exercise of interest: in his case to the recommendation of Henry Dundas, a Scottish power broker and ally of the Prime Minister.

Duncan had only five British ships of the line in his fleet, supplemented by a larger Russian fleet of twelve ships of the line and seven frigates, who tended to do what their captains (some of them Scottish) found convenient. The principal rendezvous of the North Sea Fleet was the port of Leith, near Edinburgh, in the Firth of Forth. It was to this fleet that Bligh was assigned as captain of the 24-gun armed transport, *Calcutta*. The Navy could not afford to have experienced officers on half-pay writing pamphlets, especially in defence of themselves against minor mutinies, when the whole of Europe was in mutiny against the established order.

In 1795 the Navy was desperately short of men. William Pitt, the Prime Minister, responded to the Navy's pleas for more men with the notorious 'Quota Acts' in March and April. These required the port towns and counties to provide men for the fleet, some by enticement of the King's Bounty and others by the forfeit of their liberty by whatever mischief brought them within sight of the magistrate (many of whom took advantage of Pitt's Acts to rid their neighbourhoods of those they perceived to be undesirable residents).

In October 1795 Bligh was at Leith and due to sail when a mutiny broke out on HMS *Defiance*, a 74-gun ship of the line, Captain Sir George Home (pronounced 'Hume'). Home had languished on half-pay for twelve years since the American war, his last service having been with Rodney at the Battle of the Saints. He received his commission as captain of *Defiance* by virtue of his standing with Admiral Duncan, and judging by the dash he made to the Nore to take command he was keen to be back on full pay.

In a letter to Sir Joseph Banks, Bligh describes the mutiny and what was done to put it down:

Yesterday there were several messages sent to the mutineers from Admiral Pringle, which they received in their barricaded appartments with no trifling arrogance. The grievances they wanted to have redressed were:– a New Captain, – a new Lieutenant, – liberty to go on shore – and their Grog to be mixed with less than five waters. They were talked to on these subjects by Captain Leckmere and Mr McDougall who were sent by the Admiral for this purpose to assist Captain Home, and soon after some of the Men – about seven or eight – were seized & put into Irons by the Officers of the Ship –

quietness was established until towards Night, when the Mutineers thought proper to insist on their companions being released – as they would have effected it themselves and the Captain had no marines, he thought it best to comply, at which they gave him three cheers (ML MS C218).

Having no marines was a serious problem for Home and other captains in Duncan's fleet. Duncan had written to the Admiralty constantly during the summer of 1795 pleading for marines. The red-coated 'lobster backs' were the last resort of the officers if mutiny broke out. They stood sentry in their full dress uniforms throughout the ship at all times and were paraded with fixed bayonets on the poop deck during musters (giving them a clear field of fire). *Defiance* had no marines, but a compromise was reached in July when 79 landsmen (new recruits) were assigned to *Defiance* to act as marines. During the mutiny they were easily disarmed by the seamen.

Admiral Pringle, on HMS *Asia*, tried a ruse next day which the mutineers saw through. He sent Leckmere and McDougall to the *Defiance* to tell the men that as they refused sentry duty he would have to place his own sentries on board to protect the ship, presumably from the Dutch! At first the men agreed, but they thought better of it and refused to admit the Admirals 'sentries'.

The Admiral's response was to call a meeting of the captains in port, which Bligh attended. He reported to Banks:

> Many plans were mentioned, & the best way discussed, how to subdue this mutiny, & I did not hesitate to declare that a party of Troops embarked on board of another Ship & laid alongside, was the most effectual manner that I knew of, because they would be protected, which by any other means they would not, if resistance was made.

This suggestion apparently was listened to, though whether because it was the only positive suggestion or because of Bligh's experience on *Bounty* we cannot tell.

The Admiral wrote to Lord Adam Gordon, Commander in Chief of His Majesty's forces in Scotland, to arrange for 200 troops to be made available for the assault on *Defiance*, and he ordered the captains of *Jupiter* and *Edgar* to embark the troops and place their ships alongside *Defiance*. But something, or somebody, changed Admiral Pringle's mind. Bligh was none too pleased with this turn of events:

> Suddenly the Plan was changed, and I was pitched upon to take all these Troops directly on Board of the Defiance. From this moment I heard no more of what was to be done; but set off to take command of the Boats which were filled with eighty men.

Bligh does not elaborate on why the plan was changed. Nor do the Logs give any hint or explanation; indeed they make scant or no reference to Bligh at all (PRO Adm. 51-1101; 52-2987). The other captains may have been sensibly circumspect about involving themselves, their ships or their crews. If things went wrong, the mutiny might spread, Admiralty property could be destroyed and who knows what backstabbing could occur in the subsequent enquiries?

The use of troops was a risky business. They were commanded by Major Clarkson of the South Fencible Regiment. Bligh got on with the job:

> With these two boats I proceeded in two Divisions untill close to the Ship, when from the orders I had given the respective officers, the Divisions opened and rowed to each Gangway and preceded by myself & a Major, the Commanding officer of the Soldiers in a separate Boat. Instantly was the cry of one & all – 'clear away the Guns – sink them', and we cheered the Troops not to mind this, but to come on wch they did, and got up on the poop without any hurt but a slight Bruise or two & a boat stove with the shot that were thrown out of the ports. We had now the remaining soldiers to get on board, which I effected very speedily and without any resistance which it was expected I should have met with, both in going out and coming in; but I had only a few fellows who pointed at me and said there he goes.

As Bligh was tolerably known in the fleet, the mutterings of the 'fellows' may have had a slightly baser flavour out of his earshot.

The soldiers' presence broke the resistance of the seamen, and the captains of the other ships in port arrived to witness the reinstatement of Sir George Home. The crew, however, were far from satisfied and they passed an anonymous letter to the captain – it was thrown onto the quarter-deck in the dark that night. It offered a compromise: 'Send all the soldiers out of the ship and the Royalists and we will return cheerfully to our duty' (PRO Adm. 1-5334). Home rejected this 'impertinence' and spent several days hunting down the author, eventually accusing John Graham, a seaman, of writing it. The subsequent court martial agreed with Home, and Graham was sentenced to 300 lashes.

The use of the epithet 'Royalist' is interesting. At the time the fleets were manned with a fair proportion of political prisoners, particularly from Ireland but also from among supporters of the French Revolution or the republican ideals of the American War of Independence. The fact that the several score of seamen (out of a crew of over 600) who had not supported the mutiny were branded Royalists by the mutineers indicates that there were political leanings among the leaders. Bligh was worried about the safety of the non-mutineers. He took one of them, Benjamin Cocks, into *Calcutta*, and another hundred were transferred from *Defiance* to Bligh's next ship, *Director*, on 18 March 1796, loyal seamen being at a premium at this time. (One of them was Matthew Hollister who was to play a leading role in the Nore Mutiny.) Admiral Pringle transferred several more into other ships, including twenty who went into *Jupiter*.

The local Fencibles were left on *Defiance* for several days, but because they were prohibited from serving outside Scotland troops from the 134th Regiment were embarked on *Defiance* so it could be moved to

London. The original eight leading mutineers were rearrested and a further nine arrested on various charges. They were sent to London in the frigate *Pegasus* and court-martialled in January 1796. Of the seventeen, eight were sentenced to hang, four were awarded 300 lashes each and three 100 lashes and two were acquitted. In the event, on 8 March 1796, when the eight prisoners were brought up for hanging, and the others for flogging, four were hanged. The last four awaiting their fate were reprieved, and the nine due for flogging had their sentences commuted to sixty lashes for the two worst offenders and twenty lashes for a lesser offender. As the entire punishment was witnessed in one session, the impact on those reprieved was not lessened by Sir George Home's spirit of leniency.

The causes of the mutiny were not exceptional at this time. A study of the *Defiance* Log shows trouble brewing for some time before the final outburst. Some of the Quota men from the Kirkcaldy 'volunteers' were grievously hurt to find that the Clerk of the Cheque (the Admiralty paymaster) refused them their £70 bonus on the grounds 'that neither the intention nor the terms of the Act of Parliament entitled them to it'. Sir George passed their complaints to Admiral Duncan who in turn passed them to the Admiralty (he had several other 'volunteers' making similar complaints from his other ships). The Kirkcaldy men, fishermen as it happens, were eventually refused the bounty on grounds of their age.

In addition to this issue, Home had taken upon himself the decision to water the ship's grog down from the normal three parts water to five parts. The Log shows various incidents involving drunken men fighting and general insurbordination, and life below decks was, by the accounts at the court martial, a fairly violent experience with busted noses, smashed teeth, cuts and stabbing a daily occurrence. The cry of 'no five water grog' was prominent in the mutiny.

The other issue was 'liberty', or shore leave (though I do not exclude that for some of the men the cry of 'liberty' had a deeper more political meaning). The issue of shore leave was not a trivial one. Men could be in their home ports and have no chance of seeing their wives and families ashore. The Navy feared they would desert. Only the most trustworthy of men were allowed ashore on ship's duty. They worked under the hawk eyes of the petty officers, who answered for anybody that ran. Men treated like prisoners during long years of service regarded shore duty as a temptation to desert; yet the penalties were draconian – death by hanging under the Articles of War, or at the least a severe flogging. The connection between the absence of shore leave and the provocation to desert was not obvious to the Admiralty, and the aggravation that desertion caused to captains when they reported it to their Admirals was sufficient for them to adopt a general prejudice against it.

On Sunday 4 October 1795 Robert Carter, a seaman on duty in the captain's barge, ran off before anybody could stop him. Home was furious.

The desertion reflected on him. He reacted in the same way to liberty as he did to the grog: he stopped all liberty for everybody on *Defiance*, except himself and the officers. This collective punishment went down badly, for it did not distinguish between good behaviour and bad, and, if there was no difference in the treatment either behaviour merited, there was soon no difference in the behaviour. This did not prevent their families coming out to the ship, then anchored in Leith Roads (a safe anchorage off-shore), but not all the women who took advantage of staying with their men on board were who they claimed to be, nor was it feasible for seamen's families to travel any great distance (from Kirkcaldy?) to do so. Several men petitioned Home for liberty because Leith was their home port (one of them was the unfortunate scribe John Graham). Home said no to these entreaties. Two weeks later, to the cry of 'Liberty and No Five Water Grog', and with the captain ashore on leave, the mutiny broke out, at first with some pushing and shoving between the petty officers and some men, and then in a general commotion as the cry spread along the gun deck. What happened was a foretaste of what was to afflict the entire home fleet two years later.

# 31

# Bligh's Second Mutiny

A naval blockade aims to keep the enemy's fighting ships penned in their ports. If they come out they are attacked. To combat privateers (effectively pirates, licensed by a Letter of Marque to attack an enemy country's merchant shipping), the seas were swept by frigates, and merchant ships were formed into convoys to get them safely into the Atlantic, or into port. Blockade duty was among the most boring, and because of that, the most exacting, duties in the Navy. Ships cruised just outside the enemy port – in all weathers and circumstances – for weeks, sometimes months, on end. Passing ships were chased and boarded and their cargoes checked. Occasionally the monotony might be relieved with a short cruise along the major sea lanes, or when a ship needed more sea room because of the weather. Prizes might be taken, but rarely, as only small fast ships risked running the blockade. The tyranny of purposeless petty routine and the lack of variety, plus the often appalling weather (when the enemy might dash for it) and the irksome discipline, made the seamen's lot onerous to a high degree. They were cooped up in their draughty ships like prisoners, unable to enjoy the supposed liberties they were defending. The neglect they suffered – a far more frustrating issue than flogging – eventually reaped its reward: the great fleet mutinies of 1797.

In the year running up to the Nore mutiny, Bligh commanded *Director*, a 64-gun ship of the line. He took command on 7 January 1796, *Calcutta* being decommissioned, and continued to serve in Duncan's North Sea fleet. He was not happy with this duty, or rather his wife was disaffected with it. While married they had spent more than half their lives apart. As a captain's wife she could visit him in port (she stayed for a while in Leith) but this was hardly a way to bring up their young family. In December 1795, just before Bligh went to *Director*, Elizabeth Bligh wrote to Sir Joseph Banks to see if he could arrange for her husband to get a shore duty, for instance as Captain at Greenwich Hospital. Banks obliged with a memorial to Lord Spenser emphasising Bligh's service and also his poor health. To the headaches which 'nearly killd him in his second Bread Fruit Voyage', and his health which was 'utterly ruined' by *Bounty*'s boat voyage, he now 'suffers much from Rheumatisms in the North Sea' (ML MS C218, p. 15). The Admiralty declined to move Bligh to Greenwich Hospital but informed Banks that they were about to promote him to a larger ship.

When Bligh took command of the 64-gun *Director*, with a complement of 491 men, he was 42 years old and had served in the Navy for twenty-six years. Before leaving *Calcutta* he wrote to the Admiralty to recommend Lieutenant Francis Williams for his conduct; he also complained about three other lieutenants: Thomas Russell for desertion and debts of £21 2s 6d, in August 1795; David McDowall for not taking up his appointment; and Thomas Gillespie for being delayed in taking up his appointment owing to some 'pecuniary' difficulties. His posting to *Director* helped, in Sir Joseph Banks's words, to heal 'the wound his spirit has received by the illiberal & unjust treatment his Character has met from the relatives of the Mutineers of the *Bounty*' (ibid., p. 16).

*Director* did not see action during 1796 as the interminable blockade of the Texel continued. Bligh was in constant correspondence with Banks, informing him of every development and conduct of the 'war'. While in Yarmouth he commented on the arrival of *Glatton*, the ship he was to command at the Battle of Copenhagen: 'The Glatton has only one Man wounded by Musquet Ball, the Officer of Marines. We have every reason to suppose the Carronade 68 and 32 pounders did great execution, and think much praise is due to Captain Trollop' (ibid., p. 29).

In September 1796, after returning from a cruise to the Texel, Bligh commented to Banks about the health of his crew: 'One of the Russian Ships has a number of Sick, and I understand the Squadron in general have some scurvy. I am fortunate that our Sick list contains only six & only one with scurvy, but I consider a ship healthy that has not more than five Men ill to every hundred' (ibid., p. 31). The North Sea winter was causing him problems 'but a hot climate would kill me in a month' – no doubt his promotion to *Director* proved a better medicine than a shore post at Greenwich.

The war dragged on and the cumulation of problems that had been swept under the carpet threatened to upset the furniture of State. The Navy was a long way from being manned by volunteers (though there was always a steady stream of these) and the effects of this constant infusion of dissent were bound to surface even under the regime of traditional naval discipline. The courts sent to the fleet men found guilty of offences, trivial or otherwise, and the vagrant. In addition to the normal riff-raff, there were many articulate and angry men, plus political malcontents, Irish Republicans by the score – and even men just guilty of being Irish – rebels of all kinds, nutcases and cranks of every description, inadequate souls and men of varying compatabilities for life at sea. The conditions in the fleet – which put into sharp perspective the so-called privations on board *Bounty* – were a natural source of complaint. When these were added to the doctrines of dissent, they created a dangerous recipe for sedition.

The first outbreak began in February 1797 in *Queen Charlotte* and *Royal Sovereign*. The men demanded a wage increase and drew attention to the last wage increase the Navy had received – under Charles II over 100 years before. They circulated a petition in the Channel Fleet, signed by men on thirty-eight ships, and sent it to Lord Howe, the fleet commander, in early March 1797. There was no reply from Lord Howe by the end of the month when the fleet was back in Spithead. Howe retired from command, having been ill for some time, and on 13 April the mutiny broke out.

The Admiralty ordered the ships to sea but the men refused to carry out the sailing orders from their officers. They elected delegates instead and held a meeting to decide what to do next. Once it was clear to the Admiralty that the men meant business they offered a pay rise of 5s 6d per month for Petty Officers, 4s 6d for ordinary seamen and 3s 6d for landsmen. The delegates mistrusted the offer. They recalled the mutiny in *Culloden*, Captain (later Sir) Thomas Troubridge, in 1794. When the men called off the mutiny on the promise of no retribution, Troubridge seized ten of the leaders, court-martialled them and had five of them hanged. The men at Spithead wanted an official King's Pardon to protect the lives of the leaders once the officers regained control of the ships. This was offered by the Admiralty on behalf of the King, but still the men were suspicious – nothing counted unless Parliament agreed (here we can sense the hand of a landsman with more political nous than the average seaman). The Prime Minister, Pitt, sought an early opportunity to persuade Parliament to approve measures taken to end the mutiny, but he was delayed in achieving his objective by the political problems his party was having with this notoriously difficult assembly. The delay was fatal; as ships returned home and heard about the Spithead mutiny they became infected by its demands. The mutiny spread. The men were not aware of the delicate balancing act that was the norm in the Georgian Parliament and naturally suspected that Pitt, the Admiralty and the King were equivocating in order to betray their promises. As a result the mutiny spread to Plymouth. Twenty-six ships there declared solidarity with the Spithead ships, some of them ships that had been moved from Spithead under the terms of the first settlement.

As news of the mutiny spread round the home fleets, their crews wanted to know when they were going to get the new pay rises. Admiral Duncan had a forewarning of trouble on his flagship, *Venerable*, on 30 April 1797, when there was an illegal muster of his crew to discuss their pay. On 1 May 1797 the Government sent a general order to all fleet commanders asking them to pay particular attention to formal discipline – parades, uniforms, marines and the Articles of War – and at the same time to avoid provocative behaviour. After a personal intervention by

Lord Howe, accompanied by his wife, involving a reconciliation dinner for the officers and the leaders of the mutiny, itself a unique event in the history of the Royal Navy, the Channel Fleet was got to sea again on 17 May.

Lord Howe negotiated a settlement which was agreed on 14 May 1797. Part of the settlement involved the removal from command of 114 officers named by the men, including Admiral Colpoys, Captains Griffith, Nichols, Campbell and Cook, 20 lieutenants, 8 marine officers, 3 masters, 4 surgeons, a chaplain, 17 master's mates, 25 midshipmen, 7 gunners, boatswains and carpenters, 5 marine NCOs and 3 masters-at-arms.

The Government had been anxious to collect evidence of political subversion among the seamen, and through the Duke of Portland it engaged the services of several spies for this purpose. Among these was one Aaron Graham, the man Admiral Pasley had hired to secure the release of Peter Heywood during the trial of the *Bounty* mutineers. His role this time was the opposite: to secure evidence to convict men of mutiny and sedition. He quickly set to work and sought evidence that the Spithead mutiny was a Jacobin conspiracy; in fact it was a revolt of hungry seamen.

The Nore ships sent a delegation to Spithead consisting of Charles McCarthy, Thomas Atkinson (*Sandwich*), Hinds (*Clyde*) and Matthew Hollister (*Director*). (Hinds, finding himself unguarded ashore, took the opportunity to desert from Spithead.) The wage offer had whetted their appetites. When there is no hope, men tend to live under the burden of its precedent; once hope is kindled it is not an easy emotion to control. The Spithead mutinies showed the powerful leverage the seamen had during a war. The pay increase and the extraordinary concession of the removal of named hated officers had only been won because of the solidarity of the mutineers and the dangers of the war with France (intelligence of the mutiny in France could have prompted a breakout by the no-longer blockaded French fleet). The North Sea Fleet had just returned from a blockade tour (extended by ten days in the hope of keeping the crews separated from the Nore events) and the men had not experienced the heady emotional strains of a successful confrontation with the Establishment; what seemed a generous settlement to those who had risked all to fight for it was of minimal significance to those who returned to benefit from it.

Admiral Duncan ordered Bligh to take *Director* to the Nore for a refit on 6 May 1796. At this time the other ships anchored there were in a state of ferment. On 12 May Bligh was on court-martial duty on *Inflexible*. This was a standard port chore for captains, but it removed many captains from their ships at the moment when the mutiny broke out. As soon as the news reached *Inflexible*, the court martials were adjourned and the captains hurried back to their ships.

Returning on board *Director*, Bligh was presented with a number of demands by his crew. These included the immediate removal from the ship of three of his officers, Lieutenants Ireland and Church and the Master, Mr Birch, who were accused of ill-using the men. No complaints were expressed against Bligh as captain. Bligh refused to send the three men ashore but suspended them from duty and confined them to their cabins. He remained in command of *Director* and the crew carried out his routine orders, but these did not amount to much as the ship was at anchor in a safe anchorage. The men wanted Bligh to issue them with small arms, but he refused, which alienated them.

The mutiny was run from HMS *Sandwich*, a rotting hulk of a once-proud 90-gun ship, built in 1759, which had flown Rodney's flag in the West Indies. On *Sandwich* the men had got hold of small arms, and the fact that on *Director* they had not was an affront to the militants on board. That *Sandwich* was the centre of the mutiny is not surprising. Her normal port crew was often swelled by almost a thousand 'recruits', from genuine volunteers to pressed men and sweepings from the local jails. This human cargo was crammed into the ship while the Navy decided where to send them. The surgeon in *Sandwich*, from a profession not normally easy to shock, had complained to the captain about conditions on board:

> It is absolutely necessary to reduce the numbers of men on board. Those men that are at first seized with the contagious fever, which has so alarmingly shown itself, are in general very dirty, almost naked, and in general without beds (having lost them either by their own indolence, or the villainy of their companions) ... The number of sores, scalds and other avoidable accidents, which the awkward landsmen are liable to, often degenerate into bad ulcers, which cannot readily be cured on board, owing sometimes to their own bad habits, but oftener to the foul air they breathe between decks; besides being frequently trod upon in the night from their crowded state ... sickness and contagion cannot be prevented by any physical means where fifteen or sixteen hundred men are confined in the small compass of the ship, many of whom are vitiated in their habits as filthy as their dispositions. The circumambient air is so pregnated with human effluvia that contagious fevers must inevitably be the consequence (Manwaring & Dobree, 1935, p. 123)

As these conditions and evidence of neglect were not unique in the Royal Navy, we can appreciate Bligh's dismay that his efforts to keep his seamen healthy and clean were overshadowed by sensitivities about his manners.

Thomas McCann from *Sandwich* visited *Director* and clashed verbally with Bligh when he tried to incite the crew to seize the arsenal. This made Bligh unpopular with the mutineers, and at a subsequent meeting of the Nore delegates aboard *Sandwich* Richard Parker, the 'President' of the delegates, expressed his view that the men from *Director* should do something about Bligh's continued presence on his ship. Even so it took another week before the mutineers won a majority of the *Director*'s crew for the removal of Bligh.

The Nore delegates met in a kind of 'parliament' made up of two men from each strike-bound ship. From here they issued the demands of the mutiny to the Admiralty. It also passed a disciplinary code for dealing with offenders, including opponents of the mutiny. Interestingly, the mutineers' list of punishments was no less brutal than the official ones in the Articles of War (with the exception of hanging). Flogging was imposed, as was ducking from the yard arm, the latter only slightly less injurious than keel-hauling, banned by the Navy several decades previously (Bligh, as we have seen, did not even approve of the milder forms of ducking associated with the traditional Neptune's ceremony of crossing the equator).

At this stage the Admiralty encouraged Admiral Buckner to respond in a low-key way to the Nore mutiny in the expectation that Howe's settlement would defuse the situation at the Nore. But while Howe got the Channel Fleet to sea, the situation turned worse at the Nore. For this the Admiralty and the Government were entirely to blame. At Spithead, Lord Howe personally negotiated with the leaders of the men. The pay increases were introduced in public and the oppressive officers were removed, if not publicly. But the men at the Nore were virtually ignored. Howe did meet some of them (including Hollister) at Yarmouth – only to advise them to return to duty – but there was no dining, no meetings with the Admiralty, and no offer to remove oppressive officers.

Bligh's removal from *Director* (he had been preceded, it should be noted, by other captains from their ships) coincided with a heightened mood of militancy among the Nore delegates. McCarthy of *Sandwich* fell from grace for being too moderate (he was also subjected to several personal indignities). His fate was followed by Matthew Hollister's rise to prominence. On 20 May 1797 the Nore delegates demanded that they receive 'every indulgence granted to the fleet at Portsmouth'; that upon a ship coming into harbour every man should receive 'liberty' at a time convenient to the working of the ship; that before they sailed every man should receive his arrears in pay 'down to six months'; that pressed men on board not due any pay should receive at least two months; that no officer 'turned out' of a ship should be employed in that ship again 'without the consent of the ship's company'; that men who had run, but who had returned to His Majesty's service, should be indemnified against punishment as deserters; that prize money be more equitably distributed; and that 'various alterations', including the expunging of some articles, should be made to the Articles of War in order to take out the 'terror and prejudice' of the Acts. Until these demands were met the delegates resolved not to deliver up the ships to their officers.

The demands, while just, were contrary to the custom and practice of the eighteenth-century Navy. There was little chance that they would be met. Any 'reformers' in the Establishment would be trounced by the 'reactionaries', who could argue that giving an inch (the Howe settlement at Spithead) only encouraged more arrogant, if not seditious, demands (the Nore demands).

Hollister returned to *Director* and set about removing Bligh. On 19 May 1797 Bligh wrote to the Admiralty informing them that, for the second time in his career, he had been involuntarily removed from command of his ship. He had already sent ashore Lieutenants Ireland and Church, and Mr Birch, and he was joined by three midshipmen, Purdue, Blaguire and Eldridge who also earned the disapprobation of Hollister and his supporters. Bligh particularly praised Mr Purdue 'because he did his duty like a spirited young officer' (PRO Adm. 1/516).

Howe's acceptance of the removal of unpopular officers, or officers opposing the mutineers, while a necessary concession to solve the Spithead mutiny, was now a dangerous precedent. After 19 May the situation between the two sides hardened. The delegates elected Richard Parker as their 'President' and settled down for a tough battle. Parker was an interesting personality. He bears some resemblance to Fletcher Christian. He was about 30, and had the same impetuousness and the same intelligence. His father was a grain merchant and a baker; he was not connected in the way that Fletcher was. He had been educated at Exeter Grammar School and had run away to sea. Because of his education he secured a place as a midshipman and served during the American War of Independence, at one time under Edward Riou. He claimed to have been a petty officer on HMS *Mediator* in 1783 and in peace time to have been a Master's Mate in the merchant service. It is believed that while in the merchant service he led a mutiny over food.

In the French wars Parker joined *Assurance* as a junior officer in the Channel Fleet, but he was court-martialled for disobeying an order and in consequence was disrated to AB and transferred to *Glebe* as a foremast hand. In 1794 he was discharged on medical grounds – rheumatism was the official reason. He returned to his wife's family in Braemar, Scotland and in 1797 was in Perth debtors' prison. From there he took the £30 bounty to pay off his debts and returned to the Navy. He was posted to *Sandwich* on 9 April 1797. This brought an articulate ex-officer into a ship with ready-made grievances and the example of Spithead to emulate. Parker had just enough arrogance – he once challenged Riou to a duel – and the appropriate style to be different from the simpler and more straightforward leader of the Spithead mutiny, Valentine Joyce. Parker led the Nore men to the ultimate challenge to authority and also kept the mutineers more or less under control – no mean achievement.

The Government contemplated the use of force against the Nore men. The balance of military advantage lay with the ships, not the Sheerness batteries, and using ships for the task risked spreading the mutiny if the seamen in the ships refused to fire on their beleaguered colleagues.

Evan Nepean, Secretary to the Admiralty, wrote to Duncan on 22 May 1797: 'You know the state of your fleet, I believe, as well as anyone can do, and what use could be made of it. Do you think that you could depend upon any of the ships if you were to bring them to the Nore, if it should be necessary to employ them in bringing the two or three ships of the line over there to reason?' (PRO Adm. 2/1352). Duncan replied 'yes' and 'no'. He also offered a silly suggestion: 'As to the Sandwich, you should get her cast adrift in the night and let her go on the sands, that the scoundrels may drown; for until some example is made this will not stop' (Dugan, 1966, p. 209).

The need for intelligence on the real state of the fleet became more obvious each day. However, the main concern of the King and the Admiralty at this time was the choice of ship to carry him to his honeymoon. On 26 May 1797 the Admiralty decided to send a special envoy to Duncan's fleet to provide the missing intelligence. They chose Bligh for this mission and sent him to Yarmouth with the following letter:

> Private. We send you Captain Bligh on a very delicate business on which the Government is extremely anxious to have your opinion. The welfare and almost the existence of the country may depend upon what is the event of this very important crisis. But till we know what we can look to from your squadron it will be very difficult for us to know how to act (Mackaness, 1951, p. 309).

By the time Bligh arrived in Yarmouth Duncan had demonstrated the true situation: he tried to get the fleet to sail for the Texel and found that his ships *Agamemnon*, *Repulse*, *Ardent*, *Isis*, *Glatton* and his sloops and frigates refused to sail. If the ships would not fight the Dutch they certainly would not fight their comrades at the Nore. It also told the Admiralty that the Nore mutiny was spreading to Yarmouth.

Bligh spent several days visiting as many ships as would let him on board and he talked to dozens of men among the ship's crews. On 30 May 1797 he sent the following report to Nepean:

> Secret. Memorandum by Captain Bligh for the Board of Admiralty. Arrived Yarmouth, Saturday 28th May. Admiral sailed 5 am with 12 sails. The Standard and Lion refused to obey the Admiral's orders, but afterwards complied and sailed. Nassau refused to obey the sailing order on account of pay due to the people. The ship's company observed, on being questioned whether they would resist mutiny in other ships, that every Captain should keep his own ship quiet. Montagu claims pay although but a month due. The ship's company went to their quarters and shotted their guns when the Venerable got under weigh. The ships in the road will only permit their own boats to come alongside, and no strangers. The Captain of the Marines of the Standard turned on shore and a Lieutenant of the Repulse put into the Admiral's ship by command of the people. The Glatton's Company have a remarkable loyal and good character. The delegates arrived from the Nore, but Admiral Duncan was informed of eighteen round in the Cygnet cutter, and he had given orders to prevent their communicating with any of the ships

(dated 26 May). It appeared to me very doubtful and hazardous what would be the conduct of the favourable party of seamen, if employed against the other. The Standard and Lion wanted to send delegates to the other ships, but they were refused admittance. When I received Admiral Duncan's letters for their Lordships, I thought it advisable to return without a moment's loss of time. Montagu and Nassau only in the road. Wm. Bligh (PRO Adm. 1/524 F149).

This report, and the actions of Duncan's crews, told the Admiralty that an attack on the Nore mutineers by loyal ships was not feasible.

By sailing for the Texel with only some of his fleet, Duncan had brought the mutiny to the surface. The party of delegates from the Nore in the *Cygnet*'s cutter also found out the true state of affairs at Yarmouth. Duncan ordered Lieutenant Reddy to intercept the cutter and arrest the delegates, but in a remarkable exhibition of naivety he fell for Hollister's ruse that they should be released because they had discovered that the men at Yarmouth were against the men at the Nore and that once they reported on this the Nore mutiny would collapse. Reddy agreed and allowed Hollister to inform Parker that the Nore had nothing to fear from the North Sea Fleet.

The Cabinet, on the basis of Bligh's report, tried a new initiative. It suggested that the Admiralty send someone down to Sheerness to meet the leaders of the mutiny and offer them a King's Pardon if they returned to duty. The mutineers were told that they could meet with the Lords Commissioners to accept the King's Pardon but that they could not discuss any grievances. This was rejected by the delegates. Thus the two parties did not meet. This left both sides with no new ideas.

The mutineers were trapped in floating cages off shore, with nothing to do. They received a short-lived morale-booster when eight 64-gun ships arrived to join them from Yarmouth. Admiral Buckner ordered all officers ashore and cut off all supplies going out to the ships. He also had all buoys in the Thames removed in case any ship tried to make for the open sea. The isolation tactics began to have effect. Some crews wanted to return to duty, while others, like the crew of *Director*, were 'completely under the influence of terror' from *Sandwich* and *Inflexible*, according to reports from Buckner's spies.

Buckner was told that *Director* was 'wavering' and this was confirmed by an attempted seizure of the ship from the mutineers on 30 May 1797. After a bitter fight on deck the mutineers won and the signals proclaiming the end of the mutiny were pulled down and red flags raised in their place. On 6 June another attempt was made to seize the ship. Lieutenant Roscoe read the assembled crew the meaning of the King's Pardon, and Parker came across to debate the issue and persuaded the men to stay with the mutiny. In some ships the mutineers imposed floggings (up to 36 lashes) on waverers. Other ships experienced deck brawls, and even on *Sandwich* trouble broke out. The men were on short rations and water was scarce. In a last bid to compromise, the mutineers offered to end their strike in exchange for an agreement that some officers be removed. The Admiralty refused.

Anti-mutineers in *Leopard* succeeded in seizing the ship and they removed to Gravesend under Lieutenant Robb. *Repulse* also changed hands, but a similar move in *Standard* failed. Parker ordered *Director* to chase *Repulse* and fire on her, but the men refused to obey the command and the militants had to be satisfied with firing a single gun at the escaping ship. Parker also went to *Monmouth* with a similar order and managed to get some guns fired. This exposed the weakness of the mutiny, especially to men of *Standard*, who took another vote and reinstated the captain to command the ship. *Ardent* was next to change sides and it steered from the Nore. In the next 24 hours more ships surrendered. *Agamemnon*, *Isis* and *Vestal* moved away from the Nore. Parker was now virtually a prisoner on *Sandwich*. *Monmouth* placed itself under Lieutenant Buller's command and surrendered.

The mutiny was almost over. Lord Keith, accompanied by Sir Thomas Pasley (Heywood's uncle), went round the remaining ships persuading the men to surrender. The flagship of the mutiny, *Sandwich*, surrendered and the men handed over Richard Parker, who was taken ashore in irons. Six ships remained under red flags, including *Director*. Lord Keith visited each in turn and the men hauled down the red flag. *Director* was the last ship to be visited, and without further resistance the militants gave in.

There has been some attempt to make an issue out of the fact that *Director* was the last to surrender. This was a coincidence. Lord Keith visited the ships in no apparent order of increasing militancy. That he went to *Sandwich* and *Inflexible* first before *Director* confirms the Admiralty's intelligence that these two ships were the source of the mutiny and were exerting 'terror' on the other ships, including *Director*. The loyalists on *Director* had twice tried to retake the ship and, apart from the knowledge that Hollister was on board, the Admiralty had no reason to believe there would be further resistance, as events confirmed once Lord Keith boarded. As to Bligh's standing with the men on *Director*, we shall see in a moment what he thought, and did, about them.

With the end of the mutiny the retributions began. In theory the entire crew of every ship that raised the red flag was in danger of a charge of mutiny. But to have punished everybody would have depleted the ships of crews at a time when the navy was desperate for manpower. Lord Keith, sent down as nominal second-in-command to Admiral Buckner, nevertheless directed the operation of obtaining the surrenders of the mutineers as if he was in command of the Nore. He decided on a policy of punishing a representative number of men from each ship rather than everybody involved. He chose the arbitrary figure of ten per ship, though the tenth man on some ships was not as guilty as the fortieth or fiftieth on others. When Buckner resumed command he reasserted his authority in a different way, and caused some confusion in so doing. He took the mutiny as a personal failure and, as magnanimity and failure are not happy companions, he ordered the officers to send ashore all the guilty persons, and also required them to remark on the 'good conduct of such men as have in any particular evinced the same' (PRO Adm. 1/728).

When Buckner's order arrived on *Director*, Bligh was not yet on board. His First Lieutenant, MacTaggart, whom the mutineers had tolerated throughout the mutiny, had already responded to Lord Keith's orders and sent the ten worst offenders ashore, and to comply with Buckner's orders he sent another nineteen men. Two others, Hulme and McLaurin, who were the ship's delegates, were arrested ashore by Aaron Graham who was still in the employ of the Government as a spy.

On returning on board on 16 June 1797, Bligh was not pleased with this state of affairs. He acknowledged the orders from Keith and Buckner but objected, politely, to the changes they caused in the instructions the officers were asked to carry out. On 22 June Lord Keith wrote to Bligh enquiring of the 29 men represented as having been the most violent and asking for details of the charges against them all so 'that a certain number of the worst of them may be brought to trial' (Mackaness, 1951, p. 312). In accepting the 29 names he was meeting Buckner's intentions, but in seeking details so that 'a certain number' could be charged he was complying with his own original instructions. Bligh wrote back explaining that as his First Lieutenant had complied with his original order of submitting ten names it was assumed that the remainder of the crew were pardoned. Indeed Bligh had made this clear to the crew and only awaited a pardon from Buckner. In the meantime, he told Keith, he had not complied with the order to send details of the guilt of the 19 as he thought the circumstances of the implied and reported pardon had superseded the need to do so. In short, Bligh was pressing Keith to release the 19 without further investigation and to accept the original ten as *Director*'s contribution to the required quota of guilty men.

When the pardons for the crew arrived in July *Director* still had 29 names excluded from the official list. Bligh protested to Vice-Admiral Skeffington Lutwidge, who in turn asked the Admiralty for instructions. Lutwidge told the Admiralty that Bligh had 'led the remainder of the ship's company fully to depend that there would be a pardon for all the rest, and that he was apprehensive the confinement of a further number (meaning those also excepted in the pardon) would cause a very serious dissatisfaction in the crew' (PRO Adm. 1/728, F486). The Admiralty agreed to order the release of the 19 men and told Bligh to get individual promises from his crew not to 'engage in future in mutinous assemblies, nor take an oath of any kind whatsoever excepting such as may be administered to them by persons legally authorised to do so'.

In the courts martial that followed none of the twelve prisoners from *Director* were among the 59 sentenced to death or the 36 actually hanged.

Richard Parker was hanged, but Hollister was not. Many of the men were imprisoned, several dozen were transported to New South Wales (where Bligh was to meet them when he became Governor), others were flogged and yet more were kept in the Thames prison hulks until after the victory of Admiral Duncan at Camperdown which induced a free pardon from a happy and relieved Government.

# 32

# Battle of Camperdown

With the ending of the Nore mutiny the ships caught up in the affair rejoined Admiral Duncan's motley collection of old ships, plus the eighteen ships from the Russian navy, that constituted the North Sea Fleet. Blockade duty remained unpleasant, frustrating and largely unrewarding. The ships were unable in the main to practise fleet manoeuvres, and were fortunate when they were more than a token force together. From Bligh's letters we can see how frequently he was back in port, and with all the traffic to and from the Texel, plus search-and-detain missions over a wide area of the North Sea, from Yarmouth to the Texel, to the naze of Norway, to Leith, it is obvious why Duncan was unable to mould his fleet, such as it was, into the well-trained fighting machine of the kind that Nelson put together. Individual discipline was taut; gunnery practice was at the discretion of the individual captains (Bligh was very attentive to this detail) but all-fleet manoeuvres were few. The Russian ships, some of them captained by Scotsmen, were as good as useless to Duncan. They did not recognise his command in the same way as the British ships; they were often indifferent to his signals – largely because they did not understand them – and often went away on short cruises without notice. When the battle was finally joined the Russians were on one of their unilateral absences, though this did not prevent them putting in a claim years later for a share of the prize money (Lloyd, 1963, p. 121). It was by flag signals that a fleet commander kept his ships in order and directed them in the crucial stages of the battle. Individual captains had to know what the signals meant and had to log them with the response they gave. As we shall see, Bligh's Log throughout the battle was by far the most detailed.

Jervis's victory at Cape St Vincent in February 1797 was in the traditional pre-Nelsonian style of modest gains (four enemy ships captured) for a lot of effort. Duncan was a less spectacular man than Jervis. He was 65 years old, and the son of a Provost (Mayor) of Dundee. Though he reached Post-captain at 30, he took another twenty-six years to reach flag rank, and ten more to get a fleet command. He was offered the Mediterranean command in 1795 but declined it in favour of Jervis; instead he took command of the North Sea, and in 1797, after two gruelling years of blockade duty, plus the traumas of the Nore mutiny, he was still waiting his chance for battle honours. He had been given the oldest ships, and the most disaffected of crews, and enjoyed almost total lack of support from the Admiralty (the Dutch were always regarded as a side-show to the French).

Duncan had just brought his flag ship, *Venerable* (which had not mutinied with the Nore men), back to Yarmouth when news arrived in the lugger *Speculator* that the Dutch fleet had left the Texel and were at sea. Immediate orders were given to prepare the entire North Sea fleet for sea and within hours Duncan led his ships out from Yarmouth. *Russell*, *Ardent* and *Circe* were on station off the Dutch coast but naturally did not offer battle to the Dutch under Admiral de Winter. The Dutch had sixteen ships of the line, five frigates and five brigs. Captain Trollope, the British commander of the small token force left behind to keep an eye on the Texel, kept out of range but within sight, with the intention of following them and reporting to Duncan using small cutters as messengers.

Why the Dutch came out is a mystery. Their original purpose had been to support an Irish-inspired invasion, led by Wolf Tone, but these plans had been dropped by October 1797. With no apparent military purpose the business was foolhardy, unless the Dutch thought they could beat Duncan. If they had sailed in May they would have been fighting Duncan with a much-reduced fleet due to the mutinies. But by October the men were in a different mood; now they were determined to prove their loyalty and wipe the taint of mutiny from their records. Even with their poor ships, the seamen and their officers were geared to provide that extra effort that provides the margin needed for victory. On the Dutch side the situation was not similarly conducive to victory. Although the British were bored with blockade work, they had at least been able to get sea practice, while the Dutch had been confined to port duties only. All the same, of course, the Dutch were a nation with a distinguished naval record and were unlikely to be a pushover.

There was also a personal factor, in the form of Admiral Duncan. His past record showed him to be a sound and solid commander, but lacking – mainly for want of opportunity it seems – that imaginative spark that distinguishes a winner from a plodder. At Camperdown he rose to the occasion.

The Dutch Admiral took his fleet down the Dutch coast for about forty miles and then changed his mind: he decided to return to port. De Winter knew that Duncan's fleet would intercept him before he got back to the Texel, unless bad weather, or the mercies of any British incompetence, intervened, and he chose a battle plan designed to give him the advantage of the lee shore (one toward which the wind blew, thus threatening to drive ships attacking from the open sea onto the shore). As the Dutch ships were of shallower draft than the British, they could keep closer in to the shore and thus intimidate the British captains into concerning themselves both with the battle and with the safety of their ships. Similar attempts to use shallow water to forestall British ships attacking failed at the Nile in 1798 and Copenhagen in 1801.

The Dutch were sailing in nine fathoms (54 feet) about five miles off shore. Duncan's original plan had been to form a line of attack and make a pass along the Dutch ships (the traditional battle tactic of the day). Expecting this to be the case, the Dutch formed themselves in a line to engage the British.

Duncan abandoned his original plan as the Dutch were sailing for their home port and were offering battle 'on the run' rather than forming up for a set-piece engagement. This would force Duncan to arrange his ships in a line while trying to keep up with the Dutch, and as the speed with which this difficult task could be accomplished was dictated by the slowest ship he had with him he decided to abandon the plan. There was no point being in line in time for the Dutch to slip past him on their northerly journey.

Duncan divided the British into two, one group led by himself in *Venerable* and the other by Admiral Onslow in *Monarch*. They approached the Dutch line in somewhat disorganised formations. Some part of this disorder was caused by his ships either not seeing the signals, owing to the distance, or not understanding them; another part was due to the inapplicability of the signals to what the captains understood to be the situation. However, one signal all captains understood (at their peril) was that for 'close action'. Duncan set his ships onto the Dutch line like two wolf packs, allowing them to seize the initiative and exert maximum pressure on a few points in the Dutch line. Duncan had discovered, by accident of the circumstances, something which Nelson was to demonstrate at Trafalgar: a line defence is not effective against a pronged side-on attack. Once the engagement commenced, the smoke and confusion made it impossible to direct any but the very closest of ships. De Winter's plan held him to a fixed course of action: make for port. However, this was only feasible if his ships could weather the British attack and keep roughly to their courses. Once his line was broken and his ships lost momentum, they were at the mercy of events. This is precisely what happened. His ships had to stand and fight rather than fight on the run. Duncan's brilliant improvisation to circumstances, even if clumsily carried out by his ships, gave him a decisive victory. In terms of enemy ships destroyed and captured it was magnificent by contemporary standards (Nelson was to set new standards with his victory at the Nile in 1798).

Bligh's Log on *Director* has enabled naval historians to untangle the confusing battle of Camperdown; it is much more detailed than the Logs of other ships, largely because Bligh was always meticulous in reporting what he observed and because Bligh's ship took a full part in the contest. *Director* engaged ships in the southernmost group first, and, when victory was assured, Bligh took her to the northernmost group and joined in the fighting there. In this way he not only saw a good deal of what happened but was able to claim some credit for the afternoon's victory.

His account begins:

At 7.45 ... Russell showed her double pennants and made signal for an enemy being in sight, consisting of 16 line-of-battle ships, 4 frigates and 2 brigs. At 8.30, bore up. At 9, the Russell made the signal for 16 sail of the line. At 9.10, signal for sternmost ships to make more sail. At 9.15, signal to prepare for battle. Saw a fleet to southward. Cleared ship for action. At 11.18, Director's signal to lead no 95 Vice. At 11.25, Signal for ships to engage opponents. At 11.30 bore up for the enemy per signal. At 11.36, signal for lee division to engage the centre of the enemy. At 11.38, signal for the lee division to engage the rear of the enemy. At 11.47, signal – the Admiral means to pass through the enemy's line (Bligh, Log of *Director*, 1 January-31 December 1797, PRO Adm. 51/1156, 1195, 1229, 1285, 1298; also reproduced in Jackson (ed.), 1899, vol. 1, pp. 282-8).

From the Log we can see the rapidly changing situation reflected in the signals recorded by Bligh. Confusion in the ships was considerable. In the *Belliqueux* Captain Inglis, a Scot, is reported to have reacted to the confusing signals with an outburst in his native tongue, as he threw the signal book to the deck: 'Damn ... Up wi' the hel-lem and gang into the middle o' it' (Lloyd, 1963, p. 141). This was the inspired fighting spirit that took Duncan to victory. In another of his ships, *Agincourt*, Captain John Williamson was displaying an altogether different spirit, and one he had shown before on that fateful beach at Kealakekua Bay where Captain Cook was killed. There he 'misread' Cook's signal for help as an order to pull away from the fighting; at Camperdown he understood the confusing signals as an order from Duncan not to engage the enemy.

Bligh's Log continues:

At noon, Camperdown ESE 4 or 5 leagues. Our fleet standing down in two divisions for Action. The Monarch, Russell, Director and Montagu the headmost ships. The Monarch on our larboard beam, standing towards the Dutch Vice-Admiral. Admiral Duncan nobly leading his Division towards the Dutch Commander-in-Chief. The enemy's line formed on a wind on the larboard tack about NE by E. At 12.40, the Monarch (Vice-Admiral Onslow) began to engage the Dutch Vice-Admiral in a most spirited manner. At 12.45, we began with the second ship in the rear, the Russell having just begun before us with the sternmost ship, the rest of our Division came on and on all sides there was a general firing. The Dutch gave way, and the ships became mixed, so that it required sometimes great caution to prevent firing into one another.

The break-up of the Dutch line was fatal for them. It brought two or three British ships to bear on a single Dutch ship; odds that in the circumstances were overwhelming. By 1 o'clock the Dutch rear were in grave difficulties. *Russell* and *Montagu* were either side of the *Delft*,

*Director* and *Monmouth* either side of *Alkamaar*, *Powerful* and *Adamant* attacked *Haarlem* (which *Director* attacked when it moved up the line from the starboard side) and *Monarch* and *Veteran* attacked *Jupiter*. At this time only *Beaulieu*, a frigate, and *Agincourt* had not got alongside any of the Dutch ships.

> The Dutch began to strike, and particularly one to us, but we engaged different ships, indeed, believe most of all of the enemy's rear received shot from different ships of ours. The Director was now advancing towards Vice-Admiral Onslow's ship, when we found the ship she was engaging had struck, and the rear of the enemy done up. It appeared to me now that some force was wanted in the van, as we saw five ships unengaged and apparently not hurt, and also the Dutch Commander-in-Chief without any ships of ours engaged with him. There was no time to be lost, as night was approaching and as there were enough ships in our lee division about the rear of the enemy to take possession of them, I made sail (and passed Monarch) engaging some of the centre ships, for I considered now the capture of the Dutch Commander-in-Chief's ship as likely to produce the capture of those ahead of him, and I desired my first lieutenant to inform the officers and men I was determined to be alongside the Dutch Admiral.

Bligh's observation that *Vrijheid* was not being attacked when he saw it does not mean that the Dutch Commander-in-Chief had escaped so far without a fight. From 1 o'clock several ships were engaging her, including *Venerable* and *Ardent*. For more than an hour *Venerable* had been surrounded by enemy ships which were also being engaged by other British ships. *Ardent* received appalling casualties in its engagement with *Vrijheid*. Its captain was killed in the first broadside, the master minutes later, and two lieutenants received serious wounds. As Bligh sailed *Director* towards *Vrijheid*, *Ardent* was forced off with forty men dead and nearly a hundred wounded. As a 64-gun ship, it was outgunned by the Dutch flagship, but its crew's courage in going alongside and staying there for so long undoubtedly weakened the *Vrijheid*.

It is to Bligh's credit that he saw an opportunity to move to the head of the Dutch line; he could just as easily have made a meal of accepting Dutch surrenders or simply have stood off like *Agincourt*. Bligh, however, approached *Vrijheid*:

> At 3.5, we began the action with him, lying on his larboard quarter within 20 yards, by degrees we advanced alongside, firing tremendously at him, and then across his bows almost touching, when we carried away his foremast, topmast, topgallant mast and soon after his main mast, topmast and topgallant mast, together with his mizen mast, and left him nothing standing. The wreck lying all over his starboard side, most of his guns were of no use. I therefore hauled up along his starboard side and there we finished him for at 3.55 he struck and the action ended.

De Winter denied later that he struck his flag at all and claimed that his colours were hoisted and re-hoisted as they were shot down until he ran out of flags and lines. Striking a flag (lowering it from display) was the recognised signal for surrender, and De Winter's denial that he did so, and the reason he gave for why he could not continue flying it, was a common occurrence. But by not surrendering, De Winter, under the 'rules' of sea warfare, was inviting the British to continue inflicting heavy casualties by firing into his defenceless ship. When effective resistance is impossible, continuing a slaughter is a heavy price to pay for a nation's pride. As it was, *Vrijheid* sustained 58 dead and 98 wounded.

When *Vrijheid* 'struck', Bligh sailed *Director* over to *Venerable*, which was about half a mile away at this time. This does not mean that Duncan stood off from *Vrijheid*; sailing ships cannot be controlled like modern engine-driven warships. If the wind took Duncan away, he may not have been able to close the gap without a sailing manoeuvre which might not have been possible to execute in the midst of other, enemy, ships, and he might have been forced to engage any enemy ship he moved closer to. Bligh reports that Duncan 'hailed me to take possession of the *Vrijheid*, the ship we had just beaten, and I sent my first Lieutenant on board in consequence'. De Winter was sent on board Duncan's ship, *Venerable*, as protocol demanded, and Bligh received the *Vrijheid*'s captain's second-in-command, the captain being mortally wounded and unable to be moved. 'As soon as the action ended,' writes Bligh, 'my officers came to congratulate me, and to say there was not a man killed who they knew of, and of such good fortune I had no idea, for it passed belief. We had only seven men wounded. Before we got up with the Dutch Admiral we had a share with the Veteran in making a Dutch ship strike, and we passed close to leeward of a Dutch ship of the line on fire.'

Duncan's victory was complete. With it followed the honours. He was made a baronet, Viscount Duncan of Camperdown and Baron Duncan of Lundie (in Dundee a district today is still known as Camperdown). Admiral Onslow also became a baronet, and Captains Trollope and Fairfax were knighted. Gold medals were issued to all the captains. But the price of victory was high: 228 dead and 812 wounded. The Dutch lost 540 dead and 620 wounded. But as with all naval victories of the day, once the honours and celebrations were over the Admirals and Captains got down to the usual and undignified business of squabbling over prize-money (in this case the division of £150,000). Bligh, like many others, including Admiral Nelson in a famous claim he ran for many years in dispute with his Commander-in-Chief, fought long and hard, and eventually without success, for his share of the *Vrijheid*; he had to accept his allotted share in the end.

Duncan ordered Bligh to take the Dutch ship *Gelijkeid* (Egalité), to Yarmouth, and when he arrived on 18 October he wrote to Evan Nepean at the Admiralty:

My Commander in Chief not being here, I have the honour to inform you for the information of my Lords Commissions of the Admiralty that I anchored here last night with His Majesty's ship Director and Egalite, sixty-four, a prize of the Fleet.

I took charge of her by order of Admiral Duncan from whom, owing to the badness of the weather, and having the ship in tow, we unavoidably parted company.

Two ships are observed at the back of the Sand and I have reason to hope that one of them is the Liberty [Vrijheid], Admiral De Winter's ship, as Admiral Duncan, from my having been alongside of her allowed me to take possession and I sent my first Lieutenant, Mr MacTaggart, to command her.

The Director had only seven men at all touched with the shot or splinter, three of whom only are now on the doctor's list (PRO Adm. 1/1516 Captain 'B').

While Bligh received the congratulations of Admiral Duncan and the coveted gold medal from the mint, Captain John Williamson of the *Agincourt* was tried and convicted after the battle. His court martial took place on HMS *Circe*, the attendant frigate to Duncan's squadron at Camperdown. There were two charges: disobedience to signals and not going into action; cowardice and disaffection. The trial opened on 4 December 1797 and ended on New Year's Day 1798. It was prolonged because of the complications of the evidence, which turned it into an enquiry of the battle itself. Such was the confusion about what happened that dozens of witnesses were closely questioned for hours, with their Log Books as evidence, as to who was where and who saw what. Bligh's appearance and evidence were surprisingly brief.

Bligh's testimony was not unhelpful to Williamson, though it was by no means central to the prosecution's case. The main charge was that Williamson had held his ship back during the conflict contrary to Duncan's orders. It followed that the prosecution had to prove this by evidence from the other captains; once they proved disobedience, they could then establish cowardice and disaffection.

Bligh's evidence was as follows:

Q. Did you make any observations on that day, on the Agincourt's conduct in making full sail during the action, so far as you were in a situation to observe her? A. No; I made no observation of the Agincourt, making sail. I don't recollect taking any notice of the Agincourt but once, and that merely momentary during the action, when the ships were engaged, and I fancied at that time the whole of the rear division was engaging. They seemed much crowded. Q. (By Captain Williamson). If the Agincourt had lain to a mile and half to windward of the fleet for half-an-hour, under her topsails and her main topsail aback, after the Vice-Admiral had commenced the action, would you not have seen her? A. I did not see her in that situation (*The Times*, 16 December 1797).

The Court found the charges of disobeying a signal as 'proved in part' and the other charges 'not proved'. It sentenced Williamson to remain on the bottom of the list of Post-captains (thus precluding promotion to flag rank) and declared him 'incapable of ever serving' on board any ship in the Royal Navy again. Nelson considered the sentence deplorably light: 'I would have every man believe, I shall only take my chance of being shot by the Enemy, but if I do not take that chance, I am certain of being shot by my friends.'

Williamson's naval career was ended. Why Bligh covered for him is not known. Circumstantially, I believe he did so in 1797 for the same reason that he was silent about Williamson's role in Cook's death in 1779 – there was, perhaps, some secret masonic connection between the two.

Bligh's conduct at Camperdown was criticised almost forty years later by an anonymous reviewer in the *United Service Journal* (1837, part ii, pp. 147-9). The occasion was a review of a two-volume history of the Royal Navy by Captain E.P. Brenton. Brenton had remarked that one or two of the captains at Camperdown had 'elicited the severest censure' from Admiral Duncan. The reviewer stated that Duncan 'might have said four or five, without fear of contradiction'. He names *Montagu* and *Agincourt* as being among the four or five deserving of censure and then opens a blistering attack on Bligh in *Director*, 'the most modest of the shy ships'. Bligh's report of the battle is described as 'an article concocted under the express superintendence of her Commander', and he quotes incidents on *Director*, naming the second and third lieutenants, S. Birch and W.W. Foote, as witnesses for Bligh's misconduct.

The anonymous reviewer's case is spoiled by inaccuracy in the timings and events. He misquotes Duncan's reports to suit his case and puts other facts in doubt. For example he claims that Bligh reported that the *Vrijheid* 'at four struck to us'. He did not; he claimed that the *Vrijheid* struck at 3.55. The importance of the time lies in the reviewer's quoting Duncan's Log that the *Vrijheid* struck at 3 pm: 'the Admiral's ship is dismasted and has struck, as have several others.' The implication is that Bligh was fighting a non-existent engagement with an enemy that had already surrendered.

In Duncan's despatch, written after the battle, when he had time to reflect on the exact order of events, he gives the following details:

> The action commenced about Forty Minutes past Twelve o'clock. The Venerable soon got through the Enemy's Line, and I began a close Action, with my Division in the Van, which lasted near Two Hours and a Half, when I observed all the Masts of the Dutch Admiral's Ship to go by the Board; she was, however, defended for some Time in a most gallant Manner; but being overpressed by Numbers, her Colours were struck, and Admiral De Winter was soon brought on Board Venerable (Lloyd, 1963, pp. 169-71).

Two and a half hours from 12.40 takes the time to 3.10, the time when Duncan observed the dismasting of the *Vrijheid*. Bligh's account also gives the time of the action commencing as 12.40 and his own engagement with the *Vrijheid* commencing at 3.05. He reports he dismasted *Vrijheid* in his first pass along it, and there is such a close coincidence in their reports that the reviewer's interpretation of the Admiral's Log, hastily written in the midst of a battle, must be suspect. This is more particularly so when Duncan adds that the *Vrijheid* 'was, however, defended for some Time in a most gallant Manner', and we remember that De Winter denied he struck at all. The incontrovertible fact is that Bligh's First Lieutenant led the boarding party that arranged for De Winter to be escorted to *Venerable* and the ship's second-in-command, Captain-Lieutenant Siccame, was escorted to *Director*. Duncan left the timing of the surrender imprecise in his despatch to the Admiralty as 'some Time' after 3.15; Bligh stated it precisely on two occasions, in his Log and in his Memorandum drawn up afterwards, as 3.55. I think it unlikely that he got it wrong and that the anonymous reviewer of a book forty years later got it right.

The reviewer goes on to quote 'irrefragible' witnesses, including the Second and Third Lieutenants. They reported that Bligh did not put on more sail when ordered to do so, that he silenced their criticisms and ordered one of them to go to his station below decks, that he ordered the First Lieutenant to put tarpaulins over the grates and ensure that nobody else left his station, that he held back until the Dutch ships were engaged, that he pretended that the ship was not ready for action afterwards, and that he refused to tell Lieutenant Brodie on the *Rose* cutter how many were injured because so few were.

There are several dubious points in the reviewer's claim that Bligh's conduct was open to censure over these incidents. *Director* was an older, smaller and slower ship than the 74-gun ships of the line accompanying it in the division that attacked the rear of the Dutch line. Bligh's log records that *Russell* signalled for the 'sternmost ships to make more sail'. This could not have applied to *Director* as it was then line abreast of *Monarch*, *Powerful*, *Monmouth*, *Russell* and *Montagu*. The sternmost ships were *Agincourt*, *Adamant* and *Veteran*. Knowing Bligh's temperament, he no doubt would have ordered Lieutenant Birch to his post if he dared to tell him on his own quarter-deck how to conduct his ship. When going into close action, the Lieutenant's post was on the gun deck; he had no business to be elsewhere. Hence telling MacTaggart to ensure that nobody else left his post is hardly a criticism of Bligh; men who saw officers disappearing from their posts were hardly encouraged to stay by theirs. The fact that he ordered Lieutenant MacTaggart to cover the gratings with tarpaulin confirms their proximity to close action, for this was done to protect the gun deck from falling objects and burning embers. Bligh would be open to serious criticism if he had not given this order.

His sending MacTaggart to *Vrijheid* when it struck was a strong recommendation for his First Lieutenant's promotion and evidence that Bligh was well satisfied with his conduct. Perhaps he was less satisfied with his other two lieutenants and this is the basis of their weak criticisms of him?

The most telling problem for the reviewer's claims is the alleged incident with Brodie in the *Rose* cutter. This is supposed to have passed round the fleet after the battle enquiring about the casualties and damage. But according to Duncan he sent the *Rose* to Yarmouth 'at three p.m. on the 12 instant, with a short Letter to you, immediately after the Action was ended' (Lloyd, 1963). It was standard policy to send news to the Admiralty immediately after the outcome of an engagement. The timing is important: 3 pm (the date accords with the nautical practice of running each day from twelve noon to twelve noon rather than from midnight to midnight). *Rose* could not have run round the fleet 'in the course of the night', thus undermining the factual basis of the reviewer's criticism. Nor can much be made of the casualties and damage in each ship. *Director* had its 'fore yard shot away, topsail yard badly wounded, bowsprit shot through, the foretopmast shot through the head, booms and boats shot through, stays, running rigging, and sails much cut'. As to the casualties Bligh reported, *Russell*, which distinguished itself, had the same casualties as *Director*; other ships came off far worse. In a close action, death was a lottery.

The final word ought perhaps to be left with Admiral Duncan. He wrote to Bligh in October 1798, while *Director* was back at the Nore, presumably for a refit, that he wanted him back with the North Sea Fleet: 'I have mentioned to the Admiralty that if your ship is paid off I hope they will immediately give you another as I have always observed her conducted like a Man of War' (ML MS C218, p. 59).

Much of 1798 was spent on blockade duty in the North Sea. Bligh's letters and Logs show him busy as usual with the normal tasks that blockade duty and captaining a 64-gun entailed. He sat on a court martial of 'a fellow' who had declared himself to be a 'United Irishman' along with fifteen other seamen on the same charge, who had planned to take HMS *Diomede* to the Texel. This was part of a widespread Irish rebellion, both in Ireland and on some of the King's ships, which was put down forcefully and brutally. Hundreds were killed, including those by Lord Cornwallis, a veteran of the American war, who massacred several hundred prisoners captured in the only serious engagement of the uprising. Even *Defiance* joined the list of ships allegedly endangered by Irish rebellion, though in this case the men did no more than confer together, for which some of them were hanged for their pains. The verdicts of the courts martial were savage even by naval standards: four seamen on *Caesar* were hanged, another twenty on *Defiance*, eight on *Glory*, four on *St George*, and several more on *Marlborough*. One of the *Diomede* men was hanged and another was flogged round the fleet.

Bligh was also engaged in the court martial of his Master, Joseph Ramsay, who was tried (all too familiarly) for answering him 'in a very improper manner & impertinently' and saying 'If I am not able to Work the Ship, it is better to have some person else here'. He was dismissed from the ship (PRO Adm. 1/5349). In another court martial John Heugh was tried 'for endeavouring to excite mutiny and for disobeying the lawful commands of his officers when at sea' (PRO Adm. 1/524, F227).

Later in the year Bligh took *Director* to St Helena to escort a convoy of East Indiamen home and collect some specimens for Kew Gardens. He drew a chart of the cruise and this was published in 1800 by Arrowsmith. Back in a hot climate, his illness recurred, causing him to remark in a letter to Elizabeth Bligh that 'our Native Climate agrees with me best'. On his way home he expressed the 'hope I shall now end the War' as 'my health requires to be attended to' (Rutter, 1936, pp. 194-5).

Bligh remained on *Director* until 2 July 1800, when it went out of commission and he was put on half-pay, but the Admiralty found another use for his talents. He had shown some promise as a hydrographer from a running survey of the River Humber, and one of his later assignments was to make a regular survey of Dublin harbour (PRO Adm. 1/3523). The authorities said of Bligh's survey that 'it would be of infinite importance to their navigation, it being so correct and of such authority' (PRO Adm. 1/1525). Bligh sought, and was given, permission by the Admiralty to have his surveys published, which had the side-effect, apart from the prestige, of earning him some income. He also made a sketch survey of Holyhead harbour with a view to deciding on its suitability for the Irish packet boats, and he was in correspondence with the Admiralty for payment of his expenses in May 1801.

On 13 March 1801 Bligh was back in command again, this time as Captain of HMS *Glatton*, a 54-gun ship, and one that was to take him through the bloodiest battle in British naval history, the battle of Copenhagen.

# 33

# Battle of Copenhagen

The battle of Copenhagen, in which Bligh played a not insignificant part, was the fiercest battle of Nelson's career and has been described as 'the great gamble' (Pope, 1972). It was caused by the machinations of the mad Russian Tsar Paul I, who persuaded four other Baltic kingdoms to declare the Baltic out of bounds to British commercial shipping. Britain was then at the height of its sea-power, and it was left to the amiable Danes to stand up against her in defence of its allies' declaration. The Russian Court decided to end the declaration before it embroiled the country in a war with Britain, and Paul I was strangled in his bed to remove Russia from any further provocations. Meanwhile the British and Danish naval forces met, and bled, outside Copenhagen harbour.

Nelson's determination was not matched by the manner in which the fleet was despatched and commanded to achieve its purpose of reopening the Baltic to British shipping. While the declaration barring British ships was academic during the ice-bound winter months, the imminence of a spring thaw brought the issue to a head. Either Britain dealt with any country trying to enforce the declaration, or it submitted. The former was difficult, the latter politically impossible in the broader context of the war with France.

The Admiralty ordered twenty-one ships of the line to form a fleet to deal with the Baltic crisis. This was a larger fleet than had fought at St Vincent, the Nile or Camperdown. Admiral Sir Hyde Parker was appointed to command the fleet, with Nelson designated as his second-in-command. Parker, then approaching his mid-sixties, was somewhat diverted from his duties by his new, 18-year-old, bride, the daughter of Sir Richard Onslow. He had fixed on a ball in her honour for Friday 13 March and was in consequence disinclined to take the fleet out before then.

Nelson was none too happy at this dithering, given that his own mind was distracted with Lady Hamilton, though he put duty before personal affairs. He wrote to his friend Troubridge on the Board of Admiralty an almost too frank letter expressing his disgust at Parker's behaviour, which included the memorable line: 'Consider how nice it must be laying in bed with a young wife, compared to a damned cold raw wind.' Lord St Vincent, Nelson's former commander, and now First Lord of the Admiralty (replacing Spenser) had a prejudice against subordinates who conducted 'intrigue' against their Commanders-in-Chief, but he learned of the situation at Yarmouth (the constant flow of reports and letters between captains and the Admiralty ensured that 'gossip' quickly reached the Lords Commissioners, though it was probably called 'intelligence' then as now). While Parker's fleet awaited his convenience, he privately warned him of the 'irreparable injury' his career could suffer if he delayed getting to sea much longer. Parker took the hint, cancelled the ball and sailed on the next wind out of port.

Parker's relations with Nelson were strained, perhaps because of his suspicions of Nelson's ambitions and of Nelson's role in alerting the Admiralty to the situation at Yarmouth. Eighteenth-century naval 'politics' must always be taken into account when judging the relationships of officers or reports of their conduct (a point that accounts of Bligh's career forget at the risk of being grossly misleading). Parker treated Nelson as if he did not exist or, if he did, as if he merited no attention whatsoever. Up to the eve of the battle Parker did not disclose his orders to his second-in-command.

Nelson arrived at Yarmouth on 4 March 1801; both he and Parker had been in London two weeks earlier, but they had not met. Nor did they meet while together at Yarmouth and for some days after the fleet sailed, an extraordinary state of affairs which puts Bligh's occasional discourtesies to his officers into perspective. Parker and Nelson communicated by letter, with Parker ignoring or rejecting Nelson's written recommendations. Interestingly, Nelson and St Vincent were not on close terms either at this time, as their lawyers and agents were still locked in argument about the division of prize-money between them.

The Baltic fleet was being put together as early as 12 February 1801. Of the nineteen ships chosen, fourteen were ready for sea, or at sea, and two were 'doubtful'. Among those ready for sea was HMS *Glatton*, a 54-gun converted East Indiaman, armed with the controversial carronades. These were designed to fire a larger round with a smaller charge than the normal naval guns. They had been adopted in 1780 but had passed their peak of popularity by 1800. They could fire a greater amount of shot for their length and weight and this increased the damage they could inflict on an enemy ship. Their need for closer range exposed the ship to greater damage from the enemy's guns, but their destructive power promised quicker suppression of resistance. They had another disadvantage: they increased the fire risk to the ship firing them.

The Admiralty was appointing commanders right up to the eve of the departure of the fleet. Bligh had been lobbying the Admiralty for a sea command and on 13 March he was given command of *Glatton*, relieving Captain Stephen as the fleet prepared to sail. Parker's delay ensured

Bligh's place at Copenhagen; if he had sailed on time, Stephen would have been Nelson's second, not Bligh. This last-minute change did not please Stephen, for he told Bligh that the fleet 'were astonished to hear [Bligh] was to command the Glatton' (ML MS C218).

Parker switched from procrastination to urgency and left so quickly that some of his ships remained in port, being unready for sailing. Others had to come up from the Nore, and as he did not inform them of his departure, they headed first for Yarmouth. One of them, HMS *Invincible*, approaching a by now deserted Yarmouth, hit a sand bar and sank, taking with it 400 men. But having left in a hurry, Parker's progress across the North Sea was painfully slow; he sometimes lost as much as they gained in a day's sailing.

On 19 March 1801 the fleet stood off the Danish coast, beyond the horizon, while diplomatic moves were made to persuade the Danes to accept a peaceful, i.e. British, settlement. Vansittart, a British diplomat, was sent ashore to persuade the Danes to treat for peace. Nelson, typically, thought little of this 'pen and ink' activity, and offered the opinion that 'A fleet of British men-of-war are the best negotiators in Europe'.

Vansittart returned with news that the Danes would not give up their membership of the Federation of Armed Neutrality and that they were constructing formidable defences at Copenhagen. This did little to encourage Parker's already flagging spirit, and it forced Nelson to conduct a strenuous, almost insubordinate, campaign for militant action. Parker, a more cautious man, had relied on the diplomatic measures to produce a solution; Nelson, an audacious fighting man, wanted immediate action. He preferred to overpower Britain's enemies with the Navy, and saw the Russians as lynchpin to the break-up of the Federation of Armed Neutrality. Once the Russians were defeated at sea, the Federation would collapse. But he was not fussy which end of the Baltic was tackled first.

Copenhagen is situated on the east side of an island off the east coast of Denmark. The channel on the west side of the island, between it and Fyn Island, is known as the Great Belt, and by sailing down this channel and east along the Prussian coast the fleet could approach Copenhagen from the south. Alternatively, it could approach from the north by sailing through a narrow channel between Denmark and Sweden. The Great Belt route postponed a decision on whether to attack Denmark or Russia first, because the fleet could either turn north to Copenhagen or continue east to Russia. Parker favoured the Great Belt route for this reason. He was also concerned that the fleet passing through the Sjaelland Sound would be exposed to Danish and Swedish batteries. He was persuaded, however, to change his mind, and the fleet hove-to while the arguments continued. The pilots, not for the last time, disagreed with the captains, this time on account of the dangerous shallows and shoals which they felt made the Sjaelland Sound too dangerous.

Exasperated by this dilatoriness, Nelson sought permission to take a

squadron through the narrow channel past Copenhagen and on to the
Baltic to meet the Russian fleet. Parker could sit it out at the entrance to
the Baltic while he got on with the war. His patience with the pilots
eventually snapped.

Parker wanted new orders from London for the plan to attack Russia,
so Nelson eventually persuaded him that his single squadron could
attack Copenhagen instead. On 26 March 1801 he won Parker's approval
for this bold stroke.

The ditherings and delays had affected the entire fleet by the time
Nelson got his way. When he met the captains of the ships assigned to his
squadron, which included Bligh on *Glatton*, they were far from
enthusiastic. Some of them – it is not known which – expressed doubts
about the ability of the squadron to silence the Danish guns. The Danes
had been given plenty of time to strengthen their defences, and to give
their inexperieced crews gunnery practice. Nelson spent a day convincing
everybody that they could win, and this cemented his relationships with
them all, an important factor that proved decisive in the battle.

Nelson remarked of the Danish defences: 'It only looks formidable to
those who are children of war, but to my judgment, with ten sail of the
line I think I can annihilate them; at all events, I hope to be allowed to
try' (Oman, 1947, p. 437).

The entrance to Copenhagen harbour was a narrow channel dominated
by the great Trekroner (Three Crowns) Fort. To make things more
difficult, the Danes had removed the channel buoys, and attacking ships
would have to be careful not to run aground (the pilots were of no use in a
military situation). Between the Danish line of defence and the main
channel there was a shallow known as the Middle Ground, and the
channels on either side were known as the King's Deep and Holland
Deep. Nelson's plan was to pass down the Holland Deep, out of range of
the Danish guns, and then swing up into the King's Deep to attack the
Danish defences from the south and minimise the damage that could be
done by the Trekroner guns. The British ships were too large to cross the
Middle Ground, and the Danish ships and floating batteries were
anchored on the edge of the shallows in such a way that the British could
not get behind them and use the tactics that had worked so brilliantly at
the Nile. The Danes had placed their ships carefully, forcing the British
to pass in front of them. This meant that as the Danes need only fight
from one side of their ships they could deploy their limited supply of
experienced gunners among their less experienced, but enthusiastic,
volunteers. A battle in open water was bound to invite the British to
demonstrate their superiority in gunnery. Moreover, as the Trekroner
and Lynetten forts were unsinkable, they had some confidence that they
could cripple any assault from the north.

In taking his ships down the Holland Deep, Nelson had to endure
disagreements among the pilots as to where the channel lay. Eventually

he organised the sounding of the channels, using his own men, and marked the passage with temporary buoys. While the sounding parties were working through the night, Parker and Nelson met on board HMS *London*. Parker insisted that *Ganges* and *Edgar* join the small squadron of ten ships (among which was *Isis*, whose first Lieutenant was the 31-year-old Robert Tinkler, formerly of *Bounty*; his brother-in-law, John Fryer, was also present in Parker's fleet).

Nelson took his squadron down the narrow channel and, by keeping to the Swedish side, avoided the Danish guns. He took the *Amazon* frigate, Captain Riou, for a look at the Danish defences, and in doing so became acquainted with the *Amazon*'s commander. They took an instant liking to each other and Riou worked closely with Nelson in the preparations for the battle.

Once the squadron was at the southern end of the Middle Ground, they had to survey the King's Deep, again in the dark to avoid interference from the Danish ships. Not only was the width of the King's Deep of great importance, but so was the direction of the slope of the sea bed. For Nelson's plan to succeed, each ship needed enough room beside it for another ship to pass. He intended that the first British ship into the channel would drop anchor and engage the first Danish ship or floating battery; the second ship would leapfrog round it and engage the second Danish ship, and so on. Each ship thus avoided being raked by Danish fire before it got into position.

From the disposition of the Danish defences they appear to have expected an attack down the north channel, which would have exposed each British ship to the Trekroner's guns. Nelson's plan minimised the military effect of these preparations, and enabled the 'bombs' (specially fitted warships with heavy mortars suitable for bombarding Copenhagen out of range of the Danish guns) to be brought up as a reserve to attack the ships defending the city (and perhaps to attack the city itself). Nelson's plan remained a gamble. Could he position his ships? Could they sustain the Danish guns and eventually suppress them? Could he force a Danish capitulation?

Nelson held a final conference on board *Elephant*, his flag ship, the night before the battle. Bligh was present. Having gone over his plans in detail once again, Nelson shook hands individually with each of his captains. After they left he spent most of the night dictating final orders to each captain and had them sent across to each ship by messenger. Bligh's written orders from Nelson are preserved among his papers in the Mitchell Library, along with a pen-and-ink drawing of the disposition of the ships in the battle (ML Safe 1/39). Every ship was ordered to have its sheet and spare anchors over the side 'ready to let go at a moments notice' because 'great precision is necessary in the placing the ships'. Bligh was at his best in carrying out such orders. Other captains were less fortunate, and Nelson's plan almost collapsed from the start.

*Agamemnon* ran aground on the Holland Deep side of the Middle
Ground and was out of action for the duration of the battle. This left the
58-gun *Provesteenen* uncovered and able to fire at every ship that passed
it. Nelson signalled *Polyphemus* to attack *Provesteenen* (its original target
being the last ship in the Danish line). *Edgar* (74), Captain George
Murray, was the first to open fire on the Danes, which it did as it passed
them on its way to its target, *Jylland* (54). *Isis* (50), Captain James
Walker, *Russell* (74), Captain Cumming, *Ardent* (64), Captain Thomas
Bertie, and *Glatton* (54), Captain William Bligh, followed next. Bligh
fired his carronades into the *Provesteenen*, doing much damage, and then
reloaded to fire into *Wagrien*. His target was the Danish flagship,
*Dannebrog*, and he stood 200 yards off her and began to pour in his
broadsides 'at 10.26'. *Isis* was just astern of *Glatton* attacking *Wagrien*.

In the billowing smoke of the battle *Bellona* passed too far to the
starboard and grounded on a spur running out of the Middle Ground.
This accident was partly the fault of the pilots who had insisted at
Nelson's last meeting that the slope of the King's Deep went from left to
right, with the deepest part of the channel against the Middle Ground.
This contradicted Captain Hardy's night time survey which suggested
the opposite – the deepest part of the channel was closest to the Danish
ships. In the row the pilots refused to take the ships into the channel if
their advice was not accepted. In response *Bellona*'s Master volunteered
to take the lead ship, *Edgar*, into the channel, which in consequence
removed him from *Bellona* and contributed to its grounding. Nelson had
no doubt about the competence of the pilots. He wrote that he had
'experienced in the Sound the misery of having the honour of our Country
intrusted to Pilots, who have no other thought than to keep the Ship clear
of danger, and their own silly heads clear of shot … Everybody knows
what I must have suffered; and if any merit attaches itself to me, it was in
combatting the dangers of the shallows in defiance of the Pilots' (Nelson
to St Vincent, [29th] September 1801, in Nicolas (ed.), 1844-6, vol. 4,
p. 499).

The situation worsened. *Russell* followed *Bellona* onto the Middle
Ground, taking another ship out of the battle. Instead of twelve ships
Nelson now had nine. Following behind *Russell*, he swung *Elephant*'s
helm to port to pass on the port side of the stranded ships, and
fortunately the other ships followed him. He took *Elephant* into the
vacant spot ahead of *Glatton* and joined in the attack on *Dannebrog*. He
wanted to get closer to *Dannebrog* but once the again the pilots objected,
with warnings that he would ground if he did so (despite the fact that the
Danish ships were in the same channel and ungrounded). With other
things on his mind Nelson did not argue with them, and anchored
*Elephant* where it was.

The plan was now severely disrupted and the ships behind him had to
improvise. *Ganges* (74) was next up the King's Deep and it anchored

opposite Nelson's orginal target, *Sjaelland* (74), followed by *Monarch* (74) and *Defiance*. This brought Nelson's second-in-command, Rear Admiral Thomas Graves, ahead of Nelson and between him and Admiral Parker (then some miles to the north). With all the British ships opposite the Danish ships and floating batteries, battle commenced in earnest. At the northern end of the line, the mighty fortresses of Trekroner and Lynetten were attacked by frigates under Captain Riou, instead of by line-of-battle ships. The match was grossly uneven, but Riou had no choice in the circumstances. He flung his smaller ships into action and for the next few hours stood his ground through some of the heaviest gunfire of the battle.

After a few exchanges the entire battle area was blanketed by smoke and neither side could see the other. As they were all anchored, this did not matter too much; they simply kept firing into the smoke in the direction where they knew the enemy was anchored. This stationary, stand-up, close-action battle was worse than any of the veterans had experienced. The only chance of survival was to keep firing as accurately and as often as possible at the enemy to suppress his fire first. Discipline and training were the ingredients of victory and the British crews excelled in these. The Danes made up for their lack of experience with outstanding enthusiasm and patriotism. They were also untroubled by the 'rules' of naval combat; they did not surrender a ship when they could no longer fire its guns due to heavy casualties among the gun crews – they simply replenished the crews from ashore and reopened the contest.

Exhausted British seamen found silenced, battered and smouldering wrecks suddenly reopening fire with fresh Danish volunteers. Because the British could not likewise replace their casualties, and because the 'rules' of striking colours were not being played, they had no choice but to keep up a murderous fire onto the Danish ships and batteries where normally they would have desisted, if only on humanitarian grounds (and with half an eye on minimally damaging the enemy for the prize money).

Bligh noted in his Log, after two hours of close action, and with seven of his upper guns disabled: 'At noon, the action continuing very hot, ourselves much cut up. Our opponent, the Danish Commodore, struck to us, but his seconds ahead and astern [*Elven* and *Aggerhuus*] still keep up a strong fire.' The battle continued in like manner for another two hours. Neither side could give up; the British could not withdraw without risking massive damage in collisions, grounding and exposing themselves to unreturned gunfire. Hence each side continued blasting away and taking casualties. From a distance the situation must have looked desperate, and so it did to Parker, standing off with the main fleet a few miles to the north.

In fact the situation was beginning to turn slowly in favour of the British ships. *Provensteenen* and *Wagrien* were shot into submission and boarded, though the boarders only found dead and wounded. *Rendsborg* was hit below the water line and driven out of position; it moved out of one action and, in Danish fashion, back into another action further up the line, though it was badly crippled. *Nyeborg* was blasted out of line by *Edgar* and drifted shorewards. *Hyland* fought until it was exhausted and ceased fire for lack of working guns and ammunition. *Ardent* took on three Danish ships, *Cronborg*, *Hayen* and *Elven*, firing at all three (a manoeuvre in which British gunnery supremacy was at a premium) until they were silenced after 2 pm. *Glatton* was firing its carronades into *Dannebrog* and, with less effect, at the floating batteries round it, which, being relatively unscathed, did considerable damage in return.

*Svoedfisken* was in a terrible state by noon but kept firing to the end of the battle. *Sjaelland* lost a third of its crew from the gunfire of *Ganges* and when its cables were cut by shot it drifted out of the battle. *Monarch* received the highest casualties on the British side; its captain was killed in the first minutes and command passed to Lieutenant Yelland. He worked hard and courageously against *Charlotte Anne* (26), *Sohesten* floating battery and *Holsteen* (60), as well as being under fire from the Trekroner fort. Admiral Fischer, the Danish Commander-in-Chief, was driven off his flagship, *Dannebrog*, when it was silenced by *Glatton* and *Elephant*, and he took his command to *Holsteen*, opposite *Monarch*. He was eventually driven off that ship as well and went ashore to the Trekroner fort, but by then the Danish situation was critical. *Hioelperen* surrendered right in front of Trekroner and Admiral Fischer.

Admiral Parker, moving slowly towards the battle from the north (the wind was southerly) could not see clearly what was going on; he could not advance too close to the King's Deep from the north without blocking an escape by Nelson's ships should they require to retreat. He sent Captain Otway ahead to report on the situation. But his very appearance with a fresh fleet was of concern to the Danes. Did they face a fresh hammering from a new fleet? The British 'bombs' were now also in position and threatened by their presence the capital itself. Incredibly, at this moment, Parker's caution overcame him and he decided not to await Otway's report. He ordered Signal no. 39 to be flown from his flagship. This was the signal to 'discontinue the action'.

A signal from a Commander-in-Chief is not discretionary; Nelson was under an obligation to obey. But Parker was four miles away from the battle and Nelson was in the middle of it and in full command of what was going on. If he broke off at that moment, not only would he be in difficulty extricating his ships in the narrow channel under fire from the Danish forts but he would also throw away whatever he had gained by attacking so vigorously over four hours. If he did not break off he would be in jeopardy with his superior, and anyway he could not be sure what confusion the signal would cause to the ships in his fleet.

Nelson already had a reputation for the unorthodox; at the battle of St Vincent he had disobeyed precise instructions at a crucial point in the battle, but fortunately for him his actions were endorsed by their success.

Here again Nelson acted characteristically. He ignored his Admiral's signal, saying: 'Leave off Action! Now damn me if I do!', and he made the by now famous remark, as he looked northwards with his telescope to his blind eye: 'I really do not see the signal.' But that was only for form. His signal officer saw the signal, he reported it to him, and as far as naval regulations went Nelson did not have to see the signal himself to obey it.

Captain Riou continued firing at the forts from his frigate, *Amazon*, after Parker's signal was seen at 1.15 pm. But astern of *Amazon* was the fleet's third-in-command, Admiral Graves, who was acutely embarrassed by Parker's signal, so much so that he responded with a no. 39 but kept Nelson's no. 16 (close action) flying too. He also continued to fire, thus ignoring no. 39. Riou had little option but to obey no. 39, as his two consorts, *Dart* and *Arrow*, acknowledged no. 39 when Graves flew it (in the smoke they may have missed his continuing with no. 16). Riou is reported to have declared, as he gave the orders to cease firing, 'What will Nelson think of us?' Wounded and bitter, he ordered *Amazon* to swing round and leave the battle. As the smoke cleared round the ship, the Trekroner guns were given an easy target. They fired at *Amazon*, and Captain Riou was cut in two by the full force of a shot and killed outright.

The loss of the frigates to the north was not decisive, but it did weaken the fire on the Danes. The crucial decision lay with Nelson and the ships astern of him. If they stopped firing, the Danes could claim a victory. Immediately astern of Nelson was Bligh in *Glatton*. His usually meticulous Log is vague for once: 'PM the action continuing very hot. At 2.45 it may be said to have ended.' No mention of singal no. 39. Of course, he may not have seen it, and as long as Nelson flew no. 16 he was 'covered' from repercussions, if any were to be made. Just as Nelson could be 'blind' for once, so Bligh could also be vague in his Log for once. Bligh's role as Nelson's second had a bearing on the decisions of the ships astern of him. By remaining in close action he ensured that Nelson's decision was transmitted along the line. None of the ships astern of Bligh ceased firing in response to Parker's no. 39.

By 2 pm the situation evidently was in Nelson's favour. None of his ships was seriously disabled or in distress. Some, including *Glatton*, were severely damaged. Three of them were non-combatants through grounding, and while the smaller ships to the north had ceased action, the main body of the squadron were keeping up a rapid fire on the Danes. Five of the eight Danish ships were silenced, except for an occasional maverick gun fired by enthusiastic volunteers, and three of the four floating batteries were also silenced. Many of the smaller Danish ships had ceased firing. Only the three forts, Trekroner, Lynetten and Sixtus, were firing for effect. To reduce these forts a landing by marines would be necessary, but the water between the British ships and the forts was crowded with floating wrecks and drifting ships. Nelson had by now disobeyed Parker's signal for a hour; he could not continue with the fiction that he was unaware of the Admiral's orders.

To preserve the fruits of his victory and comply with his duties to Parker, Nelson decided to offer the Danish Crown Prince a truce. He sent a message ashore under a flag of truce:

> Lord Nelson has directions to spare Denmark, when no longer resisting; but if firing is continued on the part of Denmark, Lord Nelson will be obliged to set on fire all the Floating-batteries he has taken, without having the power to save the brave Danes who have defended them.

He signed it, 'Nelson and Bronte, Vice Admiral, under the command of Admiral Sir Hyde Parker' (Oman, 1947, p. 443), thus meeting the necessities of protocol and implicating Parker in his gamble.

The action continued while the message went ashore and also while the Prince's emissary went on board *Elephant* to find out what the offer of a truce meant. Nelson explained that his object was humanitarian and that he would order a ceasefire while he took his prisoners 'out of the Prizes', landed 'all the wounded Danes' and either burnt or removed 'his prizes'. In short, he was claiming victory, the Danes having no prizes among the British ships. He added, however, that 'he will ever esteem it the greatest Victory' he ever had gain'd if this flag of truce may be the happy forerunner of a lasting and happy Union between my most Gracious Sovereign and His Majesty the King of Denmark'. Shortly after the Danes received this second note firing ceased on both sides.

After the cease fire, Nelson signalled Admiral Graves to come aboard *Elephant*, where he thanked him personally for his support during the battle. He also signalled Captain Bligh to come aboard. Bligh ever remembered, what for him was the supreme honour of his naval career, that Admiral Nelson thanked him personally on *Elephant*'s quarter-deck for his support as his second in *Glatton*.

With the temporary truce, the immediate problem was to remove the British fleet from the King's Deep. Graves took *Defiance* out first. Some of the other ships grounded, including *Elephant*, but Bligh got *Glatton* clear and anchored with Parker's squadron about 4 pm. During the evacuation, *Dannebrog*, which had been blazing with fires started by *Glatton*'s carronades, exploded. While the Danes removed their wounded the British anchored the 'bombs' just out of range of the Danish guns in case the truce broke down and further pressure was needed to conclude a peace.

Negotiations continued over the next few days, during which news of the murder of the Tsar arrived, making the differences between Denmark and Britain redundant. Nelson's gamble came off; he secured a peaceful settlement to the dispute and reopened the Baltic to British shipping.

After the battle the melancholy task of clearing the ships of the dead and wounded got under way. The 'good and gallant Captain Riou' was committed to the deep with many others. *Monarch* lost 56 killed, *Ardent*

30, *Isis* 28, *Edgar* 28, *Defiance* 26, *Glatton* 17, *Amazon* 14, *Bellona* 11, *Elephant* 9, *Blanche* 7, *Ganges* 6, *Polyphemus* 6, *Alcmene* 5, *Dart* 2, *Zephyr* 1 and *Desiree* none. *Monarch* lost 164 wounded, *Edgar* 104, *Glatton* 34 and *Elephant* 13. Interestingly, critics of Bligh at Camperdown have not raised the same criticism of Nelson at Copenhagen for having fewer casualties than an eighth of his squadron. But, unsurprisingly, Bligh has attracted criticism (what else!) for other things than his creditable conduct in battle at Copenhagen.

When captains are killed, promotions follow. Here Parker snubbed Nelson and made the promotions himself. He sent Captain Otway to the Admiralty with the official news of the victory, normally a clear invitation for the officer concerned to be honoured. Such an honour should have been in Nelson's gift for one of his own people. Parker promoted some of his own lieutenants, who had viewed the battle through their telescopes, to vacancies that in all decency, if not strict regulations, ought to have gone to those who were there. The most outrageous promotion was of one of his lieutenants to command the 74-gun *Monarch*. This promotion passed over the undoubted claims of Lieutenant Yelland, who had commanded her from the first few minutes of the action after his captain was killed, to, at the very least, a captaincy of one of the frigates. This must have caused much tension, for within a week Parker relieved his lieutenant and promoted Bligh out of *Glatton* into *Monarch*. He ordered Bligh to take *Monarch*, along with *Isis* and the Danish prize, *Holsteen*, back to Britain. Other Danish prizes were burned on Parker's orders and to the consternation of the men, including Nelson, who knew the cost of valuable prizes in their comrades' blood.

Bligh asked Nelson for a testimonial to the Admiralty, which was given on 14 April 1801:

Captain Bligh (of the Glatton who had commanded the Director at Camperdown) has desired my testimony to his good conduct, which although perfectly unnecessary, I cannot refuse; his behaviour on this occasion can reap no additional credit from my testimony. He was my second, and the moment the Action ceased, I sent for him, on board the Elephant, to thank him for his support (Mackaness, 1951, p. 328).

When Nelson heard that Bligh was returning to Britain in *Monarch* he asked him to handle a personal matter for him. This favour was to deliver a complete set of Copenhagen porcelain to 23 Piccadilly, the home of Sir William and Lady Hamilton. In his letter to Sir William he described Bligh as 'one of my seconds on the 2nd' and commended him as a 'good and brave man'.

Before he left, and while still in command of *Glatton*, Bligh was involved in a distasteful incident, though where the blame lies is not clear. *Glatton*, in common with some other ships, had several Danish officers on board as prisoners. A Danish lieutenant, Johan Udall, boarded

*Glatton* to collect the prisoners, one of whom, Lieutenant Winkler, claimed that the British captain had taken his sword from him. When Udall asked Bligh for an explanation, he was told that another prisoner, Lieutenant Lorentzen, had sold the sword to Bligh for an English pound, a fact confirmed by Lorentzen when questioned by Udall. Danish honour was at stake, and Udall ordered Winkler to present the sword as a gift to Bligh, thus wiping out the grubby business of a Danish officer's sword being sold. Lorentzen now stood on his dignity and refused to keep the pound note, though why he sold a brother officer's sword, or how he got hold of it in the first place, remains unanswered.

While the Danish Crown Prince and the British Admirals were settling the terms of the armistice, Admiral Fischer, the Commander-in-Chief of the Danish forces, was making efforts to convince everybody that he had not lost the battle and the entire British conduct of the battle was a disgrace. He latched onto the *Glatton* incident, among others, as an example of boorish British conduct (though his strictures ought to have been directed at Danes who traded in officers' swords). These disagreements can be put down to two proud forces disengaging from a bitterly fought contest, which, like all 'points decisions' in war and sport, remained controversial for being less than decisive.

Bligh took *Monarch* back to Britain and it must have been an unhappy voyage home. Midshipman Millard wrote: 'Captain Bligh was an excellent navigator, and I believe in every respect a good seaman, but his manners and disposition were not pleasant, and his appointment to the Monarch gave very general disgust to the officers' (ML MS ab 60/15). From what we know of Bligh this is a typical criticism, which by repetition must be regarded as accurate. However, Millard's specific complaints lack weight.

Bligh apparently did not think much of the pilots assigned to the ship. He called them 'dolt' and 'blockhead' and 'pretending that the ship was not safe in their hands, took charge of her himself'. In view of Nelson's views on the Baltic pilots, Bligh's action was probably justified, especially as he was on errand for Nelson as much as for the Admiralty and he would not want to place himself in the hands of people for whom he had a low regard as seamen.

Bligh also caused offence to Millard and others for inconveniencing them; he took *Monarch* to Yarmouth and transferred the wounded in boats into *Holsteen* which took them into the harbour. He did not dock *Monarch* there but continued on to the Nore, to the consternation of the officers who wanted to go ashore at Yarmouth to visit their 'connections'. The fact that the officers from the beginning of Bligh's command of *Monarch* did not bother to hide their disgust at his appointment and 'behaved but with distant civility' towards him, probably explains why Bligh was totally uninterested in their convenience.

Bligh arrived with *Monarch* and *Isis* at the Nore on 7 May 1801. He reported to the Admiralty, and *Monarch* was paid off and the officers dispersed at their own convenience. Bligh was immediately promoted into HMS *Irresistible*, a 74-gun ship of the line and Nelson's flagship at the battle of St Vincent. This promotion confirms his high standing in the Admiralty at this time, and Nelson's letter probably helped. He held this command for twelve months. It was a creditable reward for his role at Copenhagen. He had stood the stringent test of command under fire for the second time, this time under the watchful eye of Nelson. It was his last naval battle and a sound reply to his critics.

# 34

# The *Warrior* Court Martial

Bligh's command of *Irresistible* lasted until May 1802, when, following the peace of Amiens, the Navy stood many of its ships down and placed their officers on half-pay. Bligh wrote to Banks: 'I can only say I shall continue to serve as Zealously as ever until I am paid off and be ready to serve again whenever it is required as I must hereafter command ships which will be of great consequence in the battles our fleets will be subject to' (ML MS, 12 November 1801).

Not long after he was appointed to *Irresistible* Bligh was elected a Fellow of the Royal Society 'in consideration of his distinguished services to navigation'. With Sir Joseph Banks as President of the Royal Society at the time he had a ready sponsor for this undoubted honour.

Half-pay meant shore-leave, and Bligh spent much of the time at his home in Durham Place with Elizabeth and his family of six daughters. In 1802, the eldest, Harriet, married Henry Barker of Gloucester, and a grandson, William Bligh Barker, was born later in the year, but unfortunately he died at three years of age in 1805. Bligh wrote to the Admiralty on 9 March 1803 asking for employment (PRO Adm. 1/529). In the autumn of 1803 the Admiralty employed Bligh in surveying Dungeness, the coast of Flushing and Fowey Harbour, and in early 1804 he was working in the Hydrographic Department. He was responsible for several position fixes of places along the east coast (PRO Adm. 1/3522).

On 2 May 1804 he was offered command of HMS *Warrior*, a 74-gun ship of the line. His Commander-in-Chief was Lord Cornwallis. In common with other captains, he had a major problem in getting enough men to man the ship. Against a normal complement of over 500 he had only 241 men, of which, he considered, only 40 were capable seamen. In his view 'something must have been radically bad to have produced all this' undermanning of the fleet. He asked Betsy to contact a baker he had had on *Director* and offer him a post on *Warrior*. He also requested that she recommend any 'good youths' who want to be midshipmen, as he had 'but two young Men who do duty as Mids that can be trusted'. His First Lieutenant was George Johnston, but he was ill, and he told Betsy he would have asked for Lieutenant Senhouse to join him 'as he would be of real service' but he was doing so well in a frigate he could not ask him to give up his chances there (ML MS Safe 1/45). (The Senhouses were another Lake District family associated with the Christians.)

The quality of the men sent to the fleet was as below par as the quantity. The long war with the French was bound to lower standards, and it was in this situation that Bligh clashed with a Lieutenant Frazier over the almost inevitable subject of Frazier's competence and attention to duty.

On taking command of *Warrior*, Bligh had the task of fitting her out and making her ready for sea duty. He complained of the shortages of shipwrights and necessary equipment, and the amount of time he was kept busy in the routine rounds of courts martial 'the confinement from which is very irksome & prevents us from having a day to ourselves to go anywhere from our Ships' (ibid., Bligh to Mrs Bligh, 16 June 1804).

Bligh's version of his quarrel with Frazier is detailed in his letter to Vice-Admiral Collingwood requesting a court martial:

Lieutenant John Frazier from his application as being fit to serve was appointed 2nd Lieutenant of the Warrior under my command. On his joining the ship he had an habitual lameness in his ankle, which had been occasioned by the bones being broken by accident in the Merchant Service, with which he, however, asserted he was capable of doing his duty, and did so to the 18th instant, when by our shortness of water and provisions and being out nearly 14 weeks, it was to be expected we were soon to return to port. On this evening he wrote to me requesting I would apply to you for a survey on him, which I did on the 21st by enclosing his letter and remarking I thought he was the same as he had hitherto been. In consequence you directed that as he, Lieutenant Frazier, was represented to be very much in the same state as he had been for some time past, and the Warrior would probably go soon into port, it would be an accommodation to him to wait until then. Lieutenant Frazier conceiving this application of his exempted him from further service, and that keeping watch would militate against his being discharged by survey on his arrival in port and thereby he would be obliged to return and experience a winter's cruizing did refuse to do any further duty, altho he had my assurance of every indulgence. The Surgeon put him on one day, the 20th instant, in his sick-list, but the next day finding no inflammation in his ankle, and that the appearances were no other than it must at all times have been subject to, he no longer continued him under his care and in consequence I ordered him to keep watch, but he refused. On the 22nd I directed Lieutenant Johnson (1st Lieutenant) to tell him it was my orders he was to take his watch. He came on deck in consequence, but on Lieutenant Boyack asking him if he was come to relieve him, he replied 'no, I am only come up to take air.' – would not relieve him and went below soon after. At 8 next morning, the 23rd, he was again called on to relieve Lieutenant Russell and I sent him word by Mr Cosnaham, midshipman, it was my orders he should relieve him, to which he returned me an answer he was too lame. I again sent and repeated the orders to him and gave him til 9 o'clock to comply, but he refused to obey me inasmuch that he would not come on deck to keep his watch. And for which contumacy and disobedience on the 22nd and 23rd I ordered him under arrest and request he may be tried by Court Martial (PRO Adm. 1/5367, Minutes of the Court Martial).

Bligh obviously considered Frazier to be a malingerer. However, his evidence to the court martial had a flaw in it, for Mr Cinnamon, the Surgeon, testified that Frazier was indeed on his sick list until Captain Bligh ordered him to strike him off it. The Court dismissed the charges against Frazier because a man could only refuse duty if he was fit for it. This legalism highlights the fractious nature of discipline in home waters; what a man like Riou would have thought of Frazier's 'lameness' as an occasion to disobey an order in an undermanned ship is a matter of speculation.

Frazier now turned the tables on Bligh. He demanded that his captain be court-martialled, claiming that he did 'publicly on the quarter deck on his Majesty's Ship Warrior grossly insult and ill treat me being in the execution of my office by calling me a rascal, scoundrel and shaking his fist in my face and that at various times ... he behaved himself towards me and other commissioned, warrant and petty officers in the said ship in a tyrannical and oppressive and unofficerlike behaviour contrary to the rules and discipline of the Navy and in open violation of the Articles of War' (PRO Adm. 1/5368, 13 November 1804).

Bligh wrote directly to Cornwallis, who replied: 'What you state of your situation from this circumstance on board the Warrior is a very improper one for an officer of your rank to be in. Your conduct since you have been under my orders has always been perfectly to my satisfaction' (ibid., 17 January 1805).

The court martial duly assembled on board HMS *San Josef* in Torbay and lasted two days, 25 and 26 February 1805, Vice-Admiral Sir Charles Cotton presiding. After the charges were read out, the prosecution witnesses were brought in and gave their testimony. Bligh asked them questions, as did the court from time to time. The evidence in the minutes shows a confusing picture with prosecution witnesses making statements in support of Frazier and then in support of the defence.

Henry Cock, Master's Mate, recounted an incident on 9 October in which Frazier and he were discussing Cock's report that the wardroom steward was playing cards again after having had his cards taken away from him. Bligh came on deck and demanded to know why Frazier was neglecting his duty. Frazier replied: 'I beg your pardon, Sir, I am not, I am answerable for the occurrences of my watch', to which Bligh retorted: 'What, Sir, you damned rascal, you damned scoundrel, never was a man troubled with such a set of blackards as I am. Take care, Sir, I am looking out for you.' Later, in the same watch, Bligh came on deck and Frazier began to give an order to set the mainsail. Bligh told Frazier that if he ever set a sail or gave an order while he, Bligh, was on deck, he would confine him and make him rue it. Cock disclosed in cross examination that he would not have noted the incidents except that Frazier told him to do so, suggesting that Frazier as early as 9 October was collecting evidence against Bligh. Cock stood by his account under questioning but conceded that he had never sailed with a better captain than Captain Bligh.

Midshipman Samuel Knowles testified that in July or August he was mate of the watch and the captain questioned him and Frazier about the firing of the fog-signal guns. Bligh called him a 'liar' and said that he and Frazier were 'a parcel of villains and scoundrels from Lieutenants to the midshipmen ... to the quarter masters'. This outburst by Bligh is not surprising in view of his letter to Betsy a few weeks earlier about the untrustworthiness of all but two of his midshipmen. He may already have formed a similar view about Frazier's competence since he came on board. Knowles did not, however, support the assertion that Bligh had behaved 'tyrannically and oppressively' towards the officers of *Warrior*.

John Amplet, a marine, called by the prosecution was extremely diffident about supporting the charge that Bligh had called Frazier a 'rascal and a villain'. As one of the sentries doing duty outside Bligh's cabin, Amplet denied that he had heard any of the crew say that Bligh was tyrannical and oppressive. He recollected Bligh being in 'a passion' when he found the ship off station. He admitted that both Frazier and Bligh had approached him regarding his evidence, with Frazier assuring him that if he gave evidence against Bligh he would be respected by every officer on the ship. He had, he told the court, decided to tell the truth. He had never 'heard of any grievance sustained by any person ... which had not immediately been redressed with strict impartiality and justice'. He had, however, heard Bligh 'call the quarter master a damn rascal'.

Lieutenant Boyack testified against Bligh. He spoke of a large number of incidents in which Bligh called various people 'rascals and scoundrels'. But once again, he tempered his evidence with the assertion that he had never heard Frazier abused in this way. He was of the opinion that Bligh's 'expressions to his officers before the ship's company lessened their dignity as officers and was degrading in the extreme'.

Robert Cinnamon, the Surgeon, testified as he had done at Frazier's court martial that Bligh had ordered him to take him off the sick list, that he had heard Bligh call Frazier 'either a damnation or a damned impertinent fellow', and that he had also abused the Master, Mr Keltie, but he knew of no other incidents with the other officers.

The Surgeon's mate, Charles Queade, supported the Surgeon's medical testimony that Frazier was unfit for duty and also the case of Mr Jewell, the Boatswain. Bligh had called Jewell a 'rascal' and had shaken him physically when he accused him of not attending to his duty. Captain George Mortimer gave evidence on the Jewell incident. He saw Jewell pushed by Bligh, and he saw Bligh abuse Mr Waller, the carpenter. He agreed that Bligh was 'tyrannical and unofficerlike' to the ship's officers but, in contrast, he was always 'polite and attentive' to the Marine officers.

Robert Russell, the junior lieutenant, supported Frazier's charges that Bligh had abused Frazier, Johnston, Keltie and Jewell, calling the latter a 'damned vagrant'. But John Honeybone, seaman, stated he had seen Bligh being jostled by Frazier while he was taking a sextant reading. Jewell was called and he confirmed what had been said about Bligh's abusing him, adding that Bligh had threatened to get him 'in a dark corner', presumably to assault him. He said he did not take the matter seriously because Bligh was 'hot and hasty' and that he would sail with Bligh again.

Lieutenant William Pascoe said that Bligh had called various people 'rascals and vagabonds', but like others he equivocated and said he did not think him 'tyrannical, unofficerlike or oppressive'. James Keltie, the Master, said Bligh had called him a 'rascal' and a 'Jesuit', and he considered his demands that Frazier do his watch were 'cruel'. He also thought Bligh was cruel to force Waller, the carpenter, to supervise the fishing of a yard (repair it) when he was ill. The court recalled Cinnamon, the surgeon, to testify on Waller's condition. He said the man's medical condition was not too good at the time and he was very old but he did not think it an 'act of tyrany or even severity' on Bligh's part as the Carpenter had been able to leave his cabin and walk on deck. Samuel Meggs, carpenter's mate, said that Waller had volunteered to go on deck for about ten minutes to supervise the fishing of the yard and that he had not heard him complain about this afterwards.

The second day it was Bligh's turn to make a defence. He called George Johnston, First Lieutenant, who had been with him for several years, including service in *Director*. Johnston did not think Frazier had been cruelly treated, in fact he thought Bligh had been 'indulgent' in allowing Frazier to sleep in on 18 October and permitting him to do his watch sitting down on the quarter deck. He had not heard Bligh call Frazier a 'rascal and a scoundrel', nor seen him shake his fist at him or behave in a tyrannical manner. He said that Frazier had told him he only brought Bligh to court martial because Bligh had court-martialled him. He said he had never heard any complaints about Captain Bligh from the officers, and while 'not in the habit of courting the opinion of seamen' he believed they had a good opinion of Bligh. He rejected the charge that the carpenter had been badly treated and claimed that Waller had expressed the highest praise for Bligh when he had been invalided off the ship.

Johnston was candid about Bligh's manner of directing people to work. If he wanted something done that needed to be done quickly he acted energetically, 'frequently swearing at the quarter-masters or men of that description who were standing around, with a considerable motion of the hand, which was not only used to persons of that description, but generally in giving orders, when the service had been neglected for want of proper attention in the officers'. This is a good description of one of Bligh's Captain Cook-like 'heivas' or 'tornados of rage'. Johnston added that 'I never conceived it done with the intention of personally insulting any officer'. He was asked by the court to demonstrate how Bligh moved his hands when giving orders, which Johnston did.

Peter Mills, Midshipman, said that Frazier had tried to make him testify against Bligh by producing a 'play bill' or minor gambling debt with his name on it. He had refused. He said Frazier had said that if Bligh tried him he would try Bligh and that 'Captain Bligh intends to take my commission from me, but I dont care a fig for it, I will lose it, but I will have my satisfaction of him'. He said that Bligh's general conduct towards the officers was attentive and that he also took time to teach navigation to the petty officers.

William Ranwell, Master's Mate, said he regarded Bligh 'more as a friend' and knew him as being willing to help those who 'deserved it'. If he scolded anybody it was always because of their inattention to ship's duty and he never held it against the person concerned.

William Simmons, Gunner, denied that he had heard Bligh abuse him, and though he thought Bligh sometimes 'passionate and sometimes cool' he would as soon sail with him as with anybody else. Joseph Strephon, Clerk, denied that Bligh had behaved in the manner of the charges, but he had heard him reprimand the Boatswain, Mr Jewell, for being intoxicated. Frazier questioned Strephon about the incident when he was abused for giving an order when the captain was on the deck. They had been in *Spartiate* together and Strephon had referred to the fact that on that ship the officer of the watch could give orders when the captain was on deck. Strephon agreed that he had made such a remark but it did not have the construction Frazier was putting on it.

Bligh's own testimony was somewhat contrite. He pointed out that Frazier had delayed months before charging him, which itself was unfair. He then gave a candid and very illuminating portrayal of his manner when commanding:

> I candidly and without reserve avow that I am not a tame & indifferent observer of the manner in which Officers placed under my orders conducted themselves in the performance of their several duties; a signal or any communication from a commanding officer have ever been to me an indication for exertion & alacrity to carry into effect the purport thereof & peradventure I may occasionally have appeared to some of those officers as unnecessarily anxious for its execution by exhibiting any action or gesture peculiar to myself as such: Gentlemen, [I now] appeal to you, Mr President & the members of this honourable Court, who know & have experienced the arduous task of responsibility and that of the magnitude of one of His Majesty's seventy-four gun ships, which will, I am persuaded acquit me of any apparent impetuosity & would plead in extenuation for my imputed charges: attributing the warmth of temper, which I may at intervals have discovered, to my zeal for that service in which I have been employed

without an imaginary blemish on my character for upwards of thirty five years and not with any premeditated view of any personal insult to my Prosecutor or reducing the rank which he holds in it concerning an incumbent duty in our relative situations to render that rank mutual support which its dignity requires, as without such impression, discipline could not ensure obedience in ships of war.

Despite Bligh's plea the court decided that the charges were 'in part proved' and they ordered Bligh to be 'reprimanded and to be admonished to be in future more correct in his language'. Of Lieutenant Frazier nothing more is known; he was dismissed from the service, probably on account of his ankle (though trying your captain was not conducive to a career in the Navy).

Bligh was immediately restored to command of *Warrior* and set about getting rid of those who had testified against him (though he continued his habit of dining with the lieutenants in turn, conducting himself 'as if nothing had happened'). With the exception of First Lieutenant Johnston 'they are a very bad set of men as I ever heard of', particularly the Surgeon, Cinnamon, who he believed was 'the most designing wicked man ever came into the ship'. Of the Master, Keltie, he remarked, with sarcasm, that he had 'lost himself' with Hunter in *Waaksamheid* 'coming from Port Jackson to Cape of Good Hope' and 'cannot find his latitude to ten miles and he knows nothing about the variation of the compass or how to conduct a ship'. Mortimer, the Captain of Marines, also had to go – he 'made that foolish voyage to the South Sea' (ML MS, Banks). In general, Bligh concluded: 'We have such a set of low Men crept into the service that to govern a Ship is now not an easy matter altho a Captain's responsibility is as great or greater than ever' (Turnbull Library, New Zealand, 7 March 1805)

The *Warrior* court martial, whatever its verdict or the petty intentions of Frazier, provides more evidence of Bligh's manner as a captain. Some of the language attributed to Bligh has already been disclosed in his altercations with Christian, Fryer, Purcell, Bond and Ramsay. That he spoke this way is undeniable. There is a long list of abusive sentences included in the *Warrior* minutes: 'rascal and villain', 'rascal and scoundrel', 'Oh, you are a disgrace to the service, damn you', 'you lubber', 'you Jesuit', 'God damn you, Sir', 'what are you about?', 'infamous scoundrel', 'audacious rascal', 'vagrant', 'dastardly villain', 'God damn me', 'God damn you, you old thief, you are so great a liar, I would rather believe the quarter master or any other man in the ship', 'God damn you, why do you not hoist your sail?', 'damn your blood', 'he was a damn long pelt of a bitch', and so on.

Whatever the court thought of Bligh's language, it is not tenable that they were shocked: they merely admonished him to tone it down. The Navy had heard worse before (and has since). The great change in gentlemen's manners from the middle of the eighteenth century to the mid-Victorian years was not inconsiderable, as can be seen in the change in literary expression. Volleys of 'oaths and imprecations', as Fielding put it in *Tom Jones*, were expected of the country gentleman, and Tobias Smollet, in *Roderick Random*, has Captain Oakum abusing Lieutenant Bowling by calling him a 'lousy Scotch son of a whore', and Oakum in turn speaking to another officer as 'Mr. son of a bitch'. Captain Marryat, writing in 1803, said that 'oaths and blasphemy interlarded every sentence'. Some of the 'shock' at Bligh's language is akin to a schoolchild sneaking on another child's use of the daily language of the playground to a teacher. There is a sub-culture of swearing, lewdly and often, found among children of all classes, and people of all ranks (think of President Nixon's 'expletives deleted'). It is only a shocking revelation to those who have led a very sheltered life, or to those determined on a hypocritical pretence of having an outbreak of precious indignation.

*Warrior* was an unhappy place for those who did not do their duty to Bligh's exacting standards. It is a fact that Bligh's behaviour never changed over his career – he was neither better nor worse for most people than any other captain. A few people were incapable of bearing him, not because he treated them any differently from others but because his normal behaviour was 'too much' for their own personalities and their abilities. This appears to have been the case with Frazier, as it was with Christian.

The verdict was embarrassing rather than damaging. The battle of Trafalgar was in the offing and Bligh could have hoped for a role in Nelson's fleet. Sir Joseph Banks wrote to Bligh that 'Ld Nelson not only knows how you conducted your ship when it lay alongside his Lordship's at Copenhagen, but will not omit any opportunity of giving you Credit' (ML MS A78-5). But his friends in the Admiralty and Government were already moving to place him as Governor of New South Wales, where he was to have to deal with men far more resourceful and capable than Frazier.

# 35

# New South Wales

The penal colony at Botany Bay had been established in 1788 when Captain Phillip had taken a small fleet of transports carrying convicted persons (many of them incarcerated in Duncan Campbell's prison hulks) and soldiers to guard them, plus a small band of civilians, to settle the new land. By 1805 the colony had grown a little – it had also moved from Botany Bay to Sydney Cove, though the popular misnomer for it remained for many years in folk song and laments. Governor Phillip had returned to Britain in 1792 and was superseded by Governor Hunter in 1795. In the intervening three years the colony had been run by the military, and in particular had been under the influence of a young officer in the New South Wales Corps, Lieutenant John Macarthur, who had been born in England of Scottish parents in 1767.

Macarthur's motives in enlisting in the New South Wales Corps were unexceptional for young military men at the time: he wanted promotion and, as his wife Elizabeth put it in a letter to her mother, 'every reasonable expectation of reaping the most material advantages' (ML MS A2908, 8 October 1789). Macarthur was not an easy man to deal with; he was touchy, obstinate and aggressive. On his short voyage between London and Portsmouth he clashed with the ship's captain, a Mr Gilbert from the merchant service. He refused to speak to him and, when relationships went from bad to worse, he challenged him to a duel. Duelling was common in the army, and many of the disputes were over absurd and trivial matters, perceived slights of characters too haughty for their own good. Few duels, however, were lethal. Macarthur's with Gilbert resulted in injury to neither of them, though Gilbert was replaced as captain by the equally irascible, at least as far as Macarthur was concerned, Captain Trail. To keep the peace, Macarthur transferred at sea from *Neptune* to *Scarborough*. He fell dangerously ill at the Cape and was nursed back to health by Elizabeth. He never really recovered from this illness, and towards his last years he collapsed into lunacy.

Life at the virtual shanty town of Port Jackson was not encouraging on their arrival in June 1790. Everybody was on limited rations. Thus things remained for the Macarthurs until Major Grose, Commander of the

Corps, arrived in 1792. Grose was a veteran of the American war and had fought at Bunker Hill, Fort Montgomery and Monmouth Court House. He had been invalided out of the army from his wounds and saw the New South Wales Corps as a comfortable billet until his final retirement. Much of the daily administration he left to Lieutenant John Macarthur.

Macarthur devised a scheme to enrich himself and the other officers. Briefly, he speculated in cargoes, on one occasion hiring a whaler to make a round trip to the Cape to bring back goods which were sold at inflated prices. He used regimental funds for these purposes, and took advantage of the monetary position in the colony. Having sent convicts out to settle and soldiers to guard them, the Government had not considered it necessary to send out cash for use as money. The officers were paid in London not Sydney, which meant they could draw bills on London and use them to fund their commercial activities in the colony. This gave them a means of trading with visiting ships, and the fact that all ships' captains had to report to Macarthur to get permission to land anything at all gave Macarthur the opportunity to buy up the entire cargo, using bills drawn against the officers' wages on London.

When Phillip departed in November 1792, Grose became acting Lieutenant-Governor until Hunter arrived in September 1795. He dispensed with the civilian magistrates and placed all matters pertaining to law in the hands of the officers. Macarthur was appointed Inspector of Public Works, which made him virtual controller of the entire commercial life of the colony. This gave him a decisive voice in which convicts went where, to undertake what labour for whom. Grose made out land grants to the officers, and Macarthur supplied them with convict (i.e. unpaid) labour. Retired soldiers and convicted persons who had completed their sentences received land grants of 25 acres, and private civilians received more. This was one way to clear the land for agriculture to enable the colony to get on a self-sufficient footing and be less dependent on supplies arriving from Britain.

To supplement the official allowance of two labourers per land grant, the officers were able to trade for additional labour using whatever goods they acquired from their commercial monopoly of all landed cargoes. Rum was among the most popular of articles for use as 'wages'. Money was of little use – there was not much to spend it on even if it could be obtained – but rum struck an immediate chord among the convict labourers. Alcoholic escapism had its attractions; it also ensured that enough rum was consumed to keep up the demand for more.

The Governors who went out to New South Wales up to 1810 were naval officers, which lent itself to inter-service rivalry. Free settlers were very scarce and had insufficient social weight to counterbalance the economic power of the military officers. The only alternative to regimental power, entrenched economically as it was by their monopoly of cargoes and their manipulation of bills on London (welcomed by ships' captains for their security), was the civil power exercised by the Governor.

London was not altogether satisfied with the management of the colony. There was a constant stream of litigious and fractious complaints about almost everything from all quarters of the distant colony. Making decisions on these matters, with the added burden that it took up to two years for the cycle of a complaint to travel from Sydney to London and back again (the 'tyranny of distance' as Geoffrey Blainey put it), and the urgent need for attention to all the other matters affecting the management of His Majesty's Government, was an irritating diversion. And there seemed to be no end to the stream of letters, reports and complaints arriving from the tiny settlement.

Captain John Hunter's Governorship did not resolve the problems. He was speedily diverted into the internecine battles within the governing elite of the colony. He thought that the New South Wales Corps contained within it many men who would 'have been considered disgraceful to every other Regiment in His Majesty's Service' (*HRA*, First Series, vol. 1, Proceedings, December 3-30, 1795, p. 575). He did not get on well with Macarthur who appeared to be connected with a lot of the trouble he experienced.

Macarthur ceased to be an aide to Grose, though he remained in the Corps, and attended largely to his own commercial and farming affairs. He quarrelled bitterly with Richard Atkins, a close confidant of Hunter, over his policy of purchasing grain for the officers from the Government Stores at lower prices than it was sold to the free settlers (*HRA*, pp. 96-7). A long rambling correspondence ensued, much of it sent to London for the attention of government.

Macarthur, in common with other officers, grew more prosperous. By 1798 his land holdings had grown to 500 acres, and his labour force numbered forty men. He had fifty head of cattle, a dozen horses and one thousand sheep. This was no mean achievement for somebody on a salary of £100 a year. His stock alone was worth £5,000. The Government in London was not pleased with the entrepreneurial activities of the officers of the Corps. The Duke of Portland told Hunter that the 'officers engaging in traffic may be found to have disgraced his Majesty's service' (*HRA*, vol. 2, p. 38). The free settlers complained to Portland that prices rose from ship to shore from the officers' monopoly by as much as 500 to 1,000 per cent (ibid., p. 43).

Hunter was recalled to London in 1800 and Governor Philip Gidley King appointed to succeed him. Though Portland wanted the Governor to clear up the mess and set the colony on the road to commercial prosperity in the hands of civilians not soldiers, he did not make a good choice. In asking for the names of the officers who had been trading he missed the wiley Macarthur through his resigning from the Corps before the order arrived. Colonel George Johnston was the only man specifically charged with this offence.

Captain King's arrival heralded changes in the policy of the colony. Governor Hunter, Captain Kent (RN), Major Foveaux and Macarthur made offers to sell their livestock to the Government, in Macarthur's case for £4,000 (*HRA*, First Series, vol. 1, pp. 524-6). When Portland heard of Macarthur's offer he remarked sardonically: 'Considering Captain Macarthur in the capacity of an officer on duty with his regiment, I can by no means account for his being a farmer to the extent he appears to be, and I must highly disapprove of the Commanding Officer of the Corps to which he belongs allowing him or any other officer to continue in such contradictory situations and characters' (ibid., vol. 3, p. 101, Portland to King, 19 June 1801). But Portland only knew half of it. King estimated Macarthur's wealth as being 'at least £20,000'. He accused him of 'making a large fortune, helping his brother officers to make small ones (mostly at the publick expense) and sowing discord and strife' (ibid., pp. 321-2).

Macarthur wanted to return to Britain at this time, but he returned in a less respectable fashion than he had expected (though there is more than a suspicion that he deliberately provoked events to suit his plans; J.C. Garran & L. White, *Merinos, Myths and Macarthurs*, 1985). He was sent back in September 1801 under arrest for a court martial for duelling with his commanding officer, Lieutenant-Colonel Paterson, and wounding him in the shoulder. This way at least he returned at the Government's expense, taking with him two of his children, a file on the case, and some samples of wool. Arriving in England, he placed his children in a public school, faced the charges, which were dismissed, and showed samples of his wool to a Government interested in replacing the trade that had been lost when Napoleon's armies took over Spain.

Macarthur's main mission was to persuade the Government that a wool industry was possible in the colony. This he did to remarkable effect and was offered a land grant of 5,000 acres to commence his scheme, with a prospect of another 5,000 acres if he was successful. His success was mirrored by Governor King's failure to impress London with his management of the colony. There had been an influx of Irish prisoners and several outbreaks of disorder undeterred by sentences of 1,000 lashes and some hangings. The question of when, not whether, Governor King should be retired moved onto the agenda.

Macarthur and Sir Joseph Banks fell out and, given Banks's influence with the Government, it meant that if he was consulted, as he was to be, about King's replacement, he was bound to send someone equally prejudiced against Macarthur. He had already tried to stop Macarthur purchasing sheep from Kew Gardens by raising an ancient Act of Parliament prohibiting the export of sheep, but Lord Camden overruled him. He was successful, however, in modifying the original proposal that Macarthur should get 10,000 acres for the sheep project, and it was split into two, one half depending on performance.

In March 1805 Lord Camden invited Sir Joseph to consider possible names for nomination as the new Governor of New South Wales. This was a short time after the *Warrior* court martial and four months after Macarthur had sailed for Sydney. Camden wanted a man to replace King 'who had integrity unimpeached, a mind capable of providing its own resources in difficulties without leaning on others for advice, firm in discipline, civil in deportment and not subject to whimper and whine when severity in discipline is wanted to meet emergencies' (*HRNSW*, vol. 6, part 35). With the exception of 'civil in deportment', this was a perfect description of Bligh. And Banks thought so too, for he immediately wrote to Bligh asking him to accept the Governorship. As an inducement he asked Bligh to consider the advantages of a salary of £2,000 a year, a pension of £1,000 a year and the possibility that his daughters would find eligible husbands among the men who would be 'very capable of supporting wives in a creditable manner' (ibid.).

Bligh decided to accept. It meant his leaving active sea duty as a Post-captain (and his chance, which must be rated as good, of serving again with Nelson later that year at Trafalgar). There was, however, a difficult domestic decision to make. Elizabeth Bligh was against a sea voyage to New South Wales. She was 52 and had an 'extreme horror' of the sea. She had been ill recently and Bligh thought the voyage 'would be her death' (ML MS A84, 31 April 1805). They decided he should go out without her, taking his daughter Mary with him.

In April 1805, Lord Camden having been appraised that Bligh was agreeable to the appointment, recommended it to the King. On 29 April 1805 Bligh was superseded as captain of *Warrior*, and went onto half salary, this time at the Governorship's rate. His rank in the Navy was to continue, and his future son-in-law, Lieutenant Putland, was to accompany him as his aide. The voyage was to be in the *Lady Madeleine Sinclair*, under the escort of HMS *Porpoise*. The command of the convoy was given to Captain Joseph Short (PRO, Colonial Office Papers, 201/39 15).

Bligh left for New South Wales in February 1806. The voyage out was marked, and marred, by furious rows between him and Short. Bligh was senior to Short on the captains' list, and Short was dependent on the goodwill of Bligh once the ships reached the colony, which was something he neglected to consider when he rowed with the new Governor. He had sold up his property in Britain and had invested considerable sums in farming equipment and stocks, and was taking with him his wife and seven children. It is remarkable that he persisted in trying to thwart a man not given to making life easy for those who opposed him.

Short's instructions were to conduct the convoy and bring it to New South Wales and there place himself under command of Governor Bligh, who was to command all British vessels in Australian waters. The instructions were at fault. They directed Short to command 'the Porpoise on all occasions in the absence of captain Bligh', and as Bligh was travelling in the other ship, he pig-headedly interpreted that as sufficient 'absence' for him to command the convoy. Bligh informed Short, to no avail, that he was 'subject to my control and guidance' (ML MS A84, p. 127). Bligh's seniority made him nominal First Captain of the *Porpoise*. Short soon caused offence to Bligh's sense of importance and, instead of diplomatically backing off, he got himself deeply embroiled in a trial of wills.

The details of the dispute are tedious in the extreme, and somewhat farcical, with Short on one occasion firing warning shots across Bligh's ship when it did not steer as he ordered (ML MS Safe 1.45, 26 February etc. 1806). Perhaps the assessment made by Captain (later Admiral) Francis Beaufort is sufficient. He commanded HMS *Woolwich* and arrived at the Cape two days after Bligh's convoy. On the details of the dispute, which he heard from both of them, he was extremely critical: 'they were both wrong, both had acted intemperately and foolishly, both had laid themselves open to censure, which both will probably meet with, and both are equally resolved to stick to what they had already done and not to retract a single expression.' Beaufort goes on to judge the two men: 'I immediately pronounced for Capt. Bligh ... and whatever I thought of their mutual conduct, I perceived that one was a man of talents and the other an ass' (Friendly, 1977).

On reaching Sydney, Bligh wreaked his revenge. Short had arrested his Master, Daniel Lyle, for a breach of discipline and he had quarrelled with his First Lieutenant, J. S. Tetley. A court of enquiry was set up which found against Short in his rows with his officers. Short's charges against Lyle and Tetley were found not proven, and he made the mistake of then presenting formal charges against them, which demanded a second court of enquiry, leaving it open to Bligh to order him back to Britain for them to be heard at a court martial. Meanwhile Short pressed Bligh for the 600 acres land grant he had been promised by Lord Camden, but Bligh had not received any written orders to this effect and stood on the legality (though Short produced a letter from Camden's secretary supporting his assertion). He covered himself by immediately writing to Lord Camden, knowing full well that Short could not wait two years for a reply and anyway would be on his way home before then for the court martial of Lyle and Tetley. The first court of enquiry had concluded that relationships between Short and the officers of *Porpoise* were 'full of personal rancour, prejudice and partiality' (Mackaness, 1951, p. 358).

Short was ordered home, but he refused to leave *Porpoise* and Bligh had him forcibly removed into *Buffalo*. He was sent home with his pregnant and sick wife, who died on the voyage along with one of his children. At his court martial he was acquitted and the court recommended he receive compensation for his losses, including the sale of his equipment at a substantial discount in Port Jackson. He did not return to New South Wales but was posted to the Sea Fencibles and later the Marines and saw service in Canada. The court also had some hard things to say about Lyle and Tetley, who it believed had been put up to pursuing their charges by Governor Bligh (ML MS A85).

Lest we get the impression that this was an impartial act of justice, we must note that the President of the Court, Sir Isaac Coffin, was also playing politics. He used the verdict for the wholly discreditable purpose of trying to get Bligh removed as Governor and his friend Captain William Kent (who had enriched himself during Grose's administration) appointed in his place (*HRNSW*, vol. 6, p. 388, 13 December 1807). The Royal Navy was not just a passive military machine, it was every much as fractious as those engaged in civil politics in the scramble for sinecures. Banks sprang to Bligh's support and was able to tell him that 'all I hear in Lord Castlereagh's Office however is in your favour, your Talents your perseverance & your spirited conduct are spoken of in terms of praise which flatter me, you may be sure as much as they can do you' (ML MS A78-5, 25 August 1808). The intrigue against Bligh was not confined to Coffin's pushing the claims of Kent. Grose also had some hopes, and King was lobbying the Duke of Clarence to be returned to New South Wales for a second term as Governor. At £2,000 a year the Governorship was a major prize worth lobbying for. Betsy warned Bligh that 'the malice and cruelty of the people who were engaged in this business exceeds everything I ever thought men capable of'. She besought him to 'be extremely cautious and not push things to extremities with any one, for you have a great many enemies' and quoted some advice from a family friend 'about keeping your temper' (ML Safe 1.45, pp. 123-5, February 1808). Any slip on Bligh's part would cause his recall.

Unfortunately his wife's advice and warnings came too late. Bligh had already been deposed in a military putsch, masterminded by none other than John Macarthur and the officers of the New South Wales Corps. Having enemies in London was one thing – his powerful friends could assist him there – but having enemies in Sydney was something altogether different, especially if they held the power that mattered. And they did.

# 36

# Bligh's Third Mutiny

Bligh began his Governorship with some mutual land granting which was hardly the best way to start off a campaign against those who used public office to make private gain. The deal was that Governor King would stay in office after Bligh's arrival, enabling him to make land grants to Bligh of 240 acres near Sydney ('Camperdown'), 105 acres near Parramatta, ('Mount Betham') and 1,000 acres of the Hawkesbury River ('Copenhagen'). On assuming the Governorship he assigned 790 acres to Mrs King (impudently named 'Thanks'!). He also gave 600 acres to the Putlands, but forty years later his descendants had to concede these acres back to the Government in exchange for confirming his other grants. No wonder Captain King, when he got back to Britain, could see the commercial possibilities of another term as Governor in place of Bligh – the prospects were almost endless.

The colony was in a poor state. Natural disaster had been added to personal mismanagement and weakness. The Hawkesbury River, where the majority of fee settlers had established themselves, had flooded in March 1806, destroying considerable grain-producing farmland. Food prices rose and grain reached a premium, being pushed up by speculation and the illicit stills that turned seed-corn into liquid hope. Macarthur expressed condolences to the people who had lost everything, and was also concerned about the arrival of an otherwise welcome cargo of 400 tons of Bengal rice which, in his view, 'can produce no other effect than that of lessening the value of our own produce' (ML MS A256, pp. 477-9). Meat was scarce as well, and the sheep-breeding flocks of the officers excited some envy, and the suspicion that they held them off the meat market to push up prices. Wandering sheep, however, assisted by wandering thieves, tended to disappear into hungry bellies.

Three gentlemen, George Johnston for 'the military', Richard Atkins for 'the civil' and John Macarthur for the 'free inhabitants', with a legacy of bitter personal divisions between them, sent a memorial to the new Governor which was published in the *Sydney Gazette* on 24 August 1806. They asserted that they had 'an undoubting confidence, that your Excellency by a just, moderate, firm, and wise Government, will promote the happiness of all who deserve it' and that it was 'the indispensable duty of us all to combine with our endeavours ... a reverential regard to the Law, and a cheerful acquiescence in such measures as your Excellency may adopt, to improve the true interests of the colony'. While the protestations of loyalty were welcome, the hypocrisy of the memorialists caused comment. Within a few weeks Bligh received a petition from 379 independent settlers who had, in their opinion, much to complain about, and in particular they dissociated themselves and their class from John Macarthur, the self-appointed spokesman for the 'free inhabitants', who had no authority to speak for them and who was acting against their interests by speculation to enrich himself (*HRNSW*, vol. 6, pp. 188-91).

Bligh was soon in dispute with Macarthur, whose plans for a major sheep-rearing operation had been frustrated by delays initiated by King using the stratagem of applying to London for clarification of its intentions. Macarthur wanted to locate his 5,000-acre grant in a place known as the Cowpastures, about twenty miles south of Sydney. This area had acquired its name from the cattle that had wandered off in Governor Phillip's time and found a sanctuary in a secluded but fertile area. By King's time, when the lost cattle were rediscovered, they had multiplied in number. King ordered Macarthur to locate his 5,000 acres across the Nepean River from the Cowpastures.

Bligh was also unimpressed with Macarthur's concerns (probably because of his own relationship with Sir Joseph Banks). In an altercation with Macarthur he is alleged to have shouted: 'What have I to do with your sheep, Sir? What have I to do with your cattle? Are you to have such flocks of sheep and such herds of cattle as no man ever heard of before? No Sir, I have heard of your concerns, Sir, you have got 5,000 acres of land, Sir, in the finest situation in the country, but by God you shan't keep it.' Macarthur protested that he had the grant from the Privy Council and the Secretary of State. To which Bligh allegedly replied: 'Damn the Privy Council, and damn the Secretary of State, too; he commands at home, I command here' (Onslow (ed.), 1914, pp. 137-8).

The other problem was the Corps. Its officers were closely involved in commercial speculations, particularly in the rum trade (so were many in Bligh's own entourage and among his allies). Bligh wrote home about the state of the Corps in 1807, saying that 'about seventy of the privates were originally convicts, and the whole are so very much ingrafted with that order of persons as in many instances have had a very evil tendency, and is to be feared may lead to serious consequences' (*HRNSW*, vol. 6. p. 354). He suggested that the lot be removed home and replaced with regular troops.

Falling out with the military was Bligh's biggest mistake, though it was almost inevitable if he was to preserve his Governorship in respect of its reliance on meeting the wishes of London. His weakness was exploitable, for if the force that was ostensibly there to protect him and enforce his writ could not separate their private from their public duty, he was vulnerable to their displeasure and, given the right circumstances, was removable by them without their waiting for orders to that effect from London.

Bligh reported to London that 'I am aware that prohibiting the barter in spirits will meet with the marked opposition of those few who have so materially enriched themselves but it' (ibid., p. 251). However, his measures against the trade were not successful. Corrupted officers continued to pay their soldiers in kind (usually rum) instead of cash and threatened to thrash any of them who resisted (Holt, 1838). The laws against the trade were harsh but flouted. Floggings and fines were not a deterrent (the transported, apart from hanging, were already beyond being disgraced by lawbreaking).

Macarthur was determined to topple Bligh. He was not unaware of his past on *Bounty*, and guessed that a man at the centre of one mutiny was in a weak position when accounting for another. In one unguarded outburst, he warned that Bligh 'will perhaps get another voyage in his launch again' (Bartrum, 1811, p. 136). He also noted Bligh's deteriorating relationship with the Corps, which was 'galloping into a state of warfare with the Governor. And in my opinion they are most wretchedly circumstanced among themselves' (ML MS A256, pp. 481-3).

The tension between the two men had begun within a short while of Bligh's arrival. A dispute had arisen between debtors and creditors over the payment terms of promissory notes. Bligh had considerable experience of the finance of trading and when asked to intervene in the dispute he applied his common sense, to the discomfort of those, such as John Macarthur, who disagreed with him. The need for promissory notes in the form they were written was occasioned by the primitive financial facilities in the colony. Debts were denominated in sterling pounds but were repayable in kind. If a man owed ten pounds, and wheat was one pound a bushel, he could agree to pay back the ten pounds in cash, in the unlikely event that he had any, or in bushels of corn. This was fine as long as the price of corn remained stable, but once it rose or fell significantly the repayment in kind was disproportionate to the debt, favourably if the corn price fell, unfavourably if it rose.

Bligh decided that the debt was determined by its money value only and not by the quantity of the goods it mentioned. Thus, if it said ten pounds or ten bushels of corn, the debt was for ten pounds and the equivalent quantity of corn that at the time of repayment made up ten pounds. This made Bligh popular with the hard-pressed free settlers along the Hawkesbury and unpopular with holders, among them Macarthur, of their notes. Bligh's own farm bailiff, Andrew Thompson, won a case against Macarthur permitting him to pay the bushel equivalent of the money price he owed when corn had risen to 30s a bushel, though when the debt had been contracted wheat was at 7s 6d a bushel. An unsigned article appeared in the *Sydney Gazette* (5 July 1807) extolling the virtues of Bligh's proclamation (probably drafted by himself) which referred to the alternative practice as an 'evil' in which 'Shylock' will 'insist upon his bond'. Macarthur appealed his defeat in court and to Bligh, and promptly sent off a complaint to London about the decision (*HRA*, First Series, vol. 6, pp. 323-8). Neither did he leave the matter there. He also penned a reply to 'Bligh's' article under the pseudonym 'An Occulist' (if he did not write the reply himself he certainly drafted it) which argued that if the creditor is meant to lose when the price falls he ought to be able to gain if it rises (*Sydney Gazette*, 26 July 1807).

While this dispute was moving to a conclusion another was festering in the background. This concerned two spirit stills which Macarthur and Captain Abbott (second-in-command of the Corps) had imported into the colony in March 1807. These had been confiscated on Bligh's orders and were set to be sent back to Britain. The head and the worms of the stills were removed and the bodies allowed into Macarthur's warehouse to enable them to be emptied of the packages they contained. When orders arrived to remove the stills into the *Duke of Portland* for shipment to London, Macarthur argued that they were no longer stills since they were bereft of still-heads and worms – they were now just containers. In the litigation that followed, Macarthur won a technical issue that the stills had been removed by a person unauthorised for such work (*HRA*, vol. 6, pp. 174-8).

Another incident concerned the escape of a prisoner, John Hoare, in one of Macarthur's ships, *Parramatta*, on a voyage to Tahiti in June 1807, where he jumped ship and disappeared. On *Parramatta*'s return in November, the ship was arrested and moored alongside *Porpoise*. The ship's bond of £900 against allowing any prisoner to stow away was declared forfeit by Bligh. Macarthur, rather than pay the bond, declared that he had abandoned the vessel, its contents and crew. The latter were put in a fix by this action; without papers they had no permission to land, and without landing they could not look after themselves. They were now pawns in a battle of wits between Macarthur and the Governor.

Richard Atkins now entered the unfolding drama. He was Judge Advocate and a long-time enemy of Macarthur. Bligh did not think too highly of him either. He told Banks that Atkins was a 'disgrace to human Jurisprudence' (ML MS A85, 10 October 1807) and complained of him that 'sentences of Death have been pronounced in moments of intoxication; his determination is weak; his opinion floating and infirm; his knowledge of the Law insignificant and subservient to private inclination; and in confidential cases of the Crown, where due secrecy is required, he is not to be trusted with' (*HRA*, vol. 6, p. 150). Atkins wrote to Macarthur requiring him to attend and explain what he was going to do about the crew of the vessel. Macarthur's reply was to deny any involvement with the ship and to ignore Atkins's 'summons' as it was not properly drawn up. Denying ownership of the ship was a long-shot gamble (it was worth £10,000) in a dispute over a £900 bond, but Macarthur was trying to provoke Atkins and Bligh into an intemperate move.

Atkins did just this. He sent the Chief Constable of Parramatta, Mr Oakes, with a warrant to arrest Macarthur, whose response was to vow 'never' to 'submit to the horrid tyranny that was attempted' (his case being that as he had not been legally summoned he could not legally be arrested for not complying: *HRA*, vol. 6, note, 15 December 1807). Oakes took Macarthur's hastily scribbled note of defiance with him and returned to Atkins, who went straight to Bligh with it. The magistrates were convened, Atkins, Major Johnston, Robert Campbell and John Palmer, and they voted to arrest Macarthur by force if necessary.

Macarthur rode to Sydney and waited for Atkins to make the first move. He was arrested a few steps away from the Governor's residence, calmly conversing with friends, and creating a little drama at his public arrest. He was taken before the court, which released him on £1,000 bail. The next day he came before the magistrates, this time with two senior officers from the Corps on the bench, Major George Johnston and Captain Edward Abbott. Atkins wanted Macarthur found guilty of refusing a warrant, but Bligh intervened and sent a message to Atkins in the court questioning Macarthur's objection to appearing before Campbell for whom he was suing for the value of the *Parramatta*. In Bligh's view the case to be answered was not about the disputed boat but about civil disobedience. The magistrates decided to commit Macarthur to a criminal trial on 25 January but, playing into the wily Macarthur's hands, did not specify the charges. He was released on bail again and, once the Governor's intervention became public, he was able to claim 'tyranny' on the grounds that it was his right to know what he was charged with.

Other parts in the game now fell into place. In a dispute with Bligh over a plot of land he had leased under Governor King, on land set aside by Governor Phillip as not to be leased, Macarthur had started to erect a fence, having had requests for other pieces of land refused by Bligh, and refusing land offered by Bligh in another part of town. On 20 January 1808, Bligh ordered a party of workmen to take down the fence posts (ML MS C475, pp. 96-9; Bartrum, 1811, pp. 56-7). Ominously, while the posts were uprooted Macarthur watched alongside Captain Edward Abbott, one of the magistrates at whose house he was staying throughout January.

In a separate action Macarthur had appealed to Bligh to enforce payment of a fourteen-year-old bill he held in Atkins's name for £26 6s, now worth, with interest, in his view, £82 9s 5d. Bligh told him to take the matter to court, which Macarthur declined on grounds that it meant his appealing to Atkins to enforce payment of a bill on himself (*HRNSW*, vol. 6. p. 395, p. 420). Bligh's refusal to help added to the case Macarthur was creating to the effect that the Governor was partial.

On 22 January Major George Johnston asked permission to hold a mess dinner on the 24th of each month. Macarthur's trial was set for the 25th. Bligh appeared to be unaware of the connection; he even donated a large quantity of wine for the event. This gathering of all the officers of the Corps, along with some prominent citizens who were numbered among the signatories of the petition used to justify Bligh's removal from office, has a sinister ring about it in retrospect. John Macarthur, on bail, stayed throughout the dinner just outside the mess room, walking up and down. His son Edward and nephew Hannibal were inside joining in the songs and merriment.

Next day, 25 January 1808, the court met. Atkins was joined by Captain Anthony Fenn Kemp (who had stood bail for Macarthur), Lieutenant John Brabyn, William Moore, Thomas Laycock, William Minchin and William Lawson. Macarthur launched into a protest about being tried by Atkins. His intention was to make the trial an impossibility and to provoke the Governor into interfering with justice. By challenging Atkins before he was sworn in, he deprived him of legal status. When Atkins threatened to have Macarthur jailed, Captain Kemp disclosed his partiality by threatening to jail Atkins. Under the circumstances Atkins withdrew from the Court, declaring that it had no status without his presence as Judge Advocate. Kemp replied: 'We are the Court', which in other times and other places would have been regarded as seditious (they later passed this off as a misunderstanding as they believed they had court status by virtue of being sworn in). They released Macarthur on bail and had a military escort to see Macarthur safely away in case 'ruffians' were sent to murder him. They sent a message to Bligh informing him that they had accepted Macarthur's objection to Atkins and wanted him replaced (*HRA*, vol. 6. p. 221).

Atkins repaired to the Governor, who by all accounts flew in to one of his tempers. Bligh replied to the officers instructing them to return to him the papers of the trial, including the notes of the Judge Advocate. The officers refused to comply but offered to send copies. Bligh insisted once again, and again they refused. A government rests on its legitimacy in the eyes of its subjects or on the violence it can exact on dissenters. Bligh's Government had no recourse left to superior force, and to all intents and purposes his Government was ended. He tried one last resort. He wrote to Major Johnston, who was 'ill' at his farm at Annandale just outside Sydney. He claimed he was too ill to come to town (apparently having fallen off his horse on his way home from the mess dinner). As the 25th drew to a close, Bligh was left to the mercies of Macarthur and the officers of the Corps. Mercy was not a quality anybody noted in Macarthur's personality and character.

Next day Bligh sent his Provost-Marshal, William Gore, to arrest Macarthur (Gore was treated shamelessly after the rebellion for doing his duty). Macarthur submitted to the arrest and awaited developments. The six officers of the court met and reapplied for Bligh to appoint somebody other than Atkins to hear the case, and asking for Macarthur to be released from jail (*HRNSW*, vol. 6. p. 426). Bligh did neither. He sent letters to each of them requiring them to appear before him next day to explain themselves. He also informed Johnston of his actions.

By calling the officers in he placed them under an uncertain threat and gave them until 9 am next day to plan their response. Johnston, recovering miraculously from his 'illness', appeared in town and went to the barracks, not the Governor's residence. The steps to the coup were now complete. Macarthur had brought the military into direct confrontation with Bligh's Government. It only remained for the Corps to end it formally. Macarthur penned a petition:

> Sir, The present alarming state of this Colony, in which every man's property, liberty, and life are endangered, induces us most earnestly to implore you instantly to place Governor Bligh under an arrest and to assume the command of the colony. We pledge ourselves, at a moment of less agitation to come forward to support the measure with our fortunes and our lives (*HRNSW*, vol. 6. p. 434).

His signature was followed by those of John Blaxland, James Mileham, S. Lord, Gregory Blaxland, James Badgery, Nicholas Bayly, George Blaxcell and Thomas Jamison. These eight men constituted the basis for the rebellion. No objective reading of the events can conclude otherwise than that the only person whose property and liberty were at risk was Macarthur, and that all of this was brought on his head by himself. This was no popular revolt by the down-trodden masses, or of the small farmers of the Hawkesbury, nor even of the 'respectable' citizenry of the colony. It was a tussle between one factious group in an unruly penal colony and the office of the Governor (who was there to rule in the interests of everybody and the Home Government), in which the military power, intimately connected with the conspirators, adjudicated in their favour.

Bligh was arrested by Major Johnston, accompanied by the entire Corps, who marched in military order to Government House. They carried fixed bayonets and the band played the the 'Grenadier Guards'. At Government House, a small party went inside to arrest him. This took some time because they were unable to find him. In the accusations and counter-accusations that were reported Bligh was accused of cowardice because he did not immediately appear before the officers and submit to their arrest. The search party claimed that they found him hiding under a bed, an accusation he strenuously denied (evidence was given at Johnston's court martial that the gap below the bed was far too small for anybody, let alone the somewhat corpulent Bligh, to hide in). Bligh claimed that he was putting on his uniform, collecting his papers and trying to find a means of escaping to the Hawkesbury where he was sure the settlers would rally to his standard. He tried to stay out of sight of the searchers while they passed the room. When brought before Johnston he was ordered to quit his commission and hand it over. He had little choice, though he denied that he ever abandoned the King's Commission.

Macarthur was beside himself with joy. The colony without a Governor and in the hands of the Corps was a return to the days of Grose, but with everything on a much larger scale financially. He wrote to his wife: 'I have been deeply engaged all this day in contending for the liberties of this unhappy Colony, and I am happy to say I have succeeded beyond what I expected. I am too much exhausted to attempt to give you the particulars, therefore I must refer you to Edward, who knows enough to give you a general idea of what has been done. The Tyrant is now no doubt gnashing his Teeth with vexation at his overthrow. May he often have cause to do the like' (Onslow (ed.), 1914, p. 153). It suited Macarthur to paint the coup d'état in this light, as it had suited some unknown author in October 1807 to pen the revealing and provocative lines: 'O tempora! O mores! Is there no CHRISTIAN in New South Wales to put a stop to the tyranny of Governor Bligh?' (*HRNSW*, vol. 6, p. 339)

# 37

# Interregnum

Bligh was advised to return home and make his case against the usurpers. He refused to do so until he received such orders from London. It was not just pride; it was more like applying the naval tradition of not leaving your watch until relieved. He remained a Governor without authority.

Johnston assumed command as 'Lieutenant-Governor' and issued a 'General Order' dismissing all the officers of Bligh's Government, including Atkins. Friends and associates of Macarthur were appointed in their place. A court was arranged to dismiss all charges against Macarthur. It consisted of the original six officers of the court plus, as Judge Advocate, the former Surveyor-General, Grimes (who had colluded with Macarthur in the incident over the leased plot of land to which Bligh had objected). The court's legality was in such doubt that even Abbott was moved to complain to Johnston about it (*HRNSW*, vol. 6, p. 832).

With the new Government in power, they set about organising the colony in the image of their ambitions. They replaced Bligh's 'tyranny' with one as heavy as it was illegal. Poor Gore, the former Provost-Marshal, was sentenced to seven years' transportation, a savage sentence on a public servant carrying out his lawful duties (*HRNSW*, vol. 6, pp. 648-9). Crossley, a convicted forger who had trained in the law and was employed as a legal advisor to the Governor, also received seven years' transportation. When Macquarrie arrived to supersede Bligh he had with him an order from London declaring all legal proceedings of Johnston's courts null and void. This released Gore and Crossley from their sentences but came too late for the poor wretches hanged or flogged by the soldiers' rough justice (sentencing after Bligh's removal was extremely severe).

Illegal proceedings in an illegal regime create instability. The usurpers soon split into rival camps. The decisions of the court reached such extreme proportions that Johnston had to dismiss Grimes, along with two magistrates, Dr Harris and Lieutenant Symons. They had sentenced a visiting merchant Captain and his Mate to seven years' transportation in a complicated dispute involving Macarthur and Blaxland. Macquarrie described the Blaxland brothers as 'the most discontented, unreasonable and troublesome persons in the whole country' (*HRA*, vol. 7, p. 560). This case illustrated that the Government of the colony was regarded as an extension of the interests of traders, monopolists and speculators. Johnston reported to London that there were 'abundances of Evidences to be found here who will swear to anything' at a cost in 'justice' (*HRA*, vol. 6, p. 456).

Johnston decided on the expedient of sending people home, ostensibly to take despatches to London. He ordered Grimes, Harris, Minchin, Symons and Blaxland to Britain. The one man he could not get rid of was Bligh, who sat it out in Government House awaiting word from London. The imminent arrival of Lieutenant-Colonel Foveaux from Britain to take up his appointment as Lieutenant-Governor to Bligh was his last hope of reinstatement; but, as we know from Mrs Bligh's letter of January 1808, Foveaux was no friend of Bligh's and had lobbied with others in London to get him recalled after the Short court martial.

Even Macarthur's position was difficult. His 'friends' tried the ploy of raising a fund to have him sent to Britain to explain the situation to London. While happy at the honour and the £1,000 raised for his passage, Macarthur was no fool. Returning to London could expose him to legal charges for his role in the removal of the King's Governor; it would also mean leaving his commercial interests and the opportunities afforded by a friendly Government. Soon after, he was appointed to the unpaid post of 'Colonial Secretary' by Johnston. Instead of luring him away, his rivals showed him to be popular, and so Johnston appointed him over them. He must have laughed all the sixteen miles back to his farm (*HRNSW*, vol. 6, p. 513).

Criticism of Macarthur mounted and came from all sides. The free settlers sent a petition to Lieutenant-Colonel Paterson at the small penal camp at Port Dalrymple, saying, in part, 'The whole government appears to be out into the hands of John Macarthur Esqr. who seems a very improper person, he having been a turbulent and troublesome character, constantly quarrelling with His Majesty's Governors, and other principal officers, from Governor Phillip to Governor Bligh; and we believe him to be the principal agitator and promoter of the present alarming and calamitous state of the colony' (*HRNSW*, vol. 6, p. 596). They were even more unrestrained in their condemnation of Macarthur as the 'Scourge of this Colony', who by 'his monopoly and extortion' was 'highly injurious to the Inhabitants of every description' (HRA, vol. 6, pp. 572-3, 11 April 1808).

Macarthur was not ignorant of the pressures. He had a clear idea of the consequences of the petty squabbles among the leading personages in the overthrow of Bligh. He was also aware of the greed that motivated many of those who had subsequently signed the 'requisition' to Johnston to remove Bligh from office: 'I am of the opinion,' he wrote, 'that had they been given way to, the whole of the publick property would not have satisfied them' (ML MS A254, pp. 137-9; *HRNSW*, vol. 6, p. 643).

When Foveaux arrived he assumed command, and Johnston and Macarthur stood down. Foveaux refused to reinstate Bligh – he could see a heaven-sent opportunity in his arrest – and advised him to return to London. This infuriated Bligh (*HRA*, vol. 6, pp. 588-602). From this moment Bligh's stubbornness came to the fore, and he was to suffer many indignities and privations during the next twenty-two months in consequence of his determination only to leave at the express orders of London. He made an appeal to Paterson to return to Sydney to restore him to office. This Paterson did his best to avoid. He delayed returning to Sydney until January 1809. Once he arrived, Foveaux stood aside, though Paterson left him to carry on as before, with Major Johnston acting as the effective administrator of the Colony's affairs.

A plethora of notes, letters, commands, petitions and memorials were exchanged between the four senior people in the colony, Bligh, Paterson, Foveaux and Johnston, each seeking to ensure that his dissent with the next was recorded with a view to the legal implications of his actions. No accusation was too wild for it to be reported to London (somebody even accusing Bligh of having 'concubines' in Sydney – a doubtful charge, given that he was living with his daughter and was confined to Government House). Paterson wanted Bligh to go home, and he decided to increase the pressure by making his stay less comfortable. He had Bligh removed from Government House on 30 January 1809 and confined to two rooms with his daughter, Mrs Putland (her husband having died), at the Barracks. But the man who had suffered the boat voyage was hardly likely to be influenced by such inconveniences.

Paterson suggested to Bligh he go home in the merchant ship *Estramina*. Bligh set himself the task of getting on board *Porpoise*, for once on board a ship of the Royal Navy, he was sure of taking command. His commission made him commander of all ships in the area, and he had recently been promoted by London to Commodore. The Navy men had kept out of involvement in the shore mutiny, but they could not deny Bligh his command once he stepped on board. After considerable argument between the two men, Paterson agreed to allow Bligh to board *Porpoise*. At the same time both Johnston and Macarthur were negotiating to travel to Britain to respond to anything Bligh said about them when he returned (the belief being that Bligh intended to sail home in *Porpoise*). Paterson made Bligh swear that he would leave the colony and not stop at any port on his way out or return unless the King sent him back. Bligh gave his pledge on 'his honour as an officer and a gentleman', and promptly reneged on his word on board. He also arrested Lieutenant Kent for failing to support him during the mutiny and had him confined to the ship, in all for 23 months (he was court-martialled on 8 January 1811 and acquitted).

For the next year Bligh sailed *Porpoise* between the environs of Sydney and the Derwent in Tasmania. He stopped vessels approaching the colony to read the messages being sent from London and also to revictual *Porpoise*. Johnston and Macarthur sailed in *Admiral Gambier* for Britain on 29 March 1809. Macarthur left his talented wife in charge of his business interests, and by all accounts she did a magnificent job virtually singlehanded, in an age when women were given little room to do much more than take care of their children. With Bligh obviously determined to remain near the colony, Paterson issued a proclamation debarring anybody from assisting him, and two who did, Palmer and Hook, were jailed in consequence as 'wicked and evil disposed Persons implicated in the high crimes and misdemeanours' of Bligh (*Sydney Gazette*, 19 March 1809).

Paterson's period in office was notable for its plunder of the public domains. He gave more land grants (68,101 acres) in twelve months to anybody who asked for it than King managed in six years (compared to Bligh's granting of 2,180 acres, or Johnston's 5,660 acres or Foveaux's 8,325 acres). The fact that the military, their wives and children included, and the civilian friends of the Johnston regime predominated in these gifts shows the real nature of the successive military regimes after Bligh's deposition. Generous land grants were also a means of maintaining support for the illegal regimes, and Paterson's largesse in this respect indicates his insecurity.

London decided to regularise the affairs of the fractious Colony by replacing Bligh as Governor, first with Brigadier-General Nightingale, Commander-in-Chief of the 73rd Regiment. When he withdrew on health grounds, they appointed his second-in-command, Lachlan Macquarrie, on 9 May 1809. The Government supported Bligh on the grounds that only the King could legally remove a Governor. They ordered Macquarrie to place Johnston under close arrest and return him to London, and to have Macarthur put on trial in the Criminal Court in Sydney. All appointments subsequent to Bligh's arrest were to be declared void, as were all land grants, and all his officers were to be restored to their offices, with the exception of Atkins. Included in the reappointments was that of Bligh who was to be restored formally as Governor for twenty-four hours, to confirm the King's writ, before Macquarrie assumed the Governorship himself.

Macquarrie arrived in Sydney on 28 December 1809, while Bligh was off Tasmania in *Porpoise*. He could not therefore reinstate Bligh as Governor for the nominal one day. On hearing the news of Macquarrie's arrival, Bligh sped back in *Porpoise* and landed to an official reception and a guard of honour, made up of the 73rd Regiment, on 17 January 1810, nearly two years after the coup. It was a triumph of sorts, and Bligh made the most of it (*HRNSW*, vol. 7, pp. 143-4).

Relations between Macquarrie and Bligh were at first cordial, but they became strained when Macquarrie, acting on his judgment of the needs of the situation, became reliant on Foveaux for advice on the administration of the Colony. This mortally offended Bligh, who regarded Foveaux as part of the mutinous gang of usurpers, and he took it as a slight on himself. He wrote to Betsy, saying, 'It is a hard trial of my temper to be here just now' (ML MS Safe 1/45, 8 March 1810). Macquarrie was determined to keep himself out of the tensions between Bligh and the Corps, considering this a matter for the courts in Britain to decide, and he was immune to any entreaties to disgrace publicly, or treat coolly, people whom Bligh and his friends considered to be of doubtful character. He continued to involve both sides in official social engagements.

His relations with Bligh certainly cooled, for he wrote to his brother: '[Bligh] certainly is a most disagreeable Person to have any dealings, or Publick business to transact with; having no regard whatever to his promise or engagements however sacred, and his natural temper is uncommonly harsh, and tyrannical in the extreme ... [it was] an undoubted fact that he is a very improper Person to be employed in any situation of Trust or Command and he is certainly generally detested by high, low, rich and poor, but more specially by the higher Classes of People' (*JRAHS*, vol. 16, part 1, 1930, p. 27). Bligh claimed that he was under enormous strain at the time, and certainly disputed that he was not held in regard by those loyalists who had stuck by him or suffered under the military regimes.

Indeed Bligh's supporters in the Colony desired to signify their public support for him and they asked permission to hold a public meeting of the inhabitants of Sydney and the Hawkesbury district. The meeting was to be chaired by Provost-Marshal Gore, now happily restored to office and freed from the illegal transportation sentence imposed by the Corps. Macquarrie gave his permission for the meeting.

The meeting was held in Sydney and attracted a huge crowd. Both factions drummed up everybody they could. The address to Bligh was in fulsome language and made biting comments on Johnston and Macarthur (Bartrum, 1811, p. 448). The meeting dissolved in uproar, each side claiming that it had the majority. Gore announced that the address was carried and invited individuals to sign it. It received 460 signatures, which somewhat contradicts Macquarrie's view of public opinion about Bligh. Opponents of Bligh demanded a chance to put their motions to a vote, but Gore refused. They lobbied a no doubt weary Macquarrie, who ordered a new meeting to be held that afternoon for this purpose (strictly an illegal event as public meetings had to be announced in the *Gazette*). Bligh's supporters stayed away from this meeting and his opponent's motions were carried unanimously. Interestingly, nobody accepted Gore's invitation (he was in the chair) to sign their names to the anti-Bligh motion. Macquarrie refused to allow either motion to be published in the *Gazette*, but Bligh's supporters presented their signed statement of their support to him before he left Sydney.

Bligh's last duty before he left was to give his daughter Mary away at her wedding to Lieutenant-Colonel O'Connell, Macquarrie's deputy. Their engagement came as a total surprise to him. At Rio de Janeiro he wrote to Betsy to break the news to her that Mary was not coming home with him:

> A Few days before I sailed, when everything was prepared for her reception & we had even embarked, he [O'Connell] then opened the circumstance to me – I gave him a flat denial for I could not believe it. I retired with her, when I found she had approved of his address & given her Word to him. What will you not my Dear Betsy feel for my situation at the time, & when you know that nothing I could say had any effect; and at last overwhelmed with a loss I could not retrieve I had only to make the best of it – My consent could only be extorted, for it was not a free gift; however, on many proofs of the Honor, Goodness and high Character of Colonel O'Connell, and his good sense which had passed under my own trial, I did, like having no alternative, consent to her marriage, & gave her away at the ceremony consummated at Government House, under the most public tokens of respect & veneration – the Colony, except a few Malcontents, considering it the first blessing ever bestowed upon them – every creature devoted to her service, by her excellence, with respect and adoration. Thus my Dear Love, when I thought nothing could have induced our dear Child to have quitted me, have I left her behind in the finest climate in the World, which to have taken her from into the tempestuous Voyage I have performed I now believe I would have caused her death ... If I had forced her away & I had lost her on the Voyage I could never have survived it – she remains as a Pattern of Virtue and admired by everyone (ML MS Safe 1/45, 11 August 1810).

Mary, 27 at the time of her second wedding, an attractive woman by all accounts and a social success in the Colony, had stood by her father from the moment of his arrest – she herself barred the way of the troops into Government House and followed him first to the barracks and then onto *Porpoise*. Bligh held her in high regard, and she in return was fiercely loyal.

Bligh boarded *Hindostan* alone and sailed for Britain on 12 May 1810, the *Porpoise* and *Dromedary* in attendance, each carrying the officers and men of the New South Wales Corps, now renamed the 102nd Regiment of Foot. With the men of the Corps went their women and children, many from the only home they had known. Colonel Paterson died at sea (succumbing to his heavy drinking as much as to the strain of the voyage). Many others died on the passage.

*Hindostan* landed its passengers at Spithead on 25 October 1810. Bligh travelled to London to see Betsy and his children, to prepare to answer any charges brought against him and to prosecute Johnston for mutiny.

# 38

# Journey's End

At Rio, where he was changing ships, Macarthur was confident he would soon be returning to the Colony in triumph. He wrote to his wife: 'In two months I hope to be in England, and in three months after on my way back; but however short my stay there may be, or speedy the returning voyage, it will yet be to me a dreary and comfortless time.' He was to be disappointed in his expectations. What was of major significance to him – whether it was disputes about promissory notes, stills, leases on land, warrants or whatever – was of trivial import to the Establishment of a country in the depths of a war with Napoleon. In the Colony Macarthur was a major personage; in London he was out of place. While Major Johnston could rely on powerful friends, such as the Duke of Northumberland, Macarthur could rely on nobody and had to work hard to gain an audience with the people who mattered. Bligh also had the advantage of access to powerful personages, such as Sir Joseph Banks and through him the Duke of Clarence (whom he was invited to attend upon in February 1811), all of whom were knowledgeable of his services in defence of the realm at Camperdown and Copenhagen, and who knew something of the troublesome and fractious penal colony since it was founded in 1788. These men were less impressed with the leaders of the faction that had deposed the King's Governor for what appeared to be a string of minor defects. In consequence Macarthur's stay in England was prolonged from three months to eight years; and Major Johnston was tried by court martial and cashiered.

The only really good news to encourage the Macarthur-Johnston camp was the fall of Castlereagh, who had, wrote Macarthur, declared himself 'adverse to us' and had he remained in office, 'would have increased our difficulties, and, perhaps, in the end, have crushed us altogether' (Onslow (ed.) 1914, p. 183, 28 November 1809) and the succession of Spencer Percival as Prime Minister in place of the Duke of Portland. Percival was linked with close friends of the Christian family; he was intimate with Samuel Romilly, the radical lawyer who had helped Edward Christian collect his material for the 1794 *Appendix*, and he had followed Edward Law, another close friend of Edward Christian, as Attorney-General.

Macarthur and Johnston had to fret away a year until Bligh returned because the government refused to proceed without the presence of the former Governor. Macarthur used his time to prepare his case: 'I am continually engaged from morning until night with my lawyers in arranging the plan of a formidable attack on Mr. Bligh', he told his wife (ibid., p. 207, 5 December 1810). He decided to sue Bligh for £20,000 damages.

The first public move came from Johnston a month after Bligh had returned. He sent a Memorial to the Earl of Liverpool offering 'to produce incontestible evidence of his [Bligh's] tyranny and oppression of the people he was sent to govern; – of gross frauds and shameful robberies committed upon the public property entrusted to his care; and lastly I will prove, that he had been guilty of heretofore unheard of and disgraceful cowardice' (Onslow (ed.) 1914, pp. 208-10). The charge of 'cowardice' apparently refers to the absurd charge of hiding under a bed during his arrest. A week later he wrote to the Earl asking permission to move to London and leave his regiment under the command of his deputy. The Earl replied, through a secretary, with a polite refusal.

In January 1811 Lieutenant Kent requested a court martial on the charges brought by Bligh for which he had been under arrest since before *Porpoise* left Sydney. The charges were that he had sailed from Sydney without Governor Bligh's permission, had unlawfully removed Bligh's broad pennant from the mast and had let Lieutenant Symons leave the Colony without Bligh's permission. Macarthur acted as Kent's chief advisor during the three-day court martial. Kent stuck closely to the legalities of the technical offences he had allegedly committed. He was acquitted (*HRNSW*, vol. 7, pp. 495-6).

Johnston, recently promoted to Lieutenant-Colonel in the 102nd Regiment (the renamed Corps), was anxious for his trial to commence, if only to restrain his witnesses dispersing about their personal business. He got his way when his court martial was convened on 7 May 1811 at Chelsea Barracks. Lieutenant-General Keppel was President and Charles Manners-Sutton was Judge-Advocate General. Bligh was represented by a new advocate, (later Sir) Frederick Pollock. The court martial lasted until 5 June 1811, and a parade of witnesses passed before it, telling their stories and answering questions as best they could. The minutes were published by Mr Bartrum, 'who attended on behalf of Governor Bligh' in 1811 (an enlarged facsimile was published by the National Library of Australia in 1988 as *A Charge of Mutiny*). The minutes show the factual shallowness of Johnston's defence that he was acting to prevent a rebellion of an outraged citizenry (the only people outraged were Macarthur and a few 'respectable people' – most 'respectable people' supported Bligh). In the calm of cross examination, Johnston's witnesses crumble into prevarication. That the court martial of Johnston was turned into a trial of Bligh, which on the evidence

vindicates him convincingly, is perhaps the most positive defence of
Bligh's Governorship.

The decision of the court was: 'That Lieut. Col. Johnston is Guilty of the
act of Mutiny as described in the Charge, and [we] do therefore sentence
him to be Cashiered.' With this verdict both sides won something. Bligh
was vindicated but not avenged. Johnston was convicted but not
punished. Only Macarthur was left in legal jeopardy if he returned to the
Colony. To avoid this eventuality he refused to return to New South
Wales without an undertaking from the Government that he would not be
tried. The Government thought it politic to withhold such an
undertaking, thus keeping a troublesome fellow out of the Colony, until
Bligh died in 1817.

After the trial Johnston, now a civilian, took passage back to Sydney
and retired to his farm at Annandale. Before he went, the Prince Regent
remarked of his sentence:

> The Court, in passing a sentence so inadequate to the enormity of the crime
> of which the prisoner has been found guilty, have apparently been actuated
> by a consideration of the novel and extraordinary circumstances, which, by
> the evidence on the face of the proceedings, may have appeared to them to
> have existed during the administration of Gov. Bligh, both as affecting the
> tranquillity of the colony, and calling for some immediate decision. But
> although the Prince Regent admits the principle under which the Court
> have allowed this consideration to act in mitigation of the punishment
> which the crime of Mutiny would otherwise have suggested, yet no
> circumstances whatever can be recieved by His Royal Highness in full
> extenuation of an assumption of power, so subversive of every principle of
> good order and discipline as that under which Lieut.-Col. Johnston has been
> convicted (Bartrum, 1811, pp. 408-9).

This statement by the Prince Regent made Macarthur's position, if he
returned to the Colony, even more difficult, for Governor Macquarrie was
bound to take note of it in any legal deliberations. Macarthur's £20,000
civil suit against Bligh was quietly dropped, as was a threat of his to
petition parliament.

Macarthur and his family could only fume at their inability to use the
legal process in London with the same irreverent bias as they had used it
in Sydney in a series of actions that had created the whole sorry business
in the first place. Manners-Sutton, cross-examining Macarthur at
Johnston's trial, summed up the absurdity of the alleged cause of the
rebellion when he asserted: 'It seems the first cause of grievance was the
detention of that ship of yours, and the forfeiture of the bond for £900; the
next is about a post that was taken away from your ground; and these
seem to have been the principal part of all the causes of the rebellion'
(Bartrum, 1811, p. 213). It may be that Johnston was persuaded that he
was fighting the 'tyranny' of Government House in the name of 'liberty'
(in whose name many crimes against humanity have been committed),

but, in fact, when everything is boiled down to the essentials, the Corps were entrapped into actions that had the sole objective of advancing the private interests of a merchant-farmer, one John Macarthur.

But what of Bligh? He was dissatisfied with the court's sentence. Plainly he preferred a hanging. He believed that the 'Northumberland interest' had saved Johnston (he asserted that Johnston was a bastard son of the Duke!). Sir David Baird, a member of the court martial, wrote to Governor Macquarrie a couple of years later: 'I was a member of the Court Martial that tried the late commander of New South Wales (Col. Johnston). I was able to attend untill the day that sentence was to be passed & on that day I was so ill (from my wound) as to be obliged to have an operation performed – this I believe was fortunate for Johnston for I never heard as connected an evidence proving him guilty of Mutiny – without the least palliation that was in my Mind worthy of consideration' (ML MS A797, p. 79).

As it was, Bligh came out of the affair with some gratification. He was 57 years old and a senior Captain in the Royal Navy. He was due for promotion in December 1810, but this had been held back pending the outcome of Johnston's trial (though this did not prevent the army promoting Johnston). On 31 July 1811, four weeks after Johnston's guilty verdict, Bligh was gazetted Rear-Admiral of the Blue Squadron, back-dated to July 1810.

He did not engage in official duties after the trial and for once had plenty of time to be with his family. Unfortunately Betsy did not live very long. She died after a protracted illness on 15 April 1812 and was buried in the family grave at Lambeth churchyard. Bligh soon after moved his family to an imposing manor house in Farningham, near Maidstone, in Kent.

By seniority he was promoted twice more. In 1812 he became a Rear-Admiral of the White and in 1814 Vice-Admiral of the Blue, but he did not get an opportunity to fly his flag on a ship. He was consulted by the Admiralty from time to time, and also by the House of Commons on the problems of transporting convicts to New South Wales (*Report of the Select Committee on Transportation*, 1812, pp. 29-47). He also gave advice on the functioning of Vice-Admiral courts, and assisted Rear-Admiral Thomas Hamilton on the viability of a new design for a 74-gun ship.

Like many another old warrior he retired gracefully and, in contrast to the rest of his life, he left few clues as to what he was up to. He had much to cope with domestically, with four unmarried daughters, including the epileptic Anne, who ended her days at a nursing home in Bath. He continued to travel up to London as business and health permitted. On 7 December 1817 he collapsed and died, and was buried next to Betsy at Lambeth. His inscription reads:

Sacred to the Memory of William Bligh
Esquire, F.R.S. Vice-Admiral
of the Blue the celebrated navigator
who first transplanted the Bread fruit tree

from Otaheite to the West Indies
bravely fought the battles of his country
and died beloved, respected and lamented
on the 7th day of December 1817
aged 64

No mention is made of his Governorship of New South Wales.

Bligh's death did not end the controversies of his life. The rediscovery of Pitcairn helped to keep the issues of the *Bounty* mutiny alive. The saga of *Bounty* has continued ever since, which is remarkable given the trivial issues at stake and the unimportance of its mission.

Bligh was many of the things his contemporary critics accused him of – he was violent in his speech and abrasive in command. Whether he always stepped over from an irascible norm to an oppressive tyranny is a matter of conjecture. Certainly Christian, Fryer, Bond, Ramsay, Frazier and Macarthur found him unbearable. But many men have had harsh dispositions. Cook had a foul temper; Nelson, adored by his men, never flinched at ordering a flogging if a man deserved it. Bligh did not have such a disposition – he forgave seamen's transgressions (blaming their officers) as often as he punished them. He was no flogger by any standards.

The one thing that brought out the worst in him was any tendency in an officer to dereliction of duty. If he suspected that a man was not giving of his best, ensuring that everything was done properly and promptly and not relying on the mere giving of an order, he was at them noon, night and morning, chasing, nagging, carping, pressing and pushing. In this he was like the elements: any weakness in a ship's construction is ruthlessly sought out by the wind and the sea. Once they find a weak spot they mercilessly test it until it breaks.

Men who treated him deferentially received more than their due from him; those who sent him into paroxysms of rage he punished in every formal and informal way at his command. This made life hell for them and everybody around them. Observing these personal battles two hundred years later, we can be appalled at their ferocity, and the seeming triviality of their initial causes. But when emotions are stirred, human decencies are often the first victim.

It is in the rich variety of human behaviour that we find our places. Some in life's journey take, as George Tobin put it, a 'turbulent' route. Bligh was one of those men, gifted but flawed. He represented some of the finest aspects of the British character in his professional skills, his determination and his single-mindedness. He also had within him some of the more disagreeable traits of the vain, the pompous and the vindictive. If he erred it was in his predilection for Signal no. 16 (close action) in his personal relations. But it is in the whole person that he must be judged. He may not have been a saint, or as beloved as Nelson, but he was like a rock when others would have been overwhelmed. He showed this in the desperate voyage of the open boat and at the bloody battle of Copenhagen. He was a fighter, a survivor and a man of intense personal conviction and courage. His critics claimed that he was a bully, a tyrant, a coward and a thief. After sixteen years studying and thinking about the life and works of William Bligh, I still think his critics were unjust.

George Tobin, now a Captain, summed up Bligh a few days after his death, and more than twenty-seven years after serving under him in *Providence*, in a letter to Frank Bond (Mackaness, 1949, pp. 32-33, 15 December, 1817). It is an unbeatable statement of his character:

So poor Bligh, for with all his infirmities, you & I cannot but think [well] of him, has followed Portlock. He has had a busy and turbulent journey of it – no one more so, and since the unfortunate Mutiny in the 'Bounty', has been rather in the Shade. Yet perhaps was he not altogether understood, – I am sure, my dear Friend that in the Providence there was no settled system of Tyranny exercised by him likely to produce dissatisfaction. It was in those violent Tornados of temper when he lost himself, yet, when all, in his opinion, went right, when could a man be more placid & interesting? For myself I feel that I am indebted to him. It was the first Ship in which I ever sailed as an Officer – I Joined full of apprehension – I soon thought he was not dissatisfied with me – it gave me encouragement, and on the whole we journeyed smoothly on. Once or twice indeed I felt the Unbridled licence of his power of Speech, yet never without soon receiving something like an emollient plaister to heal the wound. Let our old Captain's frailties be forgotten, & view him as a man of Science and excellent practical Seaman. He has suffered much and ever in difficulty by labour and perseverance extricated himself. But his great quality was Foresight. In this I think, Bond, you will accord with me. I have seen many men in his profession with more resources, but never one with so much precaution – I mean chiefly as a Navigator.

# Bibliography

Anon. 1831. 'Obituary Notice for Captain Peter Heywood', *United Service Journal and Naval and Military magazine*, April 1831, Part 1, pp. 468-81. London.

Anon. 1837. [Review of Capt. E.P. Brenton's two-volume history of the Royal Navy], *United Service Journal*, Part 2, pp. 147-9. London.

Amis, Peter. 1957. 'The "Bounty" Timekeeper', *Horological Journal*, vol. 99, no. 1191, pp. 760-70.

Bach, John (ed.). 1986. *The Bligh Notebook: 'Rough account – Lieutenant Wm Bligh's voyage in the Bounty's Launch from the ship to Tofoa & from thence to Timor', 28 April to 14 June 1789, With a draft list of the* BOUNTY *mutineers*. 2 vols. Facsimile. Limited ed. Canberra.

Barney, Stephen. 1794. *Minutes of the Proceedings of the Court-Martial held at Portsmouth August 12 [sic] on ten persons charged with the Mutiny on Board His Majesty's Ship the Bounty with an Appendix containing A Full Account of the real Causes and Circumstances of that unhappy Transaction, the most material of which have hitherto been witheld from the Public*. London.

Barrow, Sir John. 1831. *The Eventful History of the Mutiny and Piratical Seizure of H.M.S. Bounty: its Causes and Consequences*. London. 1961 ed. Glasgow.

Bartrum, Mr. (ed.). 1811. *Proceedings of A General Court-Martial, held at Chelsea Hospital, Which Commenced on Tuesday May 7, 1811, and continued by Adjournment to Wednesday, 5th June, following, for the Trial of Lieut.-Col. Geo. Johnston, Major of the 102d Regiment, late the New South Wales Corps, on a Charge of Mutiny, Exhibited against him by the Crown, for Deposing on the 26th of January, 1808, William Bligh, Esq. F.R.S. Taken in short hand by Mr. Bartrum of Clement's Inn, Who attended on behalf of Governor Bligh, by Permission of the Court*. London. (A new 'facsimile' edition, introduced by John Ritchie, was published in Canberra in 1988.)

Beechey, Captain F.W. 1831. *Narrative of a Voyage to the Pacific and Beering's Strait, to co-operate with the Polar Expeditions; performed in His Majesty's Ship Blossom, under the command of Captain F.W. Beechey, R.N., F.R.S. &c, in the Years 1825, 26, 27, 28*. 2 vols. London.

Bligh, William. 1790. *A Narrative of the Mutiny on board His Majesty's Ship Bounty; and the subsequent voyage of part of the crew in the ship's boat, from Tofoa, one of the Friendly islands, to Timor, a Dutch Settlement in the East Indies, illustrated with charts*. London.

Bligh, William [& Captain Burney, ed.]. 1792. *A Voyage to the South Seas, undertaken by command of his Majesty, for the purpose of Conveying the Bread-Fruit Tree to the West Indies, in His Majesty's Ship the Bounty, commanded by Lieutenant William Bligh. Including an account of the mutiny on board the said ship, and the subsequent voyage of Part of the Crew in the Ship's Boat, From Tofoa, one of the Friendly islands, To Timor, a Dutch Settlement in the East indies, with seven charts, diagram and portrait*. London.

Bligh, William. 1794. *An Answer to Certain Assertions contained in the Appendix to a pamphlet, entitled Minutes of the Proceedings on the Court-Martial held at Portsmouth, August 12th, 1792, on Ten Persons charged with Mutiny on Board his Majesty's Ship the Bounty.* London.

Bligh, Lieutenant W. 1975. *The Log of H.M.S. Bounty, 1787-9.* Guildford (facsimile of London Admiralty PRO copy; limited edition).

Bligh, Lieutenant W. 1975. *The Log of H.M.S. Providence.* Guildford (facsimile of London Admiralty PRO copy; limited edition).

Bowker, R.M. and by Lt. William Bligh R.N., in his official log. 1978. *Mutiny!! Aboard H.M. Armed Transport 'Bounty' in 1789.*

Christian, Edward. 1794. 'An Appendix' in *Minutes of the Proceedings* .... [Barney], London.

Christian, Edward. 1795. *A Short reply to Captain Bligh's Answers.* London.

'Christian, Fletcher' (?). 1796. *Letters from Mr. Fletcher Christian, and a Narrative of the Mutiny On Board His Majesty's Ship Bounty, at Otaheite. With a succinct account of the Proceedings of the Mutineers with a Description of the Manners, Customs, Religious Ceremonies, Diversions, Fashions, Arts, Commerce; Method of Fighting; the Breadfruit, and every interesting particular relating to The Society Islands. Also His Shipwreck on the coast of America, and travels in that extensive country; with a history of the Gold Mines and general account of the possessions of the Spaniards. In Chili, Peru, Mexico &c.* London.

Christian, Glynn. 1982. *Fragile Paradise: the discovery of Fletcher Christian, Bounty Mutineer.* London.

Darby, Madge. 1965. *Who Caused the Mutiny on the Bounty?.* Sydney.

Darby, Madge. 1966. *The causes of the Bounty mutiny; a short reply to Mr. Rolf Du Rietz's comments,* Studia Bountyana, vol. 2. Uppsala.

Delano, Amasa. 1817. *A Narrative of Voyages and Travels, in the Northern and Southern Hemispheres: comprising Three Voyages round the World; together with a Voyage of Survey and Discovery, in the Pacific Ocean's Oriental Islands.* Boston.

Dugan, James. 1966. *The Great Mutiny.* London.

Du Rietz, Rolf E. 1965. *The Causes of the Bounty Mutiny: some comments on a book by Madge Darby,* Studia Bountyana, vol. 1. Limited ed. Uppsala.

Du Rietz, Rolf E. 1979. *Thoughts on the present state of Bligh scholarship,* Banksia, *1.* Limited ed. Uppsala.

Du Rietz, Rolf E. 1981. *Fresh Light on John Fryer of the 'Bounty',* Banksia, *2.* Limited ed. Uppsala.

Du Rietz, Rolf E. 1986. *Peter Heywood's Tahitian vocabulary and the narratives by James Morrison: Some notes on their origin and history,* Banksia, *3.* Limited ed. Uppsala.

Edwards, Edward and Hamilton, George. 1915. *Voyage of H.M.S. 'Pandora', despatched to arrest the mutineers of the 'Bounty' in the South Seas, 1790-1, being narratives of Captain Edward Edwards, R.N., the commander, and George Hamilton, the surgeon; with introduction and notes by Basil Thompson.* London.

Flinders, Matthew. 1814. *A Voyage to terra Australis; undertaken for the purpose of completing the discovery of that vast country, and prosecuted in the Years 1801, 1802, and 1803, in His Majesty's Ship the Investigator, and subsequently in the Armed Vessel Porpoise and Cumberland Schooner. With an account of the Shipwreck of the Porpoise, Arrival of the Cumberland at Mauritius, and Imprisonment of the Commander during six Years and a half in that island. 2 vols. and an Atlas.* London.

Friendly, Alfred. 1977. *Beaufort of the Admiralty*. London.

Garran, J.C. and White, L. 1985. *Merinos, Myths and Macarthurs: Australian graziers and their sheep, 1788-1900*. Sydney.

Gould, R.T. 1928. 'Bligh's Notes on Cook's Last Voyage', *The Mariner's Mirror*, vol. 14, no. 4, October, pp. 371-85.

[Greathead, S.] 'Authentic History of the Mutineers of the *Bounty*', *The Sailor's Magazine and Naval Miscellany*, 1820, vol. 1, pp. 402-6, 449-56; 1821, vol. 2, pp. 1-8.

Hamilton, George. 1793. *A Voyage Round the World in His Majesty's Frigate Pandora, Performed under the Direction of Captain Edwards In the Years 1790, 1791, and 1792*. Berwick.

*Historical Records of New South Wales*, Sydney. (*HRNSW*.)

*Historial Records of Australia*, Sydney. (*HRA*.)

Holt, Joseph. 1838. *Memoirs of Joseph Holt, General of the Irish Rebels in 1798*. 2 vols. London.

Hough, Richard. 1972. *Captain Bligh and Mr Christian: the men and the mutiny*. London. New ed. 1979.

Jackson, T. Sturges (ed.). 1899. 1900. *Logs of the Great Sea Fights, 1794-1805*. London.

'Jenny', 'Narrative', *Sydney Gazette*, 17 July 1819; *Bengal Hurkaru*, 2 October 1826.

Kennedy, Gavin. 1978. *The Death of Captain Cook*. London.

Kennedy, Gavin. 1978. *Bligh*. London.

Kennedy, Gavin (ed.). 1980. *Sir John Barrow: The Mutiny of the Bounty*. Boston.

Knight, C. 1936. 'H.M. Armed Vessel Bounty', *The Mariner's Mirror*, vol. 22, no. 2, April, pp. 183-99.

Lee, Ida. 1920. *Captain Bligh's Second Voyage to the South Sea*. London.

Ledward, Thomas Denman. 1903. 'Letters to his Family', *Notes and Queries*, 9th Series, vol. 12, 26 December, pp. 501-2.

Lloyd, Christopher. 1963. *St Vincent & Camperdown*. London.

Mackaness, George. 1931. *The Life of Vice-Admiral Bligh, R.N., F.R.S.* 2 vols. Sydney. Revised ed. 1 vol., 1951.

Mackaness, George (ed.). 1938. *A Book of the 'Bounty', William Bligh and Others*. London. (New edition, introduced by Gavin Kennedy, 1981.)

Mackaness, George, (ed.). 1949. *Some Correspondence of Captain William Bligh, R.N., with John and Francis Godolphin Bond, 1776-1811*. Sydney.

Mackaness, George. 1953. *Fresh Light on Bligh, being Some Unpublished Correspondence of Captain William Bligh, R.N., with Lieutenant Bond's Manuscript Notes made on the Voyage of H.M.S. 'Providence', 1791-1795*. Sydney.

Mackaness, George. 1960. 'Extracts from a Log-book of H.M.S. *Providence* kept by Lieut. Francis Godolphin Bond', *Journal and Proceedings of the Royal Australian Historical Society*, vol. 46, pp. 24-66.

Marden, Luis. 1957. 'I Found the Bones of the Bounty', *National Geographic Magazine*, vol. 112, no. 6, December, pp. 725-89.

Manwaring, G.E. and Dobree, Bonamy. 1935. *The Floating Republic: an account of the mutinies at Spithead and the Nore in 1797*. London.

Marshall, John. 1823-35. *Royal Naval Biography; or, Memories of the Services of all the Flag-Officers, Superannuated Rear-Admirals, Retired-Captains, Post-captains, and Commanders, Whose names appeared on the Admiralty List of Sea Officers at the commencement of the present year, or who have since been promoted; Illustrated by a Series of Historical and Explanatory Notes, Which will be found to contain an account of all the Naval Actions, and other important Events, from the Commencement of the late reign, in 1760, to the present period. With Copious Addenda*. London.

Maude, H.E. 1958. 'In Search of a Home: From the Mutiny to Pitcairn Island (1789-1790)', *Journal of the Polynesian Society*, vol. 67, no. 2, June, pp. 115-40.

Mitford, Mary Russell. 1811. *Christina, The Maid of the South Seas: a poem*. London.

Nicolas, N.H. (ed.). 1844-6. *The Dispatches and Letters of Vice-Admiral Lord Viscount Nelson, with Notes by Sir Nicholas Harris Nicolas, G.C.M.G.* 7 vols. London.

Oman, Carola. 1947. *Nelson*. London.

Onslow, Sibella Macarthur (ed.). 1914. *Some Early Records of the Macarthurs of Camden*. Sydney.

Pope, Dudley. 1963. *The Black Ship*. London.

Pope, Dudley. 1972. *The Great Gamble*. London.

Rutter, Owen (ed.). 1931. *The Court-Martial of the 'Bounty' Mutineers*. London.

Rutter, Owen (ed.). 1934. *The Voyage of the Bounty's Launch as related in William Bligh's despatch to the Admiralty and the Journal of John Fryer*. London.

Rutter, Owen, *Turbulent Journey: A Life of William Bligh, Vice-Admiral of the Blue*. London.

Rutter, Owen (ed.). 1937. *The Log of the Bounty, being Lieutenant William Bligh's Log of the proceedings of His Majesty's Armed Vessel 'Bounty', on a voyage to the South Seas to take the breadfruit from the Society Islands to the West Indies, now published for the first time from the manuscript in the Admiralty records*. 2 vols. London.

Smith, D. Bonner. 1936. 'Some Remarks about the Mutiny of the *Bounty*', *The Mariner's Mirror*, vol. 22, no. 2, April, pp. 200-37.

Tagart, Edward. 1832. *A Memoir of the late Captain Peter Heywood R.N., with extracts from his Diaries and Correspondence*. London.

Walters, S. (ed.) 1984. *The Letters of Fletcher Christian*, Guildford.

Wilkinson, C.S. 1953. *The Wake of the Bounty*. London.

# Index

WB = William Bligh; EB = Elizabeth Bligh; FC = Fletcher Christian. Alphabetical order is by name, not by title or rank.

**CARDINAL**